Praise for the
ALMANAC of ARCHITECTURE & DESIGN

"The reader who uses this book well will come away with a richer sense
of the texture of the profession and of the architecture it produces."
—Paul Goldberger
Pulitzer Prize-winning architecture critic, *The New Yorker*

"The essential and definitive tool for architecture and design facts.
Very well done and valuable."
—William Stout Architectural Books

"Indispensable for any public library, any design firm, and any school of
architecture, landscape architecture, or interior design...
solid, reliable, and remarkably complete."
—Robert Campbell
Pulitzer Prize-winning architecture critic, *The Boston Globe*

"The only source book of its kind,
this almanac is the design professional's definitive resource."
—MSN.com

"A goldmine of facts."
—HOK

"It won't tell you when the high tide will be next June 28 or
who won the 1976 World Series, but the *Almanac of Architecture & Design*
does fill you in on the field's best and little known facts...
Where else can you find one book that lists the world's tallest buildings,
average salaries for your region, and Ralph Adam Cram's birthday?"
—*Architecture* magazine

DesignIntelligence®

ALMANAC of ARCHITECTURE & DESIGN 2008

NINTH EDITION

DesignIntelligence®

ALMANAC of ARCHITECTURE & DESIGN 2008
NINTH EDITION

Edited by James P. Cramer and Jennifer Evans Yankopolus

Foreword by Marvin J. Malecha

Greenway Communications

östberg

Editors:	James P. Cramer
	Jennifer Evans Yankopolus
Assistant Editor and Consulting Architectural Historian:	Jane Paradise Wolford, PhD
Editorial and Research Staff:	Corinne Aaker, Susan Boling, Chelsie Butler, Austin Cramer, Ryan Cramer, Lee Cuthbert, Daniel Downey, Mary Pereboom, Carol Rundle, Tonya Smith
Layout:	Karen Berube, K.Designs
Index:	Kay Wosewick, Pathways Indexing

Greenway Communications,
a division of The Greenway Group
25 Technology Parkway South, Suite 101
Atlanta, GA 30092
(800) 726-8603
www.greenway.us

Publisher's Cataloging-in-Publication

Almanac of architecture & design / James P. Cramer and
Jennifer Evans Yankopolus, editors.
    2008 ed.
    p. cm.
    Almanac of architecture and design
    Includes bibliographical references and index.
    ISBN–13: 978-0-9785552-3-8
    ISBN–10: 0-9785552-3-6

    1. Architecture—Directories. 2. Architectural
design. 3. Architecture—United States. I. Title:
Almanac of architecture and design

NA9.A27 2008   720

Contents

Contents

2 LEADERSHIP IN DESIGN

3 RECORDS, RANKINGS & ACHIEVEMENTS

Contents

Foreword

Not so long ago on the timeline of human development, information moved at the speed of the human stride. It was a time when the pope's Easter message would take three months to reach the outer edges of Europe. Bits of information were measured by hand-scripted scrolls, and for many, life was measured by the number of days it took to walk from the town center. Family, village, religion, and, most particularly, social class defined personal relationships. The master builders of the time were the instruments of power, often rooted to projects passed between generations. Working together over and over again, teams of builders frequently developed into families. The migration of a building type from one part of the world to another required journeymen to be called to work on the projects of great patrons. And the world seemed an inexhaustible resource for the supremacy of human development.

Much has changed, and yet there is great dependence on many of the same conditions. Information moves with speed already incomprehensible. The development of ideas demands an agile posture that frequently moves outside social class or recognized governance structures. Information and lessons from one culture move and transform other cultures as never before. Social structures and building types are evolving to meet this new global imperative. Traditional boundaries seem irrelevant to the flow of ideas. The role of master builder has evolved to that of the master integrator of the information and means to the realization of a project. The teams to accomplish the work are forming and reforming even as the project progresses— let alone from one project to another. We now recognize that not only are the resources of our world exhaustible, but our actions are now directly reflected in the quality of our environment—and this determines the interactions of nations.

Yet we remain dependent on the patrons of our work. And just as the master builder understood his work to be the language of power for the cleric or the governor, today we reflect the aspirations of global patrons. There is also the reaction to such power and influence as clerics and priests call us to greater consciousness, and those committed to greater local determination question the implications of globalization on the lives of individuals without economic or social influence.

In this new milieu, design professionals must be better educated on the many ways of the world. They must be intellectually agile to understand that professional practice is under constant reconfiguration. And the ethical standards that guide us demand our attention as we bring together many belief systems to realize a project. The drive to continuously develop technologies is the most superficial indicator of the imperative to not only reconfigure professional practice in response to technology and societal change but also to develop new thought patterns that will inspire new forms of architectural response.

This is an amazing time for all of the design professions. How we move into this era will define our importance to future generations. Just as past generations have come to be recognized by the artifacts they created, so will we be able to put form to the ideas of our time. This will only be possible if we navigate through practice bringing dreams to realization. This *Almanac* is one chronicle of how we are going about addressing our challenges.

Marvin J. Malecha, FAIA
2009 President
The American Institute of Architects

Introduction: Globalization and Change Design

Welcome to the 2008 edition of the *Almanac of Architecture & Design*. Our objective is to provide you with the facts that you will need to understand the changing world of design and the resources to network and make timely decisions that aid your success.

We are grateful to more than 100 organizations that contribute statistics, records, and honors to our annual compendium. We hope that each reader will find this to be a useful volume and that you will let us know what other information you need. We are committed to making our future publications relevant to these changing times.

Architecture in Global Community

We are struck by the trends that are transforming professional practice worldwide. Recently the executive board of the Design Futures Council held a meeting at the Architectural Research and Design Institute at Tongji University in Shanghai to review the impact of China's growth on international design practices. The sharing of information between East and West was rich and meaningful.

Thor Kerr of BCI Asia forecasted that China would soon to be the largest construction economy in the world. We also heard informative presentations on innovation in materials and form from Zhang Lei, the chief architect at Atelier Zhang Lei and a professor at Nanjing University. Ren Lizhi, the deputy president at Tongji University, brought additional design trends reports developed by Lu Qiu. Zheng Ke and Zhang Junjie also joined us, and the architectural work of the Xian Dai Design Group, Werkhart International, and others was featured.

Several themes ran constant through our sessions: The first centered around the large-scale environmental impact that global cities will increasingly have. China is undergoing the most massive urbanization in human history with Shanghai emerging as the centerpiece with more than 20 million people. As China's most cosmopolitan city, Shanghai is home to China's financial center (Lujiazui) and the highest number of foreign corporate headquarters in the world. Shanghai is a Petri dish model of sorts from which we can learn from its successes as well as failures.

The meeting's second major theme involved new understandings about Chinese business practices and market conditions and projections about the country's effect on the global marketplace. Additionally, there was consider-able discussion about delivery strategies and the noticeable revolution under-way, evident in the stream of new products emerging from the country.

In the end, the group produced 10 recommendations for how architects and designers worldwide can cooperate to create a better quality of life for all:

1. There should be redoubled efforts, East and West, regarding sharing, mentoring, and providing the necessary resources to generation X and Y in order to develop the most talented future leadership in our industry. Incentives should encourage bright designers, engineers, and contractors into what will be a new AEC industry—one loaded with opportunities.

2. New leadership strategies should be developed and advocated. Leadership should voice the importance of design solutions that advance the global cities of the future. With urban areas under increasing stress, we should use design and leadership strategies ratcheted up beyond past attempts.

3. Fast architecture (together with quality enhancements) will require new models and organizations. Architects and designers should challenge the traditional paradigms of speed. With speed, quality should not be sacri-ficed—architects and other DFC leaders should spearhead this understand-ing more decisively worldwide.

4. The integration of disciplines and processes is unfolding at a rapid pace. Professional practice and education leaders need to embrace this change and bring forward new organizational design solutions that over-come present-day weaknesses.

5. While competitive forces can be positive and bring forward innova-tion, firm leaders are also encouraged to improve sharing and collaboration in order to advance new best practices.

6. The preservation of historic structures should be a high priority in design and real estate development. Cities are being rapidly transformed to accommodate increasing population levels, and extra care should be taken regarding heritage sites and preservation opportunities.

7. Green and sustainable design is of critical importance, and leaders are encouraged to integrate the latest technologies along with design processes. Tighter anti-pollution rules are encouraged for the built environment in China, the United States, and worldwide.

8. One of the most important priorities on a global scale is how design might better enhance the human condition in cities. This requires questioning of such issues as scale, light, structure, cost, and quality.

9. There should be new emphasis given to leadership form and style, not only content, which includes advancing persuasive leadership skills, rather than the adversarial nature our industry is known for. This proactive style should include community leadership as well as leadership and innovation in design and construction.

10. New attention should be given to the quality of communication between design and industry professionals. Communications should be structured to encourage leaders to learn from each other with a focus on criteria, processes, and achievements.

150 Years of Design Advocacy

As we put the final pages of this *Almanac* together, we are also in the midst of celebrating the American Institute of Architects' 150th anniversary. The AIA's members have been marking the organization's 150 years of service to the profession and the nation by working within communities to create a better future by design. The AIA is celebrating this milestone with a series of community-based initiatives through an ambitious program called Blueprint for America. Thousands of local AIA architects and community partners have been involved in more than 160 projects across the nation tackling regional issues as well as smaller-scale initiatives, such as downtown and neighborhood revitalization, affordable housing, adaptive reuse of historic schools, and smart growth issues.

Thanks to the efforts of McGraw-Hill Construction, the official media sponsor, and Autodesk, the official software sponsor, the AIA is not only celebrating 150 years of service but is reaching out to address the complex realities of today's world. These initiatives would not have been possible without the leadership of Norman Koonce, Norbert Young, Ron Skaggs, Arol Wolford, Tom Ventulett, George Miller, Roy Abernathy, Martha Bennett, Tony Costello, Diane Georgopulos, Beverly Hauschild-Baron, Ray (Skipper) Post and many others. As we celebrate these leaders and the AIA's 150th anniversary, we encourage everyone to support the numerous community initiatives that bring more attention to architecture and design and to quality of life.

Finally, we wish to thank the staff of the Greenway Group who have teamed together to help make this *Almanac of Architecture & Design* what it is today. Our databases are full, and our eagerness to do even more in the months and years ahead is intact. We continually strive to provide unique content for engaging and helping readers take ideas into actions—making the *Almanac* an invaluable tool not only for the business of design and architecture but also in the context of holistic community health.

Finally, let's celebrate the anniversary of one of the truly great associations in America. And thank you, AIA, for your vision for the future.

James P. Cramer   Jennifer Evans Yankopolus
jcramer@di.net   jyank@di.net

1

AWARDS & HONORS

The results of major national and international awards programs are included in this chapter along with information about their scope, purpose, and winners. Other award programs related to sustainable/green design, historic preservation, and design education can be found in their respective chapters.

Aga Khan Award for Architecture

3

The Aga Khan Trust for Culture grants the triennial Aga Khan Award for Architecture to outstanding projects, including individual buildings, restoration and reuse schemes, large-scale community developments, and environmental initiatives in the Muslim world. Submissions are reviewed for their ability to meet people's physical, social, and economic needs as well as their cultural and spiritual expectations. An award of $500,000 is apportioned among the winners.

Photos and descriptions of the winning projects are available online at *www.akdn.org.*

2007 Winners

Samir Kassir Square
Beirut, Lebanon
Vladimir Djurovic Landscape Architecture
   (Lebanon)

Rehabilitation of the City of Shibam
Shibam, Yemen
German Technical Cooperation
   (Germany)

Central Market
Koudougou, Burkina Faso
Swiss Agency for Development and
   Cooperation (Switzerland)

University of Technology Petronas
Bandar Seri Iskandar, Malaysia
Foster and Partners (UK); GDP Architects
   (Malaysia)

Restoration of the Amiriya Complex
Rada, Yemen
Selma Al-Radi (Iraq) and Yahya Al-Nasiri
   (Yemen)

Moulmein Rise Residential Tower
Singapore
WOHA Architects (Singapore)

Royal Netherlands Embassy
Addis Ababa, Ethiopia
Dick van Gameren and Bjarne
   Mastenbroek (Netherlands); ABBA
   Architects (Ethiopia)

Rehabilitation of the Walled City
Nicosia, Cyprus
Nicosia Master Plan Team (Cyprus)

School in Rudrapur
Dinajpur, Bangladesh
Anna Heringer (Austria) and Eike Roswag
   (Germany)

JURY
Homi Bhabha, Harvard University
Okwui Enwezor, San Francisco Art Institute
Homa Farjadi, Farjadi Architects (UK)
Sahel Al-Hiyari, Sahel Al-Hiyari and Partners
   (Jordan)
Shirazeh Houshiary, artist (UK)
Rashid Khalidi, Columbia University
Brigitte Shim, Shim Sutcliffe Architects (Canada)
Han Tümertekin, Mimarlar Tasarim Danismanlik
   Ltd (Turkey)
Kenneth Yeang, Llewelyn Davies Yeang and
   Hamzah & Yeang (UK/Malaysia)

Source: Aga Khan Trust for Culture

AIA Gold Medal

The Gold Medal is the American Institute of Architects' highest award. Eligibility is open to architects and non-architects, living or dead, whose contribution to the field of architecture has made a lasting impact. The AIA's board of directors grants a single gold medal each year, occasionally granting none.

For more information, visit the AIA on the Web at *www.aia.org*.

1907	Sir Aston Webb (UK)	1964	Pier Luigi Nervi (Italy)
1909	Charles F. McKim	1966	Kenzo Tange (Japan)
1911	George B. Post	1967	Wallace K. Harrison
1914	Jean Louis Pascal (France)	1968	Marcel Breuer
1922	Victor Laloux (France)	1969	William Wurster
1923	Henry Bacon	1970	R. Buckminster Fuller
1925	Sir Edwin Lutyens (UK)	1971	Louis I. Kahn
1925	Bertram Grosvenor Goodhue	1972	Pietro Belluschi
1927	Howard Van Doren Shaw	1977	Richard Neutra* (Germany/US)
1929	Milton B. Medary	1978	Philip Johnson
1933	Ragnar Östberg (Sweden)	1979	I.M. Pei
1938	Paul Philippe Cret (France/US)	1981	José Luis Sert (Spain)
1944	Louis Sullivan	1982	Romaldo Giurgola
1947	Eliel Saarinen (Finland/US)	1983	Nathaniel Owings
1948	Charles D. Maginnis	1985	William Wayne Caudill*
1949	Frank Lloyd Wright	1986	Arthur C. Erickson (Canada)
1950	Sir Patrick Abercrombie (UK)	1989	Joseph Esherick
1951	Bernard Maybeck	1990	E. Fay Jones
1952	Auguste Perret (France)	1991	Charles Moore
1953	William Adams Delano	1992	Benjamin Thompson
1955	William Marinus Dudok (Netherlands)	1993	Thomas Jefferson*
		1993	Kevin Roche
1956	Clarence S. Stein	1994	Sir Norman Foster (UK)
1957	Ralph Thomas Walker	1995	Cesar Pelli
1957	Louis Skidmore	1997	Richard Meier
1958	John Wellborn Root II	1999	Frank Gehry
1959	Walter Gropius (Germany/US)	2000	Ricardo Legorreta (Mexico)
1960	Ludwig Mies van der Rohe (Germany/US)	2001	Michael Graves
		2002	Tadao Ando (Japan)
1961	Le Corbusier (Charles Édouard Jeanneret) (Switzerland/France)	2004	Samuel Mockbee*
		2005	Santiago Calatrava (Spain)
		2006	Antoine Predock
1962	Eero Saarinen*	2007	Edward Larrabee Barnes*
1963	Alvar Aalto (Finland)		

* Honored posthumously

Source: American Institute of Architects

AIA Honor Awards

The American Institute of Architects' Honor Awards celebrate outstanding design in three areas: architecture, interior architecture, and regional and urban design. Juries for each discipline comprised of designers and executives present awards in each category.

Additional information is available from the AIA at *www.aia.org*.

2007 Architecture Winners

Canada's National Ballet School: Project Grand Jete, Stage 1: The Jarvis Street Campus
Toronto, ON, Canada
Kuwabara Payne McKenna Blumberg Architects; (Canada) Goldsmith Borgal & Company Limited Architects (Canada)

Dr. Theodore T. Alexander Jr. Science Center School
Los Angeles, CA
Morphosis

Meinel Optical Science Research Building
Tucson, AZ
richärd+bauer

Memorial to the Murdered Jews of Europe
Berlin, Germany
Eisenman Architects

Palo Verde Library/Maryvale Community Center
Phoenix, AZ
Gould Evans Associates; Wendell Burnette Architects

School of Art & Art History, University of Iowa
Iowa City, IA
Steven Holl Architects with Herbert Lewis Kruse Blunck Architecture

Solar Umbrella
Venice, CA
Pugh + Scarpa Architects

Spencertown House
Spencetown, NY
Thomas Phifer and Partners

Biomedical Science Research Building, University of Michigan
Ann Arbor, MI
Polshek Partnership Architects

Merced Central Plant, University of California
Merced, CA
Skidmore, Owings & Merrill

World Birding Center
Mission, TX
Lake/Flato Architects

ARCHITECTURE JURY

Richard Logan, Gensler (chair)
Elizabeth (Zibby) Ericson, Shepley Bulfinch Richardson & Abbott
Philip Freelon, The Freelon Group
Thomas W. Kundig, Olson Sundberg Kundig Allen Architects
Nicole Ludacka, The Architectural Offices
Kristal Peters, Howard University
Henry Siegel, Siegel & Strain Architects
Victor Trahan III, Trahan Architects
Jane Werner, Children's Museum of Pittsburgh

6

AIA Honor Awards

2007 Interior Architecture Winners

Bay School of San Francisco
San Francisco, CA
Leddy Maytum Stacy Architects

Better Business Bureau Heartland Office
Omaha, NE
Randy Brown Architects

Bloomberg LP Headquarters
New York, NY
STUDIOS Architecture

Endeavor Talent Agency
Beverly Hills, CA
NMDA, Inc. with Interior Architects

Haworth Chicago Showroom
Chicago, IL
Perkins+Will/Eva Maddox Branded
    Environments

ImageNet, Carollton
Carrollton, TX
Elliott + Associates Architects

Louis Vuitton Landmark
Hong Kong, China
Peter Marino + Associates Architects
    with dcmstudios

The Modern
New York, NY
Bentel & Bentel Architects/Planners

Pierson and Davenport Colleges
New Haven, CT
KieranTimberlake Associates

St. Mary of the Springs
Columbus, OH
Nagle Hartray Danker Kagan McKay
    Penney Architects Ltd.

Top of the Rock at Rockefeller Center
New York, NY
Gabellini Sheppard Associates; SLCE
    Architects

INTERIOR ARCHITECTURE JURY
Ann Beha, Ann Beha Architects, Inc. (chair)
Hank Hildebrandt, University of Cincinnati
James Prendergast, Goettsch Partners
Ken Wilson, Envision Design
D.B. Kim, Starwood Hotels and Resorts

School of Art and Art History, University of Iowa, Iowa City, IA, by Steven Holl Architects (Photo: Tom Jorgensen/University of Iowa)

AIA Honor Awards

2007 Regional Urban Design Winners

A Balanced Vision Plan for the Trinity
River Corridor
Dallas, TX
Chan Krieger Sieniewicz

Boston's Newest Smart Growth Corridor:
A Collaborative Vision for the
Fairmount\Indigo Line
Boston, MA
Goody, Clancy & Associates

The Carneros Inn
Napa, CA
William Rawn Associates Architects Inc.
with Caspar Mol Architecture and
Planning; Persinger Architects; RMW
architecture & interiors; Les Girouard

Crown Properties
Gaithersburg, MD
Ehrenkrantz Eckstut & Kuhn Architects

Historic Third Ward Riverwalk
Milwaukee, WI
Engberg Anderson Design Partnership

New York Stock Exchange Financial
Streetscapes and Security
New York, NY
Rogers Marvel Architects

Zoning, Urban Form, and Civic Identity:
The Future of Pittsburgh's Hillsides
Pittsburgh, PA
Perkins Eastman

REGIONAL & URBAN DESIGN JURY
J. Max Bond Jr., Davis Brody Bond (chair)
Shalom S. Baranes, Shalom Baranes Associates
David Crossley, Gulf Coast Institute
Richard (Dick) Farley, Civitas, Inc.
David L. Graham, ESG Architects

Source: American Institute of Architects

Did you know...

The following firms have won the most AIA Honor Awards since 1993:

Skidmore Owings & Merrill	.23	Morphosis	.7
Polshek Partnership Architects	.10	Perkins+Will	.7
Richard Meier & Partners, Architects	.10	Murphy/Jahn Architects	.6
Elliot + Associates Architects	.8	Pugh + Scarpa Architects	.6
Hardy Holzman Pfeiffer Associates	.8		
Herbert Lewis Kruse Blunck Architecture	.8		
William Rawn Associates Architects Inc.	.8		

Source: DesignIntelligence

AIA/HUD Secretary's Housing and Community Design Award

The Housing and Community Design Award, presented by the American Institute of Architects and the US Department of Housing and Urban Development, celebrates excellence in affordable housing, community design, and accessibility. It also emphasizes design as integral to creating thriving homes and communities. The Alan J. Rothman Housing Accessibility Award was named for the late HUD senior policy analyst who was an expert on disability issues.

Additional information can be found on the AIA's website at *www.aia.org*.

2007 Winners

Excellence in Affordable Housing Design
El Carrillo Housing Authority
Santa Barbara, CA
Cearnal Andrulaitis LLP

Creating Community Connection
Salishan Neighborhood Revitalization
Tacoma, WA
Torti Gallas & Partners with Environmental
  Works and McGranahan Architects

Community-Informed Design
High Point Community
Seattle, WA
Mithun Architects + Designers + Planners
  with Streeter and Associates

JURY
Katherine Austin, Katherine Austin Architect
Luis F. Borray, US Department of Housing and
  Urban Development
Don Carter, Urban Design Associates
Regina C. Gray, US Department of Housing and
  Urban Development
Jane F. Kolleeny, *Architectural Record*
Lisa Stacholy, LKS Architects, Inc.
LaVerne Williams, Environment Associates

Source: American Institute of Architects

Alice Davis Hitchcock Book Award

The Society of Architectural Historians has granted the Alice Davis Hitchcock Book Award annually since 1949 to North American publications that demonstrate a high level of scholarly distinction in the field of architectural history. The award is named in honor of the mother of Henry-Russell Hitchcock, a past president of the SAH and an international leader in architectural history for more than half a century.

More information is available from the SAH website, *www.sah.org*.

1949   *Colonial Architecture and Sculpture in Peru*
Harold Wethey
Harvard University Press

1950   *Architecture of the Old Northwest Territory*
Rexford Newcomb
University of Chicago Press

1951   *Architecture and Town Planning in Colonial Connecticut*
Anthony Garvan
Yale University Press

1952   *The Architectural History of Newport*
Antoinette Forrester Downing
and Vincent J. Scully
Harvard University Press

1953   *Charles Rennie Mackintosh and the Modern Movement*
Thomas Howarth
Routledge and K. Paul

1954   *Early Victorian Architecture in Britain*
Henry-Russell Hitchcock
Da Capo Press

1955   *Benjamin H. Latrobe*
Talbot Hamlin
Oxford University Press

1956   *The Railroad Station: An Architectural History*
Carroll L.V. Meeks
Yale University Press

1957   *The Early Architecture of Georgia*
Frederick D. Nichols
University of North Carolina Press

1958   *The Public Buildings of Williamsburg*
Marcus Whiffen
Colonial Williamsburg

1959   *Carolingian and Romanesque Architecture, 800 to 1200*
Kenneth J. Conant
Yale University Press

1960   *The Villa d'Este at Tivoli*
David Coffin
Princeton University Press

1961   *The Architecture of Michelangelo*
James S. Ackerman
University of Chicago Press

1962   *The Art and Architecture of Ancient America*
George Kubler
Yale University Press

1963   *La Cathédrale de Bourges et sa Place dans l'Architecture Gothique*
Robert Branner
Tardy

1964   *Images of American Living, Four Centuries of Architecture and Furniture as Cultural Expression*
Alan W. Gowans
Lippincott

1965   *The Open-Air Churches of Sixteenth*
       Century Mexico
       John McAndrew
       Harvard University Press

1966   *Early Christian and Byzantine*
       Architecture
       Richard Krautheimer
       Penguin Books

1967   *Eighteenth-Century Architecture in*
       Piedmont: the open structures of
       Juvarra, Alfieri & Vittone
       Richard Pommer
       New York University Press

1968   *Architecture and Politics in Germany,*
       1918–1945
       Barbara Miller Lane
       Harvard University Press

1969   *Samothrace, Volume III: The Hieron*
       Phyllis Williams Lehmann
       Princeton University Press

1970   *The Church of Notre Dame in Montreal*
       Franklin Toker
       McGill-Queen's University Press

1971   No award granted

1972   *The Prairie School: Frank Lloyd*
       Wright and his Midwest
       Contemporaries
       H. Allen Brooks
       University of Toronto Press

       The Early Churches of Constantinople:
       Architecture and Liturgy
       Thomas F. Mathews
       Pennsylvania State University
       Press

1973   *The Campanile of Florence Cathedral.*
       "Giotto's Tower"
       Marvin Trachtenberg
       New York University Press

1974   *FLO, A Biography of Frederick Law*
       Olmsted
       Laura Wood Roper
       Johns Hopkins University Press

1975   *Gothic vs. Classic, Architectural*
       Projects in Seventeenth-Century Italy
       Rudolf Wittkower
       G. Braziller

1976   No award granted

1977   *New Orleans Architecture Vol. V:*
       The Esplanade Ridge
       Mary Louise Christovich, Sally
           Kitredge Evans, Betsy Swanson,
           and Roulhac Toledano
       Pelican Publishing Company

1978   *Sebastiano Serlio on Domestic*
       Architecture
       Myra Nan Rosenfeld
       Architectural History Foundation

1979   *The Framed Houses of Massachusetts*
       Bay, 1625–1725
       Abbott Lowell Cummings
       Belknap Press

       Paris: A Century of Change, 1878–1978
       Norma Evenson
       Yale University Press

1980   *Rome: Profile of a City, 312–1308*
       Richard Krautheimer
       Princeton University Press

1981   *Gardens of Illusion: The Genius*
       of Andre LeNotre
       Franklin Hamilton Hazelhurst
       Vanderbilt University Press

1982   *Indian Summer: Luytens, Baker*
       and Imperial Delhi
       Robert Grant Irving
       Yale University Press

Alice Davis Hitchcock Book Award

1983 *Architecture and the Crisis of Modern Science*
Alberto Pérez-Goméz
MIT Press

1984 *Campus: An American Planning Tradition*
Paul Venable Turner
MIT Press

1985 *The Law Courts: The Architecture of George Edmund Street*
David Brownlee
MIT Press

1986 *The Architecture of the Roman Empire: An Urban Appraisal*
William L. MacDonald
Yale University Press

1987 *Holy Things and Profane: Anglican Parish Churches in Colonial Virginia*
Dell Upton
MIT Press

1988 *Designing Paris: The Architecture of Duban*
David Van Zanten
MIT Press

1989 *Florentine New Towns: Urban Design in the Late Middle Ages*
David Friedman
MIT Press

1990 *Claude-Nicolas Ledoux: Architecture and Social Reform at the End of the Ancient Régime*
Anthony Vidler
MIT Press

1991 *The Paris of Henri IV: Architecture and Urbanism*
Hilary Ballon
MIT Press

Seventeenth-Century Roman Palaces: Use and the Art of the Plan
Patricia Waddy
MIT Press

1992 *Modernism in Italian Architecture, 1890–1940*
Richard Etlin
MIT Press

1994* *Baths and Bathing in Classical Antiquity*
Fikret Yegul
MIT Press

1995 *The Politics of the German Gothic Revival: August Reichensperger*
Michael J. Lewis
MIT Press

1996 *Hadrian's Villa and Its Legacy*
William J. MacDonald and
    John Pinto
Yale University Press

1997 *Gottfried Semper: Architect of the Nineteenth Century*
Harry Francis Mallgrave
Yale University Press

1998 *The Dancing Column: On Order in Architecture*
Joseph Rykwert
MIT Press

1999 *Dominion of the Eye: Urbanism, Art & Power in Early Modern Florence*
Marvin Trachtenberg
Cambridge University Press

2000 *The Architectural Treatise in the Renaissance*
Alina A. Payne
Cambridge University Press

2001 *The Architecture of Red Vienna, 1919–1934*
Eve Blau
MIT Press

2002 *Modernism and Nation-Building:*
   Turkish Architectural Culture in
   the Early Republic
   Sibel Bozdogan
   University of Washington Press

   Marcel Breuer: The Career and the
   Buildings
   Isabelle Hyman
   Harry N. Abrams

2003 *The Chicago Auditorium Building:*
   Adler and Sullivan's Architecture
   and the City
   Joseph Siry
   University of Chicago Press

2004 *The Chicago Tribune Tower*
   Competition: Skyscraper Design and
   Cultural Change in the 1920s
   Katherine Solomonson
   Cambridge University Press

2005 *House and Home in Modern Japan:*
   Architecture, Domestic Space, and
   Bourgeois Culture, 1880–1930
   Jordan Sand
   Harvard University Press

2006 *Architecture and Nature: Creating*
   the American Landscape
   Christine Macy and
    Sarah Bonnemaison
   Routledge

2007 *Architecture and Suburbia: From*
   English Villa to American Dream
   House, 1690–2000
   John Archer
   University of Minnesota Press

* At this time the SAH altered its award schedule
  to coincide with its annual meeting; therefore,
  no award for 1993 was granted.

Source: Society of Architectural Historians

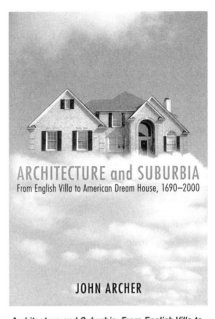

Architecture and Suburbia: From English Villa to American Dream House, 1690–2000 by John **Archer** (Photo courtesy University of Minnesota Press)

American Academy of Arts and Letters Awards

The American Academy of Arts and Letters grants its annual Academy Awards for Architecture to an American architect(s) whose work is characterized by a strong personal direction. It also presents a gold medal in the arts, rotating yearly among painting, music, sculpture, poetry, and architecture. An architect's entire career is weighed when being considered for this award.

Visit the academy's website, *www.artsandletters.org*, for more information.

Academy Awards for Architecture

1991	Rodolfo Machado and Jorge Silvetti	2002	Rick Joy
1992	Thom Mayne and Michael Rotondi, Morphosis		Office dA/Mónica Ponce de León with Nader Tehrani
1993	Franklin D. Israel	2003	Greg Lynn
1994	Craig Hodgetts and Hsin-Ming Fung		Guy Nordensen
1995	Mack Scogin and Merrill Elam	2004	Andrew Zago
1996	Maya Lin		Preston Scott Cohen
1997	Daniel Libeskind		Marion Weiss and Michael Manfredi
1998	Laurie D. Olin		James Corner
1999	Eric Owen Moss	2005	Gisue Hariri and Mojgan Hariri
2000	Will Bruder		Toshiko Mori
	Jesse Reiser and Nanako Umemoto		Massimo and Lella Vignelli
2001	Vincent James	2006	Marwan Al-Sayed
	SHoP/Sharples Holden Pasquarelli		Yung Ho Chang (China)
			Jeanne Gang
		2007	Wes Jones
			Tom Kundig
			Lebbeus Woods

Gold Medal for Architecture

1912	William Rutherford Mead	1973	Louis I. Kahn
1921	Cass Gilbert	1979	I.M. Pei
1930	Charles Adams Platt	1984	Gordon Bunshaft
1940	William Adams Delano	1990	Kevin Roche
1949	Frederick Law Olmsted Jr.	1996	Philip Johnson
1953	Frank Lloyd Wright	2002	Frank Gehry
1958	Henry R. Shepley		
1963	Ludwig Mies van der Rohe		
1968	R. Buckminster Fuller		

Source: American Academy of Arts and Letters

Annual Interiors Awards

The Annual Interiors Awards recognize interior design excellence in multiple commercial categories. A jury of design professionals selects winning projects based on aesthetics, design creativity, function, and achievement of client objectives. Winners are honored at an awards breakfast in New York, and their projects are published in *Contract* magazine.

For more information, visit *Contract*'s website at *www.contractmagazine.com.*

2007 Winners

Large Office
Cole & Weber United
Seattle, WA
Gensler

Small Office
Lehrer Architects
Los Angeles, CA
Lehrer Architects

Education
Double Jeopardy, Taubman College of
    Architecture & Urban Planning,
    University of Michigan
Ann Arbor, MI
PEG office of landscape + architecture

Public Space
General Motors Renaissance Center
Detroit, MI
Skidmore, Owings & Merrill

Small Restaurant
Lettus: Café Organic
San Francisco, CA
CCS Architecture

Restoration
Howard M. Metzenbaum U.S. Courthouse
Cleveland, OH
Westlake Reed Leskosky

Sports/Entertainment
Gopher Spot Game and Convenience
    Store, University of Minnesota
St. Paul, MN
Studio Hive

Retail
Blanc de Chine
New York, NY
S. Russell Groves

Environmental Design
Interdisciplinary Science + Technology
    Building 2, Arizona State University
Temple, AZ
richärd+bauer

Healthcare
University of Wisconsin Cancer Center at
    Johnson Creek
Johnson Creek, WI
OWP/P

Student
D-Prep
University of California, Long Beach
Christopher Petit

JURY
Ann Beha, Ann Beha Architects
Giorgio Borruso, Giorgio Borruso Design
Mark Harbick, Huntsman Architectural Group
Brigitte Preston, lauckgroup

Source: Contract

AR Awards for Emerging Architecture

The AR Awards for Emerging Architecture is an annual international competition, administered by the British publication *Architectural Review*, intended to bring wider recognition to a talented new generation of architects and designers age 45 and under. Any completed building, interior, landscape, urban site, or product design is eligible. A total of £15,000 in prize money is awarded to the winners.

Photos of the winners are available at *www.architecturalreviewawards.com*.

2006 Winners

Footbridge
Lake Austin, TX
Miró Rivera Architects

Children's Treatment Center
Hokkaido, Japan
Sou Fujimoto Architects (Japan)

Handmade School
Rudrapur, Bangladesh
Anna Heringer, (Austria) Eike Roswag
(Germany)

2006 High Commendations

Concrete pod micro space furniture
Nagoya, Japan
Kazuya Morita Architecture Studio (Japan)

House
Tokyo, Japan
Yuko Nagayama & Associates (Japan)

Mafoombey acoustic space
Helsinki, Finland
Martti Kalliala and Esa Ruskeepää with
   Martin Lukasczyk (Finland)

Restoration of Pont Trencat
Sant Celoni and Santa Maria de
   Palautodera, Spain
Xavier Font (Turkey)

Dalaman International Airport
Mugla, Turkey
Emre Arolat Architects (Turkey)

Two Houses
Hokkaido, Japan
Sou Fujimoto Architects (Japan)

Experimental House
Tsukuba, Ibaraki, Japan
Loco Architects (Japan)

Footbridge, Lake Austin, TX, by Miró Rivera Architects (Photo: Paul Finkel, courtesy of Miró Rivera Architects)

AR Awards for Emerging Architecture

2006 Honorable Mentions

House
Rathmines, Dublin, Ireland
Boyd Cody Architects (Ireland)

Walmajarri Community Centre
Djugerari, Great Sandy Desert, Western
    Australia
Iredale Pedersen Hook Architects
    (Australia)

Tan Quee Lan Apartments
Singapore
WOHA Architects (Singapore)

Aurland Lookout
Aurland, Norway
Saunders Arkitektur (Norway); Wilhelmsen
    Arkitektur (Norway)

Topographical Amnesias
Belo Horizonte, Brazil
Vazio S/A Arquitetura e Urbanismo
    (Brazil)

Tea House
Saroma, Tokoro-gun, Hokkaido, Japan
Jun Igarashi Architects (Japan)

Kastrup Sea Bath
Copenhagen, Denmark
White Arkitekter (Denmark)

Extension to Santo Stefano al Mare
    Cemetery
Santa Stefano al Mare, Italy
Aldo Amoretti, Marco Calvi, Giancarlo
    Ranalli (Italy)

Dolce & Gabbana Headquarters and
    Showrooms
Milan, Italy
+ARCH Fresa Fuenmayor Garbellini
    Tricario (Italy)

Temporary Pavilion for Archaeological
    Relics
Parco dell'Appia Antica, Villa dei Quintili,
    Rome, Italy
n!studio Ferrini Stella Architetti Associati
    (Italy)

Aqua-scape
Tokomachi-city, Niigata Prefecture, Japan
Fujiki Studio, KOU::ARC (Japan)

Windshape
Lacoste, France
nARCHITECTS

House
Enns, Volkersdorf, Austria
Bau/Kultur (Austria)

Buddhist Retreat
Wat Kao Buddhakhodom, Sri Racha,
    Chonburi Province, Thailand
Suriya Umpansiriratana (Thailand)

Hana-Tetsu Flower Shop
Osaka, Japan
Naoto Yamakuma/kt architects (Japan)

Jaegersborg Water Tower
Gentofte, Denmark
Dorte Mandrup Arkitekter (Denmark)

JURY

Christine Binswanger, Herzog & de Meuron
    (Switzerland)
Peter Davey, author (UK)
Mark Dytham, (Japan)
Paul Finch, *Architectural Review* (UK)
Kim Herforth Nielsen, 3XN (Denmark)
Benedetta Tagliabue, EMBT (Spain)

Source: Architectural Review

Architectural Photography Competition

Sponsored by the St. Louis chapter of the American Institute of Architects, the Architectural Photography Competition celebrates outstanding architectural photos by AIA members. Photos taken anywhere in the world are eligible. However, the Albert Fuller Award, named for the founder of the competition, is limited to US subjects. In addition to a cash prize, winning photos are eligible for inclusion in the American Architectural Foundation's yearly desk calendar.

Winning photos can be seen at *www.aia-stlouis.org.*

2007 Winners

First Place
"Screen"
Berlin, Germany
James Stem

Second Place
"Untitled"
Athens, Greece
Andrew Morrall

Third Place
"Liberia Figurines"
Venice, Italy
David Wood

Albert Fuller Award
"Where Snow Flies"
Ennis, MT
Henry Sorenson Jr.

**Judges Special
Commendation Awards**
"Prague Sunrise"
Prague, Czech Republic
David Metzger

"Layered Opening"
Gwalior, India
Jacob Albert

"Alhambra Tilework"
Granada, Spain
Susan Ingham

"Giza"
Egypt
Bryce Tolene

"Open Sky"
Jeju Island, South Korea
Jae Kauh

"Yellow Hydrant"
Valparaiso, Chile
Steven House

"Break Into the Rational"
Barcelona, Spain
Andrea Quilici

"Ghery's Vision"
Boston, MA
Shannon Chance

"Rough Blue"
Arequipa, Peru
Sheila Colon

"Ocean, Door, Sky"
Santorini, Greece
Andrew Morrall

Source: AIA St. Louis

Architecture Firm Award

The American Institute of Architects grants its Architecture Firm Award, the highest honor the AIA can bestow on a firm, annually to an architecture firm for consistently producing distinguished architecture. Eligible firms must claim collaboration within the practice as a hallmark of their methodology and must have been producing work as an entity for at least 10 years.

For more information, visit the AIA online at *www.aia.org*.

1962	Skidmore, Owings & Merrill	1986	Esherick Homsey Dodge and Davis
1963	*No award granted*	1987	Benjamin Thompson & Associates
1964	The Architects Collaborative		
1965	Wurster, Bernardi & Emmons	1988	Hartman-Cox Architects
1966	*No award granted*	1989	Cesar Pelli & Associates
1967	Hugh Stubbins & Associates	1990	Kohn Pedersen Fox Associates
1968	I.M. Pei & Partners	1991	Zimmer Gunsul Frasca Partnership
1969	Jones & Emmons		
1970	Ernest J. Kump Associates	1992	James Stewart Polshek & Partners
1971	Albert Kahn Associates, Inc.		
1972	Caudill Rowlett Scott	1993	Cambridge Seven Associates
1973	Shepley Bulfinch Richardson and Abbott	1994	Bohlin Cywinski Jackson
		1995	Beyer Blinder Belle
1974	Kevin Roche John Dinkeloo & Associates	1996	Skidmore, Owings & Merrill
		1997	R.M. Kliment & Frances Halsband Architects
1975	Davis, Brody & Associates		
1976	Mitchell/Giurgola Architects	1998	Centerbrook Architects and Planners
1977	Sert Jackson and Associates		
1978	Harry Weese & Associates	1999	Perkins & Will
1979	Geddes Brecher Qualls Cunningham	2000	Gensler
		2001	Herbert Lewis Kruse Blunck Architecture
1980	Edward Larrabee Barnes Associates		
		2002	Thompson, Ventulett, Stainback & Associates
1981	Hardy Holzman Pfeiffer Associates		
		2003	Miller/Hull Partnership
1982	Gwathmey Siegel & Associates, Architects	2004	Lake/Flato Architects
		2005	Murphy/Jahn Architects
1983	Holabird & Root	2006	Moore Ruble Yudell Architects & Planners
1984	Kallmann, McKinnell & Wood Architects		
		2007	Leers Weinzapfel Associates
1985	Venturi, Rauch and Scott Brown		

Source: American Institute of Architects

Clockwise from top: **Principals of Leers Weinzapfel Associates Architects, Inc.,** *from left,* **Josiah Stevenson, Andrea Leers, Jane Weinzapfel, Joe Pryse; Princeton University Chilled Water Plant Addition, Princeton, NJ** (Photo: Alan Karchmer/Esto); **Harvard University Science Center Expansion, Cambridge, MA** (Photo: Alan Karchmer/Esto)

Arnold W. Brunner Memorial Prize

The American Academy of Arts and Letters annually awards the Arnold W. Brunner Memorial Prize to architects of any nationality who have contributed to architecture as an art. The award consists of a $5,000 prize. The prize is named in honor of the notable New York architect and city planner, Arnold William Brunner, who died in 1925.

For more information, visit the academy's website at *www.artsandletters.org.*

1955	Gordon Bunshaft	1982	Helmut Jahn
	Minoru Yamasaki*	1983	Frank Gehry
1956	John Yeon	1984	Peter Eisenman
1957	John Carl Warnecke	1985	William Pedersen and
1958	Paul Rudolph		Arthur May
1959	Edward Larrabee Barnes	1986	John Hejduk
1960	Louis I. Kahn	1987	James Ingo Freed
1961	I.M. Pei	1988	Arata Isozaki (Japan)
1962	Ulrich Franzen	1989	Richard Rogers (UK)
1963	Edward C. Bassett	1990	Steven Holl
1964	Harry Weese	1991	Tadao Ando (Japan)
1965	Kevin Roche	1992	Sir Norman Foster (UK)
1966	Romaldo Giurgola	1993	Rafael Moneo (Spain)
1967	*No award granted*	1994	Renzo Piano (Italy)
1968	John M. Johansen	1995	Daniel Urban Kiley
1969	N. Michael McKinnell	1996	Tod Williams and Billie Tsien
1970	Charles Gwathmey and	1997	Henri Ciriani (France)
	Richard Henderson	1998	Alvaro Siza (Portugal)
1971	John H. Andrews (Australia)	1999	Fumihiko Maki (Japan)
1972	Richard Meier	2000	Toyo Ito (Japan)
1973	Robert Venturi	2001	Henry Smith-Miller and
1974	Hugh Hardy with Norman		Laurie Hawkinson
	Pfeiffer and Malcolm	2002	Kazuyo Sejima + Ryue Nishizawa
	Holzman		(Japan)
1975	Lewis Davis and Samuel Brody	2003	Elizabeth Diller and
1976	James Stirling (UK)		Ricardo Scofidio
1977	Henry N. Cobb	2004	Hans Hollein (Austria)
1978	Cesar Pelli	2005	Shigeru Ban (Japan)
1979	Charles Moore	2006	Jean Nouvel (France)
1980	Michael Graves	2007	Eric Owen Moss
1981	Gunnar Birkerts		

* Honorable Mention

Source: American Academy of Arts and Letters

Arthur Ross Awards

Presented annually by the Institute of Classical Architecture & Classical America, the Arthur Ross Awards celebrate the achievements and contributions of architects, painters, sculptors, artisans, landscape designers, educators, publishers, patrons, and others dedicated to preserving the classical tradition. Award categories include architecture, community design, education, landscape design, and stewardship.

A list of winners in all categories is available online at *www.classicist.org*.

Architecture Recipients

1982	Philip Trammell Shutze	1992	Sherman Pardue
1983	Edward Vason Jones		Thomas H. Beeby
	Samuel Wilson Jr.	1993	William T. Baker
1984	Rurik F. Eckstrom	1994	George M. White
	David Anthony Easton		Ernesto Buch
1985	A. Hays Town	1995	Jaquelin Robertson
	Douglas L. Greene	1996	Robert I. Cole
	David Warren Hardwicke	1997	Milton Grenfell
1986	Thomas C. Celli	1998	Joseph Dixon III
	Shahi Patel		Nell E. Davis
	Robert T. Meeker	1999	Curtis and Windham Architects
1987	Norman Neuerberg	2000	Harold H. Fisher
	David T. Mayernik	2001	John Blatteau
	Thomas N. Rajkovich	2002	Quinlan Terry (UK)
1988	Frank Garretson	2003	Ferguson & Shamamian
	David Anthony		Architects
1989	Floyd E. Johnson	2004	Merrill and Pastor Architects
1990	Allan Greenberg	2005	Demetri Porphyrios (UK)
1991	Boris Baranovich	2006	Hartman-Cox Architects
	Robert A.M. Stern	2007	Michael G. Imber Architects

Source: Institute of Classical Architecture & Classical America

ASLA Firm Award

The American Society of Landscape Architects presents its annual ASLA Firm Award to a landscape architecture firm that has produced a body of distinguished work for at least 10 years. Nominees are reviewed for their influence on the profession, their collaborative environment, the consistent quality of their work, and their recognition among fellow practitioners, teachers, allied professionals, and the general public.

Information about the winning firms is available from the ASLA's website, *www.asla.org.*

2003	Jones & Jones Architects and Landscape Architects
2004	Wallace Roberts & Todd
2005	SWA Group
2006	Olin Partnership
2007	Sasaki Associates, Inc.

Source: American Society of Landscape Architects

I have found it helpful to think of a garden as sculpture, not sculpture in the ordinary sense of an object to be viewed. But sculpture that is large enough and perforated enough to walk through. And open enough to present no barrier to movement, and broken enough to guide the experience, which is essentially a communion with the sky. This is a garden.

James Rose

ASLA Medals

25

The American Society of Landscape Architects awards its highest honor, the ASLA Medal, to individuals who have made a significant contribution to the field of landscape architecture in such areas as landscape design, planning, writing, and public service. The ASLA Design Medal recognizes landscape architects who have produced a body of exceptional design work at a sustained level for at least 10 years.

Information about the winners can be found at *www.asla.org*.

ASLA Medal

1971	Hideo Sasaki	1990	Raymond L. Freeman
1972	Conrad L. Wirth	1991	Meade Palmer
1973	John C. Simonds	1992	Robert S. (Doc) Reich
1974	Campbell E. Miller	1993	Arthur E. Bye Jr.
1975	Garrett Eckbo	1994	Edward D. Stone Jr.
1976	Thomas Church	1995	Ervin H. Zube
1977	Hubert B. Owens	1996	John Lyle
1978	Lawrence Halprin	1997	Julius Fabos
1979	Norman T. Newton	1998	Carol R. Johnson
1980	William G. Swain	1999	Stuart C. Dawson
1981	Sir Geoffrey Jellicoe (UK)	2000	Carl D. Johnson
1982	Charles W. Eliot II	2001	Robert E. Marvin
1983	Theodore Osmundson	2002	Morgan (Bill) Evans
1984	Ian McHarg	2003	Richard Haag
1985	Roberto Burle Marx (Brazil)	2004	Peter Walker
1986	William J. Johnson	2005	Jane Silverstein Ries
1987	Philip H. Lewis Jr.	2006	Cameron R.J. Man
1988	Dame Sylvia Crowe (UK)	2007	William B. Callaway
1989	Robert N. Royston		

ASLA Design Medal

2003	Lawrence Halprin
2004	M. Paul Friedberg
2005	Laurie D. Olin
2006	Steve Martino
2007	Richard Haag

Source: American Society of Landscape Architects

ASLA Professional Awards

With the annual Professional Awards program, the American Society of Landscape Architects honors the best in landscape architecture from around the globe. Recipients receive coverage in *Landscape Architecture* magazine; winners in the residential category are also featured in *Garden Design* magazine. Landmark Award recognizes a distinguished landscape architecture project completed 15 to 50 years ago that retains its original design integrity and contributes significantly to the public realm.

Photos and descriptions of the winning projects can be seen on the ASLA's website, *www.asla.org.*

2007 General Design Winners

Award of Excellence
M. Victor and Frances Leventritt Garden,
    Arnold Arboretum, Harvard University
Boston, MA
Reed Hilderbrand

Honor Awards
Curran House
San Francisco, CA
Andrea Cochran Landscape Architecture

The Red Ribbon, Tanghe River Park
Qinhuangdao City, Hebei Province, China
Turenscape and Peking University
    Graduate School of Landscape
    Architecture (China)

One North Wacker Drive
Chicago, IL
PWP Landscape Architecture

Restoration of Giant Forest
Sequoia National Park, CA
National Park Service

Mesa Arts Center
Mesa, AZ
Martha Schwartz Partners

Washington Mutual Center Roof Garden
Seattle, WA
Phillips Farevaag Smallenberg (Canada)

Swenson Science Building, University
    of Minnesota Duluth
Duluth, MN
oslund.and.assoc.

Olympic Sculpture Park
Seattle, WA
Weiss/Manfredi; Charles Anderson
    Landscape Architecture

Glacier Club
Durango, CO
Design Workshop

Harvard Graduate Student Housing
    at 29 Garden Street
Cambridge, MA
Richard Burck Associates, Inc.; Jonathan
    Levi Architects with Bergmeyer
    Associates, Inc.

NE Siskiyou Green Street
Portland, OR
Kevin Robert Perry

Mount Tabor Middle School Rain Garden
Portland, OR
Kevin Robert Perry and Brandon Wilson

2007 Residential Design Winners

Award of Excellence
Elie Saab Residence
Faqra, Lebanon
Vladimir Djurovic Landscape Architecture
    (Lebanon)

Honor Awards
Private Residence
San Francisco, CA
Andrea Cochran Landscape Architecture

Erman Residence
San Francisco, CA
Surfacedesign, Inc; James A. Lord,
    Roderick R. Wyllie, Moritz Moellers,
    Geoff di Girolamo

Malinalco House
Malinalco, Mexico
Grupo de Diseño Urbano (Mexico)

Manhattan Roof Terrace
New York, NY
Sawyer/Berson Architecture & Landscape
    Architecture

Farrar Pond Residence
Lincoln, MA
Mikyoung Kim Design

Pump House
Highland Park, TX
MESA Design Group; D.I.R.T. Studio

Sonoma Vineyard
Glen Ellen, CA
MFLA Marta Fry Landscape Associates

Woody Creek Garden
Pitkin County, CO
Design Workshop

Connecticut Country House
Westport, CT
Wesley Stout Associates

Lunada Bay Residence
Palos Verdes Peninsula, Southern
    California
Artecho Architecture and Landscape
    Architecture

2007 Analysis and Planning Winners

Award of Excellence
Hunters Point Waterfront Park Project
San Francisco, CA
Hargreaves Associates

Honor Awards
The Park and New Town upon the fish-
    ponds - The Planning of 2007 China
    International Garden Show Park Area
    in Xiamen
Xiamen, China
Atelier DYJG (China)

Wildhorse Ranch
Steens Mountain, OR
DHM Design

Atlanta BeltLine Redevelopment Plan
Atlanta, GA
EDAW Inc.

Penn Connects: A Vision for the Future
Philadelphia, PA
Sasaki Associates, Inc.

University of Balamand Campus Master
    Plan
Al Koura, Tripoli, Lebanon
Sasaki Associates, Inc.

Lower Howard's Creek Corridor
    Management Plan
Clark County, KY
Parsons Brinckerhoff with Ned Crankshaw

ASLA Professional Awards

Open Space Seattle 2100 Envisioning
Seattle's Green Infrastructure for the
Next Century
Seattle, WA

Department of Landscape Architecture,
University of Washington; Open Space
Seattle 2100 Coalition

2007 Research Winners

Award of Excellence
Defiant Gardens: Making Gardens in Wartime
Kenneth I. Helphand
Trinity University Press

Honor Awards
The Green Build-out Model: Quantifying
Stormwater Benefits of Trees and
Greenroofs in Washington, DC
Casey Trees Endowment Fund

2007 Communications Winners

Award of Excellence
TOPOS - The International Review of
Landscape Architecture and Urban
Design
Munich, Germany

Honor Awards
The Chicago Green Alley Handbook
Chicago, Illinois
Hitchcock Design Group

Cultural Landscapes as Classrooms Series
Cultural Landscape Foundation

2007 Landmark Award Winner

Charleston Waterfront Park
Charleston, SC
Sasaki Associates, Inc.

JURY

Warren T. Byrd, Nelson Byrd Woltz Landscape
Architects
William B. Calloway, SWA Group
Adele Chatfield-Taylor, American Academy in
Rome
Christopher Dimond, HNTB (chair)
Astrid Haryati, City of Chicago
Richard Hawks, State University of New York

Raymond Jungles, Raymond Jungles, Inc.
Ketzel Levine, National Public Radio
Bill Marken, *Garden Design*
Ken Smith, Ken Smith Landscape Architecture
William H. Tishler, National Trust for Historic
Preservation

Source: American Society of Landscape Architects

Mesa Arts Center, Mesa, AZ, by Martha Schwartz Partners (Photo: Shauna Gillies-Smith, courtesy of the American Society of Landscape Architects)

Auguste Perret Prize

The International Union of Architects (UIA) grants the triennial Auguste Perret Prize to an internationally renowned architect or architects for work in applied technology in architecture. The prize is named after notable French architect Auguste Perret, a leading pioneer of reinforced concrete design.

For more information, visit the UIA's website at *www.uia-architectes.org.*

1961	Felix Candela (Mexico)
	Architect's office of the British Ministry of Education (UK)*
	Architects of the Office for the Study of Industrial and Agricultural Buildings of Hungary (Hungary)*
1963	Kunio Mayekawa (Japan)
	Jean Prouvé (France)
1965	Hans Scharoun (GFR)
	Heikki and Kaija Siren (Finland)*
1967	Frei Otto and Rolf Gutbrod (GFR)
1969	Karel Hubacek (Czechoslovakia)
1972	E. Pinez Pinero (Spain)
1975	Arthur C. Erickson and team (Canada)
	J. Cardoso (Brazil)*

1978	Kiyonori Kitutake (Japan)
	Piano & Rogers (Italy/UK)
1981	Günter Behnisch (GFR)
	Jacques Rougerie (France)*
1984	João Baptista Vilanova Artigas (Brazil)
1987	Santiago Calatrava (Spain)
	Clorindo Testa (Argentina)*
1990	Adien Fainsilber (France)
1993	KHR AS Arkitekten (Denmark)
1996	Thomas Herzog (Germany)
1999	Ken Yeang (Malaysia)
2002	Sir Norman Foster (UK)
2005	Werner Sobek (Germany)

*Honorary Mentions

Source: International Union of Architects

Architecture is fantasy made of precisions.

Gio Ponti

Best of 50+ Housing Awards

The National Association of Home Builders' 50+ Housing Council annually presents the Best of 50+ Housing Awards. Winning projects are chosen for their ability to meet the needs of the ever-changing seniors' housing market, including marketability, budget, density, and program. Gold, silver, and innovation awards are presented in a range of categories based on project type and size.

A list of all winners is available online at *www.nahb.org/50plusawards*.

2007 Gold Winners

Active Adult Housing:
Overall Community
Midsize (201 to 750 Homes)
Grayson Hill
Richmond, VA
Lessard Group, Inc.

Active Adult Housing:
Overall Community
Large (Over 750 Homes)
Leisure World of Virginia
Lansdowne, VA
HLS Architects

Active Adult Housing: Clubhouse
Large (Over 6,000 Square Feet)
SaddleBrook—The Preserve Clubhouse
Tucson, AZ
SHJ Studios

Active Adult Housing: Clubhouse
Interior Design
Small (Up to 6,000 Square Feet)
Grayson Hill, Richmond, VA
Interior Concepts

Active Adult Housing:
Home Design
(Over 2,400 Square Feet)
SaddleBrook—The Preserve
Tucson, AZ
Robson Communities, Inc.

Active Adult Housing:
Attached Communities –
Overall Community
Caldwell Farm
Newbury, MA
The MZO Group

Active Adult Housing: Attached
Unit Design – For-Sale Attached
(Up to 1,700 Square Feet)
Lincoln Square Lofts
Lone Tree, CO
KEPHART

Regency at Dominion Valley
Haymarket, VA
Toll Brothers

Active Adult Housing: Attached
Unit Design – On the Boards
Pond's Edge
Egg Harbor Township, NJ
VLBJR Architects, Inc.

Active Adult Housing:
Model Home Merchandising
(Up to 1,700 Square Feet)
The Highlands of Glenmoor
Easton, PA
Feinberg & Associates

Active Adult Housing: Model
Home Merchandising
(Over 2,400 Square Feet)
Grayson Hill
Richmond, VA
Lessard Group, Inc.

Best of 50+ Housing Awards

Active Adult Housing: On the Boards Clubhouse
Large (Over 6,000 Square Feet)
Clubhouse at the Dominion
San Antonio, TX
Irwin Pancake Architects

Continuing Care Retirement Community: Overall Community
Large (Over 200 Units)
Splendido at Rancho Vistoso
Tucson, AZ
Solomon Cordwell Buenz & Associates

Continuing Care Retirement Community: Common Area Interior Design
Large (Over 200 Units)
Splendido at Rancho Vistoso
Tucson, AZ
Interior Design Associates, Inc.

Sun City Ginza East
Tokyo, Japan
Barry Design Associates

Continuing Care Retirement Community: Congregate/ Independent Living Community – Overall Community
Sun City Takarazuka
Takarazuka, Japan
BAR Architects

Continuing Care Retirement Community: Congregate/ Independent Living Community – On the Boards
Parc at Buckhead
Atlanta, GA
Design Services

Continuing Care Retirement Community: Assisted Living Residences – Overall Facility
Sunrise Connecticut Avenue
Washington, DC
BeeryRio

Continuing Care Retirement Community: Assisted Living Residences – On the Boards
Residencia Assitida
Monterrey, Nuevo Leon, Mexico
Galier.Tolson.French Design Associates

Continuing Care Retirement Community: Special Needs Housing – Overall Facility
La Vida Real Memory Care Wing
San Diego, CA
Mithun Architects + Designers + Planners

Multifamily Housing: Overall Community – Income-Qualified/ Affordable Rental Apartments)
Victory House of Palmer Park
Palmer Park, MD
Grimm + Parker Architects

Cortina d'Arroyo
Arroyo Grande, CA
RRM Design Group

Multifamily Housing: Common Area Interior Design – Income-Qualified/Affordable Rental Apartments
Cortina d'Arroyo
Arroyo Grande, CA
Linda Howard Interior Design, Inc

Multifamily Housing: On the Boards – Income-Qualified/Affordable Rental Apartments
Columbia Senior Residences at MLK
    Village
Atlanta, GA
James, Harwick + Partners

Special Judges' Award: Active Adult Innovation
Watermere at Southlake
Southlake, TX
Galier.Tolson.French Design Associates

Source: National Association of Home Builders

Best of NeoCon

The Best of NeoCon competition honors the best new products introduced to the US contract market during the past year. A jury of industry professionals selects gold, silver, editor's choice, and innovation award winners. From these, one product is chosen as the best of competition. Winners are announced at NeoCon, the interior design industry's annual showcase for the latest products and trends.

For a list of all winners, including photos, visit *Contract* online at *www.contractmagazine.com.*

2007 Best of Competition

Brazo
Haworth, Inc.

2007 Gold Winners

Architectural Products
Color
3form, Inc.

Carpet: Broadloom
Bas Relief Grid & Rib Series
Monterey Tandus

Carpet: Modular
Dressed2Kill
Shaw Contract Group

Carpet: Fiber
Antron Lumineria
Antron Carpet Fiber

Casegoods/Desks/Credenzas
Uffizi Collection
Tuohy Furniture Corp.

Conference Room Furniture
Planes
Haworth, Inc.

Design Tools
Inunison Virtual Sample Folders
Tandus

Education Solutions
Vanerum Collection
StellerPartners

Flooring Resilient
Karim Kolors
Tarkett Commercial

Furniture Systems
Marketplace
Teknion

Furniture Systems: Enhancements
Axis
Industrias Riviera

Healthcare: Fabrics
AgION Upholstery
cf stinson, Inc.

Healthcare: Furniture
Opus Overbed Table
Nurture by Steelcase

Healthcare: Seating
Pause
Brandrud

Best of NeoCon

Healthcare: Textiles
When I Grow Up
Momentum Textiles

Lighting
Brazo
Haworth, Inc.

Office Accessories
Switch Mouse
Humanscale

Seating: Benches
Rottet by Decca Bench
Decca Contract

Seating: Conference
Axos
Interstuhl Bueromoebel

Seating: Ergonomic/Desk/Task
Arria
Steelcase Inc.

Seating: Guest
Global Edition
Bernhardt Design

Seating: Sofas & Lounge
Valeri Collection
Leland International

Seating: Stacking
Elena
Barcelona Seating Collection

Software Technologies
20-20 Office Sales 2008
20-20 Technologies

Tables: Conference
Converge
Gunlocke

Tables: Occasional
The Blas Series
HBF

Tables: Training
Akira
Vecta

Technology Support
Eubiq Power Outlet
Eubiq Pte. Ltd.

Textiles: Drapery
Biedermeier Collection
Architex

Textiles: Upholstery
LUX[e]
Luna Textiles

Wall Treatments
Lusterware
Knoll Inc.

Worksurfaces: Height-Adjustable
NEXT
Baker Manufacturing

Source: Contract

Bottom Line Design Awards

Sponsored by *Business 2.0* and frog design, the Bottom Line Design Awards recognize the positive effects of experience-driven industrial design on businesses and their brands. Jurors analyze entries for such factors as sales record, brand fit, relevance to the target consumer, marketing program, utilization of technology, impact on the corporate culture, improvement over previous models, ease of use, noteworthy design, and the generation of world-of-mouth recommendations and customer loyalty.

Profiles and photos of the winning designs are available online at *www.bottomlinedesignawards.com.*

2007 Winners

Aeronautics
Eclipse 500
Eclipse Aviation, IDEO, and BMW

Architecture
LivingHomes RK1
Ray Kappe

Brand Extension
Electrolux Jeppe Utzon Barbeque
Jeppe Utzon (Denmark)

Consumer Electronics
Kodak EasyShare V570
BlueMap Design

Energy
Quietrevolution QR5
Richard Cochrane (UK)

Home Appliance
InSinkErator Evolution Excel
Continuum

Luxury Goods
WinePod
Sterling Design

Marketing
H-Racer Hydrogen Fuel Cell Car
Taras Wankewycz

Medical
Optovue RTVue
Whipsaw

Navigation
Mio DigiWalker H610
Mitac International

Promotion
FogScreen
Ismo Rakkolainen (US), Karri Palovuori
     (Finland)

JURY
Marissa Mayer, Google
Virginia Postrel, author
Mark Rolston, frog design
Ron Snyder, Crocs
Carol Wilder, The NewSchool

Source: Business 2.0 *and frog design*

Bridge Awards

The Engineers' Society of Western Pennsylvania recognizes outstanding bridge engineering with its annual Bridge Awards. Four awards—the George S. Richardson Medal, Gustav Lindenthal Medal, Eugene C. Figg Medal, Arthur G. Hayden Medal—honor bridges for various meritorious qualities, including design, technical innovation, and service to the community.

More information is available from the society's website, *www.eswp.com.*

George S. Richardson Medal

1988	Sunshine Skyway Bridge
	St. Petersburg–Bradenton, FL
1989	Honshu-Shikoku Bridge Routes
	(specifically the Kojima-
	Sakaide Route)
	Kobe–Sakaide, Japan
1990	Ben Sawyer Bridge
	Mt. Pleasant–Sullivans Island, SC
1990	Oakland Bay Bridge
	San Francisco–Oakland, CA
1991	Roosevelt Lake Bridge
	Roosevelt, AZ
1992	Lake Washington Floating Bridge
	Seattle, WA
1993	Hanging Lake Viaduct
	Glenwood Canyon, CO
1994	Natchez Trace Parkway Bridge
	Franklin, TN
1995	Normandy Bridge
	Le Havre–Honfleur, France
1996	LRFD Design Specifications
1997	George P. Coleman Bridge
	Yorktown, VA

1998	Akashi-Kaikyo Bridge
	Honshu–Awaji, Japan
1999	Confederation Bridge
	Northumberland Strait, Port
	Borden, PE–Cape
	Tormentine, NB, Canada
2000	Storrow Drive Bridge
	Boston, MA
2001	Tagus River Suspension Bridge
	Rail Addition Project
	Lisbon, Portugal
2002	Lions Gate Bridge
	Vancouver, BC, Canada
2003	Leonard P. Zakim Bunker Hill
	Bridge
	Boston, MA
2004	Al Zampa Memorial Bridge
	(New Carquinez Bridge)
	Vallejo, CA
2005	Rion–Antirion Bridge
	(Harilaos Trikoupis Bridge)
	Rion–Antirrion, Greece
2006	LRFD Unified Steel Design
	Code, William Wright, Michael
	Grubb and Don White
2007	No. 3 Yangtze River Bridge
	Nanjing, China

Gustav Lindenthal Medal

1999	Interstate H-3 Winward Viaduct Oahu, Hawaii
2000	Golden Gate Bridge San Francisco, CA
2001	Oresund Fixed Link Bridge Project Copenhagen, Denmark–Malmö, Sweden
2002	Broadway Bridge Daytona Beach, FL
2003	President JK Bridge Brasilia, Brazil

2004	Mingo Creek Viaduct (Joe Montana Bridge) Washington County, PA
2005	Viaduct of Millau Millau, France
2006	Arthur J. Ravenel Jr. Bridge Charleston, SC
2007	Penobscot Narrows Bridge and Observatory Waldo and Hancock counties, ME

Eugene C. Figg Jr. Medal for Signature Bridges

2002	Jiangyin Bridge Jiangyin, China
2003	Rama 8 Bridge Chaiyuth Na Nakorn, Bangkok, Thailand
2004	Lu Pu Bridge Shanghai, China

2005	Sundial Bridge at Turtle Bay Redding, CA
2006	Dagu Bridge Tianjin, China
2007	Royal Park Bridge Replacement West Palm Beach, FL

Arthur G. Hayden Medal

| 2003 | Duisburg Inner Harbor
Footbridge
Duisburg, Germany |
| 2004 | Esplanade Riel Pedestrian
Bridge
Winnipeg, MB, Canada |

2005	Liberty Bridge Greenville, SC
2006	Gatwick Pier 6 Airbridge London, UK
2007	Nesciobrug Ijburg, Netherlands

Source: Engineers' Society of Western Pennsylvania

Did you know...

Opened in May 2000, the Millennium Bridge is London's only pedestrian bridge. Developed by Foster and Partners with sculptor Anthony Caro, it is also the first bridge built in London since 1894, when the Tower Bridge was completed.

38

BusinessWeek/Architectural Record Awards

The BusinessWeek/Architectural Record Awards are granted annually to organizations that prove good design is good business. Sponsored by *Architectural Record* and *BusinessWeek* magazines, the award's special focus is on collaboration and the achievement of business goals through architecture. Eligible projects must have been completed within the past four years and may be submitted by any architect registered in the United States or abroad.

For more information, visit *Architectural Record* online at *www.archrecord.com*.

2007 Winners

Award of Excellence

Navy Federal Credit Union
Pensacola, FL
ASD Inc.

InterActiveCorp Headquarters
New York, NY
Gehry Partners/STUDIOS Architecture

Young Centre for the Performing Arts
Toronto, ON, Canada
Kuwabara Payne McKenna Blumberg
   Architects (Canada)

United States Census Bureau Headquarters
Suitland, MD
Skidmore, Owings & Merrill

Citation for Excellence

San Diego Padres Ballpark/Petco Park
San Diego, CA
Antoine Predock Architect

Four Seasons Centre for the
   Performing Arts
Toronto, ON, Canada
Diamond and Schmitt Architects Inc.
   (Canada)

Hearst Tower interior
New York, NY
Gensler

SJ Berwin Law Offices
London, UK
Hellmuth, Obata & Kassabaum

Gardiner Museum
Toronto, ON, Canada
Kuwabara Payne McKenna Blumberg
   Architects (Canada)

Hubbell Lighting Headquarters
Greenville, SC
McMillan Smith & Partners

Source: BusinessWeek/Architectural Record

Charter Awards

Presented by the Congress for the New Urbanism, the Charter Awards honor projects that best fulfill and advance the principles of the Charter of the New Urbanism, which defines the essential qualities of outstanding buildings and urban places. The awards recognize architecture, landscape architecture, and urban designs projects that improve the human experience and are built in harmony with their physical and social contexts.

For photos of the winning projects, visit CNU's website at *www.cnu.org.*

2007 Winners

Region, Metropolis, City, Town

Louisiana Speaks: Pattern Book
Urban Design Associates, Ltd.

City Plan 2025
Fayetteville, AR
Dover, Kohl & Partners

Long Beach, Mississippi, Concept Plan
Long Beach, MS
Ayers Saint Gross Architects + Planners

Neighborhood, District, Corridor

Salishan Neighborhood HOPE VI
Tacoma, WA
Torti Gallas and Partners

Harbor Town
Memphis, TN
Looney Ricks Kiss

Street Smart: Streetcars and Cities in the 21st Century
Nationwide
Reconnecting America

Cooper's Crossing
Camden, NJ
Torti Gallas and Partners; Urban Design Associates, Ltd.

Carneros Inn
Napa, CA
William Rawn Associates Architects Inc.

Innovista Master Plan
Columbia, SC
Sasaki Associates, Inc.

La Candelaria
Antigua, Guatemala
Castillo Arquitectos (Guatemala); Dover, Kohl & Partners

Block, Street, Building

Takoma Walk
Takoma Park, MD
Cunningham Quill Architects

Kedzie & Rockwell and Brown Line Stations
Chicago, IL
Muller & Muller, Ltd.

The Ellington
Washington, DC
Torti Gallas and Partners

Oak Plaza
Miami, FL
Cure & Penabad Studio; Khoury & Vogt Architects

Charter Awards

Katrina Cottage VIII
Infill locations, US
Stephen A. Mouzon, Architect

Courthouse Square, Theatre Way,
  and Broadway Streetscapes
Redwood City, CA
Freedman Tung & Bottomley

Lofts 590
Arlington, VA
SK&I Architectural Design Group

Habitat Trails
Rogers, AR
University of Arkansas Community
  Design Center

Chatham Square
Alexandria, VA
Lessard Group, Inc.

Cottage Square
Ocean Springs, MS
Tolar LeBartard Denmark Architects

Academic
Toward an Urban & Sustainable
  Puerto Nuevo
San Juan, Puerto Rico
University of Puerto Rico

Company Towns Revisited: Historic
  Typologies as a Model for Growth
Petit Paradis, Haiti
Notre Dame University

Connecting the City of Water to Its History
Castellamare di Stabia, Italy
University of Maryland

Saucier Town Plan
Saucier, MS
Andrews University

A Response to the Current Development
  of Valparaiso's Waterfront
Valparaiso, Chile
University of Maryland

JURY
Hillary Brown, New Civic Works
Rick Cole, City of Ventura, California
Andrés Duany, Duany Plater-Zyberk & Company
Kjell Forshed, Brunnberg & Forshed (Sweden)
Vince Graham, I'ON Group
Stefanos Polyzoides, Moule & Polyzoides (chair)
Susan Van Atta, Van Atta Associates

Source: Congress for the New Urbanism

If architects are to continue to do useful work on this planet, then surely their proper concern must be the creation of place. To make a place is to make a domain that helps people know where they are and by extension who they are.

Charles Moore

Clockwise from top: **Kedzie & Rockwell Station, Chicago, IL, by Muller & Muller, Ltd.; Carneros Inn, Napa, CA, by William Rawn Associates Architects Inc.; The Ellington, Washington, DC, by Torti Gallas and Partners** (Photos courtesy of the architects and the Congress for the New Urbanism)

Cityscape Architectural Review Awards

Cityscape, an international development conference, and the British magazine *Architectural Review*, jointly grant the Cityscape Architectural Review Awards to promote design excellence in the Middle East, Africa, Central and Eastern Asia, Australasia (excluding Japan, Australia, and New Zealand), and South America. Entries are judged on innovation, environmental awareness, and appropriateness to the site and culture.

For more information, visit Cityscape online at *www.cityscape.ae.*

2006 Winners

Residential, Built
Trevose 12 Group Housing
Singapore
Bedmar & Shi (Singapore)

Residential, Future
Breathing House
Riyadh, Saudi Arabia
Donner & Sorcinelli Architetti (Italy)

Commercial, Built
Kanyon
Istanbul, Turkey
Tabanlioglu Architecture (Turkey) with
   The Jerde Partnership

Commercial, Future
Living Wall
Amman, Jordan
Foster and Partners (UK)

Community, Built
Bishan Community Library
Bishan Place, Singapore
Look Architects (Singapore)

Community, Future
Kariobangi
South Nairobi, Kenya
Studio Bednarski Ltd (UK)

Sports & Leisure, Built
Palawan Beachfront Amenities
Sentosa, Singapore
Timur Designs (Singapore)

Sports & Leisure, Future
Citadel Square
Beirut, Lebanon
Machado and Silvetti Associates

Transport, Future
Queen Alia International Airport
Amman, Jordan
Foster and Partners (UK)

Environmental Award
Bridging the Rift
Central Arava, Israel/Wadi Araba, Jordan
Skidmore, Owings & Merrill

Islamic Architecture Award
Princess Salma Estate
Al-Shaq City, Zerqa, Jordan
Group for Design & Architectural
   Research (Jordan)

Master Planning Award
Cairo Future City
Cairo, Egypt
ACLA (UAE)

JURY
Paul Finch, *Architectural Review* (UK)
Suha Özkan, Aga Khan Award for Architecture
   (Switzerland)
Jack Pringle, Pringle Brandon (UK)
Raj Rewal, Raj Rewal Associates (India)
Fathi Rifki, American University of Sharjah (UAE)
Ken Yeang, Llewllyn Davies Yeang (Malaysia)

Source: Cityscape Architectural Review Awards

Bishan Community Library, Singapore by Look Architects (Singapore) (Photo: Patrick Bingham-Hall and Tim Nolan)

Dedalo Minosse Prize

The biennial Dedalo Minosse International Prize for Commissioning a Building honors outstanding clients of architecture. The International Prize is presented to a client for selecting an architect from any country, while the ALA-Assoarchitetti Prize honors clients who select an Italian architect. Additional awards in both categories also recognize clients who commission young architects. The prize takes its name from the Greek myth of Daedalus, the architect hired by King Minos to design a labyrinth to imprison the Minotaur.

For information and photo of these and all the winners, go to *www.assoarchitetti.it.*

2005–2006 Winners

International Prize for Commissioning a Building
Gallery in Kiyosato
Kiyosato, Yamanashi, Japan
Satoshi Okada Architects (Japan)
Joji Aonuma (developer, Japan)

International Prize for Commissioning a Building, Architect Under 40
Museum of World Culture
Gothenburg, Sweden
Brisac Gonzalez Architects (UK)
Sweden National Property Board
(developer, Sweden)

ALA-Assoarchitetti Prize
Research and Multimedia Center,
Grappa Nardini
Bassano del Grappa, Italy
Massimiliano Fuksas (Italy)
Giuseppe Nardini (developer, Italy)

ALA-Assoarchitetti Prize, Architect Under 40
School Building
Sondrio, Italy
LFL Architetti (Italy)
Administration of Provincia of Sondrio
(developer, Italy)

JURY
Stanislao Nievo, writer and environmentalist
(Italy, chair)
Paolo Caoduro, Caoduro Lucernari (Italy)
Cesare Maria Casati, l'Arca (Italy)
Bruno Gabbiani, ALA - Assoarchitetti (Italy)
Kisho Kurokawa, Kisho Kurokawa Architect &
Associates (Japan)
Richard Haslam, architectural historian (UK)
Pier Paolo Maggiora, architect (Italy)
Adriano Rasi Caldogno, Veneto Region Planning
Office (Italy)
Frederick Samitaur Smith, Samitaur Constructs
Roberto Tretti, Centro Studi per le Libere
Professioni (Italy)
Claude Vasconi, architect (Italy)

Source: Associazione Liberi Architetti

Design and Business Catalyst Awards

Co-sponsored by the Industrial Designers Society of America and *BusinessWeek* magazine, the annual Design and Business Catalyst Awards highlight the impact of good design on financial performance. The program rewards projects that consider market performance, social impact, and aesthetics. Illustrating the strategic value of design investment, the Catalyst Awards are presented in conjunction with the International Design Excellence Awards.

Photos and profiles of the winners can be found on IDSA's website, *www.idsa.org.*

2007 Winners

Bank of America "Keep the Change"
IDEO and Bank of America

Pangea Organics
IDEO and Pangea Organics

2007 Honorable Mentions

LifePort® Kidney Transporter
IDEO and Organ Recovery Systems

Master Lock Titanium Series Padlock
Continuum and Master Lock Company

Eclipse 500 Very Light Jet
IDEO and Eclipse Aviation

JURY
John Hoke III, Nike
Annette Schömmel, artheisa
Keith Yamashita, Stone Yamashita Partners

Source: Industrial Designers Society of America

Good design isn't about making things work better anymore. It's about making you feel engaged with the present.

Sam Jacobs

Design and Business Catalyst Awards

Eclipse 500 Very Light Jet by IDEO and Eclipse Aviation (Photos courtesy of IDSA)

Design for Asia Awards

The Design for Asia Awards acknowledge outstanding designs that have positively impacted the Asian lifestyle. Any designer, company, or educator worldwide is eligible to enter buildings, interiors, or products that have been launched in Asian markets. Judging criteria include creativity, usability, ergonomics, aesthetics, workmanship, ecological responsibility, and application of technology. In addition, the jury separately recognizes outstanding designs originating from the Greater China region.

For additional information, visit the award's website at *www.dfaaward.com*.

2006 Grand Award

Centennial "My Tools" Collection
SAAT Design Inc (Japan)

Banyan Tree Ringha
Jian Tang, Yunnan Province, China
Architrave (Singapore)

Kimukatsu Restaurant
Tokyo, Japan
Hironaka Ogawa & Associates (Japan)

THANN hair and skincare products
Tony Suppattranont (Thailand)

Ultra Slim Mobile Phone SGH-X820/SGH-
   X828/SPH-V9900
Samsung Electronics (Korea)

Romancecar VSE
Noriaki Okabe Architecture Network
   (Japan)

Pocket Imager Portable Projector
Samsung Electronics (South Korea)

Chocolate Phone
LG Electronics (South Korea)

iPod and iPod nano
Apple Computer

Lane Crawford at ifc mall and Pacific Place
Hong Kong, China
Yabu Pushelberg (Canada)

2006 Best Design from Greater China

One Touch Can Opener
Daka Development Ltd (Hong Kong)

Shunde Performing Arts Centre
Sunde, Guangdong Province, China
P&T Architects & Engineers Ltd.
   (Hong Kong)

7350C Scanner
BenQ Corporation (Taiwan)

Mirror 64PXL Wash
Diehl Design (Germany); Traxon
   Technologies Ltd. (Hong Kong)

Portable Speaker SBA1500
Philips Design (Hong Kong)

Three on the Bund
Shanghai, China
Michael Graves & Associates

Design for Asia Awards

2006 Special Merit Award

redwhiteblue/here/there/everywhere
anothermountainman communications
   (Hong Kong); MCCM Creations
   (Hong Kong)

JURY

Victor Lo, Hong Kong Design Centre, (Hong Kong, co-chair)
Freeman Lau, Hong Kong Design Centre (Hong Kong, co-chair)
Gary Chang, EDGE Design Institute Ltd (Hong Kong)
Kyung-won Chung, Advanced Institute of Science and Technology (South Korea)
William Harald-Wong, William Harald-Wong & Associates Sdn Bhd (Malaysia)
John Heskett, Hong Kong Polytechnic University (Hong Kong)
Tetsuyuki Hirano, Hirano & Associates, Inc (Japan)
Kuan Cheng-neng, Shih-Chien University (Taiwan)
Katherine McCoy, High Ground Tools and Strategies for Design
Henry Steiner, Steiner&Co (Hong Kong)
Wang Min, China Central Academy of Fine Arts (China)
Ralph Wiegmann, iF International Forum Design GmbH (Germany)

Source: Hong Kong Design Centre

Let the East learn from Western civilization. Let the West learn from the Eastern culture. In the world of freedom, we naturally create a relationship to each other.

Isamu Noguchi

Clockwise from top: **Lane Crawford at Pacific Place, Hong Kong, China by Yabu Pushelberg (Canada); Centennial "My Tools" Collection by SAAT Design Inc (Japan); and Portable Speaker SBA1500 by Philips Design (Hong Kong); Shunde Performing Arts Centre, Sunde, Guangdong Province, China, by P&T Architects & Engineers Ltd. (Hong Kong)** (Photos courtesy of Hong Kong Design Centre)

Design for Humanity Award

The American Society of Interior Designers grants the annual Design for Humanity Award to an individual or institution for significant design-related initiatives that have had a universal and far-reaching effect in improving the quality of the human environment. A committee appointed by the ASID board reviews the nominations, and the award is presented at ASID's annual national convention.

More information can be found on the ASID webiste, *www.asid.org.*

1990	The Scavenger Hotline	1998	William L. Wilkoff
1991	E.I. Du Pont de Nemours & Company	1999	AlliedSignal, Inc., Polymers Division
1992	The Preservation Resource Center	2000	Victoria Schomer
1993	Neighborhood Design Center	2001	ASID Tennessee Chapter, Chattanooga
1994	Elizabeth Paepcke and International Design Conference in Aspen	2002	Cynthia Leibrock
		2003	Habitat for Humanity International
1995	Cranbrook Academy of Art	2004	Architecture for Humanity and Cameron Sinclair
1996	Wayne Ruga and the Center for Health Design	2005	Patricia Moore
1997	Barbara J. Campbell, *Accessibility Guidebook For Washington, DC*	2006	The Robin Hood Foundation

Source: American Society of Interior Designers

In design, Mother Nature is our best teacher.

Van Day Truex

Designer of Distinction Award

With its Designer of Distinction Award, the American Society of Interior Designers recognizes individuals for their commitment to the profession as demonstrated by a significant, high-quality body of work that shows attention to social concerns and expresses creative, innovative concepts. Eligibility is open to members in good standing who have practiced interior design for at least 10 years.

Refer to the ASID website at *www.asid.org* for additional information.

1979	William Pahlman	1996	Joseph Minton
1980	Everett Brown	1997	Phyllis Martin-Vegue
1981	Barbara D'Arcy	1998	Janet S. Schirn
1982	Edward J. Wormley	1999	Gary Wheeler
1983	Edward J. Perrault	2000	Paul Vincent Wiseman
1984	Michael Taylor	2001	William Hodgins
1985	Norman DeHaan	2002	Hugh L. Latta
1986	Rita St. Clair		Margaret McCurry
1987	James Merrick Smith	2003	Eleanor Brydone
1988	Louis Tregre	2004	Deborah Lloyd Forrest
1994	Charles D. Gandy	2005	Barbara Barry
1995	Andre Staffelbach	2006	Penny Bonda

Source: American Society of Interior Designers

Whether it's fine arts or music or architecture, the most compelling works are finessed and manipulated so subtly that you're barely aware of the artist's hand.

Scott Johnson

Designer of the Year

Contract magazine grants the annual Designer of the Year Award to a mid-career designer whose work demonstrates extraordinary creative and innovative vision and who is poised for great success in the future. The recipient is celebrated at the Annual Interiors Award Breakfast and in an issue of the magazine.

For more information, visit *Contract*'s website, *www.contractmagazine.com.*

1980	John F. Saladino	1994	Lauren L. Rottet
1981	Michael Graves	1995	Debra Lehman-Smith
1982	Orlando Diaz-Azcuy	1996	Richard M. Brayton
1983	Joseph Rosen		Stanford Hughes
1984	Raul de Armas	1997	Carolyn Iu
1985	Francisco Kripacz		Neville Lewis
1986	Charles Pfister	1998	David Rockwell
1987	Miguel Valcarel	1999	William McDonough
	Randy Gerner	2000	Ralph Appelbaum
	Judy Swanson	2001	Shigeru Ban (Japan)
	Patricia Conway	2002	George Yabu (Canada)
1988	Carol Groh		Glenn Pushelberg (Canada)
1989	Scott Strasser	2003	Peter Pfau
1990	Karen Daroff	2004	Shashi Caan
1991	Gregory W. Landahl	2005	Kendall Wilson
1992	Gary L. Lee	2006	Mark Harbick
	Mel Hamilton	2007	Kelly Bauer
1993	Juliette Lam		Jim Richärd

Source: Contract

The most successful buildings demonstrate harmonious relationships in scale, whether externally to their surroundings, or internally to their occupants.

John F. Saladino

Elisabeth Blair MacDougall Book Award

The Society of Architectural Historians established the Elisabeth Blair MacDougall Book Award to recognize the most distinguished work of scholarship in the history of landscape architecture or garden design published in the previous two years. Named for the landscape historian and SAH past president Elisabeth Blair MacDougall, the award honors the late historian's role in developing this field of study.

For further information, contact the SAH online, *www.sah.org.*

2006   *The Nature of Authority: Villa Culture, Landscape, and Representation in Eighteenth-Century Lombardy*
Dianne Suzette Harris
Pennsylvania State University
    Press

2007   *Cultivated Power: Flowers, Culture, and Politics in the Reign of Louis XIV*
Elizabeth Hyde
University of Pennsylvania Press

Source: Society of Architectural Historians

The garden, by design, is concerned with both the interior and the land beyond the garden.

Stephen Gardiner

Emporis Skyscraper Award

Emporis, an international provider of architectural and building information, bestows their annual Skyscraper Award to an outstanding building over 100 meters (328 feet) completed in the previous year. The selection process favors solutions that provide for people's physical, social, and economic needs as well as respond to cultural and spiritual expectations. Particular attention is given to buildings that use local resources and appropriate technology in an innovative way.

More information is available from the Emporis website at *www.emporis.com.*

2006 Winners

Skyscraper of the Year
Hearst Tower
New York, NY
Foster and Partners (UK)

Runners Up (ranked in order)
The Wave
Gold Coast City, Australia
DBI Design Pty Ltd (Australia)

Eureka Tower
Melbourne, Australia
Fender Katsalidis Architects (Australia)

1180 Peachtree
Atlanta, GA
Pickard Chilton Architects, Inc.;
    Kendall/Heaton Associates Inc

Hesperia Tower
L'Hospitalet de Llobregat, Spain
Richard Rogers Partnership (UK); Alonso
    Balaguer y Arquitectos Asociados
    (Spain)

Beetham Tower
Manchester, UK
Ian Simpson Architects (UK)

Shimao International Plaza
Shanghai, China
East China Architectural Design &
    Research Institute Co. Ltd. (China);
    Ingenhoven Overdiek und Partner
    (Germany)

10 Holloway Circus
Birmingham, UK
Ian Simpson Architects (UK)

Aurora
Brisbane, Australia
Cottee Parker Architects (Australia)

Palms Fantasy Tower
Las Vegas, NV
KGA Architecture; The Jerde Partnership

Source: Emporis

Engineering Excellence Awards

The American Council of Engineering Companies' annual Engineering Excellence Awards recognize one Grand Conceptor Award and up to 23 grand and honor awards. A panel of engineers and infrastructure experts reviews submissions for uniqueness and originality, technical value to the engineering profession, social and economic considerations, complexity, and ability to meet the needs of the client.

Winning project descriptions are available online at *www.acec.org.*

2007 Winners

Grand Conceptor Award
Montgomery Point Lock and Dam
Desha County, AR
MWH Americas, Inc.

Grand Awards
Seattle Green Roof Evaluation Project
Seattle, WA
Magnusson Klemencic Associates

Louisville Metro Hazard Information
    Portal
Louisville, KY
Fuller, Mossbarger, Scott & May Engineers,
    Inc.

Hearst Tower
New York, NY
WSP Cantor Seinuk

Perry Street Bridge Replacement
Napoleon, OH
HNTB Ohio, Inc.

WaMu Center/Seattle Art Museum
    Expansion
Seattle, WA
Magnusson Klemencic Associates

Mokelumne River Project
Woodbridge, CA
Winzler & Kelly Consulting Engineers

West Side Combined Sewer Overflow
    Project
Portland, OR
Parsons Brinckerhoff

Honor Awards
The Center for Health & Healing at
    Oregon Health & Science University
Portland, OR
Interface Engineering, Inc

Guthrie on the River
Minneapolis, MN
Ericksen, Roed and Associates, Inc.

Georgia Aquarium
Atlanta, GA
Uzun & Case Engineers

Arapaho Road Bridge
Addison, TX
URS Corporation

Sweetwater Creek State Park Visitor Center
Lithia Springs, GA
Long Engineering, Inc.

Okeechobee's Innovative Surface Water
    Plant
Okeechobee, FL
LBFH, Inc., A Boyle Engineering Company

World Class Biosolids Incineration Systems
Ypsilanti, MI
Tetra Tech, Inc.

University of Virginia Meadow Creek
    Regional Storm Water Management
    Plan
Charlottesville, VA
Nitsch Engineering, Inc.

Engineering Excellence Awards

A. Alfred Taubman Student Services Center, Lawrence Technological University, Southfield, MI, by Harley Ellis Devereaux (Photo by Justin Maconochie)

Norfolk Southern Keystone Buildout
Indiana County, PA
URS Corporation

Woodrow Wilson Memorial Bridge Outer
Loop Bascule Span
Maryland, Washington, DC, and Virginia
Hardesty & Hanover

Clarian Pathology Laboratory
Indianapolis, IN
BSA LifeStructures

M.R.T. Chaloem Ratchamongkhon Line
Bangkok, Thailand
The Louis Berger Group

Upstream Passageway for the American Eel
at the St. Lawrence FDR Power Project
Massena, NY
C&S Engineers, Inc.

A. Alfred Taubman Student Services
Center, Lawrence Technological
University
Southfield, MI
Harley Ellis Devereaux

Rattlesnake Creek Pedestrian Bridge
Missoula, MT
HDR Engineering, Inc.

AquaPod™ Fish Containment System
Searsmont, ME
Kleinschmidt Associates

Source: American Council of Engineering Companies

European Prize for Urban Public Space

The European Prize for Urban Public Space is a biennial competition to celebrate and encourage the recovery and creation of cohesive spaces in Europe's cities. First awarded in 2000, the prize is presented both to the designers of the project and the sponsor institutions in order to encourage the rejuvenation of public spaces to improve the quality of urban life. A commemorative plaque is installed at each winning site.

For further information, visit the award online at *www.urban.cccb.org/prize*.

2006 Winners

Winners
Morske orgulje/Sea organ
Zadar, Croatia
Nikola Basic (Croatia)
Port Authorities Zadar (developer, Croatia)

A8ernA
Zaanstad, Netherlands
NL Architects (Netherlands)
Zaanstad Programma Management Dienst
    Stad (developer, Netherlands)

Special Prize of the Jury
ZwischenPalastNutzung/Volkspalast
Berlin, Germany
ZwischenPalastNutzung/Volkspalast
    (Germany)
Sophiensäle, HAU (developer, Germany)

Special Mentions
New Zgody Square
Krakow, Poland
Piotr Lewicki and Kazimierz Latak
    (Poland)
City of Krakow (developer, Poland)

Piazza Nera Piazza Bianca
Robbiano, Italy
Ifdesign; Franco Tagliabue Volontè; Ida
    Origgi; Chiara Toscani (Italy)
Comune di Giussano (developer, Italy)

JURY
Severi Blomstedt, Museum of Finnish
    Architecture (Finland)
Aaron Betsky, Nederlands Architectuurinstituut
    (Netherlands)
Rowan Moore, Architecture Foundation (UK)
Francis Rambert, Institut Français d'Architecture
    (France)
Carme Ribas, architect (Spain)
Dietmar Steiner, Architeckturzentrum Wien
    (Austria)
Elias Torres, architect (Spain)

Source: European Prize for Urban Public Space

A city, like a living thing, is a united and continuous whole.

Plutarch

Excellence on the Waterfront Awards

Lauding projects that convert abandoned or outmoded waterfronts into constructive spaces, the Excellence on the Waterfront Awards are presented annually by the nonprofit Waterfront Center. Judging criteria include the design's sensitivity to the water, quality and harmony, civic contribution, environmental impact, and educational components. The group also presents a Clearwater Citizens Award to recognize outstanding grassroots initiatives.

Visit the center's website, *www.waterfrontcenter.org*, for additional information.

2006 Winners

Battery Bosque, Battery Park City
New York, NY
Saratoga Associates; weisz + yoes architecture; Piet Oudolf

Royal Victoria Dock Bridge
London, UK
Lifschutz Davidson Sandilands (UK);
    Cynthia Grant Transport Design (UK)

2006 Honor Awards

Artistic, Cultural, and Education
Ocean Education Center
Dana Point, CA
Bauer and Wiley

WaterFire
Providence, RI
Barnaby Evans

Environmental Protection and Enhancement
Stanley Park Salmon Stream
Vancouver, BC, Canada
PWL Partnership Landscape Architects
    Inc. (Canada)

Industrial/Working Waterfront and Artistic
WaterWorks at Arizona Falls
Phoenix, AZ
Harries/Heder Collaborative

Commercial/Mixed-Use
National Assembly for Wales
Cardiff, Wales, UK
Richard Rogers Partnership (UK)

Parks and Recreation
Sabine-to-Bagby Promenade
Houston, TX
SWA Group

Plans
East River Waterfront Plan
New York, NY
New York City Department of City
    Planning; SHoP Architects

River Renaissance Planning
Portland
Portland, OR
City of Portland Bureau of Planning;
    Parsons Brinckerhoff

Waterfront Futures Project, Port of
    Bellingham
Bellingham, WA
City of Bellingham; PRR

WaterFire, Providence, RI, by Barnaby Evans

2006 Clearwater Award Recipients

Voices and Visions of Village Life: Patuxent Village, Warwick and Cranston, Rhode Island
Holly Ewald and Michael Bell

Women's Quiet Battle for Blue Sky and Clear Water, Tobata Women's Association
Kitakyushu, Japan

JURY
Thomas Meyer, Meyer, Scherer & Rockcastle, Ltd. (chair)
Chris Carlson, METRO
Bob Eury, Central Houston, Inc.
Ross Jefferson, Saint John Waterfront Development Partnership (Canada)
Marianna Koval, Brooklyn Bridge Park Conservancy

Source: Waterfront Center

Exhibition of School Architecture Awards

The Exhibition of School Architecture Awards, sponsored by the American Association of School Administrators, American Institute of Architects, and Council of Educational Facility Planners International, showcase how well-designed schools facilitate student achievement. The Shirley Cooper Award recognizes the project that best meets the educational needs of students. The Walter Taylor Award honors the project that best addresses a difficult design challenge.

Visit AASA's website, *www.aasa.org*, for more information.

2007 Winners

Shirley Cooper Award
Ingunnarskoli
Reykjavik, Iceland
Bruce Jilk Architects

Walter Taylor Award
Ben Franklin Elementary School
Kirkland, WA
Mahlum Architects

Honorable Mentions
ACORN Woodland
    Elementary/EnCompass Academy
Oakland, CA
Beverly Prior Architects

Tonopah High School
Tonopah AZ
DLR Group

Eagle Rock Elementary School
Eagle Point, OR
Dull Olson Weekes Architects

Auburn High School
Auburn, MA
Flansburgh Associates, Inc.

Cambridge Media Arts Studio
Cambridge, MA
HMFH Architects, Inc.

Cesar Chavez Elementary School
Long Beach, CA
LPA, Inc.

Hockaday School
Dallas, TX
Overland Partners Architects; Good Fulton
    & Farrell Architects

Hudson High School
Hudson, MA
Symmes Maini & McKee Associates

Northwest Middle School
Salt Lake City, UT
VCBO Architecture

Brown Center, Maryland Institute College
    of Art
Baltimore, MD
Ziger/Snead LLP; Charles Brickbauer
    Architects

Source: American Association of School Administrators

Gold Key Awards

For over 20 years, the Gold Key Awards for Excellence in Hospitality Design have honored outstanding hospitality projects. Judging criteria include aesthetic appeal, practicality and functionality, and innovative design concepts. The awards are presented by the International Hotel/Motel & Restaurant Show and sponsored by *Interior Design* and *HOTELS* magazines. Winners in each category are profiled in both sponsoring publications.

For eligibility requirements and an entry form, visit *www.ihmrs.com.*

2006 Winners

Best Hotel Design
Banyan Tree Ringha
Jian Tang, Yunnan Province, China
Architrave (Singapore)

Guest Room
Senso Room, Hotel Meliá Roma Aurelia
    Antica
Rome, Italy
Sol Meliá Hotels & Resorts (Spain);
    E. eG DiVeroli (Italy)

Lobby/Reception Area
Carlton Hotel
New York, NY
Rockwell Group

Lounge/Bar
Social Hollywood
Los Angeles, CA
Zeff Design

Restaurants, Casual Dining
MX
Hong Kong, China
Steve Leung Designers, Ltd. (China);
    Alan Chan Design Company (China)

Restaurants, Fine Dining
FIN Restaurant, Mirage
Las Vegas, NV
Yabu Pushelberg

Spa
Oriental Spa, Landmark Mandarin
    Oriental
Hong Kong, China
Mandarin Oriental Hotel Group Spa
    Division; Remedios Siembieda

Suite
Banyan Tree Ringha
Jian Tang, Yunnan Province, China
Architrave (Singapore)

JURY
Carol Rusche Bentel, Bentel & Bentel
John Bricker, Gensler
Sam Kapadia, Doubletree Metropolitan Hotel
Tony May, Tony May Group
Ellis O'Connor, Gramercy Park Hotel

Source: International Hotel/Motel & Restaurant Show

Gold Key Awards

Clockwise from top: **FIN Restaurant, Mirage, Las Vegas, NV, by Yabu Pushelberg (Canada); Oriental Spa, Landmark Mandarin Oriental, Hong Kong, China, by Mandarin Oriental Hotel Group Spa Division and Remedios Siembieda; and MX, Hong Kong, China, by Steve Leung Designers, Ltd. (China) and Alan Chan Design Company (China)** (Photos courtesy of the International Hotel/Motel & Restaurant Show)

GSA Design Awards

The US General Services Administration presents its biennial design awards as part of its Design Excellence Program, which seeks the best in design, construction, and restoration for all Federal building projects. The awards were developed to encourage and recognize innovative design in Federal buildings and to honor noteworthy achievements in the preservation and renovation of historic structures.

Visit GSA's website at *www.gsa.gov* for photos and descriptions of the winners.

2006 Honor Awards

Architecture
United States Courthouse
Fresno, CA
Gruen Associates/Moore Ruble Yudell
    Architects & Planners, joint venture

Architecture/On the Boards
Peace Arch Port of Entry
Blaine, WA
Bohlin Cywinski Jackson

Sustainability/Adaptive Reuse
Social Security Administration Teleservice
    Center
Auburn, WA
TVA Architects

Interior Design / Workplace Environment
Bannister Federal Complex Atrium
Kansas City, MO
BNIM Architects

2006 Citations

Architecture
Oklahoma City Federal Building
Oklahoma City, OK
Ross Barney Architects

Carl B. Stokes United States Court House
Cleveland, OH
Kallman Mckinnell & Wood Architects with
    Karlsberger

United States Border Patrol Station
Murrieta, CA
Garrison Architects

Architecture/On the Boards
Jacob K. Javits Federal Building Entry
    Pavilion
New York, NY
Lehman-Smith + Mcleish

Modernization
Des Moines Federal Building Facade
    Replacement
Des Moines, IA
SmithGroup with Designbuild Solutions

Preservation
Howard M. Metzenbaum United States
    Courthouse
Cleveland, OH
Westlake Reed Leskosky

Conservation
United States Custom House
Chicago, IL
Kellermeyer Godfryt Hart with Berglund
    Construction

64

GSA Design Awards

Lease Construction
Internal Revenue Service Center
Kansas City, MO
BNIM/360, joint venture

Sustainability/Workplace Environment
Census Bureau Headquarters
Suitland, MD
Skidmore, Owings & Merrill

Engineering and Technology
Patent and Trademark Headquarters
Alexandria, VA
Syska Hennessy Group

Fritz Lanham Federal Building
    Modernization
Fort Worth, TX
Huitt-Zollars

Graphic Design
GSA's Stewardship of Historic Buildings:
    Two Volumes
Cox & Associates

Workplace Matters
Stuart Mckee Design

Construction Excellence
Food and Drug Administration Center
    for Drug Evaluations and Research
White Oak, MD
Heery/Tishman joint venture with Centex
    Construction

JURY
William Bain, NBBJ
Randolph Croxton, Croxton Collaborative
    Architects
Kimberly Davenport, Rice University Art Gallery
Joan Goody, Goody, Clancy & Associates (chair)
Elizabeth Corbin Murphy, Chambers Murphy
    & Burge Restoration Architects
Michael Mills, Ford Farewell Mills and Gatsch
    Architects
Blake Peck, McDonough Bolyard Peck
Teresa Rainy, Skidmore Owings & Merrill
Peter Lindsay Schaudt, Peter Lindsay Schaudt
    Landscape Architecture

Source: US General Services Administration

My buildings don't speak in words but by means of their own spaciousness.

Thom Mayne

Clockwise from top: Bannister Federal Complex, Kansas City, MO, by BNIM Architects; United States Courthouse, Fresno, CA, by Gruen Associates/Moore Ruble Yudell Architects & Planners, joint venture; and Oklahoma City Federal Building, Oklahoma City, OK, by Ross Barney Architects (Photos courtesy of GSA)

Healthcare Environment Award

Since 1989, the annual Healthcare Environment Awards have recognized innovative, life-enhancing designs. The program is sponsored by the Center for Health Design, *Contract* magazine, Medquest Communications, and the American Institute of Architecture Students and is open to architects, interior designers, healthcare executives, and students. The winners are honored at the annual Healthcare Design Conference and featured in an issue of *Contract* magazine.

Additional information is available on the Web at *www.healthdesign.org*.

2007 First-Place Winners

Acute
Orange City Hospital
Orange City, IA
HGA Architects and Engineers with
  Cannon Moss Brygger & Associates

Professional Conceptual Design
Emergency Care Facility
5GStudio_collaborative

Ambulatory, Large
Moakley Building at Boston Medical
  Center
Boston, MA
Tsoi/Kobus & Associates, Inc.

Ambulatory, Small
Piedmont Physicians Group at Atlantic
  Station
Atlanta, GA
Stanley Beaman & Sears

Student
Imed: Interactive Medical Emergency
  Department
David Ruthven
Clemson University

2007 Honorable Mentions

Acute
Children's Healthcare of Atlanta at
  Scottish Rite
Atlanta, GA
Stanley Beaman & Sears

Ambulatory, Large
Advocate Lutheran General Hospital
  Center for Advanced Care
Park Ridge, IL
OWP/P

Ambulatory, Small
Brightleaf Holistic and Cosmetic Dentistry
Santa Monica, CA
M. Charles Bernstein Architects

Student
Patient Room Prototype
Phillip Benson (Canada)
Carleton University

JURY
Susan DiMotta, Perkins Eastman
Jeff Logan, Anshen+Allen
Andrea Hyde, Hyde Incorporated
Joe Kuspan, Karlsberger
Jeff Stouffer, HKS, Inc.

Source: The Center for Health Design

Orange City Hospital, Orange City, IA, by HGA Architects and Engineers and Cannon Moss Brygger & Associates (Photos courtesy of the Orange City Area Health System)

68

Henry C. Turner Prize

The Henry C. Turner Prize for Innovation in Construction Technology is presented jointly by the National Building Museum and the Turner Construction Company to recognize notable advances in construction. It honors individuals, companies, and organizations for their inventions, innovative methodologies, and exceptional leadership in construction technology. The award is named for the founder of Turner Construction, which began operation in New York City in 1902.

For additional information, refer to the museum's website at *www.nbm.org*.

2002	Leslie E. Robertson
2003	I.M. Pei
2004	Charles A. DeBenedittis
2005	US Green Building Council
2006	Paul Teicholz
2007	Gehry Partners
	Gehry Technologies

Source: National Building Museum

You cannot change the world with green buildings. You need to change to green business.

Ken Yeang

Housing Awards

The Housing Professional Interest Area of the American Institute of Architects established the Housing Awards to recognize the importance of good housing as a necessity of life, a sanctuary for the human spirit, and a valuable national resource. Licensed AIA-member architects are eligible to enter US-built projects. Winning designs are published in Architectural Record and displayed at the annual AIA National Convention and Expo.

Additional information is available from the AIA's website, *www.aia.org.*

2007 Winners

One/Two Family Custom Housing
House at the Shawangunks
New Paltz, NY
Bohlin Cywinski Jackson

1532 House
San Francisco, CA
Fougeron Architecture

Loblolly House
Taylors Island, MD
KieranTimberlake Associates

Tye River Cabin
Skykomish, WA
Olson Sundberg Kundig Allen Architects

Delta Shelter
Mazama, WA
Olson Sundberg Kundig Allen Architects

A Ranch House in the San Juan Mountains
Telluride, CO
Michael Shepherd, AIA, Architect

One/Two Family Production Housing
Danielson Grove
Kirkland, WA
Ross Chapin Architects

The 505
Houston, TX
Collaborative Designworks

Special Housing
The DESIGNhabitat 2 House
Greensboro, AL
The DESIGNhabitat 2 Studio, Auburn
    University School of Architecture;
    David W. Hinson, AIA

The Plaza Apartments
San Francisco, CA
Leddy Maytum Stacy Architects with
    Paulett Taggart Architects

Patrolia Loft
Boston, MA
Ruhl Walker Architects

Shirley Bridge Bungalows
Seattle, WA
Ron Wright and Associates/Architects

Regional Homeless Center
Los Angeles, CA
Jeffrey M. Kalban & Associates
    Architecture, Inc.

Multifamily Housing
High Point
Seattle, WA
Mithun Architects + Designers + Planners

1247 Wisconsin
Washington, DC
McInturff Architects

Housing Awards

The Union, San Diego, CA, by Jonathan S. Segal, Architect

156 West Superior Condominiums
Chicago, IL
Miller/Hull Partnership

The Union
San Diego, CA
Jonathan S. Segal, Architect

Bridgeton Hope VI
Bridgeton, NJ
Torti Gallas and Partners

Salishan Neighborhood Revitalization
Tacoma, WA
Torti Gallas and Partners

JURY
Katherine Austin, Katherine Austin, AIA,
    Architect(chair)
Don Carter, Urban Design Associates
Jane F. Kolleeny, *Architectural Record*
Lisa Stacholy, LKS Architects, Inc.
LaVerne Williams, Environment Associates

Source: American Institute of Architects

Hugh Ferriss Memorial Prize

The American Society of Architectural Illustrators annually bestows the Hugh Ferriss Memorial Prize, the highest honor conferred by the organization, for the best graphic representation of architecture. The prize is part of Architecture in Perspective, an annual international competition, traveling exhibition, and catalog comprised of the Hugh Ferriss winner as well as 60 other pieces intended to promote the field of architectural illustration.

To view the winning illustrations, visit the ASAI's website at *www.asai.org.*

1986	*Worth Square Building* Lee Dunnette	1996	*Hines France Office Tower* Paul Stevenson Oles
	The State Capitol Dome, Texas James Record	1997	*World War II Memorial* Advanced Media Design
1987	*One Montvale Avenue* Richard Lovelace	1998	*Baker Library Addition, Dartmouth College* Wei Li
1988	*Proposed Arts and Cultural Center* Thomas Wells Schaller	1999	*Five Star Deluxe Beach Hotel* Serge Zaleski
1989	*Edgar Allen Poe Memorial (detail)* Daniel Willis	2000	*1000 Wilshire Blvd.* Thomas Wells Schaller
1990	*The Interior of the Basilica Ulpia* Gilbert Gorski	2001	*The Royal Ascot, Finishing Post* Michael McCann
1991	*Affordable Housing Now!* Luis Blanc	2002	*Chicago 2020* Gilbert Gorski
1992	*BMC Real Properties Buildings* Douglas E. Jamieson	2003	*Edge City* Ronald Love
1993	*Additions and Renovations to Tuckerton Marine Research Field Station* David Sylvester	2004	*Project Japan* Michael Reardon
		2005	*Resort, Evening* Chris Grubbs
1994	*3rd Government Center Competition* Rael D. Slutsky	2006	*Arthur V. McCarthy Memorial* Dennis Allain
1995	*The Pyramid at Le Grand Louvre* Lee Dunnette	2007	*Harry's Island – The Coral Helix* Ana Carolina Monnaco

Source: American Society of Architectural Illustrators

72

I.D. Annual Design Review

Since 1954, *I.D.* magazine has been chronicling the evolution of design through its I.D. Annual Design Review, which recognizes the best in product, furniture, graphic, and environment design. A jury of leading practitioners reviews the submissions and grants awards on three levels: best of category, design distinction, and honorable mention. Winning entries are published in the magazine's annual awards issue.

For descriptions and photos, visit *I.D.*'s website, *www.idonline.com.*

2007 Best of Category Winners

Concepts
Brush & Rinse
Amron Experimental

Consumer Products
Leaf
fuseproject

Environments
Drape Wall/Drape House
SLV Design

Equipment
S2 Split-Head Framing Hammer
ATOMdesign, Inc.

Furniture
Hanabi
Nendo (Japan)

Graphics
Matthew Ritchie: Incomplete
   Projects 01–07
Purtill Family Business

Interactive
Tellme Search
Tellme Networks

Packaging
WD-40
Gad Shaanan Design (Canada)

JURY
David Alhadeff, The Future Perfect
John Bielenberg, C2 (Creative Capital)
Rodrigo Corral, Rodrigo Corral Design
Kristina DiMatteo, *Print*
Stephen Doyle, Doyle Partners
Winka Dubbeldam, ArchiTectonics
John Dunnigan, Rhode Island School of Design
Mark Frauenfelder, *Make*
Linda Hales, *Washington Post*
Natalie Jeremijenko, artist
Michael Ian Kaye, AR New York
Douglas Lloyd, Lloyd (+co)
Matilda McQuaid, Cooper-Hewitt,
   National Design Museum
Bill Moggridge, IDEO
Clement Mok, designer
Jonah Peretti, Huffington Post
Paul Priestman, Priestman Goode (UK)
Anna Rabinowicz, Parsons The New School
   for Design
Joe Rosa, Art Institute of Chicago
Paul Sahre, Office of Paul Sahre
Marc Tsurumaki, Lewis.Tsurumaki.Lewis
Tucker Viemeister, Studio Red
Zoe Wishart, Psyop, Inc.
Tobias Wong, designer

Source: I.D.

I. Donald Terner Prize

73

The biennial I. Donald Terner Prize for Innovation in Affordable Housing began in 2006, the 10th anniversary of the death of I. Donald Terner. Administered by the Center for Community Innovation at the University of California, Berkeley, the prize honors the work of Don Terner whose non-profit BRIDGE Housing Corporation has built more than 10,000 affordable housing units. The award recognizes both projects and the leadership teams behind them.

Additional information is available online at *www-iurd.ced.berkeley.edu/cci/ternerprize/*.

2006 Recipient

Winner
8 NW 8th Avenue
Seattle, WA
SERA Architects
Central City Concerns

Finalists
Burnham Building
Irvington, NY
Stephen Tilly, Architect
Jonathan Rose Companies

Mission Creek Community
San Francisco, CA
Hardison Komatsu & Tucker;
   Santos Prescott and Associates
Mercy Housing California

Tierra Del Sol
Canoga Park, CA
DE Architects
New Economics for Women

River View Master Planned Neighborhood
Guadalupe, CA
Murray Duncan Architects
People's Self-Help Housing

Plaza Apartments
San Francisco, CA
Leddy Maytum Stacy Architects;
   Paulett Taggart Architects
Public Initiatives Development Corporation

JURY
Elinor Bacon, ER Bacon Development
David Baker, David Baker + Partners
John King, San Francisco Chronicle
Greg Maher, Local Initiatives Support
   Corporation
J. Michael Pitchford, Community Preservation
   & Development Corporation
Geoffrey Wooding, Goody Clancy Associates

Source: Center for Community Innovation

Home is not just a place to sleep, home is where we house our souls.

Alexandra Stoddard

I. Donald Terner Prize

8 NW 8th Avenue, Portland, OR, by SERA Architects (Photo: Michael Mathers, courtesy of SERA Architects)

IDSA Personal Recognition Award

The Industrial Designers Society of America presents its Personal Recognition Award to designers and others whose involvement in and support of design has contributed to the profession's long-term welfare and importance. Nominees are reviewed by a nominating committee, and IDSA's officers select the final winners.

For additional information, visit the IDSA's website, *www.idsa.org*.

1968	Dave Chapman	1996	Jane Thompson
1969	John Vassos	1997	Eva Zeisel
1978	Raymond Loewy	1998	Donald Dohner
1980	William M. Goldsmith	1999	Victor Papanek
1981	George Nelson	2000	Robert Schwartz
1982	Jay Doblin	2001	Bill Stumpf
1985	Deane W. Richardson	2002	Viktor Schreckengost
1986	Carroll M. Gantz	2003	Sam Farber
1991	Budd Steinhilber	2004	Henry Dreyfuss
1992	Cooper C. Woodring		Bruce Nussbaum
	Ellen Manderfield	2005	*No award granted*
1993	Raymond Spilman	2006	Robert Blaich
	Brooks Stevens		Charles (Chuck) Harrison
1994	Belle Kogan	2007	Walter Dorwin Teague*
1995	David B. Smith		

* Honored posthumously

Source: Industrial Designers Society of America

A chair is only finished when someone sits in it.

Hans Wegner

Institute Honors for Collaborative Achievement

The American Institute of Architects presents the Institute Honors for Collaborative Achievement to individuals and groups who have advanced the architectural profession. Nominees must be living at the time of their nomination and may hail from any number of areas, including administration, art, construction, industrial design, information science, professions allied with architecture, public policy, research, education, recording, illustration, writing, and scholarship.

For a list of all past winners, visit the AIA online at *www.aia.org.*

1995–2007 Recipients

1995	Art Institute of Chicago, Department of Architecture	1999	Howard Brandston
	American Society of Architectural Perspectivists		Jeff Goldberg
			Ann E. Gray
			Blair Kamin
	Friends of Post Office Square		Ronald McKay
	University of Virginia, Curator and Architect for the Academical Village/ The Rotunda		Miami-Dade Art in Public Places
			Monacelli Press
			New York Landmarks Conservancy
		2000	Aga Khan Award for Architecture
	Albert Paley		Douglas Cooper
	UrbanArts, Inc.		Christopher Jaffe
	Yoichi Ando (Japan)		Donald Kaufman and Taffy Dahl
1996	Boston by Foot, Inc.		William Lam
	William S. Donnell		San Antonio Conservation Society
	Haley & Aldrich, Inc.		
	Toshio Nakamura (Japan)		F. Michael Wong
	Joseph Passonneau	2001†	Vernon L. Mays Jr.
	Preservation Society of Charleston		John R. Stilgoe
		2003	Kathryn H. Anthony
	Earl Walls Associates		Hervé Descottes (France)
	Paul Warchol Photography, Inc.		Gilbert Gorski
1997	Architecture Resource Center		Jane Merkel
1998	Lian Hurst Mann		J. Irwin Miller
	SOM Foundation		New York, New Visions
	William Morgan		Joan Ockman
			Martin Puryear
			Robin Hood Foundation

77

2005   ArchVoices
        Randall Arendt
        John James (Australia)
        Barbara A. Nadel
        Schoolyards to Skylines
2007   Association for Preservation
            Technology
        Bryan Bell
        Francis D.K. Ching
        Directory of African American
            Architects
        U.S. General Services
            Administration Office of the
            Chief Architect
        Harvard Design magazine
        Public Architecture
        Rocky Mountain Institute
        Witold Rybczynski

* Honored posthumously
† Beginning in 2001, the award became biennial.

Source: American Institute of Architects

Architecture is not a translation of anything. Architecture must not follow
theories, style, fashion, or technology. It exists as an entity within itself.

Will Aslop

Interior Design Competition

The Interior Design Competition is presented jointly each year by the International Interior Design Association and *Interior Design* magazine. The program was established in 1973 to recognize outstanding interior design projects and to foster new ideas and techniques. Winning projects appear in the magazine, and the best-of-competition winner receives a $5,000 cash prize.

Photos of the winners are available on IIDA's website, *www.iida.org.*

2007 Recipients

Best of Competition
Minarc House
Los Angeles, CA
Minarc

Winners
Silver Rain, a la prairie spa
Grand Cayman, Cayman Islands
D'Aquino Monaco Inc

Seyfarth Shaw
Chicago, IL
Gensler

Fornarina London
London, UK
Giorgio Borruso Design

Kimukatsu Restaurant
Tokyo, Japan
Hironaka Ogawa & Associates (Japan)

JURY
Kelly Bauer, richärd+bauer
D.B. Kim, Westin Design & Starwood Hotels
   Worldwide
David Oakey, David Oakey Designs
Richard Pollack, Pollack Architecture

Source: International Interior Design Association

[There] seems to be within all of us an innate yearning to be lifted momentarily out of our own lives into the realm of charm and make believe.

Dorothy Draper

FORNARINA, London, UK, by Giorgio Borruso Design (Photo: Benny Chan, courtesy of Giorgio Borruso Design)

International Design Excellence Awards

The annual International Design Excellence Awards, co-sponsored by *BusinessWeek* magazine and the Industrial Designers Society of America, honor outstanding industrial design projects worldwide. A jury of business executives and design professionals select as many winners as it deems warranted, evaluating entries for design innovation, benefit to the user, benefit to the client, ecological responsibility, and appropriate aesthetics and appeal. Gold, silver, and bronze awards are granted.

Descriptions and photos of all the winners are available online at *www.idsa.org.*

2007 Gold Winners

Business & Industrial Products
Crown Stacker Family - ST 3000, SX 3000, and WF 3000 Series
Crown Design Center; Formation Design Group

Premium Edge Safety Harness
General Assembly; Guardian Fall Protection

Computer Equipment
LCD Monitor Mobius (SyncMaster 971p)
Samsung Electronics (South Korea); IDEO

LOMAK - light operated mouse and keyboard
peterhaythornthwaite//creativelab (New Zealand)

Consumer Products
Fuego Outdoor Grilling System
Pentagram; Fuego

HomeHero™ Fire Extinguisher
Arnell Group

One Touch™ Can Opener
Daka Development Ltd (China)

PalmPeeler™
Chef'n Corporation

Design Concepts
DIVERTO SYNERGY 360T
Diverto Technologies BV (Netherlands); Protoscar SA (Switzerland); Delft University of Technology (Netherlands); Hunan Sunward Intelligent Machinery Co. Ltd. (China)

Verdi Lawnscaping system
Insight Product Development

Design Research
Cockpit, Cabin and Option Packages Research for the Eclipse 500 Very Light Jet
IDEO; Eclipse Aviation

Design Strategy
Gourmet Settings at Costco
Kerr & Co. (Canada); Hahn Smith Design

Ecodesign
Tesla Roadster
Lotus Design Studio (UK); Tesla Motors Inc.; Bill Moggridge

Environments
No award granted

Tesla Roadster by Lotus Design Studio (UK); Tesla Motors Inc., Bill Moggridge (Photo courtesy of Tesla Motors Inc.)

Did you know...

In the past five years, the following have won the most IDEAs:

Source: Industrial Designers Society of America

International Design Excellence Awards

Furniture
No award granted

Interaction Design
Cockpit Interaction for the Eclipse 500
    Very Light Jet
IDEO; Eclipse Aviation

Medical & Scientific Products
4D localization system
IDEO; Calypso® Medical Technologies, Inc.

Nanopoint cellTRAY
Carbon Design; Nanopoint, Inc

Packaging & Graphics
Aliph Jawbone Bluetooth Headset
    Packaging
fuseproject

Student Designs
"Smart Opt" Soldering Station
Natalie Schraufnagel
Milwaukee Institute of Art and Design

Universal Toilet
Changduk Kim and Youngki Hong
Daejin University (South Korea)

The Access
J. Ryan Eder
University of Cincinnati

Transportation
No award granted

JURY
Carole Bilson, Pitney Bowes, Inc.
Barbara Bloemink, Museum of Arts and Design
Hillary Blumberg, Martha Stewart Living
    Omnimedia
Prasad Boradkar, Arizona State University
Moira Cullen, Coca-Cola North America
Uday Dandavate, SonicRim
Robin Edman, Swedish Industrial Design
    Foundation (Sweden)
Chris Hacker, Johnson & Johnson
Andreas Haug, Phoenix Design (Germany)
Gavin Ivester, PUMA
Jonathon Kemnitzer, KEM STUDIO
Franco Lodato, University of Montreal School
    of Design (Canada)
Sigi Moeslinger, Antenna Design New York Inc.
Richard Sapper, IBM
Michael Schrage, consultant and author
Ruth Soénius, Siemens AG (Germany)
Milton Tan, Ministry of Information,
    Communications and the Arts and
    DesignSingapore Council (Singapore)
Stephen B. Wilcox, Design Science

Source: Industrial Designers Society of America

The true value of a thing evolves by using it.

Martin Bergmann

International Highrise Award

Every two years the International Highrise Award honors an outstanding tall building (100 meters or higher) located anywhere in the world that demonstrates special aesthetics, pioneering design, integration into town planning, sustainability, innovative technology, and cost-effectiveness. The jury jointly recognizes the winning project's planner, who receives 50,000 euros, and developer, who receives a sculpture. Jury commendations, which carry no monetary award, are also granted at the jury's discretion.

For further information, visit the award's website at *www.highrise-frankfurt.de*.

2006 Winners

Prize Winner
Torre Agbar
Barcelona, Spain
Ateliers Jean Nouvel (France)
Aigües de Barcelona (developer, Spain)

Commendations
Turning Torso
Malmö, Sweden
Santiago Calatrava (Spain)
HSB (developer, Sweden)

Montevideo
Rotterdam, Netherlands
Mecanoo Architecten (Netherlands)
ING Real Estate (developer, Netherlands)

Wienerberg Hochhaus
Vienna, Austria
Delugan Meissl Associated Architects
   (Austria)
Mischek (developer, Austria)

Jian Wai SOHO
Beijing, China
Riken Yamamoto & Field Shop (Japan)
Soho China Ltd. (developer, China)

JURY
Johannes Haug, DekaBank (Germany)
Hans-Gernhard Nordhoff, City of Frankfurt
   (Germany)
David Leventhal, Kohn Pedersen Fox (UK)
Peter P. Schweger, Schewger Assoziierte
   Architekten (Germany)
Werner Sobek, Werner Sobek Ingenieure
   (Germany)

Source: International Highrise Award

Did you know...

The maximum circumference of London's Swiss Re Building—or the Gherkin, as it is widely known—is only 6.5 feet less than its height.

James Beard Restaurant Design Award

The James Beard Foundation annually presents the James Beard Restaurant Design Award to the project that best demonstrates excellence in restaurant design or renovation. Architects and interior designers are eligible to enter restaurant projects completed within the preceding three years. The award is presented at the annual Beard Birthday Fortnight celebration.

Additional information can be found online at *www.jamesbeard.org*.

1995	Fifty Seven Fifty Seven New York, NY Chhada Siembieda and Partners
1996	Bar 89 New York, NY Ogawa/Depardon Architects
1997	Paci Restaurant Westport, CT Ferris Architects
1998	Monsoon Toronto, ON, Canada Yabu Pushelberg
1999	MC Squared San Francisco, CA Mark Cavagnero Associates
2000	Brasserie New York, NY Diller & Scofidio
2001	Russian Tea Room New York, NY Leroy Adventures

2002	Blackbird Restaurant Chicago, IL Thomas Schlesser & Demian Repucci
2003	L'Impero Restaurant New York, NY Vicente Wolf Associates
2004	PUBLIC New York, NY AvroKO
2005	Solea Restaurant, W Mexico City Mexico City, Mexico Studio Gaia Avec Chicago, IL Thomas Schlesser Design
2006	The Modern New York, NY Bentel & Bentel Architecture/Planners
2007	Xing Restaurant New York, NY Lewis.Tsurumaki.Lewis

Outstanding Restaurant Design recipients, *from left,* **Paul Lewis, Marc Tsurumaki, David J. Lewis**
(Photo courtesy of the James Beard Foundation)

J.C. Nichols Prize

The Urban Land Institute's J.C. Nichols Prize for Visionary Urban Development rewards individuals and institutions whose work demonstrates a high commitment to responsible development. The award's namesake, Jesse Clyde Nichols, was a visionary developer whose work embodied ULI's mission to foster responsible land use. Winners, who receive a $100,000 honorarium, may include architects, researchers, developers, journalists, public officials, planners, and academics.

For information about the winners, including how their work has advanced the development industry, go to the prize's website, *www.nicholsprize.org*.

2000	Joseph P. Riley Jr.
2001	Daniel Patrick Moynihan
2002	Gerald D. Hines
2003	Vincent J. Scully
2004	Richard D. Baron
2005	Forest City Enterprises, Inc. and Albert B. Ratner
2006	Peter Calthorpe
2007	Sir Stuart Lipton

Source: Urban Land Institute

Vital cities have marvelous innate abilities for understanding, communicating, contriving, and inventing what is required to combat their difficulties....Lively, diverse, intense cities contain the seeds of their own regeneration, with energy enough to carry over for problems and needs outside themselves.

Jane Jacobs

Jean Tschumi Prize

The Jean Tschumi Prize is awarded by the International Union of Architects (UIA) to individuals to honor significant contributions to architectural criticism or architectural education.

For more information, visit the UIA's website at *www.uia-architectes.org*.

1967	Jean-Pierre Vouga (Switzerland)	1993	Eric Kumchew Lye (Malaysia)
1969	I. Nikolaev (USSR)	1996	Peter Cook (UK)
	Pedro Ramirez Vazquez		Liangyong Wu (China)
	(Mexico)		Toshio Nakamura (Japan)*
1972	João Batista Vilanova Artigas		COMEX (Mexico)*
	(Brazil)	1999	Juhani Pallasmaa (Finland)
1975	Reyner Banham (UK)		Jennifer Taylor (Australia)*
1978	Rectory and Faculty of	2002	Manuel Tainha (Portugal)
	Architecture of the University		Elia Zenghelis (Greece)
	of Lima (Peru)		The authors of *World Architecture:*
1981	Neville Quarry (Australia)		*A Critical Mosaic* (China)*
	Jorge Glusberg (Argentina)*	2005	*QUADERNS* magazine (Spain)
	Tadeusz Barucki (Poland)*		Peter Davey (UK)
1984	Julius Posener (GDR)		Selim Khan-Magomedov
1987	Christian Norberg-Schultz		(Russia)*
	(Norway)		
	Ada Louise Huxtable (US)		* Honorary Mention
1990	Eduard Franz Sekler (Austria)		
	Dennis Sharp (UK)*		
	Claude Parent (France)*		*Source: International Union of Architects*

A bold idea, plus precision, care, and thought make a good building.

Gordon Bunshaft

John F. Nolan Award

The John F. Nolan Award recognizes senior non-design executives who have actively championed design as an important component of economic and cultural development. Administered by the Design Management Institute, the award honors John F. Nolan, who in his role as president of the Massachusetts College of Art encouraged the institute's creation and helped sustain its growth.

For further information, visit the DMI on the Internet at *www.dmi.org*.

2005   Bruce Nussbaum
2006   Masamichi Udagawa

Source: Design Management Institute

Did you know...

According to the Design Management Institute, five schools in the United States offer degree programs in design management, compared to 13 in the UK.

John M. Clancy Award

The John M. Clancy Award for Socially Responsible Housing encourages excellence in the design of urban housing for underserved populations. Named after architect John M. Clancy, whose work focused on enhancing the lives of ordinary citizens, the award honors public and private multi-family housing projects that serve diverse populations of all income levels. This biennial program is sponsored by Goody, Clancy & Associates and administered by the Boston Society of Architects/AIA.

For more information, visit the award's website, *www.johnclancyaward.org.*

2007 Winners

Honor Awards
6 North Apartments
St. Louis, MO
Trivers Associates

Mission Creek Community
San Francisco, CA
Hardison Komatsu Ivelich & Tucker

Awards for Design
Trolley Square
Cambridge, MA
Mostue & Associates Architects

Paradise Pond Apartments
Northampton, MA
PFRA + LDa Architects, Joint Venture
    Partnership

Othello Station
Seattle, WA
WRT-Solomon E.T.C

JURY
Sherry Ahrentzen, Arizona State University
Blair Kamin, *Chicago Tribune*
David Parish, Federal Home Loan Bank
Geoff Wooding, Goody Clancy & Associates

Source: Boston Society of Architects/AIA

Between the houses of childhood and death, between those of play and work, stands the house of everyday life, which architects have called many things—residence, habitation, dwelling, etc.—as if life could develop in one place only.

Rem Koolhaas

Keystone Award

Created in 1999 by the American Architectural Foundation, the Keystone Award honors individuals and organizations outside the field of architecture that have increased the value of architecture and design in our culture. The award's objective is to encourage leadership by all members of society, reflecting the increasingly important role design plays in our lives and communities. Recipients are celebrated at the annual Accent on Architecture Gala in Washington, DC.

Additional details are available from the AAF's website, *www.archfoundation.org.*

1999	Richard M. Daley
2000	Rick Lowe
2002	Joseph P. Riley Jr.
2004	US General Services Administration, Public Buildings Service
2005	Jeremy Harris
2006	Pritzker Family
2007	Save America's Treasures

Source: American Architectural Foundation

Architecture must create places as the synthesis of its various elements and aspects, where people can find themselves and thereby feel that they are human beings somewhere.

Botond Bognar

Latrobe Prize

The College of Fellows of the American Institute of Architects created the biennial Latrobe Prize to reward and promote research leading to significant advances in the architecture profession. The prize, named after Benjamin Henry Latrobe, often considered America's first professional architect, includes a $100,000 grant to support the recipient's research and subsequently report the findings in publications, exhibitions, or educational programs.

For more information, refer to the AIA's website at *www.aia.org*.

2001	Stephen J. Kieran and James H. Timberlake	2007	"On the Water, A Model for the Future: A Study of New York and New Jersey Upper Bay" Guy Nordenson with Stan Allan, Catherine Seavitt, James Smith, Michael Tantala, Adam Yarinsky, and Stephen Cassell
2003	Academy of Neuroscience for Architecture		
2005	Chong Partners Architecture, Kaiser Permanente, and the University of California, Berkeley		

Source: American Institute of Architects

Consider the momentous event in architecture when the wall parted and the column became.

Louis I. Kahn

Legend Award

Presented by *Contract* magazine, the Legend Award recognizes an outstanding individual for lifetime achievement in design. The recipient is celebrated at the Annual Interiors Award Breakfast and in an issue of the magazine.

For more information, visit *Contract*'s website, *www.contractmagazine.com.*

2002	Margo Grant Walsh
2003	Hugh Hardy
2005	Neil Frankel
2006	Niels Diffrient
2007	William E. Valentine

Source: Contract

A good chair should look as if could spring at you or take you in its arms.

Roger Banks-Pye

Lewis Mumford Prize

93

Every two years the Society for American City and Regional Planning History grants the Lewis Mumford Prize for the best book on American city and regional planning history. Selection criteria include originality, depth of research, and contribution to the field. The award is named in honor of the celebrated urban planner, historian, sociologist, and architectural critic whose influential writings addressed the effect of buildings on the human condition and the environment.

Additional information is available online at *www.dcp.ufl.edu/sacrph/*.

1993 *The New York Approach: Robert Moses, Urban Liberals, and Redevelopment of the Inner City*
Joel Schwartz
Ohio State University Press

1995 *The City of Collective Memory: Its Historical Imagery and Architectural Entertainments*
M. Christine Boyer
MIT Press

1997 *City Center to Regional Mall: Architecture, the Automobile, and Retailing in Los Angeles, 1920–1950*
Richard Longstreth
MIT Press

1999 *Boston's Changeful Times: Origins of Preservation and Planning in America*
Michael Holleran
Johns Hopkins University Press

*Remaking Chicago: The Political Origins of Urban Industrial Change**
Joel Rast
Northern Illinois University Press

2001 *Downtown: Its Rise and Fall, 1880–1950*
Robert Fogelson
Yale University Press

2003 *The Bulldozer in the Countryside: Suburban Sprawl and the Rise of American Environmentalism*
Adam Rome
Cambridge University Press

2005 *Downtown America: A History of the Place and the People Who Made It*
Alison Isenberg
University of Chicago Press

* Honorary Mention

Source: Society for American City and Regional Planning History

Library Buildings Awards

The American Institute of Architects and American Library Association present the biennial Library Buildings Awards to encourage excellence in the design and planning of libraries. Architects licensed in the United States are eligible to enter any public or private library project from around the world, whether a renovation, addition, conversion, interior project, or new construction. The jury consists of three architects and three librarians with extensive library building experience.

Additional information is available on the ALA's website at *www.ala.org*.

2007 Winners

Robin Hood Foundation Library
New York, NY
Gluckman Mayner Architects

Desert Broom Branch Library
Phoenix, AZ
richärd+bauer

Shunde Library
Foshan, China
P&T Architects and Engineers Ltd,
   with Shunde Architectural Design
   Institute/Guangdong Architecture
   Design Institute (China)

Ballard Library and Neighborhood
   Service Center
Seattle, WA
Bohlin Cywinski Jackson

Santa Monica College Library Expansion
   & Renovation, Santa Monica College
Santa Monica, CA
CO Architects

David Bishop Skillman Library,
   Lafayette College
Easton, PA
Ann Beha Architects

William J. Clinton Presidential Center
Little Rock, AR
Polshek Partnership Architects with Polk
   Stanley Rowland Curzon Porter
   Architects; Witsell Evans Rasco
   Architects and Planners; and Woods
   Carradine Architects

Fleet Library, Rhode Island School
   of Design
Providence, RI
Office dA

La Grande Bibliothéque
Montreal, QC, Canada
Patkau/Croft-Pelletier/Menkés Shooner
   Dagenais Architectes (Canada)

JURY

Edward Dean, Chong Partners Architecture
Anne M. Larsen of Massachusetts Board of
   Library Commissioners
Wendy Pautz, LMN Architects
Jefferson B. Riley, Centerbrook Architects and
   Planners (chair)
Elizabeth A. Titus, New Mexico State University
   Library
Ken S. Weil, South Huntington Library

Source: American Library Association

Library Interior Design Award

The Library Interior Design Award is a biennial competition that honors excellence in the design of library interiors and promotes innovative concepts and design excellence. Projects are judged on aesthetics, design creativity, function, and satisfaction of the client's objectives. The program is administered by the American Library Association in partnership with the International Interior Design Association.

For further information, visit the ALA on the Web at *www.ala.org*.

2006 Winners

Academic Libraries
30,000 Square Feet and Smaller
Morton College Library
Cicero, IL
Legat Architects

Academic Libraries
Over 30,000 Square Feet
University Library, University of Ontario
    Institute of Technology
Oshawa, ON, Canada
Diamond and Schmidt Architects Inc.
    (Canada)

Christopher Center for Library and
    Information Resources, Valparaiso
    University
Valparaiso, IN
EHDD Architecture

Special Merit
Baker Library, Harvard University
Cambridge, MA
Robert A.M. Stern Architects

Public Libraries
30,000 Square Feet and Smaller
Incline Village Library
Incline Village, NV
Leo A Daly and Hershenow & Klippenstein
    Architects

Quincie Douglas Branch, Tucson-Pima
    Public Library
Tucson, AZ
Richard + Bauer Architects

Honorary Mention
International District/Chinatown Branch,
    Seattle Public Library
Seattle, WA
Miller Hayashi Architects

Public Libraries
Over 30,000 Square Feet
Pierre Berton Resource Library
Vaughan, ON, Canada
Diamond and Schmidt Architects Inc.
    (Canada)

Special Merit
ImaginOn, Public Library of Charlotte and
    Mecklenburg County
Charlotte, NC
Gantt Huberman Architects with Holzman
    Moss Architecture

Single Space
Nashville Public Library Civil Rights
    Collection
Nashville, TN
Tuck Hinton Architects

Library Interior Design Award

Special Libraries
30,000 Square Feet and Smaller
Edward E. Hale Public School 106 Library
Brooklyn, NY
Rockwell Group

Innovation in Sustainable Design
Desert Broom Branch, Phoenix Public
   Library
Phoenix, AZ
Richard + Bauer Architects

On the Boards
Arabian Library, Scottsdale Public Library
   System
Scottsdale, AZ
Richard + Bauer Architects

JURY
Neil Frankel, Frankel + Coleman
Cary D. Johnson, Gensler
Susan Kent, New York Public Library
William Sannwald, consultant

Source: American Library Association

Beauty is the quality of harmonious relationships. A formula to produce it
does not exist.

Frank A. Parsons

Lighting Design Awards

Presented for lighting installations that couple aesthetic achievement with technical expertise, the Lighting Design Awards are bestowed annually by the International Association of Lighting Designers. The program emphasizes design innovation with attention to energy usage, economics, and sustainable design. One project receives the Radiance Award, the finest example of lighting design excellence among all submissions.

For additional information, visit the IALD on the Internet at *www.iald.org*.

2007 Winners

Radiance Award
Chino Cultural Complex
Chino, Nagano, Japan
Lighting Planners Associates Inc. (Japan)

Awards of Excellence
AGC Monozukuri (Quality Manufacturing)
    Training Center
Yokohama-shi, Kanagawa, Japan
Takenaka Corporation (Japan)

Manchester235
Manchester, UK
Lighting Design International (UK)

ERHA Clinic Kelapa Gading
Jakarta, Indonesia
Abdi Ahsan (Indonesia)

Information Center in the Central
    Memorial for the Murdered Jews
    of Europe
Berlin, Germany
LichtVision (Germany)

Manufactum
Munich, Germany
pfarré lighting design (Germany)

Awards of Merit
UMB Bank, Shawnee Branch
Shawnee, KS
Yarnell Associates

Public Passage
Munich, Germany
pfarré lighting design (Germany)

Berlin Main Station, Underground
    Platforms and Shopping Areas
Berlin, Germany
LichtVision (Germany)

Changi International Airport, Terminal 2
    Upgrade
Singapore
Lighting Planners Associates Inc. (Japan)

Blue Pool House
Dallas, TX
Pamela Hull Wilson

Park Hyatt Philadelphia at the Bellevue
Philadelphia, PA
Sean O'Connor Associates

Temple Emanu-El
New York, NY
Sachs Morgan Studio

Greenville Liberty Bridge
Greenville, SC
Derek Porter Studio

7 World Trade Center
New York, NY
Cline Bettridge Bernstein Lighting
    Design Inc.

Lighting Design Awards

Luz Railway Station, Museum of the
   Portuguese Language
São Paulo, Brazil
Franco & Tortes Lighting Design (Brazil)

Residential Lobby, Diana Garden Hiroo
Tokyo, Japan
Reiko Chikada and Sachi Takanaga (Japan)

Uniqa Tower
Vienna, Austria
LichtKunst Licht (Germany)

Special Citation
Kresge Foundation
Troy, MI
Lighting Design Allianc

Chicago Board of Trade Lobby Renovation
Chicago, IL
Schuler Shook

Retem Corporation Tokyo Factory
Tokyo, Japan
Reiko Chikada and Sachi Takanaga (Japan)

Sustainable Design Award
No award granted

JURY
David Becker, Point of View (Australia)
Andrea Hartranft, C.M. Kling & Associates
   (chair)
Ronald D. Kurtz, Randy Burkett Lighting
   Designers
Mark McInturff, McInturff Architects
Stephen Perkins, ForrestPerkins
Diane Soper, Lumenociti, Inc.
Galina Zbrizher, Total Lighting Solutions
   (Canada)
James Youngston, Gabler-Youngston

Source: International Association of Lighting Designers

There is one fundamental fact about lighting: Where there is no light, there is
no beauty.

Billy Baldwin

Clockwise from top: **Greenville Liberty Bridge, Greenville, SC, by Derek Porter Studio** (©Derek Porter, 2006); **Public Passage, Munich, Germany, by pfarré lighting design (Germany)** (©Andreas J. Focke); **and Manufactum, Munich, Germany, by pfarré lighting design (Germany)** (©Andreas J. Focke). (All images courtesy of IALD)

Plates 1–4: **Bloch Building at the Nelson-Atkins Museum of Art, Kansas City, MO, by Steven Holl Architects** (Photos: Roland Halbe, *except bottom right* ©Timothy Hursley. All photos courtesy of the Nelson-Atkins Museum of Art.)

Plates 5–6: **IAC Building, New York, NY, by Gehry Partners** (Photos: Albert Vecerka/Esto Photographics, courtesy of IAC)

Plates 7–8: **Davies Alpine House, Kew Gardens, London, UK, by Wilkinson Eyre Architects (UK)** (Photos courtesy of the Royal Botanical Garden, Kew)

Plate 9: **Elie Saab Residence, Faqra, Lebanon, by Vladimir Djurovic Landscape Architecture (Lebanon)**
(Photo: Geraldine Bruneel)

Plates 10–12: **FILA, New York, NY, by Giorgio Borruso Design** (Photos: Benny Chan, courtesy of Giorgio Borruso Design)

Plates 13–14: **Simone de Beauvoir Bridge, Paris, France, Feichtinger Architectes (France)** (Photos: David Boreau, courtesy of Feichtinger Architectes)

Plates 15–17: **Joondalup Library and Technology Centre, Edith Cowan University, Joondalup, WA, Australia, by JCY Architects and Urban Designers (Australia)** (Photos: Patrick Bingham-Hall, courtesy of Edith Cowan University)

Plates 18–20: **Schermerhorn Symphony Center, Nashville, TN, by David Schwarz/Architectural Services** (Photos: Tom Gatlin, courtesy of the Schermerhorn Symphony Center)

Plates 21–23: **Gardiner Museum, Toronto, ON, Canada by Kuwabara Payne McKenna Blumberg Architects (Canada)** (Photos: Shai Gill (*above right and left*) and Tom Arban (*bottom right*), courtesy of the Gardiner Museum)

Plates 24–26: **Serpentine Gallery Pavilion 2007, London, UK, by Olafur Eliasson (Germany) and Kjetil Thorsen (Norway)** (Photos: ©John Offenbach, courtesy of the Serpentine Gallery)

Plates 27–29: **Musée du Quai Branly, Paris, France, by Ateliers Jean Nouvel (France)** (Photos by Nicolas Borel, ©Musée du Quai Branly)

Plates 30–32: **Des Moines Central Library, Des Moines, IA, by David Chipperfield Architects (UK) with Herbert Lewis Kruse Blunck Architecture** (Photos: Farshid Assassi, courtesy of the Des Moines Public Library)

Plates 33–34: **Berg Oase Spa at the Tschuggen Grand Hotel, Arosa, Switzerland, by Mario Botta Architetto (Switzerland)** (Photos courtesy of the Tschuggen Group)

Plate 35: **Minneapolis Public Library, Minneapolis, MN, by Cesar Pelli & Associates, Architectural Alliance, Michaels Associates, and Ralph Appelbaum Associates** (Photo: ©Jeff Goldberg/Esto, courtesy of the Minneapolis Public Library)

Plates 36–38: **Akron Art Museum, Akron, OH, by Coop Himmelb(l)au (Austria)** (Photos: ©Roland Halbe Fotografie, courtesy of the Akron Art Museum)

Plates 39–41: **Longchamp, SoHo, New, York, NY, by Heatherwick Studio (UK)** (Photos: Nikolas Koenig)

Lynn S. Beedle Achievement Award

The Lynn S. Beedle Achievement Award recognizes individuals who have made extraordinary contributions to tall buildings and the urban environment. Candidates may be from any area of specialization, including architecture, structures, building systems, construction, academia, planning, development, or management. The award is named for the founder of the Council on Tall Buildings and Urban Habitats and its director from 1969 to 2000.

For more information, visit the CTBUH website, *www.ctbuh.org*.

2002	Lynn S. Beedle
2003	Charles A. DeBenedittis
2004	Gerald D. Hines
2005	Alan G. Davenport
2006	Ken Yeang (Malaysia)
2007	Lord Norman Foster (UK)

Source: Council on Tall Buildings and Urban Habitats

Tall buildings do not change a place—they reflect a place.

Peter Rees

Marcus Prize

The biennial Marcus Prize, through the support of the Marcus Corporation Foundation, recognizes emerging international architects. Half the $100,000 prize is awarded to the winning architect. The other half is given to the University of Wisconsin–Milwaukee School of Architecture and Urban Planning to administer the prize and to facilitate a collaboration between the winner and the university on projects that address design challenges in Milwaukee.

For additional information, visit the school's website, *www.uwm.edu.*

2005	MVRDV (Netherlands)
2007	Barkow Leibinger Architects (Germany)

Source: University of Wisconsin–Milwaukee

Good architecture never shouts. It is like a well-mannered lady that is polite to its neighbors. The order and progression of the street is more important than the individual buildings.

Hugh Newell Jacobsen

Marketing Achievement Award

The Society for Marketing Professional Services' Marketing Achievement Award, the highest honor presented by the organization, salutes professionals for their exemplary achievements and lasting contributions to the field. Nominees must be SMPS members and have demonstrated significant accomplishments in at least three of five areas: research, education, professional leadership, marketing communications, or innovative programs.

For more information, visit SMPS online at *www.smps.org.*

1987	Diane Creel	1998	Kay Lentz
1989	Weld Coxe	1999	Howard J. Wolff
1990	Joan Capelin	2000	Randolph W. Tucker
1991	Janet Goodman Aubry	2001	Jean R. Valence
1992	Thomas Page	2003	Julie Luers
1993	William Hankinson	2005	Randy Pollock
1995	Lisbeth Quebe	2006	Mitchel R. Levitt
1996	Nancy Egan	2007	Craig Park
1997	Laurin McCraken		

Source: Society for Marketing Professional Services

Marketing is too often retrospective rather than visionary.

Ian Cameron

Marketing Communications Awards

The annual Marketing Communications Awards are presented by the Society for Marketing Professional Services to recognize excellence in marketing communications by professional service firms in the design and building industry. The diverse award categories acknowledge the wide-ranging initiatives a marketing strategy can entail, including books, brochures, magazines, websites, special events, annual reports, and direct-mail campaigns. If applicable, a small-firm award winner may also be named.

Photos of all winners are available on the SMPS website, *www.smps.org*.

2007 First-place Winners

Advertising
Opus Corporation
Green Building Services, Inc.*

Annual Report
Arup

Book/Monogram
Olson Sundberg Kundig Allen Architects

Brochure
Walter P. Moore
Green Building Service Inc.*
Watchdog Real Estate Project
   Managers/Bowhaus Design Groupe*

Corporate Identity
Beverly Prior Architects

Direct-Mail Campaign
Candela
Marketlink

Feature Writing
BSA LifeStructures

Holiday Piece
Butler Rogers Baskett Architects
TGBA/Taylor Gregory Butterfield
   Architects

Internal Communications
EDAW Inc.

Magazine
Cooper Carry, Inc.

Media Relations Campaign
EYP Mission Critical Facilities
Constructive Communications, Inc.*

Newsletter,External
CG Marketing Communications
Frisbie Architects*

Newsletter, Internal
Perkins+Will

Promotional Campaign
Jones Lang LaSalle

Special Event
HMC Architects (Canada)
Elliott + Associates Architects*

Specific Project Marketing
HGA Architects and Engineers

Target Marketing
Thompson, Ventulett, Stainback &
   Associates
Kinslow, Keith & Todd, Inc.*

Marketing Communications Awards

Website
STUDIOS Architecture
Design & Co., Inc.

JURY
Richard Belle, American Council of Engineering
Companies
Elisa Cohen, Association of General Contractors
of America
Jennifer Lipner, American Society of Interior
Design
Ann Looper, American Society of Landscape
Architects
Kristen Richards, ArchNewsNow
Phil Simon, American Institute of Architects
Jeffery Yoders, Building Design & Construction

* Small-firm winner

Source: Society for Marketing Professional Services

Michelangelo Award

105

The Construction Specifications Institute's Michelangelo Award pays tribute to an exceptional individual for a lifetime of distinguished, innovative service to the design and construction industry. The recipient's career demonstrates a far-reaching effect in creating and sustaining the built environment. Only one winner may be selected each year. The honoree is celebrated at the annual CSI Show and presented with a bust of Michelangelo.

For more information, visit the CSI on the Web at *www.csinet.org*.

2005	Lawrence Halprin
2006	Charles H. Thornton
2007	*No award granted*

Source: Construction Specifications Institute

Architecture is the only art which demands wanderings through space for us to appreciate it.

Narendra Dengle

Mies van der Rohe Award

The biennial Mies van der Rohe Award highlights notable contemporary European architecture that demonstrates an innovative character and excellence in design and execution. The award consists of a cash prize of 50,000 euros and a sculpture by Xavier Corberó, a design inspired by the Mies van der Rohe Pavilion in Barcelona, Spain. Recipients of the Emerging Architect Special Mention, which celebrates young architects, receive 10,000 euros and a sculpture.

For more information, visit the foundation's website at *www.miesbcn.com.*

1988	Borges e Irmão Bank Vila do Conde, Portugal Alvaro Siza (Portugal)
1990	New Terminal Development, Stansted Airport London, UK Norman Foster & Partners (UK)
1992	Municipal Sports Stadium Badalona, Barcelona, Spain Esteve Bonell and Francesc Rius (Spain)
1994	Waterloo International Station London, UK Nicholas Grimshaw & Partners (UK)
1996	Bibliotèque Nationale de France Paris, France Dominique Perrault (France)
1999	Art Museum in Bregenz Bregenz, Austria Peter Zumthor (Switzerland)
2001	Kursaal Congress Centre San Sebastian, Spain Rafael Moneo (Spain)
	Kaufmann Holz Distribution Centre* Bobingen, Germany Florian Nagler, Florian Nagler Architekt (Germany)

2003	Car Park & Terminal Hoenheim North Strasbourg, France Zaha Hadid (UK)
	Scharnhauser Park Town Hall* Ostfildern, Germany Jürgen Mayer (Germany)
2005	Netherlands Embassy Berlin Berlin, Germany Office for Metropolitan Architecture (Netherlands)
	Basket Bar* Utrecht, Netherlands NL Architects (Netherlands)
2007	MUSAC – Contemporary Art Museum of Castilla y León León, Spain Mansilla + Tuñón (Spain)
	Faculty of Mathematics* Ljubljana, Slovenia Bevk Perovic arhitekti (Slovania)

*Emerging Architect Special Mention

Source: Mies van der Rohe Foundation

Modern Healthcare/AIA Design Awards

The annual Modern Healthcare/AIA Design Awards recognize excellence in the design and planning of new and remodeled healthcare facilities. Sponsored by *Modern Healthcare* magazine and the American Institute of Architects' Academy of Architecture for Health, all types and sizes of patient-care facilities are eligible to enter. Winners are recognized in an issue of the magazine and at the annual AAH convention.

Additional information is available online at *www.modernhealthcare.com.*

2006 Winners

Awards of Excellence, Built
Rebecca and John Moores Cancer Center, University of California at San Diego
La Jolla, CA
Zimmer Gunsul Frasca Partnership

Children's Hospital Boston
Boston, MA
Shepley Bulfinch Richardson Abbott

Honorable Mention, Built
Neonatal Intensive-Care Unit, University of California at Davis Medical Center
Sacramento, CA
Chong Partners Architecture

Reuter Children's Outpatient Center
Asheville, NC
Stanley Beaman & Sears

Peter O. Kohler Pavilion
Portland, OR
Perkins+Will; Petersen Kolberg & Associates

Orange City Hospital
Orange City, IA
HGA Architects and Engineers; Cannon Moss Brygger & Associates

Emenhiser Center at Samaritan Lebanon Community Hospital
Lebanon, OR
Clark/Kjos Architects

Banner Good Samaritan Medical Center
Phoenix, AZ
OWP/P

Citation, Built
University of Wisconsin Cancer Center at Johnson Creek
Johnson Creek, WI
OWP/P

Heart Hospital at Baptist, Baptist Medical Center
Jacksonville, FL
Cannon Design, Inc.

Brigham and Women's Hospital
Boston, MA
Payette Associates

Citation, Not Built
Inpatient Tower, Hadassah Medical Center
Jerusalem, Israel
HKS Inc.; Spector Amisar (Israel)

Source: Modern Healthcare

National Building Museum Honor Award

The National Building Museum Honor Award celebrates individuals and organizations that have made exceptional contributions to America's built environment. Each year the award is presented at an elegant gala held in the museum's Great Hall, which since 1883 has often been the site of the Presidential Inaugural Ball.

More information is available on the museum's website, *www.nbm.org.*

1986	J. Irwin Miller	1999	Harold and Terry McGraw and the McGraw-Hill Companies
1987	*No award granted*	2000	Gerald D. Hines
1988	James W. Rouse	2001	Michael D. Eisner and the Walt Disney Company
1989	Daniel Patrick Moynihan	2002	DuPont
1990	IBM	2003	National Football League and Major League Baseball
1991	The Rockefeller Family	2004	US General Services Administration
1992	The Civic Leadership of Greater Pittsburgh	2005	Forest City Enterprises
1993	J. Carter Brown	2006	Clark Construction Group
1994	James A. Johnson and Fannie Mae	2007	Related
1995	Lady Bird Johnson		
1996	Cindy and Jay Pritzker		
1997	Morris Cafritz, Charles E. Smith, Charles A. Horsky and Oliver T. Carr Jr.		
1998	Riley P. Bechtel and Stephen D. Bechtel Jr. of the Bechtel Group		

Source: National Building Museum

Did you know...

In 2007, the National Building Museum received a $600,000 grant from the Home Depot Foundation to further educational efforts toward a more sustainable built environment, including raising public awareness, sharing best practices in sustainability among design and building professionals, and using technology to reach a larger audience.

National Design Awards

109

The National Design Awards honor the best in American design. This annual program, sponsored by the Smithsonian's Cooper-Hewitt, National Design Museum, celebrates design in various disciplines as a vital humanistic tool in shaping the world and seeks to increase national awareness of design by educating the public and promoting excellence, innovation, and lasting achievement. The awards are granted for a body of work, not a specific project.

Photos and profiles of the winners are available from the award's website, *www.nationaldesignawards.org.*

2007 Recipients

Architectural Design
Office dA

Communication Design
Chipp Kidd

Corporate Achievement
Adobe Systems Incorporated

Design Mind
Denise Scott Brown and Robert Venturi

Design Patron
Maharam

Fashion Design
Rick Owens

Interior Design
Lewis.Tsurumaki.Lewis

Landscape Design
Peter Walker and Partners

Lifetime Achievement
Antoine Predock

Product Design
Jonathan Ive

Special Jury Commendation
Frank Ching

JURY
Stephen Burks, Readymade Projects
Caterina Fake, Flickr
Michael Gabellini, Gabellini Sheppard Associates
Tim Gunn, Liz Claiborne Inc.
Reed Kroloff, Tulane University
Yeohlee Teng, Yeohlee Inc.
James Wines, SITE and Penn State University

Source: Cooper-Hewitt, National Design Museum

National Design Awards

Clockwise from top: **Robert Venturi and Denise Scott Brown** (Photo: Frank Hanswijk); **Jonathan Ive** (Photo: Apple, Inc.); **Antoine Predock** (Photo courtesy Antoine Predock). (All photos courtesy Cooper-Hewitt, National Design Museum)

National Design-Build Awards

The annual National Design-Build Awards honor projects that exemplify the principles of interdisciplinary teamwork, innovation, and problem solving that characterize the design-build delivery method. Created by the Design-Build Institute of America, the competition is open to design-build projects completed within the previous three years. In addition to the National Design-Build Award, the jury may also grant Design-Build Excellence Awards and merit awards.

For a list of all winning projects, visit the DBIA's website at *www.dbia.org.*

2006 National Design-Build Award Winners

**Public Sector Building
Over $15 million**
University of Washington Research
and Technology Building
Seattle, WA
M.A. Mortenson Company

**Public Sector Building
Under $15 million**
U.S. Navy Littoral Warfare Research
Facility
Panama City, FL
The Haskell Company

**Industrial/Process Sector
Under $25 million**
D/B APTU Conversion to Hypersonic
Capabilities
Arnold AFB, TN
Caddell Construction Company, Inc.

Transportation Under $50 million
Beartooth Highway Emergency Repairs
Red Lodge, MT
Kiewit Western Co.

**Design-Build Rehabilitation/
Renovation/Restoration**
Big-D Construction Corporate Office
Salt Lake City, UT
Big-D Construction

Source: Design-Build Institute of America

Did you know...
Use of the design-build approach for the Carmen Dragon Elementary School in Antioch, CA, saved $1.5 million. The school was also completed 2.5 months faster than similarly constructed schools.

National Medal of Arts

Congress established the National Medal of Arts in 1984 to honor individuals and organizations who have encouraged the arts in America through distinguished achievement, support, or patronage. All categories of the arts are represented; although awards are not always granted in each discipline every year. Any citizen or organization may submit nominations; the president of the United States makes the final selection.

Visit the National Endowment for the Arts' website at *www.arts.endow.gov* for additional information.

Design Professional Recipients

1987	Isamu Noguchi	1998	Frank Gehry
1988	I.M. Pei	1999	Michael Graves
1989	Leopold Adler	2002	Florence Knoll Bassett
1990	Ian McHarg		Lawrence Halprin
1991	Pietro Belluschi	2004	Vincent J. Scully
1992	Robert Venturi	2006	Viktor Schreckengost
	Denise Scott Brown		
1995	James Ingo Freed		
1997	Daniel Urban Kiley		*Source: National Endowment for the Arts*

Did you know...

South-African-born Denise Scott Brown received the 2007 Vilcek Foundation Prize, a annual award with a $50,000 prize given to foreign-born individuals who have made extraordinary contributions to US society. She is the first architect to receive the award.

National Planning Excellence Awards

Through its National Planning Awards program, the American Planning Association recognizes the role cutting-edge planning achievements and outstanding individual contributions play in creating communities of lasting value. Excellence Awards are granted to outstanding initiatives by planning agencies, planning teams or firms, community groups, and local authorities.

Profiles of the winning projects can be found on the APA's website at *www.planning.org.*

2007 Winners

Best Practices
New Jersey Smart Growth Locator
Trenton, NJ

Protecting Florida's Springs: Land Use
Planning Strategies and Best
Management Practices
Tallahassee, FL

Grassroots Initiative
Corridor Housing Initiative
Minneapolis, MN

Implementation
Chattanooga Bicycle Planning
Chattanooga, TN

Public Outreach
Youngstown 2010
Youngstown, OH

Innovations in Neighborhood Planning in Honor of Jane Jacobs
Revitalization of Hannibal Square
Winter Park, FL

JURY
H. DeWitt Blackwell, Western Piedmont (NC)
    Council of Governments
Kevin Costello, Boone County (KY) Planning
    Commission
Chandra Foreman, Polk County (FL)
Regina Gray, US Department of Housing and
    Urban Development
Karen Hundt, Planning & Design Studio
Jon Kinsey, Kinsey, Probasco, Hays Development
Carlos Martin, US Department of Housing and
    Urban Development
Carol Rhea, Rhea Consulting, Inc.
Catherine Ross, Georgia Institute of Technology
David Woods, Brookhaven (NY) Department of
    Planning, Environment, and Land
    Management

Source: American Planning Association

P/A Awards

Progressive Architecture magazine first granted the P/A Awards in 1954 to recognize design excellence in unbuilt projects. *Architect* magazine now administers the annual program; a jury of designers and architects selects the winners.

For more information, visit the magazine online, *www.architectmag.com.*

2007 Winners

Calgary Centre for Global Community
Calgary, Canada
Marc Boutin Architect (Canada)

Hybrid Urban Sutures: Filling in the Gaps
  in the Medina of Fez
Fex, Morocco
Aziza Chaouni

Pittman Dowell Residence
La Crescenta, CA
Michael Maltzan Architecture

Villa Moda: New Kuwait Sports Shooting
  Club
Kuwait City, Kuwait
Office dA

2007 Citations

Bahá'í Mother Temple for South America
Santiago, Chile
Hariri Pontarini Architects (Canada)

Bab Tebbaneh School for Working
  Children and for Women
North Tripoli, Lebanon
Hashim Sarkis A.L.U.D. (Lebanon)

Campus d'Espoir
Port-au-Prince, Haiti
Studio Luz Architects

Veranda Urbanism: Community Design
  and Aging in Place, Good Shepherd
  Ecumenical Retirement Community
Little Rock, AR
University of Arkansas Community Design
  Center

JURY

Jose M. Castillo, arquitectura 911sc (Mexico)
Yung Ho Chang, Massachusetts Institute of
  Technology
Karen Fairbanks, Marble Fairbanks
Giuseppe Lignano, LOT-EK
Hadrian Predock, Predock_Frane Architects

Source: Architect

Palladio Awards

The Palladio Awards honor outstanding achievement in traditional design reflecting the creative interpretation or adaptation of the principles of the Renaissance architect Andrea Palladio. Entries are judged for their refinement and appropriateness, adherence to the program, use of materials, quality of construction and craftsmanship, and overall design excellence. Winners receive bronze trophies and are featured in *Traditional Building* magazine.

For more information, visit *Traditional Building*'s website at *www.traditional-building.com.*

2007 Commercial, Institutional, and Public Winners

Restoration/Renovation
Donald W. Reynolds Center for American
    Art & Portraiture
Washington, DC
Hartman-Cox Architects

Adaptive Reuse
1919 car dealership as an office and retail
    space
Richmond, VA
Commonwealth Architects

New Design & Construction
Barret Library at Rhodes College
Memphis, TN
Hanbury Evans Wright Vlattas + Company;
    Shepley Bulfinch Richardson Abbott

2007 Residential Winners

Restoration/Renovation
High Victorian residence
Riverdale, NY
BKSK Architects

Sympathetic Addition
Carhart Mansion
New York, NY
John Simpson & Partners (UK); Zivkovic
    Associates Architects

New Design & Construction
Chadsworth Cottage
Figure Eight Island, NC
Christine G.H. Franck, Inc.

Harborview House
Northeast Harbor, ME
Albert, Righter & Tittmann Architects, Inc.

Private Museum
Chester County, PA
Archer & Buchanan Architecture

JURY
Anne Fairfax, Fairfax & Sammons Architects
Michael Lykoudis, University of Notre Dame
Raymond Pepi, Building Conservation Associates,
    Inc.
Rob Robinson, Urban Design Associates
Thomas Gordon Smith, University of Notre
    Dame

Source: Traditional Building *magazine*

Patron's Prize

The Patron's Prize is awarded by the American Society of Interior Designers annually as merited to promote quality interior design. Eligible parties include clients (residential and commercial), organizations, government bodies, foundations, media, and museums that have significantly supported or promoted quality interior design.

For further information, contact the ASID at *www.asid.org*.

2003	Cooper-Hewitt, National Design Museum, Smithsonian Institution
2004	Herman Miller Inc.
2005	Edward A. Feiner
2006	US Green Building Council

Source: American Society of Interior Designers

The dialogue between client and architect is about as intimate as any conversation you can have, because when you're talking about building a house, you're talking about dreams.

Robert A.M. Stern

Philip Johnson Award

With its annual Philip Johnson Award, the Society of Architectural Historians recognizes outstanding architectural exhibition catalogs. This award is named in recognition of Philip Johnson, a distinguished architect and the first director of the architecture department at the Museum of Modern Art, whose 1932 exhibit and catalog, *The International Style: Architecture Since 1922* (co-authored with Henry-Russell Hitchcock), is credited with popularizing European modernism in the United States.

For more information, visit the SAH website, *www.sah.org*.

1990   *Los Angeles Blueprints for Modern Living: History and Legacy of the Case Study Houses*
Elizabeth A.T. Smith
Museum of Contemporary Art
    and MIT Press

1991   *Architecture and Its Image: Four Centuries of Architectural Representation, Works from the Collection of the Canadian Centre for Architecture*
Eve Blau and Edward Kaufman,
    eds.
Canadian Centre for
    Architecture and MIT Press

1992   No award granted

1993   *The Making of Virginia Architecture*
Charles Brownell
Virginia Museum of Fine Arts
    and the University Press of
    Virginia

Louis I. Kahn: In the Realm of Architecture
David Brownlee
Museum of Contemporary Art
    and Rizzoli International

1994   *Chicago Architecture and Design 1923–1993: Reconfiguration of an American Metropolis*
John Zukowsky
Prestel and Art Institute of
    Chicago

1995   *The Palladian Revival: Lord Burlington, His Villa and Garden in Chiswick*
John Harris
Yale University Press

1996   *The Perspective of Anglo-American Architecture*
James F. O'Gorman
Athenaeum of Philadelphia

An Everyday Modernism: The Houses of William Wurster
Marc Treib
San Francisco Museum of
    Modern Art and University of
    California Press

1997   *Sacred Realm: The Emergence of the Synagogue in the Ancient World*
Steven Fine
Yeshiva University Museum and
    Oxford University Press

Philip Johnson Award

1998	*Building for Air Travel: Architecture and Design for Commercial Aviation* John Zukowsky Art Institute of Chicago and Prestel	2003	*Richard Neutra's Windshield House* Dietrich Neumann, ed. Yale University
1999	*The Work of Charles and Ray Eames: A Legacy of Invention* Donald Albrecht Library of Congress, Vitra Design Museum, and Abrams Publishing	2004	*Central European Avant-Gardes: Exchange and Transformation, 1910–1930* Timothy O. Benson, ed. MIT Press
2000	*E.W. Godwin: Aesthetic Movement Architect and Designer* Susan Weber Soros Yale University Press	2005	*Thomas Jeckyll: Architect and Designer, 1827–1881* Susan Weber Soros and Catherine Arbuthnott Yale University Press
2001	*Mapping Boston* Alex Krieger and David Cobb, editors MIT Press	2006	*Raised to the Trade: Creole Building Arts of New Orleans** John Ethan Hankins ad Steven Maklansky New Orleans Museum of Art
2002	*Mies in Berlin* Terence Riley, Barry Bergdoll, and the Museum of Modern Art Harry N. Abrams	2007	*Machu Picchu: Unveiling the Mystery of the Incas* Richard L. Burger and Lucy C. Salazar, eds. Yale University Press

* Honorary Mention

Source: Society of Architectural Historians

Did you know...

Philip Johnson's Glass House opened to the public in 2007. It is the second Modern masterpiece, after Mies van der Rohe's Farnsworth House, in the National Trust for Historic Preservation's portfolio.

Praemium Imperiale

The Praemium Imperiale is awarded by the Japan Art Association, Japan's premier cultural institution, for lifetime achievement in the fields of painting, sculpture, music, architecture, and theater/film. The following individuals received this honor for architecture, which includes a commemorative medal and a 15,000,000 yen ($130,000) honorarium.

For more information, visit the Japan Art Association's website at *www.praemiumimperiale.org.*

1989	I.M. Pei	1999	Fumihiko Maki (Japan)
1990	James Stirling (UK)	2000	Sir Richard Rogers (UK)
1991	Gae Aulenti (Italy)	2001	Jean Nouvel (France)
1992	Frank Gehry	2002	Sir Norman Foster (UK)
1993	Kenzo Tange (Japan)	2003	Rem Koolhaas (Netherlands)
1994	Charles Correa (India)	2004	Oscar Niemeyer (Brazil)
1995	Renzo Piano (Italy)	2005	Taniguchi Yoshio (Japan)
1996	Tadao Ando (Japan)	2006	Frei Otto (Germany)
1997	Richard Meier	2007	Jacques Herzog and Pierre de
1998	Alvaro Siza (Portugal)		Meuron (Switzerland)

Source: Japan Art Association

Architecture is about exploring. Culturally, historically, psychologically, anthropologically, and topographically, every job is different. So the real risk is that as an architect you end up imposing your stamp before you understand what is the reality of a place.

Renzo Piano

1

Pritzker Architecture Prize

In 1979, Jay and Cindy Pritzker established the Pritzker Architecture Prize to inspire greater creativity in the profession and to heighten public awareness about architecture. Today, it is revered as one of the field's highest honors. The prize, which includes a $100,000 grant, is awarded each year to a living architect whose body of work represents a long-standing, significant contribution to the built environment.

Information about each of the winners is available on the award's website, *www.pritzkerprize.com.*

1979	Philip Johnson	1994	Christian de Portzamparc
1980	Luis Barragán (Mexico)		(France)
1981	James Stirling (UK)	1995	Tadao Ando (Japan)
1982	Kevin Roche	1996	Rafael Moneo (Spain)
1983	I.M. Pei	1997	Sverre Fehn (Norway)
1984	Richard Meier	1998	Renzo Piano (Italy)
1985	Hans Hollein (Austria)	1999	Sir Norman Foster (UK)
1986	Gottfried Boehm (Germany)	2000	Rem Koolhaas (Netherlands)
1987	Kenzo Tange (Japan)	2001	Jacques Herzog and Pierre de
1988	Gordon Bunshaft		Meuron (Switzerland)
	Oscar Niemeyer (Brazil)	2002	Glenn Murcutt (Australia)
1989	Frank Gehry	2003	Jørn Utzon (Denmark)
1990	Aldo Rossi (Italy)	2004	Zaha Hadid (UK)
1991	Robert Venturi	2005	Thom Mayne
1992	Alvaro Siza (Portugal)	2006	Paulo Mendes da Rocha (Brazil)
1993	Fumihiko Maki (Japan)	2007	Sir Richard Rogers (UK)

Source: The Pritzker Architecture Prize

My passion and great enjoyment for architecture, and the reason the older I get the more I enjoy it, is because I believe we—architects—can effect the quality of life of the people.

Sir Richard Rogers

Richard Rogers (Photo by Dan Stevens, courtesy of Richard Rogers Partnership and the Hyatt Foundation)

Pulitzer Prize for Architectural Criticism

Joseph Pulitzer created the Pulitzer Prize to encourage excellence in journalism, music, and letters. The Pulitzer Prize Board currently confers 21 awards, including one for distinguished journalistic criticism. First granted in 1970, the criticism award encompasses such areas as music, film, theater, fashion, visual arts, culture, and architecture; therefore, an award for architectural criticism is not necessarily bestowed each year. Since 1980 the board has also recognized the finalists, included below.

Visit the Pulitzer Prize's website at *www.pulitzer.org* for a detailed history, chronology, and archive of past winners.

Recipients

1970	Ada Louise Huxtable *New York Times*	1990	Allan Temko *San Francisco Chronicle*
1979	Paul Gapp *Chicago Tribune*	1996	Robert Campbell *Boston Globe*
1984	Paul Goldberger *New York Times*	1999	Blair Kamin *Chicago Tribune*

Finalists

1981	Allan Temko *San Francisco Chronicle*	2003	John King *San Francisco Chronicle*
1983	Beth Dunlop *Miami Herald*		Nicolai Ouroussoff *Los Angeles Times*
1988	Allan Temko *San Francisco Chronicle*	2004	Nicolai Ouroussoff *Los Angeles Times*
1997	Herbert Muschamp *New York Times*	2006	Nicolai Ouroussoff *New York Times*
2002	John King *San Francisco Chronicle*		

Source: The Pulitzer Prize Board

Pure beauty in an individual work of art is the degree to which it attains utility and the harmony of all parts in relation to each other.

Adolf Loos

RAIA Gold Medal

The highest honor bestowed by the Royal Australian Institute of Architects, the Gold Medal rewards the distinguished service of Australian architects who have designed buildings of high merit or who have otherwise advanced the profession. The recipient delivers the annual A.S. Hook Address, named for early RAIA promoter Alfred Samuel Hook, that provides insight into the life, work, and principles of the medalist and the state of the profession.

Past A.S. Hook addressesare available from *www.architecture.com.au.*

1960	Leslie Wilkinson	1985	Richard Norman Johnson
1961	Louis Laybourne-Smith	1986	Richard Butterworth
1962	Joseph Charles Fowell	1987	Daryl Jackson
1963	Sir Arthur Stephenson	1988	Romaldo Giurgola
1964	Cobden Parkes	1989	Robin Findlay Gibson
1965	Sir Osborn McCutcheon	1990	Peter McIntyre
1966	William Rae Laurie	1991	Donald Campbell Rupert Bailey
1967	William Purves Godfrey	1992	Glenn Murcutt
1968	Sir Roy Grounds	1993	Kenneth Frank Woolley
1969	Robin Boyd	1994	Neville Quarry
1970	Jack Hobbs McConnell	1995	*No award granted*
1971	Frederick Bruce Lucas	1996	John Denton
1972	Edward Herbert Farmer		Bill Corker
1973	Jørn Utzon (Denmark)		Barrie Marshall
1974	Raymond Berg	1997	Roy Simpson
1975	Sydney Edward Ancher	1998	Gabriel Poole
1976	Harry Seidler	1999	Richard Leplastrier
1977	Ronald Andrew Gilling	2000	John Morphett
1978	Mervyn Henry Parry	2001	Keith Cottier
1979	Harold Bryce Mortlock	2002	Brit Andresen
1980	John H. Andrews	2003	Peter Corrigan
1981	Colin Frederick Madigan	2004	Gregory Burgess
1982	Sir John Wallace Overall	2005	James Birrell
1983	Gilbert Ridgway Nicol	2006	Kerry Hill (Singapore)
	Ross Kingsley Chisholm	2007	Enrico Taglietti (Italy)
1984	Philip S. Cox		

Individuals are from Australia unless otherwise indicated.

Source: Royal Australian Institute of Architects

RAIC Gold Medal

The Royal Architectural Institute of Canada began its Gold Medal program in 1967 to recognize architects or individuals in related fields who have made significant contributions to Canadian architecture. As the RAIC Gold Medal is merit-based, awards are not necessarily granted annually.

For more information, visit the RAIC's website at *www.raic.org.*

1967	Jean Drapeau	1989	Raymond T. Affleck
1968	Vincent Massey	1991	Phyllis Lambert
1970	Eric R. Arthur	1992	Douglas Shadbolt
	John A. Russell*	1994	Barton Myers
1973	Serge Chermayeff (UK/US)	1995	Moshe Safdie (US)
1976	Constantinos Doxiadis (Greece)	1997	Raymond Moriyama
1979	John C. Parkin	1998	Frank Gehry (US)
1981	Jane Jacobs	1999	Douglas Cardina
1982	Ralph Erskine (Sweden)	2001	A.J. (Jack) Diamond
1984	Arthur C. Erickson	2006	Bruce Kuwabara
1985	John Bland	2007	Mario Saia
1986	Eberhard Zeidler		

*Honored posthumously
Individuals are from Canada unless otherwise indicated.

Source: Royal Architectural Institute of Canada

Architecture depends on its time. It is the crystallization of its inner structure, the slow unfolding of its form.

Ludwig Mies van der Rohe

red dot design awards

The red dot design awards is one of the world's oldest product design competitions, founded in 1955 by the Design Zentrum Nordrhein Westfalen in Essen, Germany. An international panel of jurors reviews the entries for innovation, functionality, quality, symbolic and emotional content, ergonomics, and ecological compatibility. The winners are exhibited at the museum and receive the red dot trophy, an international seal of quality.

To see photos of all the winners, visit red dot online at *www.red-dot.de.*

2007 Best of the Best

Living Rooms and Bedrooms
Yin Yang Chaise Lounge
G. Nicolas Thomkins (Switzerland)

Jotul 370 Wood Burning Stove
Hareide Designmill (Netherlands)

Andoo
EOOS Design GmbH (Austria)

MOËL upholstery
Inga Sempé (France)

Households and Kitchens
Eva Solo Bin
Tools Design (Denmark)

SERVO-DRIVE
Julius Blum GmbH (Germany)

KFN 8998 SE fridge-freezer combination
Miele & Cie. KG (Germany)

Leisure, Sports, Wellness and Caravanning
Adidas TOUR360 II Golf Shoe
Adidas (Germany)

Icaro Tech Stabilizing Jacket
Attivo Creative Resource Srl (Italy)

Raptor Avalanche Shovel
Nose AG Design Intelligence (Switzerland)

Architecture and Interior Design
HT 811-0 In-House Telephones
S. Siedle & Söhne (Germany)

Myths: Jewels Today - Seen by Stefan
    Hemmerle
Tom Postma (Netherlands)

Flash 1-7960-154 Decoration Fabric
Marty Lamers (Netherlands)

walchwindow04 window and façade system
Walch GmbH (Austria); Kumulus Netzwerk
    für Produktentwicklung (Austria)

Industry and Crafts
Hilti TE 7-C Rotary Hammer
Hilti Aktiengesellschaft (Germany);
    Busse Design Ulm (Germany)

Tegera Pro 9195 Protective Gloves
Ergonomidesign AB (Sweden)

OXO Good Grips Utility Knife
Smart Design

Transports
Crown TSP6000 Turret Stockpicker
Formation Design Group

Porsche 911 Targa
Dr. Ing. h.c. F. Porsche AG (Germany)

NEOPLAN Cityliner touring coach
NEOMAN Bus GmbH (Germany)

Bathrooms, Heating, Sanitary Installations, and Air Conditioning
Wedge Washbasin
BAGNO SASSO (Switzerland)

red dot design awards

Sundeck Bathtub
EOOS Design GmbH (Austria)

GROHE Ondus® Faucet
Grohe AG (Germany)

Life Science and Medicine
SPI MONO Torque Ratchet
Thommen Medical AG (Germany);
    Zürcher Hochschule Winterthur
    (Switzerland)

Otto Bock Lumbo TriStep Multifunctional
    Lumbar Orthosis
Otto Bock HealthCare GmbH (Germany);
    Resolut Design (Germany)

Otto Bock C-Leg® Prosthesis System
Otto Bock HealthCare GmbH (Germany)

1C30 Trias Prosthetic Foot
Otto Bock HealthCare GmbH (Germany)

Offices and Administration
Ahrend 800
Ahrend (Netherlands)

GUBI Chair II
Komplot Design (Denmark)

Media and Home Electronics
Prada Phone
LG Electronics Inc. (South Korea)

U600
Samsung Electronics (South Korea)

LMD-10A51W Portable DMB TV
Samsung Electronics (South Korea)

iPod shuffle
Apple Computer

Computers and Accessories
Freecom ToughDrive Pro
Aplustec Design (Taiwan)

Lifebook Q2010 Notebook
Fujitsu Siemens Computers (Germany)

NAVIGON 7100
platinumdesign (Germany)

Jewelry, Fashion, and Luxuries
Clinique Derma White Auto Open
    Compact
Clinique Laboratories

Pontos Décentrique GMT Limited Edition
    Wristwatch
Maurice Lacroix (Germany)

Arcade Handbag
Olbrisch und Goebel GbR (Germany)

horn by Markus T
deSIGN Markus T. GmbH (Germany)

Lighting and Lamps
Itis
Artemide Group S.p.A (Italy)

Bossa
lumini (Brazil)

Open Box
Propeller (Sweden)

JURY
Masayo Ave, architect and designer (Italy/Japan)
Rido Busse, busse design ulm (Germany)
Tony K. M. Chang, Taiwan Design Center
    (Taiwan)
Vivian Cheng Wai Kwan, Hong Kong Institute of
    Vocational Education (China)
Mårten Claesson, Claesson Koivisto Rune
    (Sweden)
Sebastian Conran, Conran & Partners (UK)
Robin Edman, Swedish Industrial Design
    Foundation (Sweden)
Roy Fleetwood, Office for Design Strategy (UK)
Kenneth Grange, Kenneth Grange Design
    Ltd.(UK)
Herman Hermsen, University of Applied Science,
    Düsseldorf (Netherlands)
Carlos Hinrichsen, Pontificia Universidad
    Católica de Chile (Chile)
Daniel Huber, Spirit Design (Austria)

Clockwise from top: **Yin Yang Chaise Lounge by G. Nicolas Thomkins (Switzerland), Jotul 370 Wood Burning Stove by Hareide Designmill (Netherlands), and Bossa by Artemide Group (Italy)** (Photos courtesy of the red dot design awards)

Florian Hufnagl, Die Neue Sammlung - Pinakothek der Moderne (Germany)

Tapani Hyvönen, ED-design Ltd. (Finland)

Zhang Jin Jie (JinR), GREEN T. HOUSE (China)

Soon-In Lee, Hong-Ik University (South Korea)

Stefan Lengyel, Moholy-Nagy University of Art and Design (Hungary)

Thomas Lockwood, Design Management Institute

Francesco Milani, Milani design & consulting AG (Switzerland)

Simon Ong, Kingsmen Creatives Ltd (Singapore)

Martin Pärn, Estonian Academy of Arts (Estonia)

Dirk Schumann, Schumann - Büro für industrielle Formentwicklung (Germany)

Nils Toft, Christian Bjorn Design (Denmark)

Danny Venlet, Venlet Interior Architecture (Belgium)

Source: Design Zentrum Nordrhein Westfalen

Religious Art & Architecture Design Awards

The annual Religious Art & Architecture Design Awards, co-sponsored by *Faith & Form* magazine and the Interfaith Forum on Religion, Art and Architecture (a professional interest area of the American Institute of Architects), reward the highest achievements in architecture, liturgical design, and art for religious spaces. Architects, liturgical consultants, interior designers, artists, and craftpersons worldwide are eligible to enter. Winning projects are featured in *Faith & Form.*

For additional information and entry forms, visit the journal's website at *www.faithandform.com.*

2006 Honor Awards

New Facilities

Pope John XXIII Church and Pastoral
    Center
Seriate, Italy
Mario Botta Architetto (Switzerland)

Friends Meetinghouse
San Antonio, TX
Lake/Flato Architects

SETRE Chapel
Kobe, Japan
Ryuichi Ashizawa Architects & Associates
    (Japan)

Divinity School Addition, Duke University
Durham, NC
Hartman-Cox Architects

Parish Center Podersdorf
Podersdorf, Austria
lichtblau.wagner architekten (Austria)

Renovation

San Fernando Cathedral Renovation and
    Cathedral Centre
San Antonio, TX
Rafferty Rafferty Tollefson Lindeke
    Architects

Restoration

Central Synagogue
New York, NY
H3 Hardy Collaboration Architecture

Liturgical/Interior Design

St. Thomas More Chapel, St. Thomas
    School of Law
Minneapolis, MN
Tylevich Studio, Inc.

Jewish Chapel at the Commodore Uriah P.
    Levy Center, U.S. Naval Academy
Annapolis, MD
Boggs & Partners Architects

Visual Arts

Living Hope of the Resurrection, Luther
    Theological Seminary
St. Paul, MN
Jeff Barber

St. Mary Magdalene, St. Joseph's Chapel
New York, NY
John Collier

Blessed Trinity Catholic Church Window
Frankenmuth, MI
Elizabeth Devereaux Architectural Glass

Bronze Doors, St. Thomas More Chapel,
    St. Thomas School of Law
Minneapolis, MN
Tylevich Studio, Inc.

Ceremonial Objects
Chuppah, Jewish Chapel at the
    Commodore Uriah P. Levy Center,
    U.S. Naval Academy
Annapolis, MD
Boggs & Partners Architects

2006 Merit Awards

New Facilities
Temple Solel
Cardiff-by-the-Sea, CA
Goldman Firth Rossi Architects

Raphael Kirche
Pforzheim, Germany
AAg Loebner Schäfer Weber (Germany)

Liturgical/Interior Design
Holy Spirit Catholic Community Church
Naperville, IL
INAI Studio

Cathedral in Eisenstadt
Eisenstadt, Austria
lichtblau.wagner architekten (Austria)

JURY
James Graham, architect
Laurie Gross, artist
Susan Pendleton Jones, clergy
Sharif Senbel, Studio Senbel Architecture +
    Design (Canada)
Rod Stephens, liturgical designer (chair)

Source: Faith & Form

Did you know...
The Baltimore Basilica, the first cathedral built in the newly formed United
States of America, reopened on Nov. 4, 2006, after being closed for more
than two years while the building underwent a $34 million restoration that
renewed Benjamin Henry Latrobe's neoclassical design.

residential architect Design Awards

The residential architect Design Awards honor the best in American housing. Projects may be submitted in one of 14 categories, though judges may eliminate, add, or combine categories—bestowing as many awards (or none) as they see fit. The jury, comprised of top residential architects, also selects the residential project of the year from among the winning entries. Winning projects are published in *residential architect* magazine.

For photos of all the winning projects, visit *www.residentialarchitect.com* online.

2007 Project of the Year

Camouflage House
Green Lake, WI
Johnsen Schmaling Architects

2007 Grand Prize Winners

Affordable Housing
No award granted

Architectural Design Detail
No award granted

Architectural Interiors
Artist's Studio
Seattle, WA
Olson Sundberg Kundig Allen Architects

Ontario 301
Washington, DC
Robert M. Gurney, FAIA, Architect

Custom House
3,500 square feet or less
No award granted

Custom House
More than 3,500 square feet
No award granted

Multifamily
Loft23
Cambridge, MA
Dimella Shaffer

The Union
San Diego, CA
Jonathan S. Segal, Architect

On the Boards
Moen Pool and Guesthouse
Des Moines, IA
Herbert Lewis Kruse Blunck Architecture

Outbuilding
Roddy/Bale Garage
Bellevue, WA
Miller/Hull Partnership

Renovation
No award granted

Modular 3, Kansas City, KS, by Studio 804 (Photos courtesy of Studio 804)

Single-Family Production, Attached

The 505
Houston, TX
Collaborative Designworks

Judges' Award

Modular 3
Kansas City, KS
Studio 804

JURY

Randy Brown, Randy Brown Architects
Anne Decker, Rill & Decker Architects
David Furman, David Furman Architecture
Val Glitsch, Val Glitsch, FAIA, Architect
Guy Peterson, Guy Peterson/Office for
    Architecture
Garth Rockcastle, Meyer, Scherer & Rockcastle

Source: residential architecture *magazine*

RIBA Royal Gold Medal

The Royal Institute of British Architects' Royal Gold Medal was inaugurated by Queen Victoria in 1848. It is conferred annually on a distinguished architect, person, or firm "whose work has promoted, either directly or indirectly, the advancement of architecture."

For additional information, visit the RIBA on the Internet at *www.riba.org*.

1848	Charles Robert Cockerell (UK)
1849	Luigi Canina (Italy)
1850	Sir Charles Barry (UK)
1851	Thomas L. Donaldson (UK)
1852	Leo von Klenze (Germany)
1853	Sir Robert Smirke (UK)
1854	Philip Hardwick (UK)
1855	Jacques Ignace Hittorff (France)
1856	Sir William Tite (UK)
1857	Owen Jones (UK)
1858	Friedrich August Stuler (Germany)
1859	Sir George Gilbert Scott (UK)
1860	Sydney Smirke (UK)
1861	Jean-Baptiste Cicéron Lesueur (France)
1862	Robert Willis (UK)
1863	Anthony Salvin (UK)
1864	Eugène Emmanuel Violett-le-Duc (France)
1865	Sir James Pennethorne (UK)
1866	Sir Matthew Digby Wyatt (UK)
1867	Charles Texier (France)
1868	Sir Henry Layard (UK)
1869	C.R. Lepsius (Germany)
1870	Benjamin Ferrey (UK)
1871	James Fergusson (UK)
1872	Baron von Schmidt (Austria)
1873	Thomas Henry Wyatt (UK)
1874	George Edmund Street (UK)
1875	Edmund Sharpe (UK)
1876	Joseph Louis Duc (France)
1877	Charles Barry Jr. (UK)
1878	Alfred Waterhouse (UK)
1879	Marquis de Vogue (France)
1880	John L. Pearson (UK)
1881	George Godwin (UK)
1882	Baron von Ferstel (Austria)
1883	Francis C. Penrose (UK)
1884	William Butterfield (UK)
1885	H. Schliemann (Germany)
1886	Charles Garnier (France)
1887	Ewan Christian (UK)
1888	Baron von Hansen (Austria)
1889	Sir Charles T. Newton (UK)
1890	John Gibson (UK)
1891	Sir Arthur Blomfield (UK)
1892	Cesar Daly (France)
1893	Richard Morris Hunt
1894	Lord Frederic Leighton (UK)
1895	James Brooks (UK)
1896	Sir Ernest George (UK)
1897	Petrus Josephus Hubertus Cuypers (Netherlands)
1898	George Aitchison (UK)
1899	George Frederick Bodley (UK)
1900	Rodolfo Amadeo Lanciani (Italy)
1901	*No award granted due to the death of Queen Victoria*
1902	Thomas Edward Collcutt (UK)
1903	Charles F. McKim
1904	Auguste Choisy (France)
1905	Sir Aston Webb (UK)
1906	Sir Lawrence Alma-Tadema (UK)
1907	John Belcher (UK)
1908	Honore Daumet (France)
1909	Sir Arthur John Evans (UK)
1910	Sir Thomas Graham Jackson (UK)
1911	Wilhelm Dorpfeld (Germany)
1912	Basil Champneys (UK)
1913	Sir Reginald Blomfield (UK)
1914	Jean Louis Pascal (France)
1915	Frank Darling (Canada)
1916	Sir Robert Rowand Anderson (UK)
1917	Henri Paul Nenot (France)
1918	Ernest Newton (UK)

1919	Leonard Stokes (UK)
1920	Charles Louis Girault (France)
1921	Sir Edwin Lutyens (UK)
1922	Thomas Hastings
1923	Sir John James Burnet (UK)
1924	*No award granted*
1925	Sir Giles Gilbert Scott (UK)
1926	Ragnar Östberg (Sweden)
1927	Sir Herbert Baker (UK)
1928	Sir Guy Dawber (UK)
1929	Victor Laloux (France)
1930	Sir Percy Scott Worthington (UK)
1931	Sir Edwin Cooper (UK)
1932	Hendrik Petrus Berlage (Netherlands)
1933	Sir Charles Reed Peers (UK)
1934	Henry Vaughan Lanchester (UK)
1935	Willem Marinus Dudok (Netherlands)
1936	Charles Henry Holden (UK)
1937	Sir Raymond Unwin (UK)
1938	Ivar Tengbom (Sweden)
1939	Sir Percy Thomas (UK)
1940	Charles Francis Annesley Voysey (UK)
1941	Frank Lloyd Wright
1942	William Curtis Green (UK)
1943	Sir Charles Herbert Reilly (UK)
1944	Sir Edward Maufe (UK)
1945	Victor Vesnin (USSR)
1946	Sir Patrick Abercrombie (UK)
1947	Sir Albert Edward Richardson (UK)
1948	Auguste Perret (France)
1949	Sir Howard Robertson (UK)
1950	Eleil Saarinen (Finland/US)
1951	Emanuel Vincent Harris (UK)
1952	George Grey Wornum (UK)
1953	Le Corbusier (Charles-Édouard Jeanneret) (Switzerland/France)
1954	Sir Arthur Stephenson (Australia)
1955	John Murray Easton (UK)
1956	Walter Gropius (Germany/US)
1957	Alvar Aalto (Finland)
1958	Robert Schofield Morris (Canada)
1959	Ludwig Mies van der Rohe (Germany/US)
1960	Pier Luigi Nervi (Italy)
1961	Lewis Mumford
1962	Sven Gottfrid Markelius (Sweden)
1963	Lord W.G. Holford (UK)
1964	E. Maxwell Fry (UK)
1965	Kenzo Tange (Japan)
1966	Ove Arup (UK)
1967	Sir Nikolaus Pevsner (UK)
1968	R. Buckminster Fuller
1969	Jack Antonio Coia (UK)
1970	Sir Robert Matthew (UK)
1971	Hubert de Cronin Hastings (UK)
1972	Louis I. Kahn
1973	Sir Leslie Martin (UK)
1974	Powell & Moya (UK)
1975	Michael Scott (Ireland)
1976	Sir John Summerson (UK)
1977	Sir Denys Lasdun (UK)
1978	Jørn Utzon (Denmark)
1979	The Office of Charles and Ray Eames
1980	James Stirling (UK)
1981	Sir Philip Dowson (UK)
1982	Berthold Lubetkin (Georgia)
1983	Sir Norman Foster (UK)
1984	Charles Correa (India)
1985	Sir Richard Rogers (UK)
1986	Arata Isozaki (Japan)
1987	Ralph Erskine (Sweden)
1988	Richard Meier
1989	Renzo Piano (Italy)
1990	Aldo van Eyck (Netherlands)
1991	Sir Colin Stansfield Smith (UK)
1992	Peter Rice (UK)
1993	Giancarlo de Carlo (Italy)
1994	Sir Michael and Lady Patricia Hopkins (UK)
1995	Colin Rowe (UK/US)
1996	Harry Seidler (Australia)
1997	Tadao Ando (Japan)
1998	Óscar Niemeyer (Brazil)
1999	Barcelona, Spain
2000	Frank Gehry
2001	Jean Nouvel (France)

RIBA Royal Gold Medal

From left, **Jacques Herzog and Pierre de Meuron** (Photos ©Adriano A. Biondo, courtesy RIBA)

2002	Archigram (UK)
2003	Rafael Moneo (Spain)
2004	Rem Koolhaas (Netherlands)
2005	Frei Otto (Germany)
2006	Toyo Ito (Japan)
2007	Jacques Herzog and Pierre de Meuron (Switzerland)

Source: Royal Institute of British Architects

Richard H. Driehaus Prize for Classical Architecture

The Richard H. Driehaus Prize annually honors an outstanding contributor to the field of traditional architecture. The eponymous award, including a $100,000 prize, was established and endowed by the founder of Chicago's Driehaus Capital Management Company, and is presented by the University of Notre Dame's School of Architecture. Winners also receive a model of the Choregic Monument of Lysikrates in Athens, Greece, known as the first use of the Corinthian order.

Additional information is available online at *www.driehausprize.org*.

2003	Léon Krier (UK)
2004	Demetri Porphyrios (Greece)
2005	Quinlan Terry (UK)
2006	Allan Greenberg
2007	Jaquelin Robertson

Source: University of Notre Dame School of Architecture

Where architecture exists it always transcends politics. Buildings can appear inhuman not through their architecture, but through their lack of architecture.

Léon Krier

Richard H. Driehaus Prize

Top: **Ertegun House, Southhampton, New York, by Jaquelin T. Robertson** (Photo: Marianne Haas); *Left: from left to right,* **Edward P. Bass, Richard H. Driehaus and Jaquelin T. Robertson.** (All images courtesy of the Notre Dame School of Architecture)

Rudy Bruner Award for Urban Excellence

The biennial Rudy Bruner Award for Urban Excellence celebrates projects that approach urban problems with creative inclusion of often competing political, community, environmental, and formal considerations. Established in 1987, the program grants one gold medal, along with a $50,000 cash prize, and four silver medals, each with a $10,000 prize. A multidisciplinary jury performs an on-site evaluation of the five finalists before selecting the gold-medal recipient.

Photos of the winners are available at *www.brunerfoundation.org*.

2007 Winners

Gold Medal
Pittsburgh Children's Museum and Family
    District
Pittsburgh, PA

Silver Medal
Artists for Humanity Epicenter
Boston, MA

Crossroads Project: Brady Street Bus
    Shelter, Urban Plaza and Marsupial
    Pedestrian Bridge
Milwaukee, WI

High Point Redevelopment
Seattle, WA

L.A. Design Center
Los Angeles, CA

Redesign of Columbus Circle
New York, NY

JURY
Manny Diaz, City of Miami, FL
Reese Fayde, Living Cities: National Community
    Development Initiative
Reed Kroloff, Tulane University
David Perry, Great Cities Institute
Josephine Ramirez, The Music Center
Robert Kroin, Boston Redevelopment Authority

Source: Bruner Foundation

Did you know...

Barry Benepe and Omar Freilla are the first recipients of the Jane Jacobs Medal, an annual $200,000 prize granted by the Rockefeller Foundation to two individuals whose visionary work has enhanced the diversity and dynamism of the urban environment, especially New York City.

Russel Wright Award

The Russel Wright Award honors individuals who are working in the tradition of the mid-20th-century design pioneer Russel Wright (1904–1976). A well-known home furnishings and housewares designer who was most prodigious in the 1930s through the 1950s, Wright strove to make well-designed domestic objects accessible to the public. Manitoga, the 75-acre wooded landscape he sculpted in Garrison, NY, is now home to the Russel Wright Design Center, the award's sponsor.

For more information, visit Manitoga's website, *www.russelwrightcenter.org*.

2000	Michael Graves	2004	Jens Risom
2001	Lella and Massimo Vignelli		Michael and Stephen Maharam
	William T. Golden		The Institute of Ecosystems
	Cooper-Hewitt National Design		Studies
	Museum, Smithsonian	2005	Knoll, Inc.
	Institution		Palisades Interstate Park
2002	Murray Moss		Commission
	Frances S. Reese	2006	Frances D. Fergusson
	Eva Zeisel		Viktor Schreckengost
2003	Jack Lenor Larsen	2007	Herman Miller Inc.
	Harvey Keyes Flad		Mitchell Wolfson Jr.
	Rob Forbes		

Source: Russel Wright Design Center

Simplicity and repose are the qualities that measure the true value of any work of art.

Frank Lloyd Wright

SADI Awards

Retail Traffic magazine annually presents the SADI (Superior Achievement in Design and Imaging) Awards to recognize outstanding retail design achievements. The jury, comprised of leading US retail architects and designers, reviews projects for criteria such as problem solving, general aesthetics, image building, and implementation. Any architecture or design firm, retailer, or developer of a new or renovated retail store, shopping center, or restaurant is eligible to enter.

More information is available on *Retail Traffic*'s website at *www.retailtrafficmag.com.*

2007 Winners

Grand SADI Award
Fornarina
London, UK
Giorgio Borruso Design

Winners
Westfield San Francisco Centre
San Francisco, CA
ka architecture; RTKL Associates Inc.

Bloomingdales
New York, NY
Mancini Duffy

Westfield Century City Dining Terrace
Los Angeles, CA
Westfield Group

Honorable Mentions
Nokia Flagship
New York, NY
Eight Inc.

LEIBER
Las Vegas, NV
Callison Architecture

Harvey Nichols
Dubai, UAE
Callison Architecture

Auto Mercado
San Jose, CA
api(+)

Waterside at Marina del Rey
Marina del Rey, CA
Perkowitz + Ruth Architects

Avenue Carriage Crossing
Collierville, TN
CMH Architects Inc.

Runners-Up
Fido, Eaton Centre
Toronto, ON, Canada
GHA shoppingscapes

Mazza Gallerie
Washington, DC
Cooper Carey, Inc.

Lotte Mia Department Store
Seoul, South Korea
FRCH Design Worldwide

NorthPark Center
Dallas, TX
OmniPlan

140

SADI Awards

JURY

Robert J. Acciarri, ADA Architects, Inc.

Mark Carter, Thompson, Ventulett, Stainback & Associates

Francis Cooke, Skidmore, Owings & Merrill

Robert A. Fiala, tda Architecture

David B. Janes, SGPA Architecture + Planning

Charlie Kridler, Gensler

Adam Kushabi, General Growth Properties

Greg Lyon, KTGY Group Inc.

Edward A. Shriver Jr., stradas

Source: Retail Traffic

Did you know...

According to the International Council of Shopping Centers, the enclosed mall is dead. Since 2005 only three new enclosed malls have opened in the United States, and no new projects are in the works. However, the council predicts 52 outdoor shopping developments to open between August 2007 and 2009.

SCUP/AIA-CAE Excellence in Planning Awards

The Society for College and University Planning and the American Institute of Architects' Committee on Architecture for Education jointly present the annual Excellence in Planning Awards to outstanding planning and design projects developed for higher education institutions. The jury considerations include the quality of the physical environment as well as the comprehensiveness of the planning process. The award is presented to all members of the project team.

Further information can be found at the SCUP website, *www.scup.org.*

2007 Honor Awards

Planning for an Established Campus
Penn Connects: A Vision for the Future, University of Pennsylvania
Philadelphia, PA
Sasaki Associates, Inc.

Planning for a District or Campus Component
The Village at 115, Case Western Reserve University
Cleveland, OH
Goody, Clancy & Associates

Planning for Preservation, Restoration, Renovation or Adaptive Reuse
Lakeshore Nature Preserve Master Plan, University of Wisconsin–Madison
Madison, WI
Ken Saiki Design

Landscape Architecture
Courtyard and Outdoor Learning Environment for Natural Sciences, Keene State College
Keene, NH
Dirtworks

Architecture for a New Building
Santiago Canyon College Library, Santiago Canyon College
Orange, CA
LPA, Inc.

Architecture for a Building Addition
Benedicta Arts Center, College of St. Benedict
St. Joseph, MN
HGA Architects and Engineers

Architecture for Restoration or Preservation
Old Capitol Fire Restoration & Building Improvements, University of Iowa
Iowa City, IA
OPN Architects

Architecture for Renovation or Adaptive Reuse
The Warehouse, Syracuse University
Syracuse, NY
Gluckman Mayner Architects

De La Guerra Dining Commons, University of California, Santa Barbara
Santa Barbara, CA
STUDIOS Architecture

142

SCUP/AIA-CAE Excellence in Planning Awards

2007 Merit Awards

Planning for an Established Campus
Occidental College Master Plan
Los Angeles, CA
Moule & Polyzoides Architects and
  Urbanists

Landscape Architecture
Pollock Road Streetscape & Utility
  Upgrades, Pennsylvania State University
State College, PA
Wallace Roberts & Todd

Architecture for a New Building
Student Union, Averett University
Danville, VA
VMDO Architects

Architecture for a Building Addition
University of Alaska Museum of the North
Fairbanks, AK
HGA Architects and Engineers

Architecture for Renovation or Adaptive Reuse
Glorya Kaufman Hall/Center for World
  Arts & Cultures
University of California, Los Angeles
Moore Ruble Yudell Architects & Planners

JURY
Stephen F Troost, Michigan State University
Daniel Friedman, University of Washington
Larry Porter, Rutgers, The State University of
  New Jersey
Dan Raih, Bruner/Cott & Associates Inc
James Richard, richärd+bauer

Source: Society for College and University Planning

Architecture is different from other forms of art in that it is created through discussion with everyone involved. The architect has to respond to demands from the other parties concerned.

Tado Ando

SEGD Design Awards

143

The Society for Environmental Graphic Design's Design Awards recognize the best in environmental design: the planning, design, and specifying of graphic elements in the built and natural environments. Eligible projects include signage, wayfinding systems, mapping, exhibit design, themed environments, retail spaces, sports facilities, and campus design. A jury of professionals reviews the entries to determine which projects best identify, direct, inform, interpret, and visually enhance our surroundings.

For a list of all winners, visit SEGD's website at *www.segd.org*.

2007 Honor Award

Thailand Creative & Design Center
Bangkok, Thailand
Graphic 49 Limited (Thailand)

National World War I Museum
Kansas City, MO
Ralph Appelbaum Associates

Arizona Cardinals Stadium
Glendale, AZ
Pentagram

Wall of Discovery, University of Minnesota
Minneapolis, MN
HGA Architects and Engineers

Los Angeles Metro
Los Angeles, CA
Metro Design Studio

Alesari
Zak Krusynski, David Roll, Kayne
    Toukonen
Kent State University

JURY

Lynn Befu, Anshen + Allen
Phil Engelke, RTKL (chair)
David Gibson, Two Twelve
Cybelle Jones, Gallagher & Associates Inc
Hal Kantner, Hellmuth, Obata & Kassabaum
Carol Newsom, Newsom Design
Alexandra Wood, Holmes Wood

Source: Society for Environmental Graphic Design

I have spent most of my life unlearning things that were proved not to be true.

R. Buckminster Fuller

SEGD Design Awards

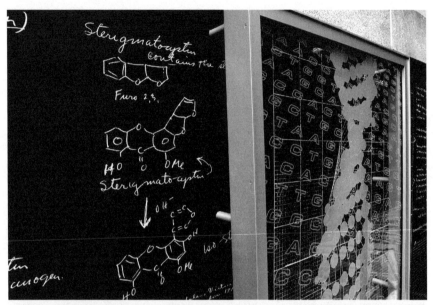

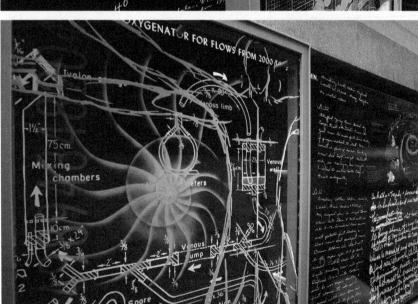

Wall of Discovery, University of Minnesota, Minneapolis, MN, by HGA Architects and Engineers
(Photos courtesy of the University of Minnesota)

Sir Patrick Abercrombie Prize

The triennial Sir Patrick Abercrombie Prize is awarded by the International Union of Architects (UIA) to an internationally renowned architect or architects for significant work in town planning and territorial development. The prize is named after the distinguished British architect and planner Sir Patrick Abercrombie, who is known for the post-World War II replanning of many British towns, most notably London.

For more information, visit the UIA's website at *www.uia-architectes.org.*

1961	Town Planning Service of the City of Stockholm (Sven Gottfrid Markelius and G. Onblahd, Sweden)
1963	Constantinos Doxiadis (Greece)
1965	Colin Buchanan and team (UK)
	T. Farkas and team (Hungary)
1967	Giancarlo de Carlo (Italy)
1969	H. Bennet and team (UK)
	Belaunde Terry (Peru)*
1972	Centre for Experimentation, Research and Training (Morocco)
1975	Iosif Bronislavovitch Orlov (USSR)
	Nilolai Ivanovitch Simonov (USSR)
1978	The City of Louvain la Neuve (Belgium)
1981	Warsaw architects (Poland) for the reconstruction of their capital
	M. Balderiotte and team (Argentina)*

1984	Hans Blumenfeld (Canada)
	Lucio Costa (Brazil)
1987	AIA Regional/Urban Design Assistance Team
	Eduardo Leira (Spain)*
	L. Bortenreuter, K. Griebel, H.G. Tiedt for the remodeling of the city center of Gera (GDR)*
1990	Edmund N. Bacon
1993	Jan Gehl (Denmark)
1996	Juan Gil Elizondo (Mexico)
1999	Karl Ganser (Germany)
	Shenzhen Urban Planning & Land Administration Bureau (China)*
2002	Group 91 Architects for the Temple Bar district in Dublin (Ireland)
2005	Nuno Portas (Portugal)
	Hermann Sträb (Germany)*

*Honorary Mention

Source: International Union of Architects

Sir Robert Matthew Prize

The International Union of Architects (UIA) grants the triennial Sir Robert Matthew Prize to an internationally renowned architect or architects whose work has improved the quality of human settlements. The prize is named after notable Scottish architect Sir Robert Matthew, who is known for his contributions to social architecture, among other achievements.

For more information, visit the UIA's website at *www.uia-architectes.org.*

1978	John F.C. Turner (UK)	1999	Martin Treberspurg (Austria)
1981	Hassan Fathy (Egypt)		Development & Construction
	Rod Hackney (UK)*		Branch of the Hong Kong
	Hardt Walther Hamer (GFR)*		Housing Department
1984	Charles Correa (India)		(China)*
1987	Housing Reconstruction Program	2002	Justin Kilcullen (Ireland)
	for the City of Mexico		Jaime Lerner (Brazil)
	(Mexico)		Kooperation GdW-BDA-DST
1990	Department of Architecture of		(Germany)*
	the Singapore Housing &	2005	Stefan Forster (Germany)
	Development Board		Xiaodong Wang (China)
	(Singapore)		
1993	Laurie Baker (UK)	*Honorary Mention	
1996	Giancarlo de Carlo (Italy)	**Jury Citation	
	Oberste Baubehörde with Hans		
	Jörg Nussberger(Germany)**	*Source: International Union of Architects*	

Did you know...

In 2007, New York City held the inaugural New Housing New York juried competition to encourage the integration of sustainability and design excellence with affordable housing.

Spiro Kostof Book Award

Awarded to publications that promote and educate the public about the history of urbanism and architecture, the Spiro Kostof Award is presented annually by the Society of Architectural Historians. An architectural historian and educator, Spiro Kostof's books on architecture and urban form, especially *The City Shaped: Urban Patterns and Meanings Through History*, are considered to have greatly advanced the profession.

More information is available from the SAH website, *www.sah.org*.

1994   *Architecture Power and National*
       Identity
       Lawrence J. Vale
       Yale University Press

1995   *In the Theatre of Criminal Justice:*
       The Palais de Justice in Second
       Empire Paris
       Katherine Fischer Taylor
       Princeton University Press

1996   *The Topkapi Scroll: Geometry and*
       Ornament in Islamic Architecture
       Gülru Necipoglu
       Getty Center for the History of
          Art and Humanities

1997   *The Projective Cast: Architecture*
       and Its Three Geometries
       Robin Evans
       MIT Press

       Auschwitz: 1270 to the Present
       Debórah Dwork and Robert Jan
          van Pelt
       Norton

1998   *The Architects and the City*
       Robert Bruegmann
       University of Chicago Press

       Magnetic Los Angeles
       Gregory Hise
       Johns Hopkins Press

1999   *City Center to Regional Mall:*
       Architecture, the Automobile and
       Retailing in Los Angeles,
       1920–1950
       Richard Longstreth
       MIT Press

       Housing Design and Society in
       Amsterdam: Reconfiguring Urban
       Order and Identity, 1900–1920
       Nancy Stieber
       University of Chicago Press

2000   *The Architecture of Red Vienna*
       1919–1934
       Eve Blau
       MIT Press

2001   *The Creative Destruction of*
       Manhattan, 1900–1940
       Max Page
       University of Chicago Press

2002   *Buildings on Ruins: The*
       Rediscovery of Rome and English
       Architecture
       Frank Salmon
       Ashgate Publishing Company

Spiro Kostof Book Award

2003   *Architecture in the Age of Printing:*
        Orality, Writing, Typography and
        Printed Images in the History of
        Architectural Theory
        Mario Carpo
        MIT Press

        Concrete and Clay: Reworking
        Nature in New York City
        Matthew Gandy
        MIT Press

2004   *Archaeologies of the Greek Past:*
        Landscape, Monuments, and
        Memories
        Susan E. Alcock
        Cambridge University Press

2005   *The Birth of City Planning in the*
        United States, 1840–1917
        Jon A. Peterson
        Johns Hopkins University Press

2006   *Modern Architecture and the End of*
        Empire
        Mark Crinson
        Ashgate Publishing

        The Image of an Ottoman City:
        Imperial Architecture and Urban
        Experience in Aleppo in the 16th
        and 17th Centuries
        Heghnar Zeitlian Watenpaugh
        Brill Academic Publishing

2007   *The Politics of Taste in Antebellum*
        Charleston
        Maurie D. McInnis
        University of North Carolina
              Press

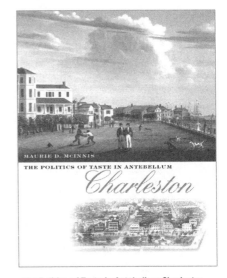

The Politics of Taste in Antebellum Charleston
by Maurie D. McInnis (Photo courtesy of the
University of North Carolina Press)

Source: Society of Architectural Historians

Star Award

The International Interior Design Association's Star Award celebrates individuals and organizations that have made extraordinary contributions to the interior design profession. As the Star Award is merit-based, it is not necessarily granted each year. Although non-members are eligible, the IIDA board of directors (the selection body) only accepts nominations from IIDA fellows, chapter presidents, and directors.

Visit the IIDA's website at *www.iida.org* for more information.

1985	Lester Dundes	1999	Michael Brill
1986	William Sullivan	2000	Eva L. Maddox
1987	Orlando Diaz-Azcuy	2001	Andrée Putman (France)
1988	Paul Brayton	2002	Karim Rashid
1989	Florence Knoll Bassett	2003	Ray Anderson
1990	Beverly Russell	2004	Kevin Kampschroer
1991	Stanley Abercrombie	2005	Target Corporation
1992	M. Arthur Gensler Jr.	2006	*Fast Company*
1993	Sivon C. Reznikoff	2007	Karen Stephenson
1994	Michael Kroelinger		
1995	Douglas R. Parker		
1997	Michael Wirtz	*Source: International Interior Designers Association*	
1998	Charles and Ray Eames		

People project meaning onto objects. If an object allows you to interact with it, then it becomes part of your being, and over time you see things in it that first you might not have seen.

Karim Rashid

Tau Sigma Delta Gold Medal

Presented annually by Tau Sigma Delta, the honor society of architecture and the allied arts, the Gold Medal honors an individual who has made outstanding contributions in the fields of architecture, landscape architecture, or an allied profession.

Information about the medal can be found on the society's website at *www.tausigmadelta.org.*

1970	Norman C. Fletcher	1990	Joseph Esherick
1971	Gunnar Birkerts	1991	Denise Scott Brown
1972	O'Neil Ford	1992	Charles Moore
1973	Arthur C. Erickson (Canada)	1993	Harold L. Adams
1974	Ian McHarg	1994	Harvey B. Gantt
1975	Hugh Asher Stubbins	1995	Peter Eisenman
1976	Vincent G. Kling	1996	Vincent J. Scully
1977	Harry Weese	1997	Cesar Pelli
1978	William Wayne Caudill	1998	William Pedersen
1979	Edmund N. Bacon	1999	William Curtis
1980	Alexander Girard	2000	Pierre Koenig
1981	Charles Moore	2001	Malcolm Holzman
1982	Moshe Safdie	2002	Cynthia Weese
1983	Ricardo Legorreta (Mexico)	2003	Michael Graves
1984	E. Fay Jones	2004	Mary Miss
1985	Pietro Belluschi	2005	Martha Schwartz
1986	Walter A. Netsch	2006	Shigeru Ban (Japan)
1987	Lawrence Halprin	2007	Sir Richard Rogers (UK)
1988	Kenneth Frampton (UK/US)		
1989	Richard Meier		

Source: Tau Sigma Delta

The sense for the perception of architecture is not the eyes—but living. Our life is its image.

Rudolph Schindler

Thomas Jefferson Award for Public Architecture

The American Institute of Architects grants the biennial Thomas Jefferson Award for Public Architecture to recognize design excellence in government and infrastructure projects. Awards are presented in three categories: private sector architects who have amassed a portfolio of distinguished public facilities, public sector architects who produce quality projects within their agencies, and public officials or others who have been strong advocates for design excellence.

For more information, visit the AIA online at *www.aia.org.*

1992	James Ingo Freed	1998	Arthur Rosenblatt
	George M. White	1999	Lewis Davis
	Daniel Patrick Moynihan		Robert Kroin
1993	Jack Brooks	2000	Charles E. Peterson
1994	Richard Dattner		Jay Chatterjee
	M.J. (Jay) Brodie	2001*	Terrel M. Emmons
	Joseph P. Riley Jr.		J. Stroud Watson
1995	Herbert S. Newman	2003	Edmund W. Ong
	Edward A. Feiner		Susan Williams
	Henry G. Cisneros	2005	Carol Ross Barney
1996	Thomas R. Aidala		Diane Georgopulos
	Douglas P. Woodlock		Charles H. Atherton
1997	John Tarantino	2007	David D. Dixon
	Richard A. Kahan		Michael A. Fitts
	Hunter Morrison		

* Beginning in 2001, the award became biennial.

Source: American Institute of Architects

We have gone beyond the stage whereby unity of language was believed to be the universal solution for architectural problems. Recognizing that complexity is the nature of the city, transformational movements take on very different forms.

Alvaro Siza

Thomas Jefferson Medal in Architecture

The Thomas Jefferson Medal in Architecture is granted jointly by the Thomas Jefferson Foundation and the University of Virginia School of Architecture for notable achievements in design or for distinguished contributions to the field of architecture. Recipients need not be architects. This award, along with the Thomas Jefferson Medal in Law, is the highest outside honor offered by the university, which does not grant honorary degrees.

For additional information, visit the school online at *www.virginia.edu/arch/*.

1966	Ludwig Mies van der Rohe	1990	Fumihiko Maki (Japan)
1967	Alvar Aalto (Finland)	1991	John Lindsay
1968	Marcel Breuer	1992	Aldo Rossi (Italy)
1969	John Ely Burchard	1993	Andrés Duany
1970	Kenzo Tange (Japan)		Elizabeth Plater-Zyberk
1971	José Luis Sert (Spain)	1994	Frank Gehry
1972	Lewis Mumford	1995	Ian McHarg
1973	Jean Labatut	1996	Jane Jacobs (Canada)
1974	Frei Otto (Germany)	1997	Jaime Lerner (Brazil)
1975	Sir Nikolaus Pevsner (UK)	1998	Jaquelin Robertson
1976	I.M. Pei	1999	Sir Richard Rogers (UK)
1977	Ada Louise Huxtable	2000	Daniel Patrick Moynihan
1978	Philip Johnson	2001	Glenn Murcutt (Australia)
1979	Lawrence Halprin	2002	James Turrell
1980	Hugh Asher Stubbins	2003	Tod Williams
1981	Edward Larrabee Barnes		Billie Tsien
1982	Vincent J. Scully	2004	Peter Walker
1983	Robert Venturi	2005	Shigeru Ban (Japan)
1984	Aga Khan (Switzerland)	2006	Peter Zumthor (Switzerland)
1985	Léon Krier (UK)	2007	Zaha Hadid (UK)
1986	James Stirling (UK)		
1987	Daniel Urban Kiley		
1988	Romaldo Giurgola	*Source: University of Virginia*	
1989	Paul Mellon		

If Thomas Jefferson visited your home, he would judge your furniture for its utility not for its antique charm.

T.J. Robsjohn-Gibbings

Tucker Design Awards

The Tucker Design Awards honor projects that demonstrate design excellence in the use of natural stone. This biennial competition, sponsored by the Building Stone Institute, is open to architects, landscape architects, interior designers, and others whose work integrates and showcases natural stone. First presented in 1977, the award is named in honor of the late Beverly R. Tucker Jr., a past president of the institute.

Contact the institute online at *www.buildingstoneinstitute.org* for more information.

2006 Winners

402 Redbud Trail
West Lake Hills, TX
Cottam Hargrave Architecture and
    Construction

Belvedere Gardens Mausoleum
Salem, VA
SMBW Architects

San Diego Padres Ballpark/Petco Park
San Diego, CA
Antoine Predock Architect with HOK
    Sport + Venue + Event

Art Collectors' Residence
Toronto, ON, Canada
Hariri Pontarini Architects (Canada)

Trinity Church Restoration
Boston, MA
Goody, Clancy & Associates

Sigmund Stern Grove Renovation
San Francisco, CA
Office of Lawrence Halprin

Liberty Bell Center, Independence
    National Historic Park
Philadelphia, PA
Bohlin Cywinski Jackson

Unified Science Center, Swarthmore
    College
Swarthmore, PA
Einhorn Yaffee Prescott with Helfand
    Architecture

Factory for Synergy Lifestyles
Karur, Tamil Nadu, India
SJK Architects (India)

Renovation/Rehabilitation of Ventilation
    Building, MTA TBTA Brooklyn Battery
    Tunnel
Brooklyn, NY
DiGeronimo PA

The Park at Lakeshore East
Chicago, IL
Site Design Group Ltd.; The Office of
    James Burnett

Prothro House Addition and Remodel
Dallas, TX
PageSoutherlandPage

Source: Building Stone Institute

Twenty-five Year Award

The American Institute of Architects' Twenty-five Year Award celebrates buildings that excel under the test of time. Eligible projects must have been completed within the past 25 to 35 years by a licensed US architect, though the buildings may be located worldwide. Winning designs are still operating under the tenets of the original program, demonstrating continued viability in function and form, and contributing meaningfully to American life and architecture.

More information is available from the AIA's website, *www.aia.org*.

1969   Rockefeller Center
        New York, NY, 1931–40
        Reinhard & Hofmeister with
            Corbett, Harrison &
            MacMurray and Hood &
            Fouilhoux

1971   Crow Island School
        Winnetka, IL, 1939
        Perkins, Wheeler & Will and
            Eliel and Eero Saarinen

1972   Baldwin Hills Village
        Los Angeles, CA, 1941
        Reginald D. Johnson with
            Wilson, Merrill & Alexander
            and Clarence S. Stein

1973   Taliesin West
        Paradise Valley, AZ, 1938
        Frank Lloyd Wright

1974   S.C. Johnson & Son
            Administration Building
        Racine, WI, 1939
        Frank Lloyd Wright

1975   Philip Johnson Residence
            (The Glass House)
        New Canaan, CT, 1949
        Philip Johnson

1976   860-880 North Lakeshore Drive
            Apartments
        Chicago, IL, 1948–51
        Ludwig Mies van der Rohe

1977   Christ Lutheran Church
        Minneapolis, MN, 1948–51
        Saarinen, Saarinen & Associates
            with Hills, Gilbertson & Hays

1978   Eames House
        Pacific Palisades, CA, 1949
        Charles and Ray Eames

1979   Yale University Art Gallery
        New Haven, CT, 1954
        Louis I. Kahn with Douglas W. Orr

1980   Lever House
        New York, NY, 1952
        Skidmore, Owings & Merrill

1981   Farnsworth House
        Plano, IL, 1950
        Ludwig Mies van der Rohe

1982   Equitable Savings and Loan
            Association Building
        Portland, OR, 1948
        Pietro Belluschi

1983   Price Tower
        Bartlesville, OK, 1956
        Frank Lloyd Wright

1984   Seagram Building
        New York, NY, 1957
        Ludwig Mies van der Rohe

1985   General Motors Technical Center
        Warren, MI, 1951
        Eero Saarinen & Associates with
            Smith, Hinchman and Grylls
            Associates

1986	Solomon R. Guggenheim Museum New York, NY, 1959 Frank Lloyd Wright		1997	Phillips Exeter Academy Library Exeter, NH, 1972 Louis I. Kahn

1986   Solomon R. Guggenheim
        Museum
        New York, NY, 1959
        Frank Lloyd Wright

1987   Bavinger House
        Norman, OK, 1953
        Bruce Goff

1988   Dulles International Airport
        Terminal Building
        Chantilly, VA, 1962
        Eero Saarinen & Associates

1989   Vanna Venturi House
        Chestnut Hill, PA, 1964
        Robert Venturi

1990   Gateway Arch
        St. Louis, MO, 1965
        Eero Saarinen & Associates

1991   Sea Ranch Condominium I
        The Sea Ranch, CA, 1965
        Moore Lyndon Turnbull
           Whitaker

1992   Salk Institute for Biological
        Studies
        La Jolla, CA, 1966
        Louis I. Kahn

1993   Deere & Company
        Administrative Center
        Moline, IL, 1963
        Eero Saarinen & Associates

1994   Haystack Mountain School of
           Crafts
        Deer Isle, ME, 1962
        Edward Larrabee Barnes
           Associates

1995   Ford Foundation Headquarters
        New York, NY, 1968
        Kevin Roche John Dinkeloo &
           Associates

1996   Air Force Academy Cadet Chapel
        Colorado Springs, CO, 1962
        Skidmore, Owings & Merrill

1997   Phillips Exeter Academy Library
        Exeter, NH, 1972
        Louis I. Kahn

1998   Kimbell Art Museum
        Fort Worth, TX, 1972
        Louis I. Kahn

1999   John Hancock Center
        Chicago, IL, 1969
        Skidmore, Owings & Merrill

2000   Smith House
        Darien, CT, 1967
        Richard Meier & Partners
           Architects

2001   Weyerhaeuser Headquarters
        Tacoma, WA, 1971
        Skidmore, Owings & Merrill

2002   Fundació Joan Miró
        Barcelona, Spain, 1975
        Sert Jackson and Associates

2003   Design Research Headquarters
           Building
        Cambridge, MA, 1969
        BTA Architects Inc.

2004   East Building, National Gallery
           of Art
        Washington, DC, 1978
        I.M. Pei & Partners

2005   Yale Center for British Art
        New Haven, CT, 1977
        Louis I. Kahn

2006   Thorncrown Chapel
        Eureka Springs, AR, 1980
        E. Fay Jones

2007   Vietnam Veterans Memorial
        Washington, DC, 1982
        Maya Lin

Source: American Institute of Architects

UIA Gold Medal

156

Every three years at its World Congress, the International Union of Architects (UIA) awards its Gold Medal to a living architect who has made outstanding achievements in the field of architecture. This honor recognizes the recipient's lifetime of distinguished practice, contribution to the enrichment of mankind, and the promotion of the art of architecture.

For more information, visit the UIA website at *www.uia-architectes.org*.

1984	Hassan Fathy (Egypt)
1987	Reima Pietila (Finland)
1990	Charles Correa (India)
1993	Fumihiko Maki (Japan)
1996	Rafael Moneo (Spain)
1999	Ricardo Legorreta (Mexico)
2002	Renzo Piano (Italy)
2005	Tadao Ando (Japan)

Source: International Union of Architects

In my opinion, comfort in architecture is given by two words. One is space. The other is light.

Santiago Calatrava

ULI Awards for Excellence

157

The Urban Land Institute's Awards for Excellence consider the full development process. Winning entries demonstrate superior design, improve the quality of the built environment, exhibit a sensitivity to the community, display financial viability, and are relevant to contemporary issues. Since it was established in 1979, the program has evolved into separate juried competitions for the Americas, Europe, and Asia Pacific. The developer responsible for each winning project is listed below.

For additional information, visit the ULI's website, *www.uli.org.*

2007 Americas Winners

2200
Seattle, WA
Vulcan, Inc.

1180 Peachtree
Atlanta, GA
Hines

The ARC (Town Hall Education Arts &
    Recreation Campus)
Washington, DC
Building Bridges Across the River

Bob and Diana Gerding Theater at the
    Armory
Portland, OR
Gerding Edlen Development

Daniel Island
Charleston, SC
The Daniel Island Company

Downtown San Diego Revitalization
San Diego, CA
Centre City Development Corp.

High Point
Seattle, WA
Seattle Housing Authority

Highlands' Garden Village
Denver, CO
Perry Rose LLC; Jonathan Rose Companies

The RAND Corporation Headquarters
Santa Monica, CA
The RAND Corporation

Urban Outfitters Corporate Office Campus
Philadelphia, PA
Philadelphia Industrial Development Corp.

AMERICAS JURY
Ronald A. Altoon, Altoon + Porter Architects
Bryce Blair, AvalonBay Communities, Inc.
Timur F. Galen, Goldman, Sachs & Company
Richard M. Gollis, The Concord Group
Veronica W. Hackett, The Clarett Group
Lee T. Hanley, Vestar Development Company
William H. Kreager, Mithun Architects +
    Designers + Planners
Isaac H. Manning, Trinity Works
J. Michael Pitchford, Community Preservation
    and Development Corporation
Frank Ricks, Looney Ricks Kiss Architects
Marilee A. Utter, Citiventure Associates
Robert M. Weekley, Lowe Enterprises, Inc.

ULI Awards for Excellence

2007 Europe Winners

Kanyon
Istanbul, Turkey
Kanyon (Turkey)

Manufaktura
Lodz, Poland
Apsys Management (Poland)

Meudon Campus
Meudon sur Seine, France
Hines France (France)

New Terminal, Madrid Barajas
    International Airport
Barajas, Spain
Estudio Lamela (Spain)

Petit Palau
Barcelona, Spain
Palau de la Musica Catalana (Spain)

EUROPE JURY
Patrick Albrand, Hines France (France)
Andrea Amadesi, IXIS AEW Italia SpA (Italy)
Ian D. Hawksworth, Capital & Counties (UK)
Anne T. Kavanagh, Cambridge Place Investment
    Management (UK)
Barbara Knoflach, SEB Asset Management
    (Germany)
Lee A. Polisano, Kohn Pedersen Fox (UK)
Andreas Schiller, Bergisch Gladbach (Germany)

2007 Asia Pacific Winners

The Ecovillage at Currumbin
Currumbin, Queensland, Australia.
Landmatters Currumbin Valley Pty Ltd
    (Australia)

Hong Kong Wetland Park
Hong Kong, China
Architectural Services Department, Hong
    Kong Special Administrative Region
    Government (China)

The Landmark Scheme
Hong Kong, China
Hongkong Land (China)

Nihonbashi Mitsui Tower
Tokyo, Japan
Mitsui Fudosan Co., Ltd (Japan)

ASIA PACIFIC JURY
Ivana Benda, Allied Architects International
    (Canada), Inc. (China)
Nicholas Brooke, Professional Property Services
    Ltd. (China)
Silas Chiow, SOM Asia (China)
Ross Holt, Landcorp (Australia)
Akio Makiyama, Forum for Urban Development,
    (Japan)
Raj Menda, RMZ Corp (India)
Yasuhiko Watanabe, Mitsubishi Estate Company
    (Japan)

Source: Urban Land Institute

USITT Architecture Awards

Sponsored by the United States Institute for Theatre Technology, the USITT Architecture Awards honor excellence in theater design. Created in 1994, the program recognizes superior design work and provides resource material about contemporary theater architecture. Submissions are evaluated for their creative image, contextual resonance, community contribution, explorations in new technologies, and functional operations.

For further information, visits the USITT's website at *www.usitt.org*.

2007 Winners

Honor Awards
The Egg, Theatre Royal Bath (renovation)
Sawclose, Bath, UK
Haworth Tompkins Architects (UK)

Young Centre for the Performing Arts
   (renovation)
Toronto, ON, Canada
Kuwabara Payne McKenna Blumberg
   Architects (Canada)

Merit Awards
Unicorn Theatre
London, UK
Keith Williams Architects (UK)

Holland Performing Arts Center
Omaha, NE
Polshek Partnership Architects; HDR, Inc.

Young Vic Theatre (renovation)
London, UK
Haworth Tompkins Architects (UK)

JURY
Kurt Schindler, ELS Architecture and Urban
   Design
Clifford Pearson, *Architectural Record*
S. Leonard Auerbach, Auerbach Pollock
   Friedlander and Auerbach Glasgow

Source: United States Institute for Theatre Technology

Great ideas arise from the small details of life.

Alvar Aalto

Veronica Rudge Green Prize in Urban Design

Established by Harvard University in 1986, the biennial Veronica Rudge Green Prize in Urban Design recognizes innovative projects that enhance public spaces and improve the quality of urban life. A panel of critics, academics, and practitioners in the fields of architecture, landscape architecture, and urban design nominate projects, which must be larger in scope than a single building and must have been constructed within the past 10 years.

Additional information can be found online at *www.gsd.harvard.edu.*

1988	Byker Redevelopment Newcastle upon Tyne, UK Ralph Erskine (Sweden)
	Malagueira Quarter Housing Project Evora, Portugal Alvaro Siza (Portugal)
1990	Urban Public Spaces of Barcelona Barcelona, Spain City of Barcelona (Spain)
1993	Hillside Terrace Complex Tokyo, Japan Fumihiko Maki (Japan)
	Master Plan and Public Buildings Monte Carasso, Switzerland Luigi Snozzi (Switzerland)
1996	Restoration of the Historic Center of Mexico City and Ecological Restoration of the District of Xochimilco Mexico City, Mexico

1998	Subway System Bilbao, Spain Sir Norman Foster and Foster and Partners (UK)
	Development of Carré d'Art Plaza Nîmes, France Sir Norman Foster and Foster and Partners (UK)
2000	Favela-Bairro Project Rio de Janeiro, Brazil Jorge Mario Jáuregui and Jorge Mario Jáuregui Architects (Brazil)
2002	Borneo-Sporenburg Housing Project Amsterdam, Netherlands West 8 Urban Design & Landscape Architecture (Netherlands)
2004	City of Aleppo Aleppo, Syria German Technical Corporation (Germany)
2006	Olympic Sculpture Park Seattle, WA Weiss/Manfredi

Source: Harvard Graduate School of Design/School of Architecture

Vincent J. Scully Prize

The National Building Museum established the Vincent J. Scully Prize to recognize exemplary practice, scholarship, or criticism in architecture, historic preservation, and urban design. The prize honors Vincent Scully, a renowned architectural scholar, mentor, critic, and educator. The award carries a $25,000 honorarium.

For more information, contact the museum online at *www.nbm.org*.

1999	Vincent J. Scully
2000	Jane Jacobs (Canada)
2001	Elizabeth Plater-Zyberk
	Andrés Duany
2002	Robert Venturi
	Denise Scott Brown
2004	Aga Khan (Switzerland)
2005	Prince of Wales (UK)
2006	Phyllis Lambert
2007	Witold Rybczynski

Source: National Building Museum

Architects are unusually poised between being practical people who deliver shelter and artists who deliver aesthetic pleasure.

Alain de Boton

Whitney M. Young Jr. Award

The American Institute of Architects bestows the Whitney M. Young Jr. Award annually upon an architect or architecturally oriented organization that has demonstrated professional responsibility related to current social issues, a challenge civil rights leader Whitney Young set forth to architects at the 1998 AIA national convention. These issues include such areas as affordable housing, the inclusion of minorities and women in the profession, disability issues, and literacy.

For more information, visit the AIA on the Internet at *www.aia.org*.

1972	Robert J. Nash		1992	Curtis J. Moody
1973	Architects Workshop of		1993	David Castro-Blanco
	Philadelphia		1994	Ki Suh Park
1974	Stephen Cram*		1995	William J. Stanley III
1975	Van B. Bruner Jr.		1996	John L. Wilson
1976	Wendell J. Campbell		1997	Alan Y. Taniguchi
1980	Leroy M. Campbell*		1998	Leon Bridges
1981	Robert T. Coles		1999	Charles F. McAfee
1982	John S. Chase		2000	Louis L. Weller
1983	Howard Hamilton Mackey Sr.		2001	Cecil A. Alexander Jr.
1984	John Louis Wilson		2002	Robert P. Madison
1985	Milton V. Bergstedt		2003	Hispanic American Construction
1986	Richard McClure Prosse*			Industry Association
1987	J. Max Bond Jr.		2004	Terrance J. Brown
1988	Habitat for Humanity		2005	Stanford R. Britt
1989	John H. Spencer		2006	Theodore C. Landsmark
1990	Harry G. Robinson III		2007	National Organization of
1991	Robert Kennard			Minority Architects

* Honored posthumously

Source: American Institute of Architects

Good urban design must be for the poor as well as for the rich.

David Appleyard

Wolf Prize for Architecture

163

The annual Wolf Prize celebrates outstanding living scientists and artists in the fields of agriculture, chemistry, mathematics, medicine, physics, and the arts—the arts category rotating among architecture, music, painting, and sculpture. In 1976 Ricardo Wolf established the Wolf Foundation, and shortly thereafter the Wolf Prize, to "promote science and arts for the benefit of mankind." The prize carries an $100,000 honorarium.

Profiles of the winners are available at *www.wolffund.org.il.*

Architecture Recipients

1983	Ralph Erskine (Sweden)
1988	Fumihiko Maki (Japan)
	Giancarlo de Carlo (Italy)
1992	Frank Gehry
	Jørn Utzon (Denmark)
	Sir Denys Lasdun (UK)
1996	Frei Otto (Germany)
	Aldo van Eyck (Netherlands)
2001	Alvaro Siza (Portugal)
2005	Jean Nouvel (France)

Source: Wolf Foundation

Each new situation requires a new architecture.

Jean Nouvel

Wood Design Awards

The Wood Design Awards annually recognize excellence in wood architecture throughout North America. Winning projects push the boundaries of conventional wood building practices and highlight the special qualities, versatility, and sheer beauty of wood as a building material, though buildings need not be constructed entirely of wood. A special award issue of *Wood Design & Building* magazine features the winning projects.

Visit *www.wooddesignandbuilding.com* for photos of the winners.

2006 Winners

Honor Awards
Ash 4 Ways
New York, NY
hanrahanMeyers architects

Craven Road Studio
Toronto, ON, Canada
Shim Sutcliffe Architects (Canada)

Hilltop Arboretum
Baton Rouge, LA
Lake/Flato Architects

Sunset Cabin
Lake Simcoe, ON, Canada
Taylor Smyth Architects (Canada)

Merit Awards
Avis Ranch Headquarters
Clyde Park, MT
Fernau & Hartman Architects Inc.

The Barn at Fallingwater
Mill Run, PA
Bohlin Cywinski Jackson

Kleinburg Pool Pavilion
Kleinburg, ON, Canada
Michael Amantea (Canada)

Milanville Bath/Guest House
Milanville, PA
Joe Levine

Open-Air Classroom, Prairie Ridge
   Environmental Education Center
Raleigh, NC
Frank Harmon Architect

Citation Awards
Environmental Education/Visitor Activity
   Center
Dingmans Ferry, PA
Bohlin Cywinski Jackson

Friends Meetinghouse
San Antonio, TX
Lake/Flato Architects

Artist Studio
Piedmont, NC
Frank Harmon Architect

Packard Komoriya Residence
Potomac, MD
Robert M. Gurney, FAIA, Architect

The Retreat
Vancouver, BC, Canada
Osburn Clarke Productions (Canada)

Wong Eckles Residence
North Kohala Island, HI
Cutler Anderson Architects

JURY
Craig Curtis, Miller/Hull Partnership
Brian MacKay-Lyons, MacKay-Lyons Sweetapple
   Architects Ltd. (Canada)
Mark McInturff, McInturff Architects

Source: Wood Design & Building

Young Architects Award

The American Institute of Architects presents the Young Architects Award to architects in the early stages of their career who have made significant contributions to the profession. The annual competition is open to AIA members who have been licensed for less than 10 years. The term *young architect* has no reference to the age of the nominees.

For a list of all past winners, visit the AIA online at *www.aia.org*.

1998–2007 Recipients

1998	J. Windom Kimsey	2004	John Burse
	Jose Luis Palacious		David Jameson
	Karin M. Pitman		Donna Kacmar
	Charles Rose		Janis LaDouceur
	Karl W. Stumpf		Kevin G. Sneed
	David Louis Swartz	2005	F. Michael Ayles
	Maryann Thompson		Jeffrey DeGregorio
	Randall C. Vaughn		Miguel Rivera
1999	Father Terrence Curry		Rick Harlan Schneider
	Victoria Tatna Jacobson		Eric Strain
	Michael Thomas Maltzan	2006	Michael Arad
	David T. Nagahiro		James Dayton
	Peter Steinbrueck		John Sangki Hong
2000	Mary Katherine Lanzillotta		Shannon Kraus
	Andrew Travis Smith		Soren Simonsen
2001	J. Scott Busby		Patrick Tighe
	P. Thomas M. Harboe	2007	Roy Abernathy
	Jeffry Lee Kagermeier		Michael P. Eberle
	Elizabeth Chu Richter		Lonnie D. Hoogeboom
	George A. Takoudes		Phillip Koski
2002	Randy G. Brown		James Mary O'Connor
	Barbara Campagna		Suzanna Wight
	Mohammed Lawal		
	Joe Scott Sandlin		
2003	Lisa M. Chronister	*Source: American Institute of Architects*	
	Paul D. Mankins		
	Paul Neuhaus		
	Ronald Todd Ray		
	Paul Woolford		

LEADERSHIP
IN DESIGN

Induction as a fellow, honorary fellow, or honorary member, or serving as president of a professional organization, is an honor commonly bestowed upon the industry's preeminent leaders. This chapter lists those noteworthy individuals along with a number of other honorific titles.

Chancellors of the American Institute of Architects College of Fellows

The chancellor of the American Institute of Architects College of Fellows is elected by the fellows to preside over the college's investiture ceremony and business affairs.

Year	Name	Year	Name
1952–53	Ralph Thomas Walker	1988	C. William Brubaker
1954–55	Alexander C. Robinson III	1989	Preston M. Bolton
1956	Edgar I. Williams	1990	William A. Rose Jr.
1957–60	Roy F. Larson	1991	Robert B. Marquis
1961–62	Morris Ketchum Jr.	1992	L. Jane Hastings
1963–64	Paul Albert Thiry	1993	John A. Busby Jr.
1965–66	G. Holmes Perkins	1994	Thomas H. Teasdale
1967–68	Norman J. Schlossman	1995	Robert T. Coles
1969–70	John Noble Richards	1996	Ellis W. Bullock Jr.
1971–72	J. Roy Carroll Jr.	1997	Jack DeBartolo Jr.
1973	Ulysses Floyd Rible	1998	Harold L. Adams
1974	Albert S. Golemon	1999	James D. Tittle
1975	Robert S. Hutchins	2000	Robert A. Odermatt
1976	William Bachman	2001	Harold Roth
1977	Philip J. Meathe	2002	C. James Lawler
1978	George Edward Kassabaum	2003	Sylvester Damianos
1979	David A. Pugh	2004	Betsey O. Dougherty
1980	Robert L. Durham	2005	Lawrence J. Leis
1981	Leslie N. Boney Jr.	2006	Ted P. Pappas
1982	William R. Jarratt	2007	Frank E. Lucas
1983	William C. Muchow	2008	Carole J. Olshavsky
1984	Bernard B. Rothschild		
1985	Donald L. Hardison		
1986	Vladimir Ossipoff		
1987	S. Scott Ferebee Jr.		

Source: American Institute of Architects

Fellows of the American Academy of Arts and Sciences

Since its founding in 1780, the American Academy of Arts and Sciences has pursued as its goal "to cultivate every art and science which may tend to advance the interest, honor, dignity, and happiness of a free, independent, and virtuous people." Its diverse membership has included the best from the arts, science, business, scholarship, and public affairs. Current members, also known as fellows, nominate and evaluate candidates for new membership.

Fellows: Design Professionals

Christopher Alexander
Edward Larrabee Barnes
Herbert Lawrence Block
Denise Scott Brown
Robert Campbell
Henry N. Cobb
Charles Correa* (India)
Carl Theodor Dreyer* (Denmark)
Peter Eisenman
Sir Norman Foster* (UK)
Kenneth Frampton
Frank Gehry
Lawrence Halprin
Steven Holl
Robert S.F. Hughes
Ada Louise Huxtable
Gerhard M. Kallmann
Rem Koolhaas* (Netherlands)
Phyllis Lambert* (Canada)
Ricardo Legorreta* (Mexico)
Maya Lin
Fumihiko Maki* (Japan)
N. Michael McKinnell
Richard Meier

Henry A. Millon
William Mitchell
Rafael Moneo* (Spain)
Oscar Niemeyer* (Brazil)
I.M. Pei
Renzo Piano* (Italy)
James Stewart Polshek
Kevin Roche
Elizabeth Barlow Rogers
Robert Rosenblum
Moshe Safdie
Vincent J. Scully
Alvaro Siza* (Portugal)
Robert A.M. Stern
Kenzo Tange* (Japan)
Billie Tsien
Robert Venturi
Tod Williams

*Foreign honorary members

Source: American Academy of Arts and Sciences

Fellows of the American Institute of Architects

Fellowship in the American Institute of Architects recognizes members who have contributed notably to the advancement of the architecture profession. As an international counterpart, foreign architects may be granted honorary fellowship. For those who have demonstrated distinguished service to architecture and the allied arts and sciences and who are not otherwise eligible for membership in the AIA, the organization grants honorary membership.

171

2007 Fellows

Mustafa Kemal Abadan
Peter Anderson
Jeffrey Anderzhon
Wagdy Anis
Douglas W. Ashe
Paula Baker-Laporte
Ron Budzinski
Mark Cavagnero
Edward J. Cazayoux
James Chaffers
Lawrence A. Chan
Joseph R. Coleman
Harold E. Davis Jr.
William L. Diefenbach
Charles Dilworth
Frank E. Dittenhafer II
Cornelius R. DuBois
Kent Duffy
Roger Duffy
Steve Dumez
William Edgerton
Michael A. Enomoto
Richard Farley
Bradford White Fiske
Michael T. Foster
John T. Friedman
Andrea Cohen Gehring
Glenn Goldman
John Grable
Sally Grans
Frank J. Greene
Bert Gregory
Nells Hall
Helen Hatch

William J. Higgins
Harley Hightower
John K. Holton
C.T. Hsu
David Jameson
Paul G. Johnson
Randolph Jones
Paul Katz
Daniel Kelley
Thomas P. Kerwin
Ronald B. Kull
Frank Christopher Lee
Paula Loomis
Gary D. Lynn
Michael Thomas Maltzan
Leonardo Marmol
Ron McCoy
Robert Meckfessel
D.B. Middleton
Kevin G. Montgomery
Jeff Oberdorfer
Patricia O'Leary
Greg Papay
Clyde Porter
Ronald B. Radziner
Patrick Rand
Margaret Rietveld
Herbert Roth
Anne Schopf
Linda Sobuta
Joseph Spear
Ross G. Spiegel
Edmund P. Stazicker
Henry Stolzman

Fellows of the American Institute of Architects

Larry Strain
Barry Svigals
L. Brooke Sween-McGloin
Paulett Taggart

Richard Thompson
Calvin Tsao
Adam Yarinsky
Donald T. Yoshino

2007 Honorary Fellows

Emilio Ambasz
Victor Cañas (Costa Rica)
David Chipperfield (UK)
Francine M.J. Houben (Netherlands)
Victor Manuel Legorreta (Mexico)

Adolfo Natalini (Italy)
Dominique Perrault (France)
Eduardo Souto de Moura (Portugal)
Chris Wilkinson (UK)

2007 Honorary Members

Ron Bogle
Amory Lovins
Elizabeth Mitchell
Lorna McRae Parsons
Edward F. Sanderson

Stephen A. Wynn
L. William Zahner

Source: American Institute of Architects

Architecture is the reaching out for the truth.

Louis I. Kahn

Fellows of the American Institute of Certified Planners

Fellowship in the American Institute of Certified Planners is one of the highest honors the AICP can bestow upon a member. The AICP grants fellowships every two years to members who have achieved excellence in professional practice, teaching and mentoring, research, public and community service, and leadership.

2006–08 Fellows

William Anderson
Barbara Becker
Tom Beckwith
Brian J.L. Berry
Gary Binger
Roger D. Blevins
Mary Anne G. Bowie
David S. Boyd
Lee Brown
Brian Campbell
Donald K. Carter
Elaine Costello
John M. DeGrove
Donald L. Elliott
Lawrence Epstein
W. Paul Farmer
Steven P. French
Harlan Hanson
Marcy Kaptur
Larry Keating
David N. Kinsey
Naphtali H. Knox
Alan Kreditor
Roberta Longfellow

Cheryl H. Matheny
Anne F. McBride
Robert D. Mitchell
Emil R. Moncivais
Sarah S. More
Michael J. Munson
Jack L. Nasar
A. Paul Norby
Myles Rademan
Jaquelin Robertson
Donald Rothblatt
Richard Rothman
James A. Segedy
Brian K. Smith
Judith G. Stoloff
Lisa S. Verner
Joseph L. Vining
Karen S. Walz
John P. Whalen
Richard M. Wozniak
Byrnes K. Yamashita

Source: American Institute of Certified Planners

Fellows of the American Society of Interior Designers

The American Society of Interior Designers grants fellowship, the highest honor bestowed on its members, to those who have made notable and substantial contributions to the interior design profession or ASID. Those who have been professional ASID members for at least 10 continuous years are eligible for nomination. For individuals who have advanced the interior design profession but are not interior designers, ASID grants honorary fellowship.

2006 Fellows

Jan Bast
Tama Duffy Day
Barbara S. Marini
Sharon S. Staley

2006 Honorary Fellows

No new inductees

Source: American Society of Interior Designers

It is not true that what is useful is beautiful. It is what is beautiful that is useful. Beauty can improve people's way of life and thinking.

Anna Castelli Ferrieri

Fellows of the American Society of Landscape Architects

The American Society of Landscape Architects grants fellowship to members of at least 10 years who have made outstanding contributions to the profession in such areas as works of landscape architecture, administrative work, knowledge, and service. The ASLA grants honorary membership to recognize those outside the profession who have performed notable service to the landscape architecture field.

175

2007 Fellows

Todd P. Bennitt
Gene Bressler
George B. Briggs
Kenneth R. Brooks
Robert A. Close
Andrea C. Cochran
Roger G. Courtenay
Brian J. Dougherty
Angela D. Dye
William T. Eubanks III
Bonnie Fisher
Douglas E. Hoerr
M. Elise Huggins
David Kamp
Barrett L. Kays
Owen C. Lang
Jeff S. Lee

Mia G. Lehrer
Brian C. McCarter
Lee R. McLaren
Tooru Miyakoda (Japan)
Jonathan Mueller
Robert R. Page
Martin Poirier
Gary D. Scott
Kevin M. Shanley
Keith E. Simpson
William P. Vitek
Lawrence W. Walquist Jr.
Susan K. Weiler
Joanne M. Westphal
Joseph Yee
Len Zickler

2007 Honorary Members

Gerald W. Adelmann
Ross C. Anderson
Gary Hack
Mike Houck
Jo Luck
Meg Maguire
Bill Marken
Roger Milliken

Steven Peck
Witold Rybczynski
Susan Szenasy
Doug Tompkins
Roger Ulrich

Source: American Society of Landscape Architects

Fellows of the Design Futures Council

Fellowship in the Design Futures Council is granted annually to individuals who have provided noteworthy leadership to the advancement of design, design solutions, or the design professions. DFC fellows are recognized for their significant contributions to the understanding of changing trends, new research, and applied knowledge that improve the built environment and the human condition.

Ava J. Abramowitz, George Washington University

Harold L. Adams, RTKL Associates Inc.

David M. Adamson, Office of Government Commerce (UK)

Ray Anderson, Interface, Inc.

Rodrigo Arboleda, MIT Media Lab

Peter Beck, Beck Group

Robert J. Berkebile, BNIM Architects

Phillip Bernstein, Autodesk

Friedl Bohm, NBBJ

John Seely Brown, Xerox Research PARC

Janine M. Benyus, author

Santiago Calatrava, architect (Spain)

Robert Campbell, *Boston Globe*

John Cary, Public Architecture

Steve Chu, Lawrence Berkeley National Laboratory

James P. Cramer,[†] Greenway Group

Michael Crichton, author and film director

Nigel Dancey, Foster and Partners (UK)

Sylvester Damianos, Damianosgroup

Clark Davis, HOK

Williston (Bill) Dye, TSA, Inc.

Philip J. Enquist, Skidmore, Owings & Merrill

Richard Farson, Western Behavioral Sciences Institute

Edward A. Feiner, Skidmore, Owings & Merrill

Martin Fischer, Stanford University

Tom Fisher, University of Minnesota

Edward Friedrichs, Friedrichs Group

Steve Fiskum, Hammel, Green and Abrahamson

James Follett, Gensler

Sir Norman Foster, Foster and Partners (UK)

Harrison Fraker, University of California, Berkeley

Neil Frankel, Frankel + Coleman

Roger E. Frechette III, Skidmore, Owings & Merrill

R. Buckminster Fuller,* engineer, inventor, educator, and architectural innovator

Thomas D. Galloway*, Georgia Institute of Technology

Frank Gehry, Gehry Partners

M. Arthur Gensler Jr., Gensler

Milton Glaser, graphic designer

Roger Godwin, architect and interior designer

Paul Goldberger, *The New Yorker*

Al Gore, author and former US vice president

David Gottfried, WorldBuild Technologies Inc.

Zaha Hadid, Zaha Hadid Architects (UK)

Jeremy Harris, Urban Strategy Institute

Paul Hawken, Natural Capital Institute

H. Ralph Hawkins, HKS, Inc.

Jerry Hobbs, AC Neilson, vnu

Carl Hodges, Seaphire International

Robert Ivy, *Architectural Record*

Jane Jacobs,* author (Canada)

Louis I. Kahn,* architect and educator

Tom Kelly, IDEO

Stephen J. Kieran, Kieran Timberlake Associates

A. Eugene Kohn, Kohn Pedersen Fox Associates

Norman L. Koonce, American Institute
of Architects
Theodore C. Landsmark, Boston
Architectural College
Gary Lawrence, Arup
Amory B. Lovins, Rocky Mountain Institute
Lucinda Ludwig,* Leo A Daly
Chris Luebkeman, Arup (UK)
Janet Martin, Communication Arts, Inc.
Bruce Mau, Bruce Mau Design
William McDonough, William McDonough
+ Partners
Alisdair McGregor, Arup
Sandra Mendler, HOK
Raymond F. Messer, Walter P. Moore
Engineers + Consultants
Gordon E. Mills, Durrant
Douglas R. Parker, Design Workshop
Alexander (Sandy) Pentland, MIT Media
Lab
B. Joseph Pine II, Strategic Horizons LLP
Daniel H. Pink, author
Witold Rybczynski, University of
Pennsylvania
Moshe Safdie, Moshe Safdie and Associates
Jonas Salk,* Salk Institute and architectural
patron

Adele N. Santos, Massachusetts Institute
of Technology
Peter Schwartz, Global Business Network
Katherine Lee Schwennsen, Iowa State
University
Terrence J. Sejnowski, Salk Institute
Scott Simpson, The Stubbins Associates
Karen Stephenson, Harvard University and
NetForm International
RK Stewart, Gensler
W. Cecil Steward, University of Nebraska–
Lincoln and Joslyn Castle Institute
Sarah Susanka, Susanka Studios
Richard Swett, former US ambassador
to Denmark
Jack Tanis, Steelcase Inc.
April Thornton, consultant
James Timberlake, Kieran Timberlake
Associates
Alan Traugott, CJL Engineering
Robert Tucker, The Innovation Resource
John Carl Warnecke, architect
Jon Westling, Boston University
Gary Wheeler, Gensler
Arol Wolford, Tectonic, Inc.
Richard Saul Wurman, author and
architect

* Deceased
† Resident fellow and foresight advisor

Source: Design Futures Council

There is nothing in a caterpillar that tells you it's going to be a butterfly.

R. Buckminster Fuller

Fellows of the Industrial Designers Society of America

Membership in the Industrial Designers Society of America's Academy of Fellows is conferred by a two-thirds majority vote of its board of directors. Fellows must be society members in good standing who have earned the special respect and affection of the membership through distinguished service to the society and to the profession as a whole.

2007 Fellows

JohnPaul Kusz
George McCain
Robert Schwartz

Source: Industrial Designers Society of America

Marketing asks the questions, design provides the answers.

Carl Gustav Magnusson

Fellows of the International Interior Design Association

Fellowship in the International Interior Design Association is a recognition of members who have demonstrated outstanding service to the IIDA, the community, and the interior design profession. For those who are not interior designers and have made substantial contributions to the interior design profession, IIDA grants honorary membership.

2007 Fellows

Kelly Bauer
William Clegg

2007 Honorary Members

No new inductees

Source: International Interior Design Association

All rooms ought to look as if they were lived in, and to have, so to say, a friendly welcome ready for the incomer.

William Morris

Presidents of the American Institute of Architects

1857–76	Richard Upjohn
1877–87	Thomas Ustick Walter
1888–91	Richard Morris Hunt
1892–93	Edward H. Kendall
1894–95	Daniel H. Burnham
1896–98	George B. Post
1899	Henry Van Brunt
1900–01	Robert S. Peabody
1902–03	Charles F. McKim
1904–05	William S. Eames
1906–07	Frank M. Day
1908–09	Cass Gilbert
1910–11	Irving K. Pond
1912–13	Walter Cook
1914–15	R. Clipston Sturgis
1916–18	John L. Mauran
1919–20	Thomas R. Kimball
1921–22	Henry H. Kendall
1923–24	William B. Faville
1925–26	Dan E. Waid
1927–28	Milton B. Medary
1929–30	Charles H. Hammond
1931–32	Robert D. Kohn
1933–34	Earnest J. Russell
1935–36	Stephen F. Voorhees
1937–38	Charles D. Maginnis
1939–40	Edwin Bergstrom
1941–42	Richmond H. Shreve
1943–44	Raymond J. Ashton
1945–46	James R. Edmunds Jr.
1947–48	Douglas W. Orr
1949–50	Ralph Thomas Walker
1951–52	A. Glenn Stanton
1953–54	Clair W. Ditchy
1955–56	George B. Cummings
1957–58	Leon Chatelain Jr.
1959–60	John Noble Richards
1961–62	Philip Will Jr.
1963	Henry L. Wright
1964	J. Roy Carroll Jr.
1965	A. Gould Odell Jr.
1966	Morris Ketchum Jr.
1967	Charles M. Nes Jr.
1968	Robert L. Durham

1969	George Edward Kassabaum
1970	Rex W. Allen
1971	Robert F. Hastings
1972	Max O. Urbahn
1973	S. Scott Ferebee Jr.
1974	Archibald C. Rogers
1975	William (Chick) Marshall Jr.
1976	Louis DeMoll
1977	John M. McGinty
1978	Elmer E. Botsai
1979	Ehrman B. Mitchell Jr.
1980	Charles E. Schwing
1981	R. Randall Vosbeck
1982	Robert M. Lawrence
1983	Robert C. Broshar
1984	George M. Notter Jr.
1985	R. Bruce Patty
1986	John A. Busby Jr.
1987	Donald J. Hackl
1988	Ted P. Pappas
1989	Benjamin E. Brewer Jr.
1990	Sylvester Damianos
1991	C. James Lawler
1992	W. Cecil Steward
1993	Susan A. Maxman
1994	L. William Chapin II
1995	Chester A. Widom
1996	Raymond G. (Skipper) Post Jr.
1997	Raj Barr–Kumar
1998	Ronald A. Altoon
1999	Michael J. Stanton
2000	Ronald L. Skaggs
2001	John D. Anderson
2002	Gordon H. Chong
2003	Thompson E. Penney
2004	Eugene C. Hopkins
2005	Douglas L. Steidl
2006	Katherine Lee Schwennsen
2007	RK Stewart
2008	Marshall E. Purnell
2009	Marvin J. Malecha

Source: American Institute of Architects

Presidents of the American Society of Interior Designers

1974–75	Norman DeHaan
1974–76	Richard W. Jones
1977	H. Albert Phibbs
1978	Irving D. Schwartz
1979	Rita St. Clair
1980	Wallace R. Jonason
1981	Jack Lowery
1982	Martin Ellinoff
1984	William Richard Waley
1985	Gail Adams
1986	Janet S. Schirn
1987	Joy E. Adcock
1988	Charles D. Gandy
1989	Elizabeth B. Howard
1990	Robert John Dean
1991	Raymond Kennedy
1992	Martha Garriott Rayle
1993	B.J. Peterson

1994–95	Gary Wheeler
1995–96	Penny Bonda
1996–97	Kathy Ford Montgomery
1997–98	Joyce Burke-Jones
1998–99	Rosalyn Cama
1999–00	Juliana M. Catlin
2000–01	Terri Maurer
2001–02	Barbara Nugent
2002–03	H. Don Bowden
2003–04	Linda Elliot Smith
2004–05	Anita Baltimore
2005–06	Robert Wright
2006–07	Suzan Globus
2007–08	Rita Carson Guest

Source: American Society of Interior Designers

When I began designing machines I also began to think that these objects, which sit next to each other and around people, can influence not only physical conditions but also emotions. They can touch the nerves, the blood, the muscles, the eyes and the moods of people.

Ettore Sottsass

Presidents of the American Society of Landscape Architects

1899–01	John C. Olmsted*
1902	Samuel Parsons Jr.*
1903	Nathan F. Barrett*
1904–05	John C. Olmsted*
1906–07	Samuel Parsons Jr.*
1908–09	Frederick Law Olmsted Jr.*
1910–11	Charles N. Lowrie*
1912	Harold A. Caparn
1913	Ossian C. Simonds*
1914	Warren H. Manning*
1915–18	James Sturgis Pray
1919–22	Frederick Law Olmsted Jr.*
1923–27	James L. Greenleaf
1927–31	Arthur A. Shurcliff
1931–35	Henry Vincent Hubbard
1935–41	Albert D. Taylor
1941–45	S. Herbert Hare
1945–49	Markley Stevenson
1949–51	Gilmore D. Clarke
1951–53	Lawrence G. Linnard
1953–57	Leon Zach
1957–61	Norman T. Newton
1961–63	John I. Rogers
1963–65	John Ormsbee Simonds
1965–67	Hubert B. Owens
1967–69	Theodore Osmundson
1969–71	Campbell E. Miller
1971–73	Raymond L. Freeman
1973–74	William G. Swain
1974–75	Owen H. Peters
1975–76	Edward H. Stone II
1976–77	Benjamin W. Gary Jr.
1977–78	Lane L. Marshall
1978–79	Jot D. Carpenter

1979–80	Robert L. Woerner
1980–81	William A. Behnke
1981–82	Calvin T. Bishop
1982–83	Theodore J. Wirth
1983–84	Darwina L. Neal
1984–85	Robert H. Mortensen
1985–86	John Wacker
1986–87	Roger B. Martin
1987–88	Cheryl L. Barton
1988–89	Brian S. Kubota
1989–90	Gerald D. Patten
1990–91	Claire R. Bennett
1991–92	Cameron R.J. Man
1992–93	Debra L. Mitchell
1993–94	Thomas P. Papandrew
1994–95	Dennis Y. Otsuji
1995–96	Vincent Bellafiore
1996–97	Donald W. Leslie
1997–98	Thomas R. Dunbar
1998–99	Barry W. Starke
1999–00	Janice Cervelli Schach
2000–01	Leonard J. Hopper
2001–02	Rodney L. Swink
2002–03	Paul F. Morris
2003–04	Susan L.B. Jacobson
2004–05	Patrick A. Miller
2005–06	Dennis B. Carmichael
2006–07	Patrick W. Caughey
2007–08	Perry Howard
2008–09	Angela D. Dye

*Charter member

Source: American Society of Landscape Architects

Presidents of the Association of Collegiate Schools of Architecture

1912–21	Warren Laird	University of Pennsylvania
1921–23	Emil Lorch	University of Michigan
1923–25	William Emerson	Massachusetts Institute of Technology
1925–27	Francke Bosworth Jr.	Cornell University
1927–29	Goldwin Goldsmith	University of Kansas
1929–31	Everett Meeks	Yale University
1931–34	Ellis Lawrence	University of Oregon
1934–36	Roy Childs Jones	University of Minnesota
1936–38	Sherely Morgan	Princeton University
1938–40	George Young Jr.	Cornell University
1940–42	Leopold Arnaud	Columbia University
1942–45	Wells Bennett	University of Michigan
1945–47	Loring Provine	University of Illinois at Urbana–Champaign
1947–49	Paul Weigel	Kansas State College
1949–51	B. Kenneth Johnstone	Carnegie Institute of Technology
1951–53	Thomas FitzPatrick	Iowa State College
1953–55	Lawrence Anderson	Massachusetts Institute of Technology
1955–57	Elliott Whitaker	Ohio State University
1957–59	Buford L. Pickens	Washington University
1959–61	Harlan E. McClure	Clemson College
1961–63	Olindo Grossi	Pratt Institute
1963–65	Henry Kamphoefner	North Carolina State College
1965–67	Walter Sanders	University of Michigan
1967–69	Robert L. Bliss	University of Utah
1969–71	Charles E. Burchard	Virginia Polytechnic Institute and State University
1971–72	Alan Y. Taniguchi	Rice University and University of Texas, Austin
1972–73	Robert S. Harris	University of Oregon
1973–74	Sanford Greenfield	Boston Architectural Center
1974–75	Don P. Schlegal	University of New Mexico
1975–76	Bertram Berenson	University of Illinois at Chicago
1976–77	Donlyn Lyndon	Massachusetts Institute of Technology
1977–78	Dwayne Nuzum	University of Colorado at Boulder
1978–79	William Turner	Tulane University
1979–80	Robert Paschal Burns	North Carolina State University
1980–81	Richard C. Peters	University of California, Berkeley
1981–82	Eugene Kremer	Kansas State University
1982–83	O. Jack Mitchell	Rice University
1983–84	Charles C. Hight	University of North Carolina at Charlotte
1984–85	Wilmot G. Gilland	University of Oregon
1985–86	George Anselevicius	University of New Mexico
1986–87	Blanche Lemco van Ginkel	University of Toronto
1987–88	J. Thomas Regan	University of Miami
1988–89	Robert M. Beckley	University of Michigan

Presidents of the Association of Collegiate Schools of Architecture

1989–90	Marvin J. Malecha California State Polytechnic University, Pomona
1990–91	John Meunier Arizona State University
1991–92	Patrick Quinn Rensselaer Polytechnic Institute
1992–93	James Barker Clemson University
1993–94	Kent Hubbell Cornell University
1994–95	Diane Ghirardo University of Southern California
1995–96	Robert Greenstreet University of Wisconsin–Milwaukee
1996–97	Linda W. Sanders California State Polytechnic University, Pomona
1997–98	John M. McRae Mississippi State University
1998–99	R. Wayne Drummond University of Florida
1999–00	Jerry V. Finrow University of Washington
2000–01	Tony Schuman New Jersey Institute of Technology
2001–02	Frances Bronet Rensselaer Polytechnic Institute
2002–03	Bradford C. Grant Hampton University
2003–04	Geraldine Forbes Isais Woodbury University
2004–05	Rafael Longoria University of Houston
2005–06	Stephen Schreiber University of South Florida
2006–07	Theodore C. Landsmark Boston Architectural Center
2007–08	Kim Tanzer University of Florida
2008–09	Marleen Kay Davis University of Tennessee, Knoxville

Source: Association of Collegiate Schools of Architecture

Architecture doesn't come from theory. You don't think your way through a building.

Arthur Erickson

Presidents of the Council of Architectural Component Executives

The Council of Architectural Component Executives is comprised of the CEOs of the staffed chapters and components of the American Institute of Architects.

1971	Julian B. Serrill AIA Iowa	1992	Eleanor McNamara AIA Georgia
1972	Don Edward Legge Texas Society of Architects/AIA	1993	Martha Murphree AIA Houston
1973–75	Fotis Karasoutis Florida Association of American Institute of Architects	1994	Paul W. Welch Jr. AIA California Council
1976–77	Dan Sheridan American Institute of Architects Minnesota	1995	John W. Braymer Virginia Society AIA
		1996	Suzanne K. Schwengels AIA Iowa
1978–79	Des Taylor Texas Society of Architects/AIA	1997	Connie C. Wallace AIA Tennessee
1980–81	Ann Stacy AIA Michigan	1998	Peter A. Rand American Institute of Architects Minnesota
1982	James P. Cramer American Institute of Architects Minnesota	1999	Gayle Krueger AIA Nebraska
1983	Lowell Erickson Boston Society of Architects/AIA	2000	Timothy D. Kent AIA North Carolina
1984	Sandra Stickney AIA East Bay	2001	Janet D. Pike AIA Kentucky

1985	George A. Allen
	Florida Association of the
	  American Institute of
	  Architects
		2002	Karen Lewand
			AIA Baltimore

		2003	David P. Lancaster Texas Society of Architects/AIA
1986	Brent L. Davis AIA Southern Arizona	2004	Saundra Stevens AIA Oregon/AIA Portland
1987	Barbara J. Rodriguez AIA New York State	2005	Elizabeth Mitchell AIA Utah/AIA Salt Lake
1988	Linda Young AIA Kansas City	2006	David A. Crawford AIA North Carolina
1989	Kathleen Davis AIA Orange County	2007	Bonnie Larson Staiger AIA North Carolina
1990	Rae Dumke AIA Michigan/AIA Detriot	2008	Frederic Bell AIA New York
1991	Beverly Hauschild-Baron American Institute of Architects Minnesota	2009	William M. Babcock AIA Wisconsin

Source: American Institute of Architects

Presidents of the Industrial Designers Society of America

1965	Henry Dreyfuss	1989–90	Peter W. Bressler
1966	Joseph Marshall Parriott	1991–92	Charles Pelly
1967–68	Robert H. Hose	1993–94	David D. Tompkins
1969–70	Tucker Madawick	1995–96	James M. Ryan
1971–72	William M. Goldsmith	1997–98	Craig Vogel
1973–74	Arthur J. Pulos	1999–00	Mark Dziersk
1975–76	James F. Fulton	2001–02	Betty Baugh
1977–78	Richard Hollerith	2003–04	Bruce Claxton
1979–80	Carroll M. Gantz	2005–06	Ronald B. Kemnitzer
1981–82	Robert G. Smith	2007–08	Michelle Berryman
1983–84	Katherine J. McCoy		
1985–86	Cooper C. Woodring		
1987–88	Peter H. Wooding		

Source: Industrial Designers Society of America

Design is directed toward human beings. To design is to solve human problems by identifying them and executing the best solution.

Ivan Chermayeff

Presidents of the International Interior Design Association

1994–95	Marilyn Farrow
1995–96	Judith Hastings
1996–97	Beth Harmon-Vaughan
1997–98	Karen Guenther
1998–99	Neil Frankel
1999–00	Carol Jones
2000–01	Richard N. Pollack
2001–02	Cary D. Johnson
2002–03	Anita L. Barnett
2003–04	Lewis Goetz
2004–05	John A. Lijewski
2005–06	Eric Engstrom
2006–07	Pamela Light
2007–08	John Mack
2008–09	Mitchell Sawasy

187

Source: International Interior Design Association

Did you know...

The International Interior Design Association was founded in 1994 as the result of a merger of the Institute of Business Designers, the International Society of Interior Designers, and the Council of Federal Interior Designers.

Presidents of the International Union of Architects

1948–53	Sir Patrick Abercrombie (UK)
1953–57	Jean Tschumi (Switzerland)
1957–61	Hector Mardones-Restat (Chili)
1961–65	Sir Robert Matthew (UK)
1965–69	Eugène Beaudouin (France)
1969–72	Ramon Corona Martin (Mexico)
1972–75	Georgui M. Orlov (Russia)
1975–78	Jai Rattan Bhalla (India)
1978–81	Louis DeMoll
1981–85	Rafael de la Hoz (Spain)
1985–87	Georgi Stoilov (Bulgaria)
1987–90	Rod Hackney (UK)
1990–93	Olufemi Majekodunmi (Nigeria)
1993–96	Jaime Duro Pifarré (Spain)
1996–99	Sara Topelson de Grinberg (Mexico)
1999–02	Vassilis C. Sgoutas (Greece)
2002–05	Jaime Lerner (Brazil)
2005–08	Gaétan Siew (Mauritius)

Honorary Presidents

1948–53	Auguste Perret (France)
1953–57	Sir Patrick Abercrombie (UK)
1969–02	Pierre Vago (France)

Source: International Union of Architects

The uniqueness of place must be allowed to surface—for architecture involves the actuality of things and speaks to the senses—it cannot rely on image alone.

Kerry Hill

Presidents of the National Council of Architectural Registration Boards

1920–22	Emil Loch		1977	Charles A. Blondheim Jr.
1923–24	Arthur Peabody		1978	Paul H. Graven
1925	Miller I. Kast		1979	Lorenzo D. Williams
1926–27	W.H. Lord		1980	John R. Ross
1928	George D. Mason		1981	Dwight M. Bonham
1929–30	Clarence W. Brazer		1982	Thomas H. Flesher Jr.
1931–32	James M. White		1983	Sid Frier
1933	A.L. Brockway		1984	Ballard H.T. Kirk
1933	A.M. Edelman		1985	Robert E. Oringdulph
1934–35	Joseph W. Holman		1986	Theodore L. Mularz
1936	Charles Butler		1987	Robert L. Tessier
1938–39	William Perkins		1988	Walter T. Carry
1940–41	Mellen C. Greeley		1989	George B. Terrien
1942–44	Louis J. Gill		1990	Herbert P. McKim
1945–46	Solis Seiferth		1991	Charles E. Garrison
1947–49	Warren D. Miller		1992	Robert H. Burke Jr.
1950	Clinton H. Cowgill		1993	Harry G. Robinson III
1951	Roger C. Kirchoff			William Wiese II, *Honorary*
1952–54	Charles E. Firestone			*Past President*
1954–55	Fred L. Markham		1994	Robert A. Fielden
1956–58	Edgar H. Berners		1995	Homer L. Williams
1959–60	Walter F. Martens		1996	Richard W. Quinn
1961	A. Reinhold Melander		1997	Darrell L. Smith
1962	Chandler C. Cohagen		1998	Ann R. Chaintreuil
1963	Paul W. Drake		1999	Susan May Allen
1964	Ralph O. Mott		2000	Joseph P. Giattina Jr.
1965	C.J. Paderewski		2001	William Bevins
1966	Earl L. Mathes		2002	C. Robert Campbell
1967	George F. Schatz		2003	Robert A. Boynton
1968–69	Howard T. Blanchard		2004	Frank M. Guillot
1970	Dean L. Gustavson		2005	H. Carleton Godsey Jr.
1971	William J. Geddis		2006	Robert E. Luke
1972	Daniel Boone		2007	Douglas K. Engebretson
1973	Thomas J. Sedgewick		2008	Gordon E. Mills
1974	E.G. Hamilton Jr.		2009	Jeffrey A. Huberman
1975	John (Mel) O'Brien Jr.			
1976	William C. Muchow			

189

Source: National Council of Architectural Registration Boards

Presidents of the Royal Architectural Institute of Canada

1907–10	A.E. Dunlop
1910–12	E.S. Baker
1912–16	J.H.G. Russell
1916–18	J.P. Ouellet
1918–20	A. Frank Wickson
1920–22	David R. Brown
1922–24	Lewis H. Jordan
1924–26	John S. Archibald
1926–29	J.P. Hynes
1929–32	Percy E. Nobbs
1932–34	Gordon M. West
1934–36	W.S. Maxwell
1936–38	W.I. Somerville
1938–40	H.L. Fetherstonbaugh
1940–42	Burwell R. Coon
1942–44	Gordon McL. Pirts
1944–46	Forsey Page
1946–48	David Chas
1948–50	A.J. Hazelgrove
1950–52	J. Roxburgh Smith
1952–54	Robert Schofield Morris
1954–56	A.J.C. Paine
1956–58	D.F. Kertland
1958–60	Maurice Payette
1960–62	Harland Steele
1962–64	John I. Davies
1964–65	F. Bruce Brown
1965–66	Gérard Venne
1966–67	Charles A.E. Fowler
1967–68	James F. Searle
1968–69	Norman H. McMurrich
1969–70	William G. Leithead
1970–71	Gordon R. Arnott
1971–72	Jean-Louis Lalonde
1972–73	C.F.T. Rounthwaite
1973–74	Allan F. Duffus
1974–75	Bernard Wood
1975–76	Fred T. Hollingsworth

1976–77	Charles H. Cullum
1977–78	W. Donald Baldwin
1978–79	Gilbert R. Beatson
1980–81	David H. Hambleton
1981–82	J. Douglass Miller
1982–83	G. Macy Dubois
1983–84	Patrick Blouin
1984–85	W. Kirk Banadyga
1985–86	Brian E. Eldred
1986–87	Rudy P. Ericsen
1987–88	Terence J. Williams
1988–89	Alfred C. Roberts
1989–90	Essy Baniassad
1990–91	Richard Young
1991–92	David W. Edwards
1992–93	Roy W. Willwerth
1993–94	J. Brian Sim
1994–95	Paul-André Tétreault
1995–97	Bill Chomik
1997–98	Barry J. Hobin
1998–99	Eva Matsuzaki
1999–00	Eliseo Temprano
2000–01	David Simpson
2001–02	Diarmuid Nash
2002–03	Ronald Keenberg
2003–04	Bonnie Maples
2004–05	Christopher Fillingham
2005–06	Yves Gosselin
2006–07	Vivian Manasc
2007–08	Kiyoshi Matsuzaki
2008–09	Paule Boutin

Individuals are Canadian unless otherwise indicated.

Source: Royal Architectural Institute of Canada

Presidents of the Royal Australian Institute of Architects

1929–30	Alfred Samuel Hook
1930–31	William Arthur Blackett
1931–32	Philip Rupert Claridge
1932–33	Lange Leopold Powell
1933–34	Charles Edward Serpell
1934–35	Arthur William Anderson
1935–36	Guy St. John Makin
1936–37	James Nangle
1937–38	Louis Laybourne-Smith
1938–39	Frederick Bruce Lucas
1939–40	Otto Abrecht Yuncken
1940–42	William Ronald Richardson
1942–44	John Francis Scarborough
1944–46	Roy Sharrington Smith
1946–48	William Rae Laurie
1948–50	Jack Denyer Cheesman
1950–52	Cobden Parkes
1952–54	Robert Snowden Demaine
1954–56	Edward James Weller
1956–57	William Purves Godfrey
1957–59	Wilfried Thomas Haslam
1959–60	Kenneth Charles Duncan
1960–61	Thomas Brenan Gargett
1961–62	Henry Ingham Ashworth
1962–63	James Campbell Irwin
1963–64	Max Ernest Collard
1964–65	Raymond Berg
1965–66	Gavin Walkley
1966–67	Mervyn Henry Parry
1967–68	Acheson Best Overend
1968–69	Jack Hobbs McConnell
1969–70	John David Fisher
1970–71	Ronald Andrew Gilling
1971–72	Kenneth William Shugg
1972–73	Henry Jardine Parkinson
1973–75	Peter McIntyre
1975–76	Harold Bryce Mortlock

1976–77	Blair Mansfield Wilson
1977–78	E. Gresley Cohen
1978–79	John M. Davidson
1979–80	Geoffrey Lawrence
1980–81	Alexander Ian Ferrier
1981–82	Michael Laurence Peck
1982–83	Richard Norman Johnson
1983–84	David Alan Nutter
1984–85	Richard Melville Young
1985–86	Roland David Jackson
1986–87	Graham Alan Hulme
1987–88	Robert Darwin Hall
1988–89	Dudley Keith Wilde
1989–90	Ronald Barrie Bodycoat
1990–91	Robert Lindsay Caufield
1991–92	Jamieson Sayer Allom
1992–93	Robert Cheesman
1993–94	James Taylor
1994–95	Virginia Louise Cox
1995–96	Peter Robertson Gargett
1996–97	John Stanley Castles
1997–98	Eric Graham Butt
1998–99	Graham Humphries
1999–00	Nigel Warren Shaw
2000–01	Edward Robert Haysom
2001–02	Graham Jahn
2002–03	Caroline Pidcock
2003–04	David Parken
2004–05	Warren Kerr
2005–06	Bob Nation
2006–07	Carey Lyon
2007–08	Alec Tzannes
2008–09	Howard Tanner

191

Individuals are Australian unless otherwise indicated.

Source: Royal Australian Institute of Architects

Presidents of the Royal Institute of British Architects

1835–59	Earl de Grey
1860	Charles Robert Cockerell
1861–63	Sir William Tite
1863–65	Thomas L. Donaldson
1865–67	A.J.B. Beresford Hope
1867–70	Sir William Tite
1870–73	Thomas Henry Wyatt
1873–76	Sir Gilbert George Scott
1876–79	Charles Barry Jr.
1879–81	John Whichcord
1881	George Edmund Street
1882–84	Sir Horace Jones
1884–86	Ewan Christian
1886–87	Edward l'Anson
1888–91	Alfred Waterhouse
1891–94	J. Macvicar Anderson
1894–96	Francis C. Penrose
1896–99	George Aitchison
1899–02	Sir William Emerson
1902–04	Sir Aston Webb
1904–06	John Belcher
1906–08	Thomas Edward Collcutt
1908–10	Sir Ernest George
1910–12	Leonard Stokes
1912–14	Sir Reginald Blomfield
1914–17	Ernest Newton
1917–19	Henry Thomas Hare
1919–21	Sir John William Simpson
1921–23	Paul Waterhouse
1923–25	J. Alfred Gotch
1925–27	Sir Guy Dawber
1927–29	Sir Walter Tapper
1929–31	Sir Banister Fletcher
1931–33	Sir Raymond Unwin
1933–35	Sir Giles Gilbert Scott
1935–37	Sir Percy Thomas
1937–39	H.S. Goodhart-Rendel
1939–40	E. Stanley Hall
1940–43	W.H. Ansell
1943–46	Sir Percy Thomas
1946–48	Sir Lancelot Keay
1948–50	Michael T. Waterhouse
1950–52	A. Graham Henderson
1952–54	Sir Howard Robertson
1954–56	C.H. Aslin
1956–58	Kenneth M.B. Cross
1958–60	Sir Basil Spence
1960–62	Lord W.G. Holford
1962–64	Sir Robert Matthew
1964–65	Sir Donald Gibson
1965–67	Viscount Lionel Brett Esher
1967–69	Sir Hugh Wilson
1969–71	Sir Peter Shepheard
1971–73	Sir Alex Gordon
1973–75	F.B. Pooley
1975–77	Eric Lyons
1977–79	Gordon Graham
1979–81	Bryan Jefferson
1981–83	Owen Luder
1983–85	Michael Manser
1985–87	Larry Rolland
1987–89	Rod Hackney
1989–91	Max Hutchinson
1991–93	Richard C. MacCormac
1993–95	Frank Duffy
1995–97	Owen Luder
1997–99	David Rock
1999–01	Marco Goldschmied
2002–03	Paul Hyett
2003–05	George Ferguson
2005–07	Jack Pringle
2007–09	Sunand Prasad

Individuals are British unless otherwise indicated.

Source: Royal Institute of British Architects

RECORDS, RANKINGS, & ACHIEVEMENTS

This chapter contains numerous rankings and ratings for professional reference and diversion. The results of the Most Popular Historic Houses ranking can be found in the Design & Historic Preservation chapter on page 374; the list of the tallest buildings in the world is located in the Building Types chapter on page 302.

Firm Anniversaries

The following currently practicing US architecture firms were founded in 1908, 1933, 1958, and 1983 respectively.

Firms Celebrating their 100th Anniversary
Harley Ellis Devereaux, Southfield, MI
Joseph & Joseph Architects, Louisville, KY
Kahler Slater Architects, Milwaukee, WI
Rogers, Burgun, Shahine and Deschler, Inc., New York, NY
Somdal-Associates Architecture-Interior Design, Shreveport, LA

Firms Celebrating their 75th Anniversary
Durrant, Dubuque, IA
Horner & Shifrin, Inc., Saint Louis, MO
Talley & Smith Architecture Inc., Shelby, NC
VSRiggi Architects, Dunmore, PA

Firms Celebrating their 50th Anniversary
AEDIS, Inc., San Jose, CA
Blitch Knevel Architects, Inc., New Orleans, LA
BOORA Architects, Portland, OR
David W. Osler Associates, Inc. Architects, Ann Arbor, MI
Frank Schlesinger Associates Architects, Washington, DC
GBBN Architects, Cincinnati, OH
GVA - George Vaeth Associates, Inc., Columbia, MD
Heimsath Architects, Austin, TX
Horst Terrill & Karst Architects, Topeka, KS
Hugh Newell Jacobsen Architect, Washington, DC
Image Group, Inc., Moorhead, MN
Pahl Architecture, Denver, CO
QPK Design, Syracuse, NY
Wakely Associates, Mount Pleasant, MI

Firms Celebrating their 25th Anniversary
AE Design Group, Southington, CT
Array Healthcare Facilities Solutions, King of Prussia, PA
Becker Morgan Group, Inc., Salisbury, MD
Blackburn Architects, Washington, DC
Boulder Associates, Inc., Boulder, CO
Braun & Steidl Architects Inc., Akron, OH
BSW International, Tulsa, OK
Cearnal Andrulaitis LLP, Santa Barbara, CA
Cogen Architects, New York, NY
Connolly Architects Inc., Milwaukee, WI
Curtis Gelotte Architects, Kirkland, WA
Dahlquist & Lutzow Architects, Ltd., Elgin, IL
David L. Sommers, AIA, Architects, Kent, OH
Davis Architectural Group, Cambridge, OH
Design West Architects, Pullman, WA
Dindo Architect, New York, NY
Dugan/Otero Architects, Rocky Mount, NC
Dull Olson Weekes Architects, Portland, OR
E. Lynn App Architects, Inc., Englewood, OH
ENVISION Architects, Albany, NY
Facilities Planning Collaborative Inc., New York, NY
French + Ryan, Inc., Georgetown, DE
Furnstahl & Simon Architects, New York, NY
Ganthner Melby Architects and Planners, Reno, NV
Gries Architectural Group, Inc., Neenah, WI
Harrison Phillips Architect, Denver, CO
HCP Architects, Albany, NY
JE Design Architects & Environmental Planners, Mesa, AZ
Juniper Russell and Associates, Inc., Newton, MA
Kaesler Architecture, Golden, CO
KAHickman Architects and Interior Designers, Round Rock, TX

195

Firm Anniversaries

Kodet Architectural Group, Ltd.,
   Minneapolis, MN
KSS Architects, Princeton, NJ
M. John Lew Architects, State College, PA
Mayse & Associates, Inc., Dallas, TX
McCall Sharp Architecture, Springfield, OH
Michael J. Burns Architects, Ltd.,
   Moorhead, MN
Michael Shepherd AIA Architect,
   Telluride, CO
Nicholas Dickinson & Associates,
   Augusta, GA
NAC Architecture, Spokane, WA
Pacific Design Associates Inc., Modesto, CA
**Panich, Noel + Associates, Architects and
   Engineers**, Athens, OH
Pegram Associates Inc., Myrtle Beach, SC
Pingel & Associates, Architects,
   Bensenville, IL
Poulos + Associates Architects, Inc.,
   Sandusky, OH
Rafael Viñoly Architects, New York, NY

Ronald Schmidt & Associates,
   Englewood, NJ
Rossini Architecture, Inc., Atlanta, GA
Roth & Sheppard Architects, Denver, CO
SALA Architects, Inc., Minneapolis, MN
Spatial Designs, Mason City, IA
Sugimura & Associates Architects,
   Campbell, CA
Svigals and Partners, New Haven, CT
TAM+CZ, Architects, Fresno, CA
Taylor Architecture, Santa Monica, CA
Thomas Hacker Architects Inc.,
   Portland, OR
Tsoi/Kobus & Associates, Inc.,
   Cambridge, MA
US Cost Incorporated, Atlanta, GA
William Rawn Associates Architects Inc.,
   Boston, MA
Yarrington Architectural Group,
   Bridgewater, NJ
YHR Partners, Moorhead, MN
Zehren and Associates, Vail, CO

Source: DesignIntelligence

Architecture and urbanism, always together. It's not the individual buildings but the aggregation of buildings, the urban setting, that really defines great architectural cultures.

Jaquelin Robertson

Firm Statistics: Architecture

	Number of Establishments[1]	Annual Payroll ($1,000s)	Paid Employees[2]
Alabama	229	86,268	1,654
Alaska	54	32,369	464
Arizona	568	184,829	3,470
Arkansas	150	76,040	1,640
California	3,450	1,742,056	26,764
Colorado	775	229,935	3,884
Connecticut	337	146,785	2,336
Delaware	42	16,980	299
District of Columbia	159	172,897	2,497
Florida	1,799	549,393	10,217
Georgia	631	323,465	5,392
Hawaii	192	67,531	1,187
Idaho	139	31,529	716
Illinois	1,188	478,449	8,340
Indiana	296	129,861	2,552
Iowa	122	45,133	866
Kansas	180	69,317	1,296
Kentucky	161	50,606	1,020
Louisiana	267	70,222	1,566
Maine	120	35,352	704
Maryland	441	199,311	3,444
Massachusetts	785	475,115	7,574
Michigan	566	246,622	4,523
Minnesota	430	230,321	3,970
Mississippi	111	34,965	779
Missouri	438	261,900	4,471
Montana	134	35,056	718
Nebraska	98	68,925	1,228
Nevada	173	80,251	1,339
New Hampshire	73	21,536	383
New Jersey	725	278,294	4,988
New Mexico	175	50,345	1,157
New York	2,154	1,039,739	16,650
North Carolina	621	234,070	4,490

Firm Statistics: Architecture

	Number of Establishments[1]	Annual Payroll ($1,000s)	Paid Employees[2]
North Dakota	41	13,251	295
Ohio	678	315,417	5,853
Oklahoma	201	79,431	1,576
Oregon	344	129,645	2,533
Pennsylvania	744	432,692	7,639
Rhode Island	86	21,707	448
South Carolina	270	89,367	1,571
South Dakota	45	11,189	266
Tennessee	286	154,188	2,560
Texas	1,450	702,669	11,617
Utah	210	62,929	1,395
Vermont	91	19,861	429
Virginia	567	274,178	4,535
Washington	716	297,618	5,237
West Virginia	45	15,949	383
Wisconsin	309	128,808	2,481
Wyoming	48	10,481	222
US Total	**23,914**	**10,554,847**	**181,618**

[1] All numbers are 2004.
[2] Paid employees for the pay period including March 12.

Source: US Census Bureau

Firm Statistics: Number of
Establishments

199

Architecture

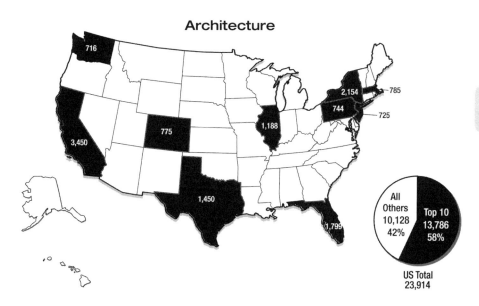

Industrial Design

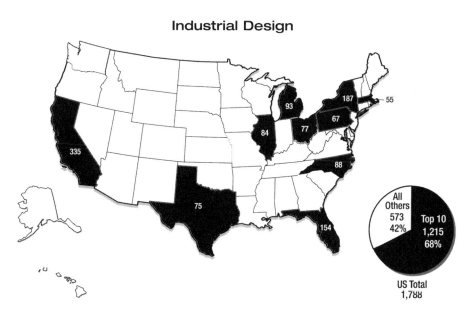

Source: DesignIntelligence

Firm Statistics: Industrial Design

	Number of Establishments[1]	Annual Payroll ($1,000s)	Paid Employees[2]
Alabama	4	Withheld	0–19
Alaska	1	Withheld	0–19
Arizona	23	2,520	74
Arkansas	4	Withheld	0–19
California	335	124,514	1,922
Colorado	31	7,720	147
Connecticut	30	7,456	100
Delaware	2	Withheld	0–19
District of Columbia	n/a	n/a	n/a
Florida	154	11,369	300
Georgia	41	9,633	179
Hawaii	1	Withheld	0–19
Idaho	4	Withheld	100–249
Illinois	84	22,014	381
Indiana	23	Withheld	20–99
Iowa	7	Withheld	0–19
Kansas	12	Withheld	20–99
Kentucky	10	Withheld	20–99
Louisiana	7	Withheld	0–19
Maine	8	Withheld	20–99
Maryland	26	5,106	135
Massachusetts	55	27,886	364
Michigan	93	45,749	996
Minnesota	38	12,263	217
Mississippi	2	Withheld	0–19
Missouri	15	4,455	124
Montana	2	Withheld	0–19
Nebraska	7	Withheld	20–99
Nevada	20	3,052	19
New Hampshire	13	5,874	73
New Jersey	55	23,811	528
New Mexico	9	Withheld	20–99

	Number of Establishments[1]	Annual Payroll ($1,000s)	Paid Employees[2]
New York	187	79,753	1,155
North Carolina	88	16,792	311
North Dakota	n/a	n/a	n/a
Ohio	77	Withheld	500–999
Oklahoma	4	Withheld	0–19
Oregon	41	50,395	706
Pennsylvania	67	28,989	581
Rhode Island	14	Withheld	20–99
South Carolina	9	Withheld	0–19
South Dakota	1	Withheld	0–19
Tennessee	13	Withheld	20–99
Texas	75	32,897	499
Utah	12	Withheld	20–99
Vermont	3	Withheld	0–19
Virginia	22	Withheld	100–249
Washington	24	Withheld	100–249
West Virginia	2	Withheld	0–19
Wisconsin	32	14,750	318
Wyoming	1	Withheld	0–19
US Total	**1,788**	**536,998**	**9,129**

[1] All numbers are 2004.
[2] Paid employees for the pay period including March 12.
  Data was withheld from certain fields to avoid disclosing data of individual companies.

Source: US Census Bureau

Firm Statistics: Interior Design

	Number of Establishments[1]	Annual Payroll ($1,000s)	Paid Employees[2]
Alabama	105	Withheld	250–499
Alaska	14	Withheld	20–99
Arizona	249	28,481	770
Arkansas	54	Withheld	100–249
California	1,563	305,397	7,040
Colorado	365	43,318	1,076
Connecticut	163	22,714	479
Delaware	35	Withheld	100–249
District of Columbia	51	35,058	527
Florida	1,609	154,550	4,525
Georgia	442	63,792	1,453
Hawaii	31	Withheld	100–249
Idaho	42	Withheld	100–249
Illinois	627	86,637	2,110
Indiana	193	19,191	617
Iowa	65	Withheld	100–249
Kansas	75	Withheld	100–249
Kentucky	107	8,331	324
Louisiana	107	7,032	277
Maine	25	Withheld	20–99
Maryland	262	33,581	875
Massachusetts	278	39,576	819
Michigan	292	Withheld	500–999
Minnesota	211	24,453	657
Mississippi	46	Withheld	100–249
Missouri	176	18,918	547
Montana	35	Withheld	20–99
Nebraska	49	Withheld	100–249
Nevada	116	20,479	428
New Hampshire	29	Withheld	20–99
New Jersey	388	43,834	1,343
New Mexico	46	Withheld	20–99

	Number of Establishments[1]	Annual Payroll ($1,000s)	Paid Employees[2]
New York	1,184	225,222	3,819
North Carolina	334	28,244	1,134
North Dakota	14	Withheld	20–99
Ohio	292	40,627	1,174
Oklahoma	95	Withheld	250–499
Oregon	123	14,413	426
Pennsylvania	294	45,874	1,039
Rhode Island	37	6,553	165
South Carolina	160	12,885	507
South Dakota	16	1,030	51
Tennessee	160	17,517	487
Texas	742	99,427	2,808
Utah	95	6,003	219
Vermont	16	Withheld	20–99
Virginia	329	38,956	1,148
Washington	206	23,142	652
West Virginia	20	Withheld	20–99
Wisconsin	114	Withheld	250–499
Wyoming	9	Withheld	20–99
US Total	**12,090**	**1,515,235**	**37,496**

[1] All numbers are 2004.
[2] Paid employees for the pay period including March 12.
  Data was withheld from certain fields to avoid disclosing data of individual companies.

Source: US Census Bureau

Firm Statistics: Number of Establishments

204

Interior Design

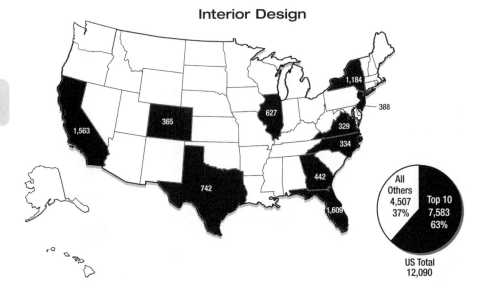

Landscape Architecture

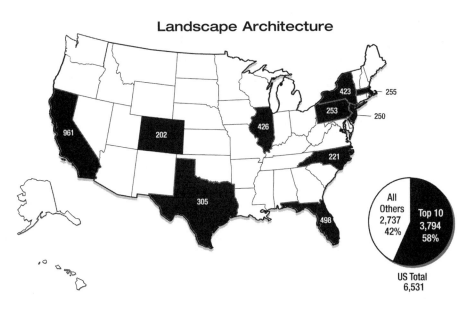

Source: DesignIntelligence

Firm Statistics: Landscape Architecture

	Number of Establishments[1]	Annual Payroll ($1,000s)	Paid Employees[2]
Alabama	46	8,483	360
Alaska	10	Withheld	2,099
Arizona	169	56,332	1,485
Arkansas	29	3,227	128
California	961	359,813	8,723
Colorado	202	57,626	1,223
Connecticut	90	17,037	334
Delaware	23	Withheld	2,099
District of Columbia	16	4,231	79
Florida	498	155,043	3,898
Georgia	194	40,879	1,113
Hawaii	38	13,168	299
Idaho	39	3,925	90
Illinois	426	95,226	1,864
Indiana	79	8,046	289
Iowa	30	4,465	89
Kansas	26	6,613	204
Kentucky	48	7,527	295
Louisiana	58	8,844	382
Maine	38	4,530	101
Maryland	152	32,724	839
Massachusetts	255	64,931	1,059
Michigan	187	54,948	1,287
Minnesota	96	16,694	367
Mississippi	31	5,087	199
Missouri	82	11,667	420
Montana	32	2,626	58
Nebraska	26	Withheld	20–99
Nevada	47	20,604	530
New Hampshire	36	7,310	425
New Jersey	250	45,815	850
New Mexico	47	6,136	213

205

Firm Statistics: Landscape Architecture

	Number of Establishments[1]	Annual Payroll ($1,000s)	Paid Employees[2]
New York	423	90,350	1,497
North Carolina	221	42,951	1,387
North Dakota	9	664	32
Ohio	157	36,858	934
Oklahoma	52	6,039	211
Oregon	96	Withheld	500,999
Pennsylvania	253	62,437	1,356
Rhode Island	31	3,625	71
South Carolina	93	16,666	535
South Dakota	16	Withheld	20–99
Tennessee	106	17,959	578
Texas	305	83,118	2,233
Utah	58	6,022	154
Vermont	26	Withheld	20–99
Virginia	139	33,595	841
Washington	165	31,585	718
West Virginia	11	Withheld	20–99
Wisconsin	91	19,957	426
Wyoming	18	Withheld	20–99
US Total	**6,531**	**1,575,383**	**543,373**

[1] All numbers are 2004.
[2] Paid employees for the pay period including March 12.
  Data was withheld from certain fields to avoid disclosing data of individual companies.

Source: US Census Bureau

Leading Architecture Firms

DesignIntelligence, the monthly journal of the Design Futures Council, an AEC industry think tank, analyzed the brand positions of firms, including peer perception, building-type studies, media coverage, and revenue levels to determine the profession's leaders. The following excerpt from the 2006 study ranks US architecture firms by size based on annual revenue and by media popularity based on the frequency with which they appeared in *Architectural Record*, *Architecture*, and *Metropolis* magazines.

207

Additional analyses from this study can be found in the 2006 Brand Equity Analysis report available at *www.di.net*.

Top Architecture Firms by Size

1. Gensler
2. Hellmuth, Obata & Kassabaum
3. Skidmore, Owings & Merrill
4. HKS Inc.
5. Perkins+Will
6. RTKL Associates Inc.
7. Leo A Daly
8. NBBJ
9. SmithGroup
10. Callison Architecture

Media Popularity

Architectural Record
1. Renzo Piano Building Workshop (Italy)
2. Office for Metropolitan Architecture (Netherlands)
3. Frank Gehry
   Moshe Safdie and Associates
5. Skidmore, Owings & Merrill

Architecture
1. Herzog & de Meuron (Switzerland)
   Skidmore, Owings & Merrill
3. Arup (UK)
4. Perkins+Will
5. Renzo Piano Building Workshop (Italy)
   Santiago Calatrava (Spain)

Metropolis
1. Skidmore, Owings & Merrill
2. Office for Metropolitan Architecture (Netherlands)
3. Morphosis
4. Charles and Ray Eames
5. Renzo Piano Building Workshop Italy)
   Kohn Pedersen Fox Associates

Source: DesignIntelligence

National Historic Planning Landmarks

Every year the American Institute of Certified Planners, the American Planning Association's professional and educational arm, grants National Historic Planning Landmark status to no more than three historically significant projects. To be eligible, projects must be at least 25 years old, have initiated a new direction in planning, made a significant contribution to the community, and be available for public use and viewing. Newly designated sites are indicated in bold.

For additional information, visit the AICP's website, *www.planning.org*.

Arizona
The Salt River Project (1911)

California
Bay Conservation and Development Commission and Creation of the San Francisco Bay Plan (1965–69)
East Bay Regional Park District, San Francisco (1934)
Los Angeles County "Master Plan of Highways" (1940) and "Freeways for the Region" (1943)
Napa County Agricultural Preserve (1968)
Petaluma Plan (1971–72)
San Francisco Zoning Ordinance (1867)

Colorado
The Denver Parks and Parkway System (1906+)
Speer Boulevard, Denver

Connecticut
The Nine Square Plan of New Haven (1639)

District of Columbia
Euclid v. Ambler, US Supreme Court (1926)
Federal Housing Assistance "701" Program (Federal Housing Act of 1954)
First National Conference on City Planning (1909)
The McMillan Commission Plan for Washington, DC (1901)
National Resources Planning Board (1933–43)
Plan of Washington, DC (1791)

Florida
City of Sanibel (1974)

Georgia
Plan of Savannah (1733)

Hawaii
Hawaii's State Land Use Law (1961)

Illinois
The American Society of Planning Officials (ASPO, 1934)
The Chicago lakefront (1836–present)
Local Planning Administration (1941)
Merriam Center, Chicago (1930+)
Plan of Chicago (1909)
Plan of Park Forest (1948)
Plan of Riverside (1869)

Indiana
New Harmony (1814–27)

Kentucky
Lexington Urban Service Area (1958)

Louisiana
Plan of the Vieux Carre, New Orleans (1721)

Maryland
Columbia (1967+)
Greenbelt (A Greenbelt Town, 1935+)
Plan of Annapolis (1695)

Massachusetts
Billerica Garden Suburb, Lowell (1914)
Emerald Necklace Parks, Boston (1875+)
Founding of the Harvard University
    Graduate Planning Program (1929)

Michigan
Kalamazoo Mall (1956)

Missouri
Country Club Plaza, Kansas City (1922)
Founding of the American City Planning
    Institute (1917)
Kansas City Parks Plan (1893)

Montana
Yellowstone National Park (1872)

New Jersey
Radburn at Fair Lawn (1928–29)
Society for the Establishment of Useful
    Manufactures Plan for Paterson
    (1791–92)
*Southern Burlington County NAACP
    v. Township of Mount Laurel* (1975)
Yorkship Village, Camden (1918)

New Mexico
The Laws of the Indies (1573; 1681)

New York
Bronx River Parkway and the Westchester
    County Parkway System (1907+)
Central Park, New York City (1857)
First Houses, New York City (1935–36)
Forest Hills Gardens, Long Island (1911+)
Founding of the American City Planning
    Institute (1917)
Grand Central Terminal, New York City
    (1903–13)
Long Island Parkways (1885) and Parks
    (1920s)
New York City Zoning Code (1916)
New York State Adirondack Preserve
    & Park (1892)
New York State Commission on Housing
    and Regional Planning (1923–26)

Niagara Reservation State Park (1885)
Regional Plan of New York & Environs
    (1929)
Second Regional Plan of the Regional Plan
    Association of New York (1968)
Sunnyside Gardens, Long Island (1924+)
University Settlement House and the
    Settlement House Movement (1886)

North Carolina
Blue Ridge Parkway (1935+)

Ohio
Cincinnati Plan of 1925
Cleveland Group Plan (1903)
Cleveland Policy Plan (1974)
Founding of Ohio Planning Conference
    (1919)
Greenhills (1935+)
Miami Valley Region's Fair Share Housing
    Plan of 1970
Plan of Mariemont (1922)

Oregon
Oregon's Statewide Program for Land Use
    Planning (1973)

Pennsylvania
Plan of Philadelphia (1683)

Rhode Island
College Hill Demonstration of Historic
    Renewal, Providence (1959)

South Carolina
First American Historic District,
    Charleston (1931)

Tennessee
Plan of Metro Government, Nashville/
    Davidson County (1956)
Tennessee Valley Authority (1933+)
Town of Norris (1933)

Texas
"A Greater Fort Worth Tomorrow" (1956)
Paseo del Rio, San Antonio (1939–41)

National Historic Planning Landmarks

Utah
Plat of the City of Zion (1833)

Virginia
Blue Ridge Parkway (1935+)
Jeffersonian Precinct, University of
   Virginia (1817)
Monument Avenue Historic District,
   Richmond (1888)
The New Town of Reston (1962)
Roanoke Plans (1907; 1928)

West Virginia
Appalachian Trail (1921+)

Wisconsin
Greendale (1935+)
Wisconsin Planning Enabling Act (1909)

Wyoming
Yellowstone National Park (1872)

Source: American Institute of Certified Planners

Only architecture that considers human scale and interaction is successful architecture.

Jan Gehl

National Historic Planning Pioneers

Every year the American Institute of Certified Planners, the American Planning Association's professional and educational arm, names up to three National Historic Planning Pioneers who have made significant contributions to American planning. Recipients have excelled in planning practice, education, and/or theory on a national scale with long-term beneficial results. Their contributions must have occurred no less than 25 years ago. New inductees are indicated in bold.

For additional information, visit the AICP's website, *www.planning.org.*

211

Charles Abrams
Frederick J. Adams
Thomas Adams
Sherry Arnstein
Edmund N. Bacon
Frederick H. Bair Jr.
Harland Bartholomew
Edward M. Bassett
Edward H. Bennett
Alfred Bettman
Walter H. Blucher
Ernest John Bohn
Daniel H. Burnham
F. Stuart Chapin Jr.
Charles H. Cheney
Paul Davidoff
Frederic A. Delano
Earle S. Draper
Simon Eisner
Carl Feiss
George Burdett Ford
Paul Goodman
Percival Goodman
Aelred Joseph Gray
Frederick Gutheim
S. Herbert Hare
Sid J. Hare

Elisabeth Herlihy
John Tasker Howard
Henry Vincent Hubbard
Theodora Kimball Hubbard
Harlean James
T.J. Kent Jr.
George Edward Kessler
Pierre Charles L'Enfant
Kevin Lynch
Benton MacKaye
Ian McHarg
Albert Mayer
Harold V. Miller
Corwin R. Mocine
Arthur Ernest Morgan
Robert Moses
Lewis Mumford
Jesse Clyde Nichols
John Nolen
Charles Dyer Norton
Charles McKim Norton
Frederick Law Olmsted Sr.
Frederick Law Olmsted Jr.
Lawrence M. Orton
The Outdoor Circle
Harvey S. Perloff
Clarence Arthur Perry

Gifford Pinchot
Planners for Equal
   Opportunity, 1964–1974
John Reps
Jacob Riis
Charles Mulford Robinson
James W. Rouse
Charlotte Rumbold
Mel Scott
Ladislas Segoe
Flavel Shurtleff
Mary K. Simkhovitch
Robert E. Simon Jr.
William E. Spangle
Clarence S. Stein
Telesis, 1939–1953
Rexford Guy Tugwell
Lawrence T. Veiller
Francis Violich
Charles Henry Wacker
Lillian Wald
Gordon Whitnall
Donald Wolbrink
Edith Elmer Wood
Henry Wright
Catherine Bauer Wurster

Source: American Institute of Certified Planners

Number of Registered Architects

Registered architects in each state are divided into two categories: resident and reciprocal, or non-resident, registrants. Based on current population levels, the chart below also calculates the per capita number of resident architects in each state. The following information is from the National Council of Architectural Registration Boards' 2006 survey.

State	Resident Architects	Reciprocal Registrations	Total	Population[1]	Per capita # of Resident Arch. (per 100,000)
Alabama	769	1,602	2,371	4,599,030	17
Alaska	231	318	549	670,053	34
Arizona	2,026	3,531	5,557	6,166,318	33
Arkansas‡	454	919	1,373	2,810,872	16
California	16,894	4,958	21,852	36,457,549	46
Colorado	2,988	3,624	6,612	4,753,377	63
Connecticut	1,538	2,792	4,330	3,504,809	44
Delaware*	100	1,000	1,100	853,476	12
DC‡	2,811	399	3,210	581,530	483
Florida	4,862	4,458	9,320	18,089,888	27
Georgia†	2,180	1,497	3,677	9,363,941	23
Hawaii	954	1,187	2,141	1,285,498	74
Idaho	487	222	709	1,466,465	33
Illinois	5,300	3,442	8,742	12,831,970	41
Indiana	1,250	1,835	3,085	6,313,520	20
Iowa	466	1,211	1,677	2,982,085	16
Kansas	936	1,566	2,502	2,764,075	34
Kentucky†	662	1,622	2,284	4,206,074	16
Louisiana	1,050	1,680	2,730	4,287,768	24
Maine	388	1,052	1,440	1,321,574	29
Maryland†	2,637	2,435	5,072	5,615,727	47
Massachusetts‡	3,308	2,802	6,110	6,437,193	51
Michigan	5,664	4,476	10,140	10,095,643	56
Minnesota	1,749	1,490	3,239	5,167,101	34
Mississippi	313	1,400	1,713	2,910,540	11
Missouri	1,920	2,846	4,766	5,842,713	33
Montana	376	847	1,223	944,632	40

State	Resident Architects	Reciprocal Registrations	Total	Population[1]	Per capita # of Resident Arch. (per 100,000)
Nebraska	600	2,500	3,100	1,768,331	34
Nevada	572	3,123	3,695	2,495,529	23
New Hampshire	297	1,411	1,708	1,314,895	23
New Jersey	2,942	4,705	7,647	8,724,560	34
New Mexico	702	1,308	2,010	1,954,599	36
New York	8,356	5,768	14,124	19,306,183	43
North Carolina	2,158	3,197	5,355	8,856,505	24
North Dakota	123	545	668	635,867	19
Ohio	3,516	3,490	7,006	11,478,006	31
Oklahoma	727	1,293	2,020	3,579,212	20
Oregon	1,453	1,188	2,641	3,700,758	39
Pennsylvania‡	7,313	3,726	11,039	12,440,621	59
Rhode Island	279	1,258	1,537	1,067,610	26
South Carolina	1,003	2,734	3,737	4,321,249	23
South Dakota	106	619	725	781,919	14
Tennessee	1,358	2,123	3,481	6,038,803	22
Texas	6,889	3,582	10,471	23,507,783	29
Utah‡	2,100	n/a	2,100	2,550,063	82
Vermont	279	698	977	623,908	45
Virginia	2,705	3,852	6,557	7,642,884	35
Washington	3,663	1,932	5,595	6,395,798	57
West Virginia	120	1,119	1,239	1,818,470	7
Wisconsin	1,622	3,185	4,807	5,556,506	29
Wyoming	108	810	918	515,004	21
US Total	**111,304**	**109,377**	**220,681**	**299,398,484**	**37**

[1] 2006 population estimate from the US Census Bureau
* Counts are estimates based on data from prior years.
† Counts based on 2005 ratios.
‡ Counts based on 2006 ratios.

Source: National Council of Architectural Registration Boards and DesignIntelligence

Number of Registered Architects

(Top 10 Shown)

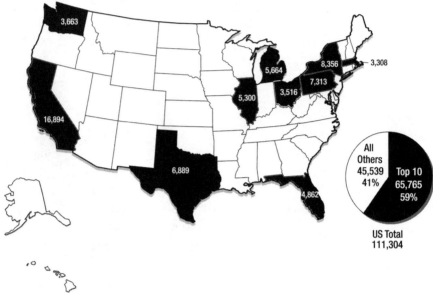

3,663

5,664

8,356

3,308

7,313

5,300

3,516

16,894

6,889

4,862

All
Others
45,539
41%

Top 10
65,765
59%

US Total
111,304

Source: DesignIntelligence

Oldest Practicing Architecture Firms in North America

The following firms were founded prior to 1900 (their specific founding dates indicated below) and are still operational today.

1827	The Mason & Hanger Group, Inc. Lexington, KY
1832	Lockwood Greene Spartanburg, SC
1853	Luckett & Farley Architects, Engineers and Construction Managers, Inc. Louisville, KY
1853	SmithGroup Detroit, MI
1868	Jensen and Halstead Ltd. Chicago, IL
1868	King & King Architects Manlius, NY
1870	Harriman Associates Auburn, ME
1871	Scholtz-Gowey-Gere-Marolf Architects & Interior Designers Davenport, IA
1873	Graham, Anderson, Probst, & White Chicago, IL
1873	River Bluffs Architects St. Joseph, MO
1874	Shepley Bulfinch Richardson and Abbott Boston, MA
1878	The Austin Company Kansas City, MO
1878	Ballinger Philadelphia, PA
1880	Beatty Harvey & Associates, Architects New York, NY

1880	Green Nelson Weaver, Inc. Minneapolis, MN
1880	Holabird & Root Chicago, IL
1880	Zeidler Partnership Architects Toronto, Canada
1881	Keffer/Overton Architects Des Moines, IA
1883	Ritterbush-Ellig-Hulsing Bismarck, ND
1883	SMRT Architecture Engineering Planning Portland, ME
1885	Cromwell Architects Engineers Little Rock, AR
1885	HLW International New York, NY
1887	Bradley & Bradley Rockford, IL
1889	Architectural Design West, Inc. Salt Lake City, UT
1889	CSHQA Architects/Engineers/ Planners Boise, ID
1889	MacLachlan, Corneliu & Filoni, Inc. Pittsburgh, PA
1889	Wank Adams Slavin Associates New York, NY
1890	Kendall, Taylor & Company, Inc. Billerica, MA
1890	Mathes Brierre Architects New Orleans, LA

215

Oldest Practicing Architecture Firms in North America

1890	Plunkett Raysich Architects Milwaukee, WI
1891	SSP Architectural Group Somerville, NJ
1892	Bauer Stark + Lashbrook, Inc. Toledo, OH
1892	FreemanWhite, Inc. Raleigh, NC
1893	Foor & Associates Elmira, NY
1894	Colgan Perry Lawler Architects Nyack, NY
1894	Freese and Nichols, Inc. Fort Worth, TX
1894	Parkinson Field Associates Austin, TX
1895	Brooks Borg Skiles Architecture Engineering Des Moines, IA
1895	Albert Kahn Associates, Inc. Detroit, MI
1896	Hummel Architects Boise, ID
1896	Kessels DiBoll Kessels & Associates New Orleans, LA

1896	Lehman Architectural Group Fairfield, NJ
1897	Baskervill Richmond, VA
1897	LHRS Architects, Inc. Huntington, IN
1898	Beardsley Design Associates Auburn, NY
1898	BSA, Inc. Green Bay, WI
1898	Burns & McDonnell Kansas City, MO
1898	Eckles Architecture New Castle, PA
1898	Emery Roth & Sons New York, NY
1898	Foss Associates Fargo, ND & Moorhead, MN
1898	PageSoutherlandPage Austin, TX
1899	William B. Ittner, Inc. St. Louis, MO

Source: DesignIntelligence

Architecture is to masonry what poetry is to literature.

Anon

Pathways in American Planning History: A Thematic Chronology: 1682–2000

This chronology is a compilation of significant events in the broad American movement known as planning, which embraces not only urban planning but its many sister professions, among them architecture and landscape architecture. Although it constitutes a single timeline, letter symbols permit the grouping of the entries into eight themes: laws and administrative acts, publications and addresses, housing and community planning, economic development, urban form and design, conservation and the environment, regional planning, and the history of the planning profession.

217

This chronology is adapted with permission from a fully interactive version available online at *www.planning.org/pathways*. Comments and suggestions for future revisions can be sent to the author, Albert Guttenberg, at *a-gutten@uiuc.edu*.

> *From the beginning of our national life, various forms of planning have been in evidence...The Constitution itself was an economic-political plan on a grand scale...The Constitutional Convention was...a large-scale planning board.*
> —Final Report of the National Planning Board, 1934

1682 Philadelphia is founded by William Penn. Its design is that of a rectangular grid with a central park and four smaller parks, one in each quadrant. **UD**

1733 Founder James Oglethorpe's plan for Savannah, GA, is a more elaborate grid with a main axis and interlinking gardens and squares. **UD**

1785 The Ordinance of 1785 provides for the rectangular land survey of the Old Northwest, which has been called "the largest single act of national planning in our history and...the most significant in terms of continuing impact on the body politic" by Daniel J. Elazar. **LA** **ED**

1791 In his *Report on Manufactures*, US Secretary of the Treasury Alexander Hamilton argues for protective tariffs for manufacturing industry as a means of promoting industrial development in the young republic. **ED** **BA**

Pierre L'Enfant's Baroque design for the new nation's capitol lays grand radial avenues and ceremonial spaces over a grid. **UD**

1818 In a speech before Congress, Henry Clay proposes a plan (called the American System) to allocate federal funds to promote the development of the national economy by combining tariffs with internal improvements, such as roads, canals, and other waterways. **ED** **BA**

Pathways in American Planning History

1825 The Erie Canal is completed. This artificial waterway connects the northeastern states with the newly settled areas of what was then the West, facilitating the economic development of both regions. **ED** **RP**

1839 The National Road terminates in Vandalia, IL. Begun in 1811 in Cumberland, MD, it helps open the Ohio Valley to settlement. **ED**

1855 The first model tenement is built in Manhattan. **HC**

1859 New York City's Central Park, designed by Frederick Law Olmsted Sr. and Calvert Vaux, opens to the public and becomes a model for many other American city parks. **UD**

1862 The Homestead Act opens the public domain lands to settlers for a nominal fee and a five-year residency requirement. **LA** **ED** **HC**

1862 With the Morrill Act, Congress authorizes land grants from the public domain to the states. Proceeds from the sale are to be used to found colleges offering instruction in agriculture, engineering, and other practical arts. **ED** **LA**

1864 The New York City Council of Hygiene of the Citizens Association mounts a campaign to raise housing and sanitary standards. **HC**

George Perkins Marsh, known as the father of environmentalism, publishes *Man and Nature*. This seminal book explores the destructive impact of human activity on the natural environment and inspires future conservation movements. **BA** **CE**

1868 Frederick Law Olmsted Sr. and Calvert Vaux begin the planning of Riverside, IL, a planned suburban community stressing rural as opposed to urban amenities. **HC**

1869 The Union Pacific and the Central Pacific railroads meet at Promontory Point, UT, on May 10 to complete the first transcontinental railroad. **ED**

1873 In *Landscape Architecture as Applied to the Wants of the West*, H.W.S. Cleveland advocates laying out town streets according to the land's natural contours rather than by the mechanical replication of a rigid grid. **BA** **UD**

1878 John Wesley Powell's *Report on the Lands of the Arid Region of the United States* is published. It includes a proposed regional plan that would both foster settlement of the arid West and conserve scarce water resources. **CE** **RP** **ED** **BA**

Frederick Law Olmsted Sr. inaugurates his city-shaping system of Boston urban parks. **UD**

1879 In his influential book *Progress and Poverty*, Henry George presents an argument for diminishing extremes of national wealth and poverty by means of a single tax (on land) that would capture the "unearned increment" of national development for public uses. **BA**

The Dumbbell Tenement, so called because of its shape, debuts. It is a form of multifamily housing widely built in New York until the end of the century and notorious for the poor living conditions (lack of light, air, and space) it imposed on its inhabitants. **HC**

The US Geological Survey is established to survey and classify all public domain lands. ED CE

1880   Ellen Collins applies the method of friendly rent collection (an approach to better housing developed years earlier by Octavia Hill in England) to her tenement houses on Water Street in Manhattan's 4th Ward, an immigrant slum. The idea was to provide decent low-rent housing at a modest profit while taking a sympathetic interest in the tenants' lives and teaching them good housekeeping practices. HC

1884   Pullman, IL, a model industrial town by George Pullman for his workers, is completed. HC

1885   The 10-story Home Insurance Building by William Le Baron Jenney is completed in Chicago. Made possible by the use of steel frames and the invention of the elevator, it is reputed to be the first skyscraper. UD

1888   In Richmond, VA, Frank Sprague establishes the first, successful city-wide electric streetcar system, foreshadowing the coming of the streetcar suburbs. UD

1889   Jane Addams begins her 20-year settlement-house career at Hull House on Halsted Street in Chicago. HC

1890   The year conventionally regarded as the beginning of the Art Nouveau period, an international style that flourished until WWI and that affected all arts including architecture (curvilinear ornamentation on building facades based on natural forms—leaves, flowers, vines). Louis Sullivan's designs for many buildings are representative of that style in America. UD

How the Other Half Lives, by Jacob Riis, is published and becomes a powerful stimulus to housing and neighborhood reform. BA HC

1891   The General Land Law Revision Act gives the President the power to create forest preserves by proclamation in the public domain. CE LA

1892   The Sierra Club is founded to promote the protection and preservation of the natural environment. John Muir, a Scottish-American naturalist and a major figure in the history of American environmentalism, is the leading founder. CE

1893   The World's Columbian Exposition in Chicago commemorating the 400th anniversary of the discovery of the New World is a source of the City Beautiful Movement and the urban planning profession. PP UD

219

KEY

BA	Books, Articles, Reports, Speeches	LA	Laws and Administrative Acts
CE	Conservation and the Environment	PP	History of the Planning Profession
ED	Economic Development	RP	Regional Planning
HC	Housing and Community Planning	UD	Urban Form and Design

Pathways in American Planning History

1896 In the first significant legal case concerning historic preservation, the *United States v. Gettysburg Electric Railway Co.*, the US Supreme Court rules that the acquisition of the national battlefield at Gettysburg serves a valid public purpose. CE LA

1897 Under the Forest Management Act, Congress authorizes some control by the Secretary of the Interior over the use and occupancy of forest preserves. CE LA

1898 Ebenezer Howards's famous Garden City diagrams appear in his book *Tomorrow: A Peaceful Path to Real Reform*. A source of the Garden City Movement, the book is reissued in 1902 as *Garden Cities of Tomorrow*. BA HC UD

Gifford Pinchot becomes the Chief Forester of the United States in the Department of Agriculture. From this position he publicizes the cause of forest conservation. CE

1901 The New York State Tenement House Law is the legislative basis for the revision of city codes that outlaw tenements such as the Dumbbell Tenement. Lawrence T. Veiller is the leading reformer. HC LA

The McMillan Commission is formed to update and complete L'Enfant's plan for Washington, DC. Among its accomplishments is a legal 160-foot height limit to preserve the city's skyline. UD

1902 The US Reclamation Act creates a fund from the sale of public land in the arid states in order to supply water to that region through the construction of water storage and irrigation works. RP CE LA ED

1903 Letchworth is constructed. It is the first English Garden City and a stimulus to the New Town movement in America (e.g. Greenbelt Towns, Columbia, MD). HC

President Theodore Roosevelt appoints a Public Lands Commission to propose rules for orderly land development and management in the west. RP CE LA

1906 The Antiquities Act of 1906 is the first law to institute federal protection for preserving archaeological sites. It provides for the designation as National Monuments areas already in the public domain that contain "historic landmarks, historic and prehistoric structures, and objects of historic or scientific interest." CE LA

1907 The founding of the New York Committee on the Congestion of Population, led by its secretary, Benjamin Marsh, fosters the movement to decentralize New York's dense population. HC

President Roosevelt establishes an Inland Waterway Commission to encourage multipurpose planning in waterway development: navigation, power, irrigation, flood control, water supply. CE LA

1908 State governors, federal officials, and leading scientists assemble for the White House Conservation Conference to deliberate about the conservation of natural resources. **CE**

1909 The first National Conference on City Planning is held in Washington, DC, bringing together the leaders of the housing and city planning movements. **PP**

Daniel H. Burnham's Plan of Chicago is published. It is the first metropolitan plan in the United States. Key figures in its creation include Frederick A. Delano, Charles Henry Wacker, and Charles Dyer Norton. **RP** **BA**

Possibly the first course in city planning to be offered in the United States is inaugurated in Harvard College's Landscape Architecture Department. It is taught by James Sturgis Pray. **PP**

1911 Frederick Winslow Taylor publishes *The Principles of Scientific Management*, a fountainhead of the efficiency movements in this country, including efficiency in city government. **BA**

1912 Walter D. Moody's *Wacker's Manual of the Plan of Chicago* is adopted as an eighth-grade textbook on city planning by the Chicago Board of Education. This is possibly the first formal instruction in city planning below the college level. **BA** **PP**

1913 A chair in civic design, the first of its kind in the United States, is created in the Department of Horticulture at the University of Illinois at Urbana–Champaign for Charles Mulford Robinson, one of the principal promoters of the World's Columbian Exposition. **PP** **UD**

1914 Flavel Shurtleff writes *Carrying Out the City Plan*, the first major textbook on city planning. **BA** **PP**

The Panama Canal is completed and opened to world commerce. **ED**

Harland Bartholomew, later the country's best-known planning consultant, becomes the first full-time employee of a city planning commission (Newark, NJ). **PP**

1915 Scottish biologist Patrick Geddes, known as the father of regional planning and the mentor of Lewis Mumford, publishes *Cities in Evolution*. **BA** **RP**

221

KEY

BA	Books, Articles, Reports, Speeches	**LA**	Laws and Administrative Acts
CE	Conservation and the Environment	**PP**	History of the Planning Profession
ED	Economic Development	**RP**	Regional Planning
HC	Housing and Community Planning	**UD**	Urban Form and Design

Pathways in American Planning History

1916   The Lake Forest (IL) Improve-ment Trust is established to build Market Square, reputed to be the first automobile-centered shopping district in the United States. **UD**

Nelson P. Lewis publishes *Planning of the Modern City*. **BA** **PP**

The nation's first comprehensive zoning resolution is adopted by the New York City Board of Estimates under the leadership of George McAneny and Edward M. Bassett, the latter known as the father of zoning. It soon spreads nationwide and influences urban design by setting legal limits to allowable land use. **HC** **LA** **UD**

The National Park Service is established with sole responsibility for conserving and preserving resources of special value. **CE** **LA**

1917   Frederick Law Olmsted Jr. becomes the first president of the newly founded American City Planning Institute, a forerunner of the American Institute of Planners and American Institute of Certified Planners. **PP**

1918   The US Housing Corporation and Emergency Fleet Corporation are established and operate at major shipping centers to provide housing for World War I workers. They influence later endeavors in public housing. **HC** **LA**

1919   Three early unifunctional regional authorities, the Metropolitan Sewerage Commission, the Metropolitan Water Board, and the Metropolitan Park Commission, are combined to form the Boston Metropolitan District Commission. **RP**

1920   A year conventionally regarded as the beginning of the Art Deco era, the period between the two world wars that left its mark on the look of many American cities (streamlining, angles, neon, etc.). Among its iconic structures are New York's Rockefeller Center, some Miami Beach hotels, and San Francisco's Golden Gate Bridge. **UD**

1921   New Orleans designates the Vieux Carre Commission, the first historic preservation commission in the United States. **CE**

1922   The Los Angeles County Regional Planning Commission, the first of its kind in the United States, is created. (Hugh Pomeroy is the head of the staff.) **PP** **RP**

The Regional Plan of New York is inaugurated under Thomas Adams. **RP**

In *Pennsylvania Coal Co. v. Mahon*, the first decision to hold that a land-use restriction constitutes a taking, the US Supreme Court notes "property may be regulated to a certain extent, [but] if regulation goes too far it will be recognized as a taking," thus acknowledging the principle of a regulatory taking. **LA**

The J.C. Nichols Country Club Plaza, a group of leased stores planned as a unit and managed under single ownership, is created in the vicinity of Kansas City, MO. **UD**

1923 Ground is broken for construction of Mariemont, OH, in suburban Cincinnati. Some of its features (short blocks, mixture of rental, and owner-occupied housing) foreshadow the contemporary New Urbanism movement. Mary Emery is its founder and benefactor; John Nolen is the planner. `HC`

1924 The US Department of Commerce under Secretary Herbert Hoover issues a Standard State Zoning Enabling Act. `LA`

Work begins on Sunnyside Gardens, a planned neighborhood designed by Clarence S. Stein and Henry Wright and built by the City Housing Corporation under Alexander Bing, in Queens, NY. `HC`

1925 The "Regional Plan" issue of *Survey Graphic* is published containing influential essays on regional planning by Lewis Mumford and other members of the Regional Planning Association of America (e.g., Catherine Bauer). `BA` `RP`

Cincinnati, OH, becomes the first major American city officially to endorse a comprehensive plan. `PP`

Ernest Burgess's Concentric Zone model of urban structure and land use is published in *The City*. `BA`

In April, the American City Planning Institute and the National Conference on City Planning publish Vol. 1, No. 1 of *City Planning*, the ancestor of the present-day *Journal of the American Planning Association*. `BA` `PP`

1926 In the *Village of Euclid v. Ambler Realty* the constitutionality of zoning is upheld by the US Supreme Court. (The case is argued by Alfred Bettman.) `LA`

1928 The US Department of Commerce under Secretary Herbert Hoover issues a Standard City Planning Enabling Act. `LA` `PP`

Robert Murray Haig's monograph "Major Economic Factors in Metropolitan Growth and Arrangement" is published in volume I of *The Regional Survey of New York and Its Environs*. It views land use as a function of accessibility. `BA` `RP`

Construction of Radburn, NJ, is begun. This planned community designed by Clarence S. Stein and Henry Wright, a forerunner of the New Deal's Greenbelt towns, is inspired by Howard's Garden City concept. `HC`

223

KEY

`BA`	Books, Articles, Reports, Speeches	`LA`	Laws and Administrative Acts
`CE`	Conservation and the Environment	`PP`	History of the Planning Profession
`ED`	Economic Development	`RP`	Regional Planning
`HC`	Housing and Community Planning	`UD`	Urban Form and Design

Pathways in American Planning History

Benton MacKaye, known as the father of the Appalachian Trail, publishes *The New Exploration*. In this book, he proposes plans for defending an earlier, more gentle form of New England urbanism from the spread of a rampant metropolitanism emanating mainly from Boston. BA CE

1929 Clarence Arthur Perry's monograph on the Neighborhood Unit is published in Volume VII of *The Regional Survey of New York and Its Environs*. BA HC

In the first instance of rural zoning, Wisconsin law authorizes county boards "to regulate, restrict, and determine the areas within which agriculture, forestry, and recreation may be conducted." LA

The stock market crash in October ushers in the Great Depression and fosters ideas of public planning on a national scale. ED

Architect Robert H.H. Hugman presents a plan to the civic authorities of San Antonio, TX, for the redevelopment of the San Antonio River, the seed of the city's famous Riverwalk (Paseo del Rio). UD

1931 The National Land Utilization Conference convenes in Chicago. Three hundred agricultural experts deliberate on rural recovery programs and natural resource conservation. CE ED

1932 The Federal Home Loan Bank System is established to shore up shaky home financing institutions. HC

The Reconstruction Finance Corporation is established at the outset of the Great Depression to revive economic activity by extending financial aid to failing financial, industrial, and agricultural institutions. ED

In *The Disappearing City*, Frank Lloyd Wright elevates America's penchant for urban sprawl into a design principal. He titles it Broadacre City. BA UD

1933 President Franklin Delano Roosevelt is inaugurated. The New Deal begins with a spate of counter-depression measures. ED

The Home Owners Loan Corporation is established to save homeowners facing loss through foreclosure. HC

The National Planning Board is established in the Department of the Interior to assist in the preparation of a comprehensive plan for public works under the direction of Frederick A. Delano, Charles Merriam, and Wesley Mitchell. Its last successor agency, the National Resources Planning Board, will be abolished in 1943. CE ED PP

The Civilian Conservation Corps is established to provide work for unemployed youth and to conserve the nation's natural resources. CE

The Federal Emergency Relief Administration is set up under the leadership of Harry Hopkins to organize relief work in urban and rural areas. LA

The Tennessee Valley Authority is created to provide for unified and multipurpose rehabilitation and redevelopment of the Tennessee Valley, America's most famous experiment in river-basin planning. Senator George Norris of Nebraska fathers the idea, and David Lilienthal is its most effective implementer. `CE` `ED` `RP` `LA`

The Agricultural Adjustment Act is passed to regulate agricultural trade practices, production, prices, and supply areas (and therefore land use) as a recovery measure. `ED`

1934 The American Society of Planning Officials, an organization for planners, planning commissioners, and planning-related public officials, is founded. `PP`

The National Housing Act establishes the Federal Savings and Loan Insurance Corporation for insuring savings deposits and the Federal Housing Administration for insuring individual home mortgages. `HC` `LA`

The Taylor Grazing Act is passed to regulate the use of the range in the West for conservation purposes. `CE` `RP` `LA`

The "Final Report" by the National Planning Board on its first year of existence includes a section entitled "A Plan for Planning" and an account of the "Historical Development of Planning in the United States." The latter views American planning history in the context of US political and economic history. `BA` `PP`

Robert Moses is appointed as the New York City Park Commissioner. From this post and in later years as the head of other city and state offices, he will build beaches, parkways, bridges, and tunnels that will radically change the face and form of the nation's largest city. His preference for highways over public transportation will influence a generation of engineers, architects, and urban planners who will spread his philosophy across the country. `UD`

1935 The Resettlement Administration is established under Rexford Guy Tugwell, a Roosevelt "braintruster," to carry out experiments in land reform and population resettlement. This agency built the three Greenbelt towns (Greenbelt, MD; Greendale, WI; and Greenhills, OH), forerunners of the present-day New Towns, Columbia, MD, and Reston, VA. `HC` `LA`

225

KEY

`BA` Books, Articles, Reports, Speeches	`LA` Laws and Administrative Acts
`CE` Conservation and the Environment	`PP` History of the Planning Profession
`ED` Economic Development	`RP` Regional Planning
`HC` Housing and Community Planning	`UD` Urban Form and Design

Pathways in American Planning History

The National Resources Committee publishes *Regional Factors in National Planning*, a landmark in regional planning literature. **BA** **CE** **RP**

With the Soil Conservation Act, Congress moves to make prevention of soil erosion a national responsibility. **CE** **LA**

The Historic Sites, Buildings and Antiquities Act, a predecessor of the National Historic Preservation Act, is passed. It requires the secretary of the interior to identify, acquire, and restore qualifying historic sites and properties and calls upon federal agencies to consider preservation needs in their programs and plans. **CE** **LA**

The Social Security Act is passed to create a safety net for the elderly. Frances Perkins, the secretary of labor and the first woman Cabinet member, is a principal promoter. **LA**

Congress authorizes the construction of the Grande Coulee Dam on the Columbia River in central Washington state. Finished in 1941, it is the largest concrete structure in the United States and the heart of the Columbia Basin Project, a regional plan comparable in its scope to the TVA. The project's purposes are irrigation, electric power generation, and flood control in the Pacific Northwest. **ED** **RP**

1936 The Hoover Dam on the Colorado River is completed. It creates and sustains population growth and industrial development in Nevada, California, and Arizona. **ED** **RP**

1937 *Our Cities: Their Role in the National Economy*, a landmark report by the Urbanism Committee of the National Resources Committee, is published. (Ladislas Segoe heads the research staff.) **BA** **PP**

The 1937 US Housing Act (Wagner-Steagall bill) sets the stage for future government aid by appropriating $500 million in loans for low-cost housing. It ties slum clearance to public housing . **HC** **LA**

The Farm Security Administration, successor to the Resettlement Administration, is established to administer many programs to aid the rural poor. **LA**

1938 The American Institute of Planners (formerly the American City Planning Institute), states as its purpose "...the planning of the unified development of urban communities and their environs, and of states, regions and the nation, as expressed through determination of the comprehensive arrangement of land uses and land occupancy and the regulation thereof." **PP**

1939 Homer Hoyt's influential sector theory of urban growth appears in his monograph *The Structure and Growth of Residential Neighborhoods in American Cities*. **BA** **HC**

1941 *Local Planning Administration* by Ladislas Segoe, first of the Green Book series, appears. **BA** **PP**

Robert Walker's *Planning Function in Urban Government* is published. The author advocated making the planning staff an arm of the city government rather than of a citizens planning board or commission. **BA** **PP**

1944 Under the Bretton Woods (N.H.) Agreement, the United States and allies meet to establish the International Bank for Reconstruction and Development (also known as the World Bank). ED

The Serviceman's Readjustment Act (the GI bill) guarantees loans for homes to veterans under favorable terms, thereby accelerating the growth of suburbs. HC LA

1947 The Housing and Home Financing Agency (the predecessor to HUD) is created to coordinate the federal government's various housing programs. HC LA

Construction of Park Forest, IL, and Levittown, NY, is begun. Park Forest is "the first post-World War II suburb to include a shopping center." HC

US Secretary of State George C. Marshall uses his Harvard College commencement address to propose the Marshall Plan for the reconstruction of postwar Europe. ED RP

Communitas is published. This classic text by Paul and Percival Goodman explores three community paradigms and their possible physical-spatial forms. BA HC UD

1949 The 1949 Housing Act (the Wagner-Ellender-Taft bill), the first US comprehensive housing legislation, is aimed to construct about 800,000 units. It also inaugurates the urban redevelopment program. HC LA

The National Trust for Historic Preservation is created and chartered by Congress. CE

1950 Pittsburgh is the first major American city to demolish and redesign a large part of its downtown. The finished project, comprising parks, office buildings, and a sports arena, is named The Golden Triangle. UD

Northgate Mall opens near Seattle, WA. It is reputed to be the first shopping center to be called a "mall," a name which denotes a string of stores lining both sides of a pedestrian lane. UD

1954 In *Berman v. Parker*, the US Supreme Court upholds right of the Washington, DC, Redevelopment Land Agency to condemn properties that are unsightly, though nondeteriorated, if required to achieve the objectives of a duly established area redevelopment plan. LA CE

In *Brown v. Board of Education* (Topeka, KS), the US Supreme Court upholds school integration. LA

KEY

BA	Books, Articles, Reports, Speeches	LA	Laws and Administrative Acts
CE	Conservation and the Environment	PP	History of the Planning Profession
ED	Economic Development	RP	Regional Planning
HC	Housing and Community Planning	UD	Urban Form and Design

Pathways in American Planning History

The Housing Act of 1954 stresses slum prevention and urban renewal rather than slum clearance and urban redevelopment as in the 1949 Housing Act. It also stimulates general planning for cities with a population under 25,000 by providing funds under Section 701 of the act, which is later extended by legislative amendments to foster statewide, interstate, and substate regional planning. **PP** **RP** **LA** **HC**

The Council of Government movement begins in the Detroit area with the formation of a Supervisors' Inter-County Committee, composed of representatives from each county in southeastern Michigan for the purpose of confronting areawide problems. This movement soon spreads nationwide. **RP**

1956 Congress passes the multibillion-dollar Federal Aid Highway Act to create an interstate highway system linking all state capitals and most cities with a population of 50,000 or more. **LA** **ED**

Southdale Center Mall, the first fully covered shopping center with climate control is built in Edina, MN, by Victor Gruen. **UD**

Convoked by architect José Luis Sert, some of America's foremost architects, city planners, social scientists, and public intellectuals gather at a conference at Harvard's Graduate School of Design to define urban design. **UD**

1957 F. Stuart Chapin Jr. publishes *Urban Land Use Planning*, the first textbook on the subject. **BA**

Education for Planning, a seminal, book-length inquiry by Harvey S. Perloff into the "appropriate intellectual, practical and 'philosophical' basis for the education of city and regional planners...," is published. **PP** **BA**

1958 The Seagram Building by Ludwig Mies van der Rohe is erected on New York's Park Avenue. Considered a masterpiece of the international glass-box style, it is widely imitated and influences the appearance of many American cities. **UD**

1959 "A Multiple Land Use Classification System" by Albert Guttenberg appears in *The Journal of the American Institute of Planners*. It advances the understanding of land use, a key planning concept by defining and classifying its major dimensions. **BA**

Congress establishes the Advisory Commission on Intergovernmental Relations with members drawn from various branches of government. It serves primarily as a research agency and think tank in the area of intergovernmental relations. **LA** **RP**

The St. Lawrence Seaway is completed. This joint US-Canada project creates, in effect, a fourth North American seacoast, opening the American heartland to sea-going vessels. **ED** **RP**

The construction of Victor Gruen's Burdick Mall in Kalamazoo, MI, brings the idea of the mall downtown to serve as a means of attracting new life to a declining central city. **UD**

1960 In *The Image of the City* author Kevin Lynch identifies the basic elements of a city's "imageability" (paths, edges, nodes, etc.). It represents a new and growing emphasis by the design professions on the way city dwellers perceive and use their urban environment. **BA** **UD**

The Philadelphia Comprehensive Plan for 1980 is published. It proposes a form that includes a hierarchy of roads, centers, and other people-serving community facilities ascending from the neighborhood to the metropolitan level. **UD** **BA**

1961 The National Capital Planning Commission publishes *The Nations Capital: A Plan for the Year 2000,* advocating a model for long-term regional growth. The metropolitan form it proposes is sectoral and directional: alternate corridors of growth and conservation. **UD** **BA**

In *The Death and Life of Great American Cities,* Jane Jacobs includes a critique of planners. Among other criticisms, she faults Ebenezer Howard's Garden City concept and the modernist Radiant City ("towers-in-a-park") idea for confusing urban design with suburban design. **BA** **PP** **UD**

Richard Hedman and Frederick H. Bair Jr. publish *And On the Eighth Day,* a book of cartoons poking fun at the planning profession by two of its own. **BA** **PP**

Hawaii becomes the first state to institute statewide zoning. **LA**

A Delaware River Basin Commission representing the states of New York, New Jersey, and Pennsylvania is created to foster joint management of the river's water resources. **RP**

1962 The urban growth simulation model emerges in the Penn-Jersey Transportation Study. **RP**

"A Choice Theory of Planning," a seminal article in the *Journal of American Institute of Planners* by Paul Davidoff and Thomas Reiner, lays the basis for an advocacy planning concept. **BA**

Rachel Carson's book *Silent Spring* is published and wakes the nation to the deleterious effects of pesticides on animal, plant, and human life. **BA** **CE**

The Fairfax County Board of Supervisors establishes Virginia's first residential planned community zone, clearing the way for the creation of Reston, a full-scale, self-contained New Town 18 miles from Washington, DC. **HC**

229

KEY

BA	Books, Articles, Reports, Speeches	**LA**	Laws and Administrative Acts
CE	Conservation and the Environment	**PP**	History of the Planning Profession
ED	Economic Development	**RP**	Regional Planning
HC	Housing and Community Planning	**UD**	Urban Form and Design

Pathways in American Planning History

Lewis Mumford, an internationally renowned social critic and the American planning professions' leading intellectual, wins the National Book Award for his *The City in History*. **BA**

1963 Construction of Columbia, MD, a New Town, is begun at a site about halfway between Washington, DC, and Baltimore, MD. It will feature some class integration and the neighborhood principle. **HC**

1964 T.J. Kent Jr. publishes *The Urban General Plan*, which details the purpose, scope, and use of the urban general, or comprehensive, plan. **BA** **PP**

The Civil Rights Act outlaws discrimination based on race, creed, and national origin in places of public accommodation. **LA**

The Federal Bulldozer by Martin Anderson indicts the then current urban renewal program as counterproductive to its professed aims of increased low- and middle-income housing supply. With Herbert J. Gans's *The Urban Villagers* (1962), a study of the consequences of urban renewal for community life in a Boston West End Italian-American community, it contributes to a change in urban policy. **BA** **HC**

In a commencement speech at the University of Michigan, President Lyndon Johnson declares war on poverty and asks the assembled to join the battle for a Great Society (equality for all, more housing, better schools and neighborhoods, improved transportation, a poison-free environment). His vision is metropolitan-wide embracing city, suburbs, and countryside. **ED** **HC** **BA**

1965 A White House Conference on Natural Beauty in America is convened on May 24, owing much to the interest and advocacy of the First Lady, Lady Bird Johnson. **CE**

Housing and urban policy achieve cabinet status when the Housing and Home Finance Agency is succeeded by the Department of Housing and Urban Development. Robert Weaver becomes HUD's first secretary and the nation's first African-American Cabinet member. **HC** **LA**

Congress passes the Water Resources Management Act authorizing federal multi-state river basin commissions. **LA** **RP**

The Public Work and Economic Development Act is passed by Congress. It establishes the Economic Development Administration to extend coordinated, multifaceted aid to lagging regions to foster their redevelopment **ED** **LA** **RP**

The Appalachian Regional Planning Act establishes a region comprising all of West Virginia and parts of 12 other states plus a planning commission with the power to frame plans and allocate resources. **ED** **LA** **RP**

John Reps publishes *The Making of Urban America*, the first comprehensive history of American urban planning beginning with colonial times. **BA**

1966 The Demonstration Cities and Metropolitan Development Act launches the "model cities" program, an interdisciplinary attack on urban blight and poverty. It is a centerpiece of President Lyndon Johnson's "Great Society" program. **HC** **LA**

230

With Heritage So Rich, a seminal historic preservation book, is published by the US Conference of Mayors. **CE** **BA**

The National Historic Preservation Act is passed. It establishes the National Register of Historic Places and provides, through its Section 106, for the protection of preservation-worthy sites and properties threatened by federal activities. This act also creates the national Advisory Council on Historic Preservation and directs that each state appoint a State Historic Preservation Officer. **CE** **LA**

Section 4(f) of the Department of Transportation Act provides protection to parkland, wildlife refuges, and other preservation-worthy resources in building national roads. **CE** **LA**

1967   The (Louis B.) Wetmore Amendment drops the final phrase in the 1938 American Institute of Planners' declaration of purpose, which ties it to the comprehensive arrangement and regulation of land use. The effect is to broaden the scope and membership of the profession by including social planners as well as physical planners. **PP**

The planning profession marks its 50th anniversary with a celebratory conference in Washington, DC. For the occasion, Russell Van Nest Black prepares a monograph entitled *Planning and the Planning Profession 1917–1967*. **PP** **BA**

In his book *Design of Cities*, Edmund N. Bacon explains his philosophy of design based on his study of great urban design achievements of the past and shows how it applies to the revived design of mid-20th-century Philadelphia. **BA** **UD**

1968   To implement the Intergovernmental Relations Act of 1968, the Office of Management and Budget issues Circular A-95 requiring state and substate regional clearinghouses to review and comment on federally assisted projects to facilitate coordination among the three levels of government. **LA** **RP**

1969   Reflecting the rising tide of environmentalism, Ian McHarg, in his book, *Design with Nature*, presents a method for tying urban land use planning to underlying natural features (soil type, contour, etc.). **BA** **UD**

231

KEY ──

BA Books, Articles, Reports, Speeches	**LA** Laws and Administrative Acts
CE Conservation and the Environment	**PP** History of the Planning Profession
ED Economic Development	**RP** Regional Planning
HC Housing and Community Planning	**UD** Urban Form and Design

Pathways in American Planning History

The National Environmental Policy Act requires an "environmental impact statement" for every federal or federally-aided state or local major action that might significantly harm the environment. **CE** **LA**

Mel Scott publishes *American City Planning Since 1890*, which is reissued in 1995 by the American Planning Association. **BA** **PP**

1970 The First Earth Day is celebrated on January 1. **CE**

The Federal Environmental Protection Agency is established to administer the main provisions of the 1970 Clean Air Act. **CE** **LA** **RP**

The Miami Valley (Ohio) Regional Planning Commission Housing Plan is adopted, the first such plan in the nation to allocate low- and moderate-income housing on a "fair share" basis. **HC** **RP**

Arcosanti, an experimental community, is founded by Italian architect Paolo Soleri in the Arizona desert 70 miles north of metropolitan Phoenix. **UD**

The Uses of Disorder, by historian and social critic Richard Sennett, advocates the lifting of all current codes, statutes ordinances, and other city legal constraints as a means of arriving at a more just and viable overall physical and social urban form. **BA** **UD**

1971 The American Institute of Planners adopts a Code of Ethics for professional planners. **PP**

Learning from Las Vegas, the product of a study by Robert Venturi, Denise Scott Brown, and Steven Izenour, finds aesthetic order and value in America's commercial strips. **BA** **UD**

1972 The Coastal Zone Management Act is adopted. **CE** **RP** **LA**

General revenue sharing is inaugurated under the US State and Local Fiscal Assistance Act. **LA**

In *Golden v. Planning Board of Ramapo*, the New York high court allows the use of performance criteria as a means of slowing community growth. **LA**

Demolition of St. Louis' notorious Pruitt-Igoe low-income housing project symbolizes a nationwide move away from massive, isolating, high-rise structures to a more humane form of public housing architecture: low-rise, less isolated, dispersed. **HC**

1973 The Endangered Species Act authorizes federal assistance to state and local jurisdictions to establish conservation programs for endangered plant and animal species. **CE** **LA**

1974 The Housing and Community Development Act replaces the categorical grant with the block grant as the principal form of federal aid for local community development. **LA** **HC**

1975 The Cleveland Policy Plan Report shifts the emphasis from traditional land-use planning to advocacy planning. **BA** **PP**

1976 The Historic Preservation Fund is established. CE

Faneuil Hall in Boston, an early festival marketplace on the site of the old Quincy Market, stimulates like projects in many of the nation's obsolete central business districts. UD

Water Tower Place opens on Michigan Avenue in Chicago. It is the nation's first vertical mall. UD

1977 The first exam for American Institute of Planners membership is conducted. PP

A Pattern Language by Christopher Alexander, Sara Ishikawa, Murray Silverstein, and others introduces an influential system of rules for structuring the built environment from the level of the region to the individual building. BA

Postmodernism is widely popularized by the publication of Charles Jencks' book *The Language of Postmodern Architecture*. The style is defined by its difference from modernism: it is eclectic rather than monolithic, ironic rather than idealistic, ornamental rather than functional. BA UD

1978 In *Penn Central Transportation Co. v. City of New York*, the US Supreme Court upholds New York City's Landmark Preservation Law as applied to Grand Central Terminal. In this landmark decision, the Court finds that barring some development of air rights is not a taking when the interior of the property could be put to lucrative use. LA CE

The American Institute of Planners and the American Society of Planning Officials merge to become the American Planning Association. PP

1979 John Reps becomes the second member of the planning profession (Lewis Mumford was the first) to win the National Book Award, with his *Cities of the American West*. BA PP

1980 The Reagan Revolution begins, and the planning profession is challenged to adapt to a new (counter-New Deal) policy environment: reduced federal domestic spending, privatization, deregulation, and a phase-out of some earlier planning aids (e.g., sewer grants) and planning programs (e.g., Title V Regions). ED

233

KEY

BA	Books, Articles, Reports, Speeches	LA	Laws and Administrative Acts
CE	Conservation and the Environment	PP	History of the Planning Profession
ED	Economic Development	RP	Regional Planning
HC	Housing and Community Planning	UD	Urban Form and Design

Pathways in American Planning History

The Superfund Bill (Comprehensive Response, Compensation and Liability Act) is passed by Congress, creating a liability for persons discharging hazardous waste into the environment. By taxing polluting industries, a trust fund is established for the cleanup of polluted sites in cases where individual responsibility is not ascertainable. **CE** **LA**

The Association of Collegiate Schools of Planning (ACSP) is established to represent the academic branch of the planning profession. **PP**

1981 The ACSP issues Volume 1, Number 1 of *The Journal of Education and Planning Research*. **BA** **PP**

1982 The Portland (Oregon) Public Services Building by Michael Graves is completed. It is considered by some to be the first postmodern building in the United States. **UD**

1983 In a case focusing on Mt. Laurel, NJ, the New Jersey Supreme Court rules that all 567 municipalities in the state must build their "fair share" of affordable housing, a precedent-setting blow against racial segregation. **LA** **HC** **RP**

1984 Construction begins on Seaside, FL, one of the earliest examples of New Urbanism (designed by Andrés Duany and Elizabeth Plater-Zyberk). Unlike most earlier planned communities, New Urbanism emphasizes urban features—compactness, walkability, mixed use—and promotes a nostalgic architectural style reminiscent of the traditional urban neighborhood. The movement has links to the anti-sprawl, smart growth movement. **HC**

1986 The First National Conference on American Planning History is convened in Columbus, OH, and leads to the founding of the Society for American City and Regional Planning History the following year. **PP**

1987 In *First English Evangelical Lutheran Church v. County of Los Angeles*, the US Supreme Court finds that even a temporary taking requires compensation. In *Nollan v. California Coastal Commission*, it finds that land-use restrictions, to be valid, must be tied directly to a specific public purpose. **LA**

1989 The Planning Accreditation Board is recognized by the Washington-based Council on Post Secondary Education to be the sole accrediting agency in the field of professional planning education. **PP**

1991 Passage of the Intermodal Surface Transportation Efficiency Act includes provisions for a National Scenic Byways Program and for transportation enhancements, each of which includes a historic preservation component. **CE** **LA**

1992 In *Lucas v. South Carolina Coastal Council*, the US Supreme Court limits local and state governments' ability to restrict private property without compensation. **LA**

1993 The Enterprise Zone/Empowerment Community proposal is signed into law. It aims tax incentives, wage tax credits, special deductions, and low-interest financing to a limited number of impoverished urban and rural communities to jumpstart their economic and social recovery. **ED**

1994   In *Dolan v. City of Tigard*, the US Supreme Court rules that a jurisdiction must show that there is a "rough proportionality" between the adverse impacts of a proposed development and the exactions it wishes to impose on the developer. **LA**

The North American Free Trade Agreement between the United States, Canada, and Mexico begins on Jan. 1 with the purpose of fostering trade and investment among the three nations by removing or lowering non-tariff as well as tariff barriers. **ED** **LA** **RP**

1999   The American Institute of Certified Planners inaugurates a College of Fellows to recognize distinguished individual contributions by longer-term AICP members. **PP**

2000   President Clinton creates eight new national monuments in five western states: Canyons of the Ancients (CO); Cascade-Siskiyou (OR); Hanford Reach (WA); Ironwood Forest, Grand Canyon-Parashant, Agua Fria (AZ); Grand Sequoia, California Coastal (CA). He also expands one existing national monument in California (Pinnacles). **CE**

235

Source: Albert Guttenberg, FAICP. © Albert Guttenberg. Reprinted with permission.

KEY

BA Books, Articles, Reports, Speeches	**LA** Laws and Administrative Acts
CE Conservation and the Environment	**PP** History of the Planning Profession
ED Economic Development	**RP** Regional Planning
HC Housing and Community Planning	**UD** Urban Form and Design

Top Ranked Buildings

The following rankings provide a glimpse into the minds of architects, architecture critics, and the general public as they reflected at various points in history on the question of what are the best buildings.

1885 Poll by American Architect and Building News

1. Trinity Church
   Boston, MA, 1877
   H.H. Richardson

2. US Capitol
   Washington, DC, 1793–1865
   William Thornton, Benjamin Henry
     Latrobe, Charles Bulfinch, Thomas
     Ustick Walter

3. Vanderbilt House
   New York, NY, 1883
   Richard Morris Hunt

4. Trinity Church
   New York, NY, 1846
   Richard Upjohn

5. Jefferson Market Courthouse
   New York, NY
   Frederick Withers & Calvert Vaux,
     1877

6. Connecticut State Capitol
   Hartford, CT, 1879
   Richard Upjohn

7. Albany City Hall
   Albany, NY, 1883
   H.H. Richardson

8. Sever Hall, Harvard University
   Cambridge, MA, 1880
   H.H. Richardson

9. New York State Capitol
   Albany, NY, 1886
   H.H. Richardson

10. Town Hall
    North Easton, MA, 1881
    H.H. Richardson

Source: American Architect and Building News

100 Years of Signature Buildings, 1857–1956

In 1956 *Architectural Record* asked a panel of 50 architects and scholars to name "about 20 buildings in existence today whose overall significance, in your opinion, has been most important in the stage-by-stage development of our architecture."

1. Wainwright Building
   St. Louis, MO, 1891
   Louis Sullivan

1. Carson Pirie Scott
   Chicago, IL, 1904
   Louis Sullivan

2. Rockefeller Center
   New York, NY, 1940
   Reinhard & Hofmeister; Corbett,
     Harrison & MacMurray; Hood &
     Fouilhoux

3. Lever House
   New York, NY, 1952
   Skidmore, Owings & Merrill

4. Trinity Church
   Boston, MA, 1877
   H.H. Richardson

5. PSFS Building
   Philadelphia, PA, 1931
   Howe & Lescaze

6. General Motors Technical Center
   Warren, MI, 1957
   Saarinen, Saarinen & Associates

7. Lake Shore Apartments
   Chicago, IL, 1951
   Ludwig Mies van der Rohe

8. S.C. Johnson & Son Administration
   Building
   Racine, WI, 1936
   Frank Lloyd Wright

9. Daily News Building
   New York, NY, 1930
   Howells & Hood

9. Monadnock Block
   Chicago, IL, 1981
   Burnham & Root

9. TVA Norris Dam & Powerhouse
   Clinch River, Anderson County, TN, 1936
   Roland Wank

10. Boston Public Library
    Boston, MA, 1989
    McKim, Mead and White

10. State Fair Livestock Pavilion
    (now Dorton Arena)
    Raleigh, NC, 1952
    Matthew Nowicki and William Dietrick

11. First Church of Christ, Science
    Berkeley, CA, 1910
    Bernard Maybeck

12. Crow Island School
    Winnetka, IL, 1940
    Saarinen & Saarinen with Perkins,
        Wheeler & Will

12. Manufacturers Trust Building
    New York, NY, 1954
    Skidmore, Owings & Merrill

12. Woolworth Building
    New York, NY, 1913
    Cass Gilbert

13. Nebraska State Capitol
    Lincoln, NE, 1926
    Bertram Grosvenor Goodhue

13. Unity Temple
    Oak Park, IL, 1908
    Frank Lloyd Wright

14. United Nations Secretariat
    New York, NY, 1950
    W.K. Harrison & Consultants

14. S.C. Johnson & Son Laboratory Building
    Racine, WI, 1949
    Frank Lloyd Wright

15. Kresge Auditorium, Massachusetts Institute
        of Technology
    Cambridge, MA, 1955
    Eero Saarinen and Associates

15. Lincoln Memorial
    Washington, DC, 1917
    Henry Bacon

16. Equitable Savings and Loan Association
        Building
    Portland, OR, 1948
    Pietro Belluschi

17. Allegheny County Buildings
    Pittsburgh, PA, 1887
    H.H. Richardson

17. Cranbrook School
    Bloomfield Hills, MI, 1930
    Eliel Saarinen

17. Minerals & Metals Research Building,
        Illinois Institute of Technology
    Chicago, IL, 1943
    Ludwig Mies van der Rohe

17. University Club
    New York, NY, 1900
    McKim, Mead and White

18. Alcoa Building
    Pittsburgh, PA, 1952
    Harrison & Abramovitz

237

Top Ranked Buildings

19. Museum of Modern Art
New York, NY, 1939
Philip L. Goodwin and Edward Durrell
Stone

20. 100 Memorial Drive Apartments
Cambridge, MA, 1950
Kennedy, Koch, DeMars, Rapson &
Brown

20. Dodge Truck Plant
Detroit, MI, 1938
Albert Kahn Associated Architects
and Engineers

20. Central Lutheran Church
Portland, OR, 1951
Pietro Belluschi

20. Experimental School
Los Angeles, CA, 1935
Richard Neutra (Germany/US)

20. Pennsylvania Station
New York, NY, 1906
McKim, Mead and White

JURY

Max Abramovitz
James S. Ackerman
Wayne Andrews
Leopold Arnaud
Turpin C. Bannister
Pietro Belluschi
Marcel Breuer
Gordon Bunshaft
John E. Burchard
Alan Burnham
Leslie Cheek Jr.
Kenneth J. Conant

George Bain Cummings
John Ekin Dinwiddle
Donald D. Egbert
Walter Gropius (Germany/US)
Talbot F. Hamlin
Henry-Russell Hitchcock
Arthur C. Holden
Joseph Hudnut
Philip Johnson
Edgar Kaufman
George Fred Keck
Morris Ketchum Jr.
A. Lawrence Kocker
Ernest J. Kump
Maurice Lavanoux
Edwin Bateman Morris Jr.
Hugh Morrison
Richard Neutra (Germany/US)
Eliot Noyes
G. Holmes Perkins
Antonin Raymond
Earl H. Reed
Henry Hope Reed
John W. Root
Paul Rudolph
Eero Saarinen
Paul Schweikher
Vincent Scully
G.E. Kidder Smith
Edward Steese
Hugh Asher Stubbins
Walter Taylor
William Wurster
Minori Yamaski

The remaining panel of 50 architects and scholars returned anonymous ballots.

Source: Architectural Record, *June 1956–May 1957*

100 Years of Signature Houses, 1857–1956

As part of the 1956 "100 Years of Signature Buildings" series, *Architectural Record* ranked houses separate from other buildings.

1. Fallingwater
   Mill Run, PA, 1936
   Frank Lloyd Wright

1. Robie House
   Chicago, IL, 1909
   Frank Lloyd Wright

2. Taliesin West
   Scottsdale, AZ, 1937
   Frank Lloyd Wright

4. Henry Villard Houses
   New York, NY, 1885
   McKim, Mead and White

5. Avery Coonley House
   Riverside, IL, 1908
   Frank Lloyd Wright

5. William Watts Sherman House
   Newport, RI, 1876
   H.H. Richardson

6. Gamble House
   Pasadena, CA, 1908
   Greene and Greene

7. Glass House
   New Caanan, CT, 1950
   Philip Johnson

7. Ward Willitts House
   Highland Park, IL, 1902
   Frank Lloyd Wright

8. Walker Guest House
   Sanibel Island, FL, 1953
   Paul Rudolph

9. Ellen Scripps House
   La Jolla, CA, 1917
   Irving Gill

9. Lovell House
   Los Angeles, CA, 1929
   Richard Neutra (Germany/US)

9. Weston Havens House
   Berkeley, CA, 1940
   Harwell Hamilton Harris

10. Farnsworth House
    Plano, IL, 1951
    Ludwig Mies van der Rohe
    (Germany/US)

JURY

Same as the 100 Years of Signature Buildings poll

Source: Architectural Record, *June 1956–May 1957*

239

Top Ranked Buildings

Top Works of Architecture, 1891–1991

The following ranking resulted from a readers' poll conducted by *Architectural Record* in 1991 regarding the best buildings worldwide of the past century.

1. Fallingwater
   Mill Run, PA, 1936
   Frank Lloyd Wright

2. Villa Savoye
   Poissy, France, 1931
   Le Corbusier (Switzerland/France)

3. Barcelona Pavilion
   Barcelona, Spain, 1929
   Ludwig Mies van der Rohe
   (Germany/US)

4. Notre Dame du Haut
   Ronchamp, France, 1955
   Le Corbusier (Switzerland/France)

5. Kimbell Art Museum
   Fort Worth, TX, 1972
   Louis I. Kahn

6. Robie House
   Chicago, IL, 1909
   Frank Lloyd Wright

7. Seagram Building
   New York, NY, 1954–58
   Ludwig Mies van der Rohe

8. Chrysler Building
   New York, NY, 1930
   William Van Alen

9. Rockefeller Center
   New York, NY, 1940
   Reinhard & Hofmeister; Corbett,
   Harrison & MacMurray; Hood &
   Fouilhoux

10. Lever House
    New York, NY, 1952
    Skidmore, Owings & Merrill

11. Wainwright Building
    St. Louis, MO, 1891
    Louis Sullivan

12. Pompidou Center
    Paris, France, 1977
    Piano & Rogers (Italy/UK)

13. S.C. Johnson & Son Administration
    Building
    Racine, WI, 1939
    Frank Lloyd Wright

14. Unity Temple
    Oak Park, IL, 1908
    Frank Lloyd Wright

15. Bauhaus
    Dessau, Germany, 1926
    Walter Gropius (Germany/US)

16. Carson Pirie Scott
    Chicago, IL, 1904
    Louis Sullivan

17. Dulles International Airport, Terminal
    Building
    Chantilly, VA, 1962
    Eero Saarinen & Associates

18. Sydney Opera House
    Sydney, Australia, 1973
    Jørn Utzon (Denmark)

19. Salk Institute
    La Jolla, CA, 1966
    Louis I. Kahn

19. Glasgow School of Art
    Glasgow, Scotland, UK, 1909
    Charles Rennie Mackintosh (UK)

Source: Architectural Record, *July 1991*

2000, Top 10 Buildings of the Century

At the 2000 AIA convention, attendees were asked to vote for their top 10 favorite structures of the century.

1. Fallingwater
   Mill Run, PA, 1936
   Frank Lloyd Wright

2. Chrysler Building
   New York, NY, 1930
   William Van Alen

3. Seagram Building
   New York, NY, 1958
   Ludwig Mies van der Rohe
      (Germany/US)

4. Thorncrown Chapel
   Eureka, AR, 1980
   E. Fay Jones

5. Dulles International Airport,
      Terminal Building
   Chantilly, VA, 1962
   Eero Saarinen & Associates

6. Salk Institute
   La Jolla, CA, 1966
   Louis I. Kahn

7. Vietnam Veterans Memorial
   Washington, DC, 1982
   Maya Lin

8. Robie House
   Chicago, IL, 1909
   Frank Lloyd Wright

9. East Wing, National Gallery
   Washington, DC, 1978
   I.M. Pei & Partners

10. S.C. Johnson & Son Administration
      Building
   Racine, WI, 1939
   Frank Lloyd Wright

Source: American Institute of Architects

2001, Architecture Critics' Top Rated Buildings

US architecture critics rated the top US buildings in a 2001 study conducted by Columbia University's National Arts Journalism Program.

1. Brooklyn Bridge
   New York, NY, 1883
   John Augustus Roebling

2. Grand Central Terminal
   New York, NY, 1913
   Warren & Wetmore; Reed & Stem

3. Chrysler Building
   New York, NY, 1930
   William Van Alen

4. Monticello
   Charlottesville, VA, 1769–84; 1796–1809
   Thomas Jefferson

5. University of Virginia
   Charlottesville, VA, 1826
   Thomas Jefferson

6. Robie House
   Chicago, IL, 1909
   Frank Lloyd Wright

7. Carson Pirie Scott Building
   Chicago, IL, 1904
   Louis Sullivan

8. Empire State Building
   New York, NY, 1931
   Shreve, Lamb & Harmon

Top Ranked Buildings

9. S.C. Johnson & Son Administration
   Building
   Racine, WI, 1939
   Frank Lloyd Wright

10. Unity Temple
    Oak Park, IL, 1908
    Frank Lloyd Wright

Source: The Architecture Critic, *National Arts Journalism Program, Columbia University*

2002, Great Architectural Works of the 21st Century

In 2002, *USA Weekend* magazine asked a panel of jurors to determine the great architectural works of the 21st century (listed alphabetically).

3Com Midwest Headquarters
Rolling Meadows, IL, 1999
Valerio Dewalt Train Associates

Quadracci Pavilion, Milwaukee Art Museum
Milwaukee, WI, 2001
Santiago Calatrava (Spain) with Kahler
   Slater Architects

Rose Center for Earth and Space,
   American Museum of Natural History
New York, NY, 2000
Polshek Partnership Architects

Sandra Day O'Connor US Courthouse
Phoenix, AZ, 2001
Richard Meier & Partners Architects

Westside Light Rail Transit System
Portland, OR, 1998
Zimmer Gunsul Frasca Partnership

JURY
William Gilchrist, City of Birmingham, AL
Carol Ross Barney, Ross Barney + Jankowski
   Architects
Marilyn Taylor, Skidmore, Owings and Merrill
Thomas Ventulett, Thompson, Ventulett,
   Stainback and Associates
Sarah Susanka, residential architect and author

Source: USA Weekend, *Sept. 1, 2002*

2006, Most Important Houses in America

A panel of architects, builders, and home enthusiasts convened by *Fine Homebuilding* in 2006 selected the following 25 buildings as the most important houses in America (listed chronologically).

Ashley House
Deerfield, MA, 1730
John Wells

Monticello
Charlottesville, VA, 1768–79, 1793–1809
Thomas Jefferson

Isaac Small House
Truro, MA, c. 1780
Royal Barry Willis

Roseland Cottage
Woodstock, CT, 1848
Joseph Collin Wells

Watts Sherman House
Newport, RI, 1875
H.H. Richardson

W.G. Low House
Bristol, RI, 1887
McKim, Mead and White

Biltmore
Ashville, NC, 1889
Richard Morris Hunt

Gamble House
Pasadena, CA, 1908
Greene and Greene

Sears Kit House
Nationwide, 1908–1937
Sears, Roebuck and Company

Schindler House
West Hollywood, CA, 1921
Rudolph Schindler (Austria/US)

Wharton Esherick House and Studio
Paoli, PA, 1926–1966
Wharton Esherick

Gregory Farmhouse
Scotts Valley, CA, 1928
William Wurster

Cyrus McCormick Jr. House
Santa Fe, NM, 1931
John Gaw Meem

Jacobs I House
Madison, WI, 1936
Frank Lloyd Wright

Wallen II House
Kensington, CA, 1937
Bernard Maybeck

Fallingwater
Mill Run, PA, 1938
Frank Lloyd Wright

Levittown Ranch
Levittown, NY, 1949
Levitt and Sons

Farnsworth House
Plano, IL, 1951
Ludwig Mies van der Rohe (Germany/US)

Hedgerow Houses
Sea Ranch, CA, 1966
Joseph Esherick

Integral Urban House
Berkeley, CA, 1973
Sim van der Ryn

Unit One/Balcomb House
Santa Fe, NM, 1976
Walter Lumpkin

Seaside
Seaside, FL, 1986
Duany Plater-Zyberk & Company

Wright Guest House
The Highlands, WA, 1987
James Cutler Architects

Harris (Butterfly) House
Hale County, AL, 1997
Rural Studio

McMansions
Nationwide, 1980s–present
Various architects, builders, and developers

Source: Fine Homebuilding, *Spring/Summer 2006*

Top Ranked Buildings

America's Favorite Architecture

The American Institute of Architects, in conjunction with its 150th anniversary, conducted a public poll of the 150 best works of architecture. The full list is available at *www.aia150.org.*

1. Empire State Building
   New York, NY, 1931
   Shreve, Lamb & Harmon

2. White House
   Washington, DC, 1800
   James Hoban

3. Washington National Cathedral
   Washington, DC, 1907–1990
   George Frederick Bodley (UK),
   Henry Vaughan and Philip Frohman

4. Thomas Jefferson Memorial
   Washington DC, 1943
   John Russell Pope

5. Golden Gate Bridge
   San Francisco, CA, 1937
   Irving F. Morrow and Gertrude C.
   Morrow

6. US Capitol
   Washington, DC, 1793–1865
   William Thornton, Benjamin Henry
   Latrobe, Charles Bulfinch, Thomas
   Ustick Walter

7. Lincoln Memorial
   Washington, DC, 1917
   Henry Bacon

8. Biltmore
   Asheville, NC, 1889
   Richard Morris Hunt

9. Chrysler Building
   New York, NY, 1930
   William Van Alen

10. Vietnam Veterans Memorial
    Washington, DC, 1982
    Maya Lin

Source: American Institute of Architects

Architecture is, and always will be, concerned, roughly, with carefully balancing horizontal things on top of vertical things.

Reyner Banham

244

Top Urban Planning Books

Planetizen, a public-interest information exchange for the urban planning, design, and development communities, has prepared a list of the top 20 urban planning books currently in print. The titles (listed alphabetically) were selected by Planetizen editors based on suggestions from professionals, academics, and book reviews. Planetizen also maintains an annual list of the top 10 planning titles published in the previous year.

For additional information, reviews of each book, and winners of the annual Top 10 Planning Books, visit *www.planetizen.com/books/*.

Top 20 Urban Planning Titles

The American City: What Works and What Doesn't
Alexander Garvin
McGraw-Hill, 1996

Cities of Tomorrow: An Intellectual History of Urban Planning and Design in the Twentieth Century
Peter Geoffrey Hall
Blackwell, 1998; updated edition, Blackwell, 1996

The City in History: Its Origins, Its Transformations, and Its Prospects
Lewis Mumford
Harcourt, Brace & World, 1961

Civilizing American Cities: Writings on City Landscapes
Frederick Law Olmsted Sr., S. B. Sutton, editor
MIT Press, 1971

The Death and Life of Great American Cities
Jane Jacobs
Random House, 1961

Design With Nature
Ian McHarg
Natural History Press, 1969

Edge City: Life on the New Frontier
Joel Garreau
Doubleday, 1991

The Essential William H. Whyte
Albert Lafarge, editor
Fordham University Press, 2000

The Geography of Nowhere: The Rise and Decline of America's Man-Made Landscape
James Howard Kunstler
Simon & Schuster, 1993

Good City Form
Kevin Lynch
MIT Press, 1981

Great Streets
Allan B. Jacobs
MIT Press, 1995

The Image of the City
Kevin Lynch
MIT Press, 1960

Nature's Metropolis: Chicago and the Great West
William Cronon
WW Norton & Company, 1991

The Next American Metropolis: Ecology, Community, and the American Dream
Peter Calthorpe
Princeton Architectural Press, 1993

A Pattern Language: Towns, Buildings, Construction
Christopher Alexander, Sara Ishikawa, and Murray Silverstein
Oxford University Press, 1977

Top Urban Planning Books

Planning in the USA: Policies, Issues, and Processes
Barry Cullingworth
Routledge, 1997

The Power Broker: Robert Moses and the Fall of New York
Robert A. Caro
Vintage, 1975

The Practice of Local Government Planning (The Green Book)
Charles J. Hoch, Linda C. Dalton,
    Frank S. So, editors
National Planning League, 1915; 3rd
    edition, International City County
    Management Association, 2000

Silent Spring
Rachel Carson
Houghton Mifflin, 1962

The Urban Villagers
Herbert J. Gans
The Free Press, 1969

Note: The original publication details, rather than currently available reprint editions, are cited above.

Source: Planetizen - The Planning and Development Network - www.planetizen.com

The street is the river of life of the city, the place where we come together, the pathway to the center.

William H. Whyte

Women in Architecture Timeline

Currently less than 25 percent of practicing US architects are women, a level of participation that was traversed by some genuine trailblazers. Once encouraged to pursue interiors work and stick to the domestic arts, women architects are now designing landmark buildings, running their own firms, and assuming leadership positions. The following timeline notes some of the significant achievements between 1865 and 2005 in women's struggle to enter the US architectural profession.

1865 The Massachusetts Institute of Technology is founded and along with it the United States' first architecture program, which is only open to men.

1869 Although she has no formal architectural training, Harriet Irwin receives a patent for an architectural innovation, a hexagonal house intended to be more space efficient and easier to clean, having eliminated the sharp corners. She will design and build at least two more houses in the Charlotte, NC, area.

1876 At the Philadelphia Centennial, Mary Nolan wins an award for her Nolanum construction blocks, hollow, interlocking bricks that are fireproof, pest proof, nonabsorbent, and insulating and require neither paint nor wallpaper.

1878 Mary L. Page graduates from the School of Architecture at the University of Illinois, Urbana–Champaign. She is the first woman to earn an architecture degree from an American university.

1880 Margaret Hicks graduates from Cornell University. Two years prior, her sketch of a Workman's Cottage were published in *American Architect and Building News*.

1881 At age 25, Louise Blanchard sets up architectural shop in Buffalo, NY, with Robert Bethune. Seven years later (now married) Louise Blanchard Bethune is the first woman elected to membership in the American Institute of Architects. The following year she becomes the AIA's first female fellow.

1891 Sophia Hayden, who graduated from the Massachusetts Institute of Technology the year before, wins a competition to design the Woman's Building for the 1893 World's Columbian Exposition in Chicago. She is selected for the project by the all-female Board of Lady Managers, who opened the competition to women only.

1894 To date, only eight women in the United States are known to have completed four-year programs in architecture.

After two years of tests and receiving a degree in civil engineering from the University of California, Berkeley, Julia Morgan is accepted to L'Ecole des Beaux Arts in Paris. In 1902 at the age of 29, she becomes the first woman to graduate from this prestigious institution.

Women in Architecture Timeline

1895 Marion Mahony Griffin, a graduate of the Massachusetts Institute of Technology and the first woman licensed to practice architecture in the state of Illinois, begins working in Frank Lloyd Wright's Oak Park office, serving his chief draftsperson.

1900 To date, 39 female graduates are known to have completed formal four-year architectural training programs in the United States.

1901 The Fred Harvey Company, a vendor of hospitality services in the Southwest, hires teacher and California School of Design graduate Mary Jane Colter (1869–1958). A high-school graduate at the age of 14, she soon becomes the company's chief architect, a position she holds until 1948.

1909 Theodate Pope Riddle designs Westover School in Middlebury, CT. Cass Gilbert writes that it is "the most beautifully planned and designed…girls' school in the country."

1910 In one of the earliest-known female partnerships, Ida Annah Ryan (MIT class of 1905) asks Florence Luscomb (MIT class of 1908) to join her practice in Waltham, MA.

Half of the architecture programs in the United States still deny entry to women.

1911 Anna Wagner Keichline graduates from Cornell University's architecture program and becomes the first registered woman architect in Pennsylvania. She will later patent seven inventions, including K Brick, a hollow fireproof clay brick that is a precursor to the modern concrete block.

1913 Lois Lilly Howe (MIT class of 1890) and Eleanor Manning (MIT class of 1906) form Howe & Manning, the first architecture firm founded by women in Boston and the second in the nation. Mary Almy (MIT class of 1922) joins the firm in 1926. They specialize in domestic architecture and champion the cause of urban and low-income housing.

1915 Henry Atherton Frost, a professor of architecture at Harvard University, and landscape architect Bremer Pond open the Cambridge School of Architecture and Landscape Architecture to offer graduate training for women since they are denied entry in Harvard's Graduate School of Design due to the school's male-only policy.

1919 William Randolph Hearst inherits a quarter million acres in San Simeon, CA. His alleged conversation with architect Julia Morgan begins, "Miss Morgan, we are tired of camping out in the open at the ranch in San Simeon, and I would like to build a little something." Twenty years later, the Hearst Castle is done. Between 1919 and 1939, Morgan travels to the site via train more than 550 times for weekend work sessions.

1921 Elizabeth Martini forms the Chicago Drafting Club, later the Women's Architectural Club. The group organizes displays for the Woman's World Fairs of 1927 and 1928 and sponsors an International Exhibition of Women in Architecture and the Allied Arts at Chicago's 1933 World's Fair.

248

1923 Alberta Pfeiffer graduates at the head of her class at the School of Architecture at the University of Illinois, Urbana–Champaign and is the first woman to win the American Institute of Architects' School Medal (now the Henry Adams Medal). She works in New York for several years before establishing a practice in Hadlyme, CT, that she runs until retiring in 1977.

1931 After visiting the Bauhaus the year before, Eleanor Raymond designs the Rachel Raymond House (now demolished) in Belmont, MA. It is New England's first Modernist dwelling as well as the first Modernist design in the United States by a woman. During her career, her residential designs pioneer the use of solar technology, plywood, and Masonite.

1934 *Modern Housing*, a book by housing reformer Catherine Bauer (1905–1964), espouses European social philosophies of architecture, particularly as related to low-income housing. She later helps develop the US Housing Act of 1937, which provides federal funding for low-income housing.

1938 The Cambridge School of Architecture and Landscape Architecture becomes the Graduate School of Architecture and Landscape Architecture at Smith College. Within four years the program will be shut down due to budgetary constraints.

1944 At age 25, Natalie de Blois graduates from Columbia University's School of Architecture and joins Skidmore, Owings & Merrill's New York office. Following a hiatus in the 1950s when she receives a Fullbright Fellowship to attend the L'Ecole des Beaux-Arts in Paris, she returns to SOM and works directly with Gordon Bunshaft as a senior designer. After more than 20 years in this position, she is promoted to the level of associate. She never becomes a partner.

1945 Sarah Pillsbury Harkness, a 1940 graduate of the Smith College Graduate School of Architecture and Landscape Architecture, becomes a founding member, with Walter Gropius and others, of the Architects Collaborative in Cambridge, MA.

1946 Florence Knoll and her husband Hans form Knoll Associates (now Knoll Inc.), offering modern furniture by well-known designers. During her career, Knoll revolutionizes the look and function of the American office, winning the National Medal of Arts in 2002 for "profoundly influenc[ing] post-World War II design."

1948 *Architectural Record* runs a two-part article, "A Thousand Women in Architecture," profiling 18 of the 1,119 women trained to practice architecture, according to research by the Women's Architectural Association and the deans of architecture schools across the United States.

Women in Architecture Timeline

1955 Pietro Belluschi, the dean of the Massachusetts Institute of Technology School of Architecture, writes in an essay titled "The Exceptional One": "I know some women who have done well at it, but the obstacles are so great that it takes an exceptional girl to make a go of it. If she insisted upon becoming an architect I would try to dissuade her. If then she was still determined, I would give her my blessing that she could be that exceptional one."

1956 Lutah Maria Riggs, a 1919 graduate of the University of California, Berkeley and the first licensed female architect in California, produces her most famous work, Santa Barbara's Vedanta Temple, a design inspired by early South Indian wood temples.

1958 Architect Rose Connor combs the records of the Architecture Examining Boards of all the states and finds a total of 320 registered women architects. This represents one percent of the total number of registered architects in the United States at this time. No women are registered in seven states.

1960 Beverly Willis establishes Willis and Associates in San Francisco. Though she began her architecture career in 1954, Willis never attends architecture school and does not become a licensed architect until 1966. Still, she produces many significant projects in that city, and in the early 1970s, her firm becomes a pioneer in the use of computer-aided design.

Joan Edelman Goody marries fellow architect Marvin E. Goody, and they become partners in the Boston firm Goody, Clancy & Associates. In a 1998 interview with the *Boston Globe Magazine*, Goody says the 60-plus member firm is "probably half women now. I was lucky. I married a very supportive architect husband, and I had wonderful partners."

1962 Two years after publishing her seminal work, *The Death and Life of Great American Cities*, Jane Jacobs organizes the Committee to Save the West Village and succeeds in defeating an urban renewal plan for New York's historic Greenwich Village. Many such groups are formed in the 1960s as two pieces of legislation, the Housing Act of 1949 and the Highway Trust Act of 1956, trigger an aggressive alteration of the urban landscape.

1963 Ada Louise Huxtable is named the architecture critic of *The New York Times*, the first such staff position at any US newspaper. Huxtable will receive the Pulitzer Prize for distinguished criticism in 1970.

1972 Denise Scott Brown turns down the deanship of the School of Art and Architecture at Yale University to continue her work with the firm of Venturi & Rauch (now Venturi, Scott Brown & Associates, Inc.). With Robert Venturi and Steven Izenour she writes *Learning from Las Vegas*, one of the seminal texts of postmodernism.

1973 Beverly Willis becomes chair of the Federal Construction Council, comprised of directors of all construction departments within the federal government and charged with overseeing joint agency cooperation

Sharon E. Sutton receives her MArch degree from the Columbia University Graduate School of Architecture and Planning. She will go on to become the first African-American woman to be a full professor in an accredited architecture program. In 1996 she is presented with the Association of Collegiate Schools of Architecture Distinguished Professor Award.

1977 Laurinda Spear, with her husband Bernardo Fort-Brescia, forms Arquitectonica, a Miami firm known for its unconventional modernism. The firm will expand to New York, Los Angeles, Paris, Hong Kong, Shanghai, Manila, Lima, Buenos Aires, and San Paulo.

1980 M. Rosaria Piomelli becomes the first woman dean of a US architecture school when she is tapped to head the College of Architecture at the City College of New York, CUNY.

Elizabeth Plater-Zyberk and her husband Andrés Duany found Duany Plater-Zyberk & Company and quickly establish themselves as experts in New Urbanism and town planning, which they pioneer with their design for the soon-to-be-famous town of Seaside, FL.

1981 The American Institute of Architects' two surveys (1974 and 1981) of women architects reveal that a majority have experienced discriminatory practices in school and in the workplace. Despite these negative responses, seven out of 10 say that if they had the option of changing careers they would choose architecture again.

While still an undergraduate at Yale University, architecture student Maya Lin wins a competition to design the Vietnam Veterans Memorial on the Mall in Washington, DC. She is 21 years old.

Illinois architect Carol Ross Barney founds Carol Ross Barney Architects (now Ross Barney Architects). Aimed squarely at the commercial market, the firm insinuates itself into the fabric of Chicago and becomes one of the city's largest female-owned practices.

1983 The American Institute of Architects begins collecting data on the gender and race of its members.

1985 The International Archive of Women in Architecture (http://spec.lib.vt.edu/iawa/) is established at Virginia Polytechnic Institute and State University. Its purpose is to collect the professional papers of women architects, landscape architects, designers, architectural historians, critics, and urban planners and the records of women's architectural organizations from around the world.

Women in Architecture Timeline

Norma Merrick Sklarek becomes the first African-American woman in the United States to form her own firm, Siegel–Sklarek-Diamond. She is also the first African-American woman to become a licensed architect and to be inducted as a fellow of the American Institute of Architects.

1986 Collaborating since 1977, Billie Tsien and Tod Williams officially establish Tod Williams Billie Tsien + Associates in New York City. Tsien's background in the fine arts and a keen interest in crossing disciplinary boundaries has informed the firm's body of high-profile, acclaimed projects.

1987 Skidmore, Owings & Merrill elects Marilyn Jordan Taylor to partner. She joined SOM in 1971. She is twice named to *Crain*'s list of the Most Influential Women in New York. Currently, Taylor is the only female partner at SOM.

1991 Architects Debra Lehman-Smith and James McLeish form Lehman-Smith + McLeish in Washington, DC. By the end of the decade, *Contract Design* magazine names the firm (now Lehman Smith McLeish) one of the 20 Best Interior Design firms since 1975.

1992 American Institute of Architect President W. Cecil Steward convenes a Task Force on Diversity.

L. Jane Hastings becomes the first woman Chancellor of the American Institute of Architects' College of Fellows.

1993 Susan A. Maxman becomes the first female president of the American Institute of Architects.

Elizabeth Plater-Zyberk, is named dean of the University of Miami School of Architecture. She establishes a master of architecture program in suburb and town design.

1995 Chicago architect Sally Lynn Levine's multi-media exhibit "ALICE (Architecture Lets in Chicks, Except) Through the Glass Ceiling," opens in San Francisco, exploring the status of women in the field of architecture.

1998 Ann R. Chaintreuil becomes the first female president of the National Council of Architectural Registration Boards.

Minneapolis architect Sarah Susanka writes the bestseller *The Not So Big House.* Upon the book's publication, *US News & World Report* pronounces her an "innovator in American culture." In 2001, *Fast Company* names her to its list of "Fast 50" innovators who have changes society.

2001 According to the National Architectural Accrediting Board's annual survey of accredited architecture programs, females comprise 16 percent of the 1,038 tenured architecture school faculty, 37 percent of architecture students, and 34 percent of architecture graduates.

Cornell University's College of Architecture, Art and Planning announces the appointment of Nasrine Seraji-Bozorgzad as chair of its Department of Architecture. She is the first woman to head a department of architecture in the Ivy League.

Following the terrorist attacks of 9/11, Beverly Willis and Metropolis magazine editor-in-chief Susan Szenasy form Rebuild Downtown Our Town (R.Dot).

Architect Sandra Mendler, vice president and sustainable design principal at HOK, is named the recipient of the inaugural Sustainable Design Leadership Award for her leadership and commitment to environmental issues in the design profession.

2002 Toshiko Mori is named chair of the Harvard Graduate School of Design's Department of Architecture.

2003 The 2003 *AIA Firm Survey* concludes that despite a period of economic weakness women have made significant gains over previous studies: 20 percent of the licensed architects in the United States are women, compared to 14 percent in 1999.

2004 Zaha Hadid wins the Pritzker Architecture Prize, considered the Nobel Prize of architecture. She is the only female recipient in the award's 27-year history and only one of two female architects to be granted a major architecture prize (Gae Aulenti received the Praemium Imperiale in 1991). To date, no female has received the AIA Gold Medal or the RIBA Royal Gold Medal.

253

2005 Marilyn Jordon Taylor, a partner at Skidmore, Ownings & Merrill's New York office, becomes chair of the Urban Land Institute—the only woman, as well as the only architect, to hold this position.

Source: DesignIntelligence

World's Best Skylines

This list ranks the impressiveness of the world's skylines by calculating the density and height of each city's skyscrapers. All buildings taller than 295 feet (90 meters)—excluding spires—contribute points to its home city's score equal to the number of feet it exceeds this benchmark height.

An explanation of how the ranking is calculated, as well as a ranking of more than 100 skylines, can be found at *http://homepages.ipact.nl/ ~egram/skylines.html.*

	Skyline	Points	# Bldgs. over 295 ft/90 m
1	Hong Kong, China	86,190	3,051
2	New York, NY (incl. Jersey City, Fort Lee, Guttenburg)	35,781	863
3	Dubai, UAE	21,758	328
4	Tokyo, Japan (incl. Kawaguchi, Kawasaki, Ichikawa)	20,319	615
5	Shanghai, China	19,228	582
6	Chicago, IL	17,045	333
7	Bangkok, Thailand	13,433	445
8	Guangzhou, China	10,865	347
9	Chongqing, China	9,093	340
10	Singapore	8,527	323
11	Kuala Lumpur, Malaysia (incl. Petaling Jaya, Subang Jaya)	8,080	210
12	Seoul, South Korea	7,660	270
13	Shenzhen, China	7,564	228
14	Manila, Philippines (metro area)	6,669	190
15	Toronto, ON, Canada (incl. Mississauga)	6,282	222
16	Moscow, Russia	5,755	158
17	Osaka, Japan (incl. Sakai, Amagasaka)	5,573	143
18	Miami, FL (incl. Miami Beach)	5,100	115
19	Beijing, China	5,038	240
20	Panama City, Panama	5,014	131
21	Sydney, Australia (incl. North Sydney, Chatswood, Bondi, St. Leonards)	4,792	140
22	Nanjing, China	4,782	101
23	Houston, TX (incl. Pasadena)	4,776	114
24	Jakarta, Indonesia	4,544	177
25	São Paulo, Brazil	4,119	291

Source: Egbert Gramsbergen and Paul Kazmierczak

BUILDING
TYPES

Listings of architecturally significant aquariums, airports, art museums, convention centers, sports stadiums, and the world's tallest buildings along with their requisite architectural statistics are available in this chapter.

Airports: 1990–2007

Airports have evolved over the last century from small, utilitarian structures to sprawling, multi-purpose complexes. Engineering challenges, the popularity of regional airlines, the need to accommodate larger jets, and expansion in Asia have resulted in the construction of countless new airport terminals since 1990. Many of those noteworthy for their architecture or engineering are listed in the following chart.

Airport	Location	Architect	Opened
Astana International Airport (KZT), Passenger Terminal	Astana, Kazakhstan	Kisho Kurokawa Architect & Associates (Japan)	2005
Barcelona International Airport (BCN), South Terminal	Barcelona, Spain	Taller de Arquitectura (Spain)	2005
Beihai Fucheng Airport (BHY), Domestic Terminal	Beihai, Guangxi, China	Llewelyn-Davies Ltd. (UK)	2000
Ben Gurion Airport (TLV), Airside Complex, Terminal 3	Tel Aviv, Israel	Moshe Safdie and Associates and TRA Architects—a joint venture	2004
Ben Gurion Airport (TLV), Landside Complex, Terminal 3	Tel Aviv, Israel	Skidmore, Owings & Merrill; Moshe Safdie and Associates; Karmi Associates (Israel); Lissar Eldar Architects (Israel)—a joint venture	2002
Bilbao Airport (BIO), Terminal Building	Bilbao Spain	Santiago Calatrava (Spain)	2000
Buffalo Niagara International Airport (BUF), Passenger Terminal	Cheektowaga, NY	Cannon Design, Inc.; William Nicholas Bodouva + Associates; and Kohn Pedersen Fox Associates—a joint venture	1997
Central Japan International Airport (NGO)	Tokoname City, Aichi Prefecture, Japan	Nikken Sekkei (Japan); Azusa Sekkei (Japan); Hellmuth, Obata & Kassabaum/Arup (UK), a joint venture	2005
Charles de Gaulle Airport (CDG), Terminal 2E*	Paris, France	Aéroports de Paris (France)	2003
Charles de Gaulle Airport (CDG), Terminal 2F	Paris, France	Aéroports de Paris (France)	1998
Chek Lap Kok International Airport (HKG)	Lantau Island, Hong Kong, China	Foster and Partners (UK)	1998
Chicago-O'Hare International Airport (ORD), Terminal 5	Chicago, IL	Perkins & Will with Heard & Associates	1994
Chongqing Jiangbei International Airport (CKG)	Chongqing, China	Llewelyn-Davies Ltd. (UK) with Arup (UK)	2004

* Since the partial collapse of Terminal 2E on May 23, 2004, the building has been closed while the remaining roof structure is demolished and rebuilt.

Airports: 1990–2007

Airport	Location	Architect	Opened
Cologne/Bonn Airport (CGN), Terminal 2	Cologne, Germany	Murphy/Jahn Architects	2000
Copenhagen International Airport (CPH), Terminal 3	Copenhagen, Denmark	Vilhelm Lauritzen AS (Denmark)	1998
Dallas-Fort Worth International Airport (DFW), Terminal D	Dallas/Fort Worth, TX	HNTB Architecture; HKS, Inc.; Corgan Associates, Inc.	2005
Denver International Airport (DEN)	Denver, CO	Fentress Bradburn Architects	1995
Detroit Metropolitan Wayne County Airport (DTW), McNamara Terminal	Romulus, MI	SmithGroup	2002
Dubai International Airport (DXB), Terminal 3	Dubai, UAE	Paul Andreu Architecte (France)	2007
Dusseldorf International Airport (DUS)	Dusseldorf, Germany	JSK Architekten (Germany); Perkins & Will	2001–03
EuroAirport Basel-Mulhouse-Freiburg (BSL), South Terminal	Saint Louis Cédex, France	Aegerter and Bosshardt (Switzerland)	2005
Frankfurt Airport (FRA), Terminal 2	Frankfurt, Germany	Perkins & Will; JSK Architekten (Germany)	1994
Fukuoka International Airport (FUK), International Terminal	Hakata-ku, Fukuoka City, Japan	Hellmuth, Obata & Kassabaum; Azusa Sekkei (Japan); Mishima Architects (Japan); MHS Planners, Architects & Engineers Co. (Japan)	1999
Gardermoen Airport (GEN)	Oslo, Norway	AVIAPLAN (Norway) and Niels Torp Architects (Norway)	1998
Graz International Airport (GRZ), Passenger Terminal	Graz, Austria	Pittino & Ortner Architekturbüro (Austria)	2005
Graz International Airport (GRZ), Passenger Terminal expansion	Graz, Austria	Riegler Riewe Architekten (Austria)	1994
Guangzhou Baiyun International Airport (CAN)	Guangdong, China	Parsons Brinckerhoff with URS Corporation	2004
Hamburg Airport (HAM), New Terminal 1	Hamburg, Germany	gmp Architekten (Germany) with von Gerkan, Marg & Partner Architekten (Germany)	2005
Hamburg Airport (HAM), Terminal 4 (now Terminal 2)	Hamburg, Germany	von Gerkan, Marg & Partner Architekten (Germany)	1991
Haneda Airport (HND), Terminal 2	Tokyo, Japan	Cesar Pelli & Associates; Jun Mitsui & Associates Inc. Architects (Japan)	2004
Heathrow Airport (LHR), Pier 4A	London, UK	Nicholas Grimshaw & Partners (UK)	1993
Heathrow Airport (LHR), Europier	London, UK	Richard Rogers Partnership (UK)	1992

258

Airport	Location	Architect	Opened
Inchon International Airport (ICN), Integrated Transportation Center	Seoul, South Korea	Terry Farrell and Partners (UK)	2002
Incheon International Airport (ICN)	Seoul, South Korea	Fentress Bradburn Architects with BHJW and Korean Architects Collaborative International (South Korea)	2001
Jinan International Airport (TNA)	Jinan, China	Integrated Design Associates	2005
John F. Kennedy International Airport (JFK), American Airlines Terminal, Phase 1	Jamaica, NY	DMJM Harris	2005–2007
John F. Kennedy International Airport (JFK), Terminal 4	Jamaica, NY	Skidmore, Owings & Merrill	2001
John F. Kennedy International Airport (JFK), Terminal 1	Jamaica, NY	William Nicholas Bodouva + Associates	1998
Jorge Chávez International Airport (LIM), New Terminal	Lima, Peru	Arquitectonica	2005
Kansai International Airport (KIA)	Osaka Bay, Japan	Renzo Piano Building Workshop (Italy) with Nikken Sekkei (Japan), Aéroports de Paris (France), Japan Airport Consultants Inc. (Japan)	1994
King Fahd International Airport (DMM)	Dammam, Saudi Arabia	Minoru Yamasaki Associates (Japan)	1999
Kuala Lumpur International Airport (KUL)	Kuala Lumpur, Malaysia	Kisho Kurokawa Architect & Associates (Japan) with Akitek Jururancang (Malaysia)	1998
Learmonth International Airport (LEA)	Exeter, Australia	JCY Architects and Urban Designers (Australia)	1999
Lester B. Pearson International Airport (YYZ), New Terminal 1	Toronto, ON, Canada	Skidmore, Owings & Merrill; Moshe Safdie and Associates; Adamson Associates Architects (Canada)	2004
Lester B. Pearson International Airport (YYZ), Pier F at Terminal 1	Toronto, ON, Canada	Architects Canada (Moshe Safdie and Associates; Skidmore, Owings & Merrill; Adamson Associates Architects (Canada)	2007
Logan International Airport (BOS), Terminal A	Boston, MA	Hellmuth, Obata & Kassabaum with C&R/Rizvi, Inc.	2005
Madrid Barajas International Airport (MAD), Terminal 3	Madrid, Spain	Richard Rogers Partnership (UK) with Estudio Lamela (Spain)	2005

Airports: 1990–2007

Airport	Location	Architect	Opened
Malaga Airport (AGP), Pablo Ruiz Picasso Terminal	Malaga, Spain	Taller de Arquitectura (Spain)	1991
McCarran International Airport (LAS), Satellite D	Las Vegas, NV	Leo A Daly; Tate & Snyder	1998
Ministro Pistarini International Airport (EZE), Terminal A	Buenos Aires, Argentina	Estudio M/SG/S/S (Spain) with Urgell/Fazio/Penedo/ Urgell (Spain)	2000
Munich International Airport (MUC), Terminal 2	Munich, Germany	K+P Architekten und Stadtplaner (Germany)	2003
Munich Airport (MUC), Airport Center	Munich, Germany	Murphy/Jahn Architects	1999
Munich International Airport (MUC)	Munich, Germany	Von Busse & Partners (Germany)	1992
Orlando International Airport (MCO), Airside 2	Orlando, FL	Hellmuth, Obata & Kassabaum	2000
Ottawa International Airport (YOW), Passenger Terminal	Ottawa, ON, Canada	Brisbin Brook Beynon Architects (Canada); Stantec Inc.	2003
Philadelphia International Airport (PHL), International Terminal A-West	Philadelphia, PA	Kohn Pedersen Fox Associates	2003
Pointe à Pitre Le Raizet International Airport (PTP)	Pointe à Pitre, Guadeloupe	Aéroports de Paris (France)	1996
Ronald Reagan Washington National Airport (DCA), North Terminal	Washington, DC	Cesar Pelli & Associates; Leo A Daly	1997
San Francisco International Airport (SFO), International Terminal	San Francisco, CA	Skidmore, Owings & Merrill with Del Campo & Maru and Michael Willis Architects	2000
San Pablo Airport (SVQ)	Seville, Spain	Rafael Moneo (Spain)	1992
Seattle-Tacoma International Airport (SEA), Central Terminal	Seattle, WA	Fentress Bradburn Architects	2005
Seattle-Tacoma International Airport (SEA), Concourse A	Seattle, WA	NBBJ	2004
Sendai International Airport (SDJ)	Natori, Japan	Hellmuth, Obata & Kassabaum; Nikken Sekkei (Japan)	1998
Shanghai Pudong International Airport (PVG)	Shanghai, China	Aéroports de Paris (France)	1999
Shanghai Pudong International Airport (PVG), Terminal 2	Shanghai, China	Shanghai Xian Dai Architectural Design Group (China)	2007
Shenzhen Baoan International Airport (SZX), Domestic Terminal	Shenzhen, China	Llewelyn-Davies Ltd. (UK)	2001

Airport	Location	Architect	Opened
Southampton Airport (SOU)	Southampton, UK	Manser Associates (UK)	1994
Stansted Airport (STN)	London, UK	Foster and Partners (UK)	1991
Suvarnabhumi Airport (BK)	Samut Prakarn (Bangkok), Thailand	MJTA (Murphy/Jahn Architects; TAMS Consultants Inc.; ACT Engineering)	2006
Zurich Airport (ZRH), Airside Centre	Zurich, Switzerland	Nicholas Grimshaw & Partners (UK) with Itten+Brechbühl (Switzerland)	2004

Source: DesignIntelligence

Aquariums

The opening of Boston's New England Aquarium in 1969 ushered in a new age for aquariums, combining the traditional ideas found in the classic aquariums of the early 20th century with new technology and revised educational and research commitments. Aquariums have since proliferated. The following pages highlight the major free-standing aquariums in the United States.

Aquarium	Location	Opened	Cost
Alaska SeaLife Center	Seward, AK	1998	$56 M
Aquarium of the Bay	San Francisco, CA	1996	$38 M
Aquarium of the Pacific	Long Beach, CA	1998	$117 M
Audubon Aquarium of Americas	New Orleans, LA	1990	$42 M
Belle Isle Aquarium	Royal Oak, MI	1904	$175,000
Birch Aquarium at Scripps Institution of Oceanography, UCSD	La Jolla, CA	1992	$14 M
Colorado's Ocean Journey	Denver, CO	1999	$94 M
Flint RiverQuarium	Albany, GA	2004	$30 M
Florida Aquarium	Tampa, FL	1994	$84 M
Georgia Aquarium	Atlanta, GA	2005	$280 M
Great Lakes Aquarium	Duluth, MN	2000	$34 M
John G. Shedd Aquarium	Chicago, IL	1930	$ 3.25 M ($45 M addition)
Maritime Aquarium at Norwalk	Norwalk, CT	1988	$11.5 M ($9 M addition)
Monterey Bay Aquarium	Monterey, CA	1984	$55 M ($57 M addition)
Mystic Aquarium	Mystic, CT	1973	$1.74 M ($52 M expansion)
National Aquarium	Washington, DC	1931	n/a
National Aquarium in Baltimore	Baltimore, MD	1981	$21.3 M ($35 M 1990 addition $66 M 2005 addition)

Total Square Ft. (original/current)	Tank Capacity (orig./current, in gal.)	Architect
115,000	400,000	Cambridge Seven Associates with Livingston Slone
48,000	707,000	Esherick Homsey Dodge and Davis
156,735	900,000	A joint venture of Hellmuth, Obata & Kassabaum and Esherick Homsey Dodge and Davis
110,000	1.19 M	The Bienville Group: a joint venture of The Mathes Group, Eskew + Architects, Billes/Manning Architects, Hewitt Washington & Associates, Concordia
10,000	32,000	Albert Kahn Associates, Inc.
34,000	150,000	Wheeler Wimer Blackman & Associates
107,000	1 M	Odyssea: a joint venture of RNL Design and Anderson Mason Dale Architects
30,000	175,000	Antoine Predock Architect with Robbins Bell Kreher Inc.
152,000	1 M	Hellmuth, Obata & Kassabaum and Esherick Homsey Dodge and Davis
500,000	8 M	Thompson, Ventulett, Stainback & Associates
62,382	170,000	Hammel, Green and Abrahamson
225,000/395,000	1.5 M/3 M	Graham, Anderson, Probst, & White (Lohan Associates, 1991 addition)
102,000/135,000	150,000	Graham Gund Architects Inc. (original building and 2001 addition)
216,000/307,000	900,000/1.9 M	Esherick Homsey Dodge and Davis (original building and 1996 addition)
76,000/137,000	1.6 M/2.3 M	Flynn, Dalton and van Dijk (Cesar Pelli & Associates, 1999 expansion)
13,500	32,000	York & Sawyer Architects
209,000/324,000/ 389,400	1 M/1.5 M/ 1.578 M	Cambridge Seven Associates (Grieves & Associates, 1990 addition; Chermayeff, Sollogub and Poole, 2005 addition)

Aquariums

Aquarium	Location	Opened	Cost
New England Aquarium	Boston, MA	1969	$8 M ($20.9 M 1998 addition $19.3 M 2001 expansion)
New Jersey State Aquarium	Camden, NJ	1992	$52 M
New York Aquarium at Coney Island	Brooklyn, NY	1957	n/a
Newport Aquarium	Newport, KY	1999	$40 M ($4.5 M expansion)
North Carolina Aquarium at Fort Fisher	Kure Beach, NC	1976	$1.5 M ($17.5 M expansion)
North Carolina Aquarium at Pine Knoll Shores	Pine Knoll Shores, NC	1976	$4 M ($25 M expansion)
North Carolina Aquarium on Roanoke Island	Manteo, NC	1976	$1.6 M ($16 M expansion)
Oklahoma Aquarium	Tulsa, OK	2003	$15 M
Oregon Coast Aquarium	Newport, OR	1992	$25.5 M
Ripley's Aquarium	Myrtle Beach, SC	1997	$40 M
Ripley's Aquarium of the Smokies	Gatlinburg, TN	2000	$49 M
Seattle Aquarium	Seattle, WA	1977	n/a ($20 M expansion)
South Carolina Aquarium	Charleston, SC	2000	$69 M
Steinhart Aquarium	San Francisco, CA	1923	n/a
Tennessee Aquarium	Chattanooga, TN	1992	$45 M ($30 M addition)
Texas State Aquarium	Corpus Christi, TX	1990	$31 M ($14 M addition)
Virginia Aquarium & Science Center	Virginia Beach, VA	1986	$7.5 M ($35 M expansion)
Waikiki Aquarium	Honolulu, HI	1955	$400,000
Wonders of Wildlife at the American National Fish and Wildlife Museum	Springfield, MO	2001	$34 M

Source: DesignIntelligence

Total Square Ft. (original/current)	Tank Capacity (orig./current, in gal.)	Architect
75,000/1 M	1 M	Cambridge Seven Associates (Schwartz/Silver Architects, 1998 addition; E. Verner Johnson and Associates, 2001 expansion)
120,000	1 M	The Hillier Group
150,000	1.8 M	n/a
100,000/121,200	1 M/1.01 M	GBBN Architects (original and 2005 expansion)
30,000/84,000	77,000/455,000	Cambridge Seven Associates (BMS Architects, 2002 expansion)
29,000/93,000	25,000/433,000	Hayes, Howell & Associates (BMS Architects, 2006 expansion)
34,000/68,000	5,000/400,000	Lyles, Bissett, Carlisle and Wolff Associates of North Carolina Inc. with Cambridge Seven Associates (BMS Architects, 2000 expansion)
71,600	500,000	SPARKS
51,000	1.4 M	SRG Partnership
87,000	1.3 M	Enartec
115,000	1.3 M	Helman Hurley Charvat Peacock/Architects, Inc.
68,000/86,000	753,000/873,000	Fred Bassetti & Co. (Miller/Hull Partnership and Mithun Architects + Designers + Planners, 2007 expansion)
93,000	1 M	Eskew + Architects with Clark and Menefee Architects
22,566	300,000	Lewis P. Hobart
130,000/190,000	400,000/1.1 M	Cambridge Seven Associates (Chermayeff, Sollogub & Poole, 2005 addition)
43,000/73,800	325,000/725,000	Phelps, Bomberger, and Garza (Corpus Christi Design Associates, 2003 addition)
41,500/120,000	100,000/800,000	E. Verner Johnson and Associates (original building and 1996 expansion)
19,000	152,000	Hart Wood and Edwin A. Weed with Ossipoff, Snyder, and Rowland
92,000	500,000	Cambridge Seven Associates

265

Art Museums

By some calculations there are more than 16,000 museums in the United States. While the collections they hold are often priceless, the facilities that contain them are frequently significant, especially amidst the recent museum-building boom led by world-class architects. The following chart, while not comprehensive, lists architecturally significant US art museums.

Museum	Location	Architect (original)
Akron Art Museum	Akron, OH	Dalton, van Dijk, Johnson & Partners (conversion of the original 1899 post office)
Albright-Knox Art Gallery	Buffalo, NY	Edward B. Green
Allen Memorial Art Museum	Oberlin, OH	Cass Gilbert
American Folk Art Museum	New York, NY	Tod Williams Billie Tsien & Associates
Amon Carter Museum	Ft. Worth, TX	Philip Johnson
Anchorage Museum of History and Art	Anchorage, AK	Kirk, Wallace, and McKinley with Schultz/Maynard
Art Institute of Chicago	Chicago, IL	Shepley, Rutan, and Coolidge
Art Museum of South Texas	Corpus Christi, TX	Philip Johnson
Arthur M. Sackler Museum	Cambridge, MA	James Stirling Michael Wilford and Associates (UK)
Asian Art Museum	San Francisco, CA	Gae Aulenti (Italy) with Hellmuth, Obata & Kassabaum, LDa Architects, and Robert Wong Architects (adapted the 1917 main library by George Kelham)
Baltimore Museum of Art	Baltimore, MD	John Russell Pope
Barnes Foundation	Merion, PA	Paul Philippe Cret
Bass Museum of Art	Miami, FL	B. Robert Swartburg (adapted the 1930 Miami Beach Library by Russell Pancoast)
Bellevue Art Museum	Bellevue, WA	Steven Holl Architects
Berkeley Art Museum + Pacific Film Archive	Berkeley, CA	Mario J. Ciampi & Associates
Birmingham Museum of Art	Birmingham, AL	Warren, Knight and Davis
Brooklyn Museum	Brooklyn, NY	McKim, Mead, and White

Opened	Architect (expansion)
1981	Coop Himmelb(l)au (Austria) with Westlake Reed Leskosky, 2007 John S. and James L. Knight Building
1905	Skidmore, Owings & Merrill, 1961 addition
1917	Venturi, Scott Brown and Associates, 1977 addition
2001	—
1961	Johnson/Burgee Architects, 1977 expansion; Philip Johnson/Alan Ritchie Architects, 2001 expansion
1968	Kenneth Maynard Associates, 1974 addition; Mitchell/Giurgola Architects with Maynard and Partch, 1986 addition
1893	Skidmore, Owings & Merrill, 1977 Arthur Rubloff Building; Hammond, Beebe and Babka, 1988 Daniel F. and Ada L. Rice Building
1972	Legorreta + Legorreta (Mexico) with Dykema Architects, 2006 William B. and Maureen Miller Building
1985	—
2003	—
1929	John Russell Pope, 1937 Jacobs Wing; Wrenn, Lewis & Jancks, 1950 May Wing, 1956 Woodward Wing and 1957 Cone Wing; Bower Lewis & Thrower Architects, 1994 West Wing for Contemporary Art
1925	—
1964	Arata Isozaki & Associates (Japan) with Spillis Candela DMJM, 2002 expansion
2001	—
1970	—
1959	Warren, Knight and Davis, 1965 west wing, 1967 east wing, 1974 expansion, 1979 addition, and 1980 expansion; Edward Larrabee Barnes Associates, 1993 expansion
1897–1927	Prentice & Chan, Ohlhausen, 1978 addition; Arata Isozaki & Associates (Japan) and James Stewart Polshek & Partners, 1991 Iris and B. Gerald Cantor Auditorium; Polshek Partnership Architects, 2004 front entrance and public plaza addition

Art Museums

Museum	Location	Architect (original)
Butler Institute of American Art	Youngstown, OH	McKim, Mead and White
Cincinnati Art Museum	Cincinnati, OH	James McLaughlin
Cleveland Museum of Art	Cleveland, OH	Benjamin Hubbell and W. Dominick Benes
Colorado Springs Fine Arts Center	Colorado Springs, CO	John Gaw Meem
Columbus Museum of Art	Columbus, OH	Richards, McCarty and Bulford
Contemporary Art Museum St. Louis	St. Louis, MO	Allied Works Architecture
Contemporary Arts Museum, Houston	Houston, TX	Gunnar Birkerts and Associates
Corcoran Gallery of Art	Washington, DC	Ernest Flagg
Cranbrook Art Museum	Cranbrook, MI	Eliel Saarinen
Dallas Museum of Art	Dallas, TX	Edward Larrabee Barnes Associates
Dayton Art Institute	Dayton, OH	Edward B. Green
de Young Museum	San Francisco, CA	Herzog & de Meuron (Switzerland) with Fong & Chan Architects
Denver Art Museum	Denver, CO	Gio Ponti (Italy) with James Sudler Associates
Denver Museum of Contemporary Art	Denver, CO	Adjaye/Associates (UK)
Des Moines Art Center	Des Moines, IA	Eliel Saarinen
Detroit Institute of Arts	Detroit, MI	James Balfour
Elvehjem Museum of Art	Madison, WI	Harry Weese
Everson Museum of Art	Syracuse, NY	I.M. Pei & Associates
Figge Art Museum	Davenport, IA	David Chipperfield Architects (UK) with Herbert Lewis Kruse Blunck Architecture
Fogg Art Museum	Cambridge, MA	Coolidge, Shepley, Bulfinch, and Abbott
Frances Lehman Loeb Art Center	Poughkeepsie, NY	Cesar Pelli & Associates
Fred Jones Jr. Museum of Art	Norman, OK	Howard and Smais
Frederick R. Weisman Art Museum	Minneapolis, MN	Frank O. Gehry and Associates, Inc.
Freer Gallery Art	Washington, DC	Charles Adams Platt
Frist Center for the Visual Arts	Nashville, TN	Tuck Hinton Architects (adapted the 1934 US Post Office by Marr and Holman Architects)

Opened	Architect (expansion)
1919	Paul Boucherie, 1931 north and south wings; C. Robert Buchanan & Associates, 1967 addition; Buchanan, Ricciuti & Associates, 1986 west wing addition
1886	Daniel H. Burnham, 1907 Schmidlapp Wing; Garber and Woodward, 1910 Ropes Wing and 1930 Emery, Hanna & French Wings; Rendigs, Panzer and Martin, 1937 Alms Wing; Potter, Tyler, Martin and Roth, 1965 Adams-Emery Wing
1916	J. Byers Hays and Paul C. Ruth, 1958 addition; Marcel Breuer and Hamilton P. Smith, 1971 addition; Dalton, van Dijk, Johnson & Partners, 1984 addition
1936	—
1931	Van Buren and Firestone, Architects, Inc., 1974 addition
2003	—
1972	—
1897	Charles Adams Platt, 1927 expansion
1941	Rafael Moneo (Spain), 2002 addition
1984	Edward Larrabee Barnes Associates, 1985 decorative arts wing and 1991 Nancy and Jake L. Hamon Building
1930	Levin Porter Associates, Inc., 1997 expansion
2005	—
1971	Studio Daniel Libeskind with Davis Partnership Architects, 2006 Frederic C. Hamilton Building
2006	—
1948	I.M. Pei & Associates, 1968 addition; Richard Meier & Partners Architects, 1985 addition
1888	Cret, Zantzinger, Borie and Medary, 1927 addition; Harley, Ellington, Cowin and Stirton, with Gunnar Birkerts and Associates, 1966 south wings; Harley, Ellington, Cowin and Stirton, 1966 north wing; Michael Graves & Associates with SmithGroup, 2007 expansion
1970	—
1968	—
2005	—
1927	—
1993	—
1971	Hugh Newell Jacobsen, 2005 Mary and Howard Lester Wing
1993	—
1923	—
2001	—

269

Art Museums

Museum	Location	Architect (original)
Frye Art Museum	Seattle, WA	Paul Albert Thiry
Grand Rapids Art Museum	Grand Rapids, MI	Workshop Hakomori Yantrasast with Design +
Herbert F. Johnson Museum of Art	Ithaca, NY	I.M. Pei & Partners
High Museum of Art	Atlanta, GA	Richard Meier & Partners Architects
Hirshhorn Museum and Sculpture Garden	Washington, DC	Skidmore, Owings & Merrill
Hood Museum of Art	Hanover, NH	Charles Moore and Centerbrook Architects and Planners
Hunter Museum of American Art	Chattanooga, TN	Mead and Garfield (architects of the 1905 mansion adapted to a museum
Indiana University Art Museum	Bloomington, IN	I.M. Pei & Partners
Indianapolis Museum of Art	Indianapolis, IN	Richardson, Severns, Scheeler and Associates
Institute for Contemporary Art	Boston, MA	Diller Scofidio + Renfro
Iris & B. Gerald Cantor Center for Visual Arts	Stanford, CA	Percy & Hamilton Architects with Ernest J. Ransome
J. Paul Getty Museum	Los Angeles, CA	Richard Meier & Partners Architects
Joslyn Art Museum	Omaha, NE	John and Alan McDonald
Kemper Museum of Contemporary Art and Design	Kansas City, MO	Gunnar Birkerts and Associates
Kimbell Art Museum	Fort Worth, TX	Louis I. Kahn
Kreeger Museum	Washington, DC	Philip Johnson with Richard Foster
Lois & Richard Rosenthal Center for Contemporary Art	Cincinnati, OH	Zaha Hadid Architects (UK) with KZF Design
Mead Art Museum	Amherst, MA	McKim, Mead and White
Memphis Brooks Museum of Art	Memphis, TN	James Gamble Rogers with Carl Gutherz
Menil Collection	Houston, TX	Renzo Piano Building Workshop (Italy) with Richard Fitzgerald & Partners
Metropolitan Museum of Art	New York, NY	Calvert Vaux and J. Wrey Mould
Milwaukee Art Museum	Milwaukee, WI	Eero Saarinen with Maynard Meyer

Opened	Architect (expansion)
1952	Olson Sundberg Kundig Allen Architects, 1997 expansion
2007	—
1973	—
1983	Renzo Piano Building Workshop (Italy) with Lord, Aeck and Sargent, Inc., 2005 addition
1974	—
1985	—
1952	Derthick, Henley and Wilkerson Architects, 1975 addition; Randall Stout Architects with Derthick, Henley and Wilkerson Architects and Hefferlin + Kronenberg Architects, 2005 in 1952) addition
1982	—
1970	Edward Larrabee Barnes Associates and John M.Y. Lee, 1990 Mary Fendrich Hulman Pavilion; Browning Day Mullins Dierdorf Architects, 2005 expansion
2006	—
1894	Polshek Partnership Architects, 1999 addition
1997	—
1931	Foster and Partners (UK), 1994 Walter and Suzanne Scott Pavilion
1994	—
1972	—
1967	—
2003	—
1949	—
1916	Walk Jones and Francis Mah, 1973 addition; Skidmore, Owings & Merrill with Askew, Nixon, Ferguson & Wolf, 1989 expansion
1987	—
1880	Theodore Weston, 1888 SW wing; Richard Morris Hunt and Richard Howland Hunt, 1902 Central Fifth Avenue facade; McKim, Mead and White, 1906, side wings along Fifth Avenue; Brown, Lawford & Forbes, 1965 Thomas J. Watson Library; Kevin Roche John Dinkeloo & Associates, 1975 Lehman Wing, 1979 Sackler Wing, 1980 American Wing, 1981 Michael C. Rockefeller Wing for Primitive Art, 1988 European Sculpture and Decorative Art Wing
1957	Kahler, Fitzhugh and Scott, 1975 addition; Santiago Calatrava (Spain) with Kahler Slater Architects, 2001 Quadracci Pavilion

271

Art Museums

Museum	Location	Architect (original)
Minneapolis Institute of Arts	Minneapolis, MN	McKim, Mead and White
Modern Art Museum of Fort Worth	Fort Worth, TX	Tadao Ando (Japan)
Munson-Williams-Proctor Arts Institute	Utica, NY	Philip Johnson
Museum of Contemporary Art, Chicago	Chicago, IL	Josef Paul Kleihues (Germany)
Museum of Contemporary Art/Denver	Denver, CO	Adjaye/Associates
Museum of Contemporary Art, Los Angeles (at California Plaza)	Los Angeles, CA	Arata Isozaki & Associates (Japan)
Museum of Contemporary Art, San Diego	La Jolla, CA	Irving Gill (originally designed as a residence in 1916)
Museum of Fine Arts, Boston	Boston, MA	Guy Lowell
Museum of Fine Arts, Houston	Houston, TX	William Ward Watkin
Museum of Modern Art	New York, NY	Philip L. Goodwin and Edward Durrell Stone & Associates
Nasher Museum of Art	Durham, NC	Rafael Viñoly Architects
Nasher Sculpture Center	Dallas, TX	Renzo Piano Building Workshop (Italy) with Peter Walker and Partners
National Gallery of Art, East Building	Washington, DC	I.M. Pei & Partners
National Gallery of Art, West Building	Washington, DC	John Russell Pope
National Portrait Gallery and American Art Museum	Washington, DC	Faulkner, Stenhouse, Fryer (adapted the 1836–67 Old Patent Office Building by Robert Mills and Thomas Ustick Walter)
Nelson Fine Arts Center	Tempe, AZ	Antoine Predock Architect
Nelson-Atkins Museum of Art	Kansas City, MO	Wight and Wight
Nevada Museum of Art	Reno, NV	Will Bruder Architects
New Orleans Museum of Art	New Orleans, LA	Samuel Marx
Oakland Museum of California	Oakland, CA	Kevin Roche John Dinkeloo & Associates
Parrish Art Museum	Southampton, NY	Grosvenor Atterbury
Pennsylvania Academy of the Fine Arts	Philadelphia, PA	Frank Furness and George W. Hewitt
Philadelphia Museum of Art	Philadelphia, PA	Horace Trumbauer with Zantzinger, Borie, and Medary

272

Opened	Architect (expansion)
1915	Kenzo Tange Associates (Japan), 1974 addition; Michael Graves & Associates with RSP Architects, 2006 Target Wing
2002	—
1960	Lund McGee Sharpe Architecture, 1995 Education Wing
1996	—
2007	—
1986	—
1941	Mosher & Drew, 1950 transition to museum; Mosher & Drew, 1959 Sherwood Auditorium; Venturi, Scott Brown and Associates, 1996 expansion and renovation
1909	Guy Lowell, 1915 Robert Dawson Evans Wing; John Singer Sargent, 1921, 1925 Rotunda and Colonnade; Guy Lowell, 1928 Decorative Arts Wing; Hugh Stubbins & Associates, 1968 Forsyth Wickes Galleries and 1970 George Robert White Wing; I.M. Pei & Partners, 1981 West Wing
1924–26	Kenneth Franzheim, 1953 Robert Lee Blaffer Memorial Wing; Mies van der Rohe, 1958 Cullinan Hall and 1974 Brown Pavilion; Isamu Noguchi (Japan), 1986 Lillie and Hugh Roy Cullen Sculpture Garden; Rafael Moneo (Spain), 2000 Audrey Jones Beck Building
1939	Philip Johnson, 1964 east wing; Cesar Pelli & Associates, 1984 tower; Taniguchi Associates (Japan) with Kohn Pedersen Fox Associates and Cooper, Robertson & Partners, 2004 expansion and 2006 Lewis B. and Dorothy Cullman Education Building
2005	—
2003	—
1978	—
1941	—
1968	Foster + Partners (UK) with SmithGroup, 2007 Robert and Arlene Kogod Courtyard
1989	—
1933	Steven Holl Architects with BNIM Architects, 2007 Bloch Building
2003	—
1911	August Perez with Arthur Feitel, 1971 Wisner Education Wing, City Wing, and Stern Auditorium; Eskew Filson Architects with Billes/Manning Architects, 1993 expansion
1969	—
1897	Grosvenor Atterbury, 1902 and 1913 wings
1876	—
1928	—

273

Art Museums

Museum	Location	Architect (original)
Phoenix Art Museum	Phoenix, AZ	Alden B. Dow
Portland Art Museum	Portland, OR	Pietro Belluschi
Portland Museum of Art Building	Portland, ME	John Calvin Stevens
Princeton University Art Museum	Princeton, NJ	Ralph Adams Cram
Pulitzer Foundation for the Arts	St. Louis, MO	Tadao Ando (Japan)
Renwick Gallery	Washington, DC	James Renwick Jr.
Rodin Museum	Philadelphia, PA	Paul Philippe Cret and Jacques Gréber
Saint Louis Art Museum	St. Louis, MO	Cass Gilbert
San Diego Museum of Art	San Diego, CA	William Templeton Johnson with Robert W. Snyder
San Francisco Museum of Modern Art	San Francisco, CA	Mario Botta (Italy)
Santa Barbara Museum of Art	Santa Barbara, CA	David Adler (adapted the 1914 Old Post Office designed by Francis Wilson)
Seattle Art Museum	Seattle, WA	Venturi, Scott Brown and Associates
Shaw Center for the Arts	Baton Rouge, LA	Schwartz/Silver Architects with Eskew+Dumez+Ripple and Jerry M. Campbell Associates
Sheldon Memorial Art Gallery	Lincoln, NE	Philip Johnson
Solomon R. Guggenheim Museum	New York, NY	Frank Lloyd Wright
Speed Art Museum	Louisville, KY	Arthur Loomis
Tacoma Art Museum	Tacoma, WA	Antoine Predock Architect with Olson Sundberg Kundig Allen Architects
Terra Museum of American Art	Chicago, IL	Booth Hansen Associates
Toledo Museum of Art	Toledo, OH	Green & Wicks with Harry W. Wachter
UCLA Hammer Museum of Art	Los Angeles, CA	Edward Larrabee Barnes Associates
Wadsworth Atheneum Museum of Art	Hartford, CT	Ithiel Town and Alexander Jackson Davis

Opened	Architect (expansion)
1959	Alden B. Dow, 1965 east wing; Tod Williams Billie Tsien & Associates, 1996 and 2006 expansions
1932	Pietro Belluschi, 1939 Hirsch Wing; Pietro Belluschi, with Wolff, Zimmer, Gunsul, Frasca, and Ritter, 1970 Hoffman Wing; Ann Beha Architects, 2000 expansion; Ann Beha Architects with SERA Architects, 2005 expansion
1911	I.M. Pei & Partners, 1983 Charles Shipman Payson
1922	Steinman and Cain, 1966 expansion; Mitchell/Giurgola Architects, 1989 Mitchell Wolfson Jr. Wing
2001	
1859	John Carl Warnecke & Associates and Hugh Newell Jacobsen, 1971 restoration
1929	
1903	
1926	Robert Mosher & Roy Drew, Architects, 1966 west wing; Mosher, Drew, Watson & Associates with William Ferguson, 1974 east wing
1995	
1941	Chester Carjola, 1942 Katherine Dexter McCormick Wing; Arendt/Mosher/Grants Architects, 1961 Preston Morton Wing and 1962 Sterling Morton Wing; Paul Gray, 1985 Alice Keck Park Wing; Edwards & Pitman, 1998 Peck Wing
1991	Allied Works Architecture with NBBJ, 2007 expansion
2005	—
1963	—
1959	Gwathmey Siegel & Associates Architects, 1992 addition
1927	Nevin and Morgan, 1954 Preston Pope Satterwhite Wing; Brenner, Danforth, and Rockwell, 1973 north wing; Robert Geddes, 1983 south wing
2003	—
1987	—
1912	Edward B. Green and Sons, 1926 wing and 1933 expansion; Frank O. Gehry and Associates, Inc., 1992 Center for the Visual Arts addition; SANAA, Ltd. (Japan), 2006 Glass Pavilion
1990	—
1844	Benjamin Wistar Morris, 1910 Colt Memorial and 1915 Morgan Memorial; Morris & O'Connor 1934 Avery Memorial; Huntington, Darbee & Dollard, Architects, 1969 Goodwin Wing

275

Art Museums

Museum	Location	Architect (original)
Walker Art Center	Minneapolis, MN	Edward Larrabee Barnes Associates
Wexner Center for the Arts	Columbus, OH	Eisenman Architects with Richard Trott & Partners
Whitney Museum of American Art	New York, NY	Marcel Breuer and Associates
Yale Center for British Art	New Haven, CT	Louis I. Kahn
Yale University Art Gallery	New Haven, CT	Louis I. Kahn

Source: DesignIntelligence

Left to right: **Institute of Contemporary Art, Boston, MA, by Diller Scofidio + Renfro Architects** (Photo: Peter Vanderwarker, courtesy of the ICA); **Seattle Art Museum addition, Seattle, WA, by Allied Works Architecture** (Photo: © Richard Barnes, courtesy of the Seattle Art Museum)

Opened	Architect (expansion)
1971	Herzog & de Meuron (Switzerland) with Hammel, Green and Abrahamson, 2005 expansion
1989	—
1966	Gluckman Mayner Architects, 1998 expansion
1977	—
1953	—

Convention Centers

In the past decade public spending on convention centers has doubled to $2.4 billion annually, and since 1990 convention space in the US has increased by more than 50 percent. The following is *DesignIntelligence*'s list of the largest US convention centers with their requisite architectural statistics.

Convention Center	Location	Opened	Exhibit Halls (sq. ft.)
America's Center	St. Louis, MO	1977	502,000
AmericasMart Atlanta	Atlanta, GA	1961	276,000
Anaheim Convention Center	Anaheim, CA	1967	815,000
Atlantic City Convention Center	Atlantic City, NJ	1997	518,300
Austin Convention Center	Austin, TX	1992	246,097
Baltimore Convention Center	Baltimore, MD	1979	300,000
Boston Convention and Exhibition Center	Boston, MA	2004	516,000
Charlotte Convention Center	Charlotte, NC	1995	280,000
Cobo Conference/Exhibition Center	Detroit, MI	1960	700,000
Colorado Convention Center	Denver, CO	1990	584,000
Dallas Convention Center	Dallas, TX	1973	726,726
David L. Lawrence Convention Center	Pittsburgh, PA	2003	313,400
Donald E. Stephens Convention Center	Rosemont, IL	1974	840,000
Ernest N. Morial Convention Center	New Orleans, LA	1985	1.1 M
Fort Worth Convention Center	Fort Worth, TX	1968	253,226

Architect (original)	Architect (expansion)
Hellmuth, Obata & Kassabaum	Hellmuth, Obata & Kassabaum, 1993 and 1995 expansions
Edwards and Portman, Architects (Merchandise Mart)	Edwards and Portman, Architects, 1968 Merchandise Mart addition; John Portman & Associates, Architects, 1979 Apparel Mart, 1986 Merchandise Mart addition, 1989 Apparel Mart addition, 1992 Gift Mart
Adrian Wilson & Associates	HNTB Architecture, 1974, 1982, 1990, and 1993 expansions; HOK Sport + Venue + Event, 1999–2001 expansion
Wallace Roberts & Todd	—
PageSoutherlandPage	Austin Collaborative Venture (PageSoutherlandPage; Cotera Kolar Negrete & Reed Architects; Limbacher & Godfrey Architects), 2002 expansion
NBBJ with Cochran, Stephenson & Donkervoet	LMN Architects with Cochran, Stephenson & Donkervoet, 1996 expansion
HNTB Architecture/Rafael Viñoly Architects, joint venture	—
Thompson, Ventulett, Stainback & Associates with The FWA Group	—
Giffels & Rossetti	Sims-Varner & Associates, 1989 expansion
Fentress Bradburn Architects	Fentress Bradburn Architects, 2004 expansion
Harrell + Hamilton Architects (adapted and expanded the 1957 Dallas Memorial Auditorium by George L. Dahl Architects and Engineers Inc.)	OmniPlan, 1984 expansion; JPJ Architects, 1994 expansion; Skidmore, Owings & Merrill and HKS Inc., 2002 expansion
Rafael Viñoly Architects	—
Anthony M. Rossi Limited	Anthony M. Rossi Limited, subsequent expansions
Perez & Associates and Perkin & James	Perez & Associates and Billes/Manning Architects, 1991 expansion; Convention Center III Architects (Cimini, Meric, Duplantier Architects/Planners, Billes/Manning Architects, and Hewitt Washington & Associates), 1999 expansion
Parker Croston	Carter & Burgess, Inc. and HOK Sport + Venue + Event, 2003 addition

Convention Centers

Convention Center	Location	Opened	Exhibit Halls (sq. ft.)
George R. Brown Convention Center	Houston, TX	1987	893,590
Georgia World Congress Center	Atlanta, GA	1976	1.4 M
Greater Columbus Convention Center	Columbus, OH	1993	426,000
Hawaii Convention Center	Honolulu, HI	1996	204,249
Henry B. Gonzalez Convention Center	San Antonio, TX	1968	440,000
Indianapolis Convention Center & RCA Dome	Indianapolis, IN	1972	308,700
Jacob K. Javits Convention Center	New York, NY	1986	814,000
Kansas City Convention Center	Kansas City, MO	1976	388,800
Las Vegas Convention Center	Las Vegas, NV	1959	2 M
Long Beach Convention & Entertainment Center	Long Beach, CA	1978	224,000
Los Angeles Convention Center	Los Angeles, CA	1972	720,000
Mandalay Bay Convention Center	Las Vegas, NV	2003	934,731
McCormick Place	Chicago, IL	1971	2.6 M

Architect (original)	Architect (expansion)
Goleman & Rolfe Associates, Inc.; John S. Chase; Molina & Associates; Haywood Jordan McCowan, Inc.; Moseley Associates with Bernard Johnson and 3D/International	Golemon & Bolullo Architects, 2003 expansion
Thompson, Ventulett, Stainback & Associates	Thompson, Ventulett, Stainback & Associates, 1985 and 1992 expansions, Thompson, Ventulett, Stainback & Associates with Heery International, Inc., 2003 expansion
Eisenman Architects with Richard Trott & Partners	Eisenman Architects, Karlsberger, and Thompson, Ventulett, Stainback & Associates, 2001 expansion
LMN Architects with Wimberly Allison Tong & Goo	—
Noonan and Krocker; Phelps and Simmons and Associates	Cerna Raba & Partners, 1986 expansion; Thompson, Ventulett, Stainback & Associates with Kell Muñoz Architects and Haywood Jordon McCowan, Inc, 2001 expansion
Lennox, James and Loebl (Lennox, Matthews, Simmons and Ford; James Associates; Loebl Schlossman Bennett & Dart)	Blackburn Architects and Browning Day Mullins Dierdorf Architects with Hellmuth, Obata & Kassabaum, 1993 and 2001 expansions
I.M. Pei & Partners	—
C.F. Murphy Associates with Seligson Associates, Hormer and Blessing, and Howard Needles Tammen & Bergendoff	Convention Center Associates, Architects; BNIM Architects; HNTB Architecture, 1994 expansion
Adrian Wilson & Associates with Harry Whitney Consulting Architect	Jack Miller & Associates, 1967 South Hall; Adrian Wilson & Associates, 1971 C3 expansion; Jack Miller & Associates, 1975 C4 expansion; JMA Architecture, 1980 C5 expansion and 1990 expansion; Domingo Cambeiro Corp. Architects, 1998 North Hall and 2002 South Hall
Killingsworth, Brady, Smith and Associates	Thompson, Ventulett, Stainback & Associates, 1994 expansion
Charles Luckman & Associates	Pei Cobb Freed & Partners with Gruen Associates, 1993 expansion; Gruen Associates, 1997 Kentia Hall addition
Klai Juba Architects	—
C.F. Murphy Associates	Skidmore, Owings & Merrill, 1986 North Hall; Thompson, Ventulett, Stainback & Associates with Architects Enterprise, 1996 South Hall; Thompson, Ventulett, Stainback & Associates and Mc4West, 2007 West Hall

281

Convention Centers

Convention Center	Location	Opened	Exhibit Halls (sq. ft.)
Miami Beach Convention Center	Miami Beach, FL	1958	503,000
Minneapolis Convention Center	Minneapolis, MN	1989–91	475,000
Moscone Center	San Francisco, CA	1981	741,308
Orange County Convention Center	Orlando, FL	1983	2.1 M
Oregon Convention Center	Portland, OR	1990	315,000
Pennsylvania Convention Center	Philadelphia, PA	1993	440,000
Phoenix Convention Center	Phoenix, AZ	1985	252,000
Reliant Center	Houston, TX	2004	706,213
Reno-Sparks Convention Center	Reno, NV	1965	381,000
Salt Palace Convention Center	Salt Lake City, UT	1996	515,000
San Diego Convention Center	San Diego, CA	1989	615,701
Tampa Convention Center	Tampa, FL	1990	200,000
Washington Convention Center	Washington, DC	2003	703,000
Washington State Convention and Trade Center	Seattle, WA	1988	205,700

Source: DesignIntelligence

Architect (original)	Architect (expansion)
B. Robert Swartburg	Gilbert M. Fein, 1968 Hall D; Edward Durrell Stone & Associates, Gilbert M. Fein, and Watson, Deutschmann, Kruse & Lyon, 1974 addition; Thompson, Ventulett, Stainback & Associates with Borrelli, Frankel, Biltstein, 1989 and 1991 expansions
Leonard Parker Associates; Setter Leach & Lindstrom; LMN Architects	Convention Center Design Group (Leonard Parker Associates; Setter Leach & Lindstrom; LMN Architects), 2001 expansion
Hellmuth, Obata & Kassabaum	Gensler/DMJM Associate Architects, joint venture, 1992 North Hall; Gensler/Michael Willis Architects/ Kwan Henmi Architecture, joint venture, 2003 West Hall
Helman Hurley Charvat Peacock/Architects, Inc.	Hellmuth, Obata & Kassabaum and Vickey/Ovresat Assumb Associates, Inc., 1989-90 expansion; Hunton Brady Pryor Maso Architects and Thompson, Ventulett, Stainback & Associates, 1996 expansion; Helman Hurley Charvat Peacock/Architects, Inc., Thompson, Ventulett, Stainback & Associates, Inc. and Hunton Brady Pryor Maso Architects, 2003 expansion
Zimmer Gunsul Frasca Partnership	Zimmer Gunsul Frasca Partnership, 2003 expansion
Thompson, Ventulett & Stainback Associates with Vitetta Group and Kelly/Maiello Architects and Planners (including the adaption of the 1893 Reading Terminal Headhouse by Wilson Brothers and F.H. Kimball)	—
GSAS, Architects and Planners, Inc. with Howard Needles Tammen & Bergendoff	Leo A Daly/HOK Sport + Venue + Event with van Dijk Westlake Reed Leskosky, 2006 expansion
Hermes Reed Architects	
Richard Neutra with Lockard, Casazza & Parsons	Parsons Design Group, 1981 North Hall; Sheehan, Van Woert Architects, 1991 East Hall; LMN Architects, 2002 expansion
Thompson, Ventulett, Stainback & Associates with GSBS Architects	Leonard Parker Associates with MHTB Architects, 2000 expansion; Edwards & Daniels Architects, Inc., 2006 expansion
Arthur Erickson Architect with Deems Lewis McKinley	HNTB Architecture with Tucker Sadler Architects, 2002 expansion
Hellmuth, Obata & Kassabaum	—
TVS–D&P–Mariani PLLC (Thompson, Ventulett, Stainback & Associates; Devrouax & Purnell Architects; and Mariani Architects Engineers)	—
TRA Architects	LMN Architects, 2001 expansion

283

Minor League Ballparks

Half of today's AAA ballparks were built within the last 10 years, and baseball's other minor leagues have also seen quite a bit of building activity, their increasingly sophisticated ballpark designs following the trend of the major leagues. The following charts list all the AAA ballparks and their requisite architectural statistics, as well as other minor-league ballparks that have opened since 2000.

AAA Ballparks

Team	League/Affiliation	Stadium	Location
Albuquerque Isotopes	Pacific Coast/Florida Marlins	Isotopes Park	Albuquerque, NM
Buffalo Bisons	International/Cleveland Indians	Dunn Tire Park	Buffalo, NY
Charlotte Knights	International/Chicago White Sox	Knights Stadium	Fort Mill, SC
Colorado Springs Sky Sox	Pacific Coast/Colorado Rockies	Security Services Field	Colorado Springs, CO
Columbus Clippers	International/Washington Nationals	Cooper Stadium	Columbus, OH
Durham Bulls	International/ Tampa Bay Devil Rays	Durham Bulls Athletic Park	Durham, NC
Fresno Grizzlies	Pacific Coast/San Francisco Giants	Grizzlies Stadium	Fresno, CA
Indianapolis Indians	International/Pittsburgh Pirates	Victory Field	Indianapolis, IN
Iowa Cubs	Pacific Coast/Chicago Cubs	Principal Park	Des Moines, IA
Las Vegas 51s	Pacific Coast/Los Angeles Dodgers	Cashman Field	Las Vegas, NV
Louisville Bats	International/Cincinnati Reds	Louisville Slugger Field	Louisville, KY
Memphis Redbirds	Pacific Coast/St. Louis Cardinals	AutoZone Park	Memphis, TN
Nashville Sounds	Pacific Coast/Milwaukee Brewers	Herschel Greer Stadium	Nashville, TN
New Orleans Zephyrs	Pacific Coast/New York Mets	Zephyr Field	New Orleans, LA
Norfolk Tides	International/Baltimore Orioles	Harbor Park	Norfolk, VA
Oklahoma RedHawks	Pacific Coast/Texas Rangers	AT&T Bricktown Ballpark	Oklahoma City, OK
Omaha Royals	Pacific Coast/Kansas City Royals	Rosenblatt Stadium	Omaha, NE
Ottawa Lynx	International/Philadelphia Phillies	Lynx Stadium	Ottawa, ON, Canada
Pawtucket Red Sox	International/Boston Red Sox	McCoy Stadium	Pawtucket, RI

Architect	Opened	Cost (original)	Capacity (current)	Naming Rights (amt. & expiration)
HOK Sport + Venue + Event	2003	$25 M	11,075	—
HOK Sports Facilities Group	1988	$40 M	21,050	$2.5 M (8 yrs.)
Odell & Associates	1990	$12 M	10,002	—
HNTB Architecture	1988	$3.7 M	8,500	$1.5 M (12 yrs.)
Osborn Engineering Company (Trautwein Associates, Architects and Planners, 1977 renovation)	1932	$450,000 ($6 M, 1977 renovation)	15,000	—
HOK Sports Facilities Group	1995	$16 M	10,000	—
HOK Sport + Venue + Event	2002	$46 M	12,500	—
HOK Sports Facilities Group	1996	$18 M	15,696	—
HOK Sports Facilities Group	1992	$11.5 M	11,000	$2.5 M (Indefinite)
Tate & Snyder	1983	$26 M	9,334	—
HNTB Architecture and K. Norman Berry & Associates	2000	$26 M	13,131	—
Looney Ricks Kiss in association with HOK Sports Facilities Group	2000	$46 M	14,320	$4.5 M (15 yrs.)
Stoll-Reed Architects Inc.	1977	$1 M	10,130	—
HOK Sports Facilities Group	1997	$25 M	10,000	—
HOK Sports Facilities Group	1993	$16 M	12,067	—
Architectural Design Group	1998	$32.4 M	13,066	Undisclosed
Leo A Daly	1948	$750,000	21,871	—
Brian W. Dickey Architect	1993	$17 M	10,332	—
Mark Linenthal and Thomas E. Harding (Heery International, Inc., 1999 renovation)	1942	$1.2 M ($16 M, 1999 renovation)	10,031	—

Minor League Ballparks

AAA Ballparks

Team	League/Affiliation	Stadium	Location
Portland Beavers	Pacific Coast/San Diego Padres	PGE Park	Portland, OR
Richmond Braves	International/Atlanta Braves	The Diamond	Richmond, VA
Rochester Red Wings	International/Minnesota Twins	Frontier Field	Rochester, NY
Round Rock Express	Pacific Coast/Houston Astros	Dell Diamond	Round Rock, TX
Sacramento River Cats	Pacific Coast/Oakland A's	Raley Field	Sacramento, CA
Salt Lake Bees	Pacific Coast/Los Angeles Angels of Anaheim	Franklin Covey Field	Salt Lake City, UT
Scranton-Wilkes Barre	International/New York Yankees	PNC Field	Moosic, PA
Syracuse Sky Chiefs	International/Toronto Blue Jays	Alliance Bank Stadium	Syracuse, NY
Tacoma Rainiers	Pacific Coast/Seattle Mariners	Cheney Stadium	Tacoma, WA
Toledo Mud Hens	International/Detriot Tigers	Fifth Third Field	Toledo, OH
Tucson Sidewinders	Pacific Coast/Arizona Diamondbacks	Tucson Electric Park	Tuscon, AZ

Other New Minor League Ballparks: 2000–07

Team	League/Affiliation	Stadium	Location
Aberdeen IronBirds	Class A New York-Penn League/ Baltimore Orioles	Ripken Stadium	Little Aberdeen, MD
Arkansas Travelers	Class AA Texas League/Los Angeles Angeles of Anaheim	Dickey-Stephens Park	North Little Rock, AR
Brooklyn Cyclones	Class A New York-Penn League/ New York Mets	KeySpan Park	Brooklyn, NY
Camden Riversharks	Independent Atlantic League	Campbell's Field	Camden, NJ
Casper Rockies	Rookie Pioneer League/ Colorado Rockies	Mike Lansing Field	Casper, WY
Cedar Rapids Kernels	Class A Midwest League/ Los Angeles Angels of Anaheim	Veterans Memorial Stadium	Cedar Rapids, IA
Chattanooga Lookouts	Class AA Southern League/ Cincinnati Reds	AT&T Field	Chattanooga, TN

Architect	Opened	Cost (original)	Capacity (current)	Naming Rights (amt. & expiration)
A.E. Doyle (Ellerbe Becket with Fletcher, Farr, Ayotte, PC, Inc., 2001 renovation)	1926	$502,000 ($38.5 M, 2001 renovation)	18,000	$7.1 M (10 yrs.)
Baskervill	1985	$8 M	12,134	—
Ellerbe Beckett	1997	$35.3 M	10,868	$3.5 M (20 yrs.)
HKS Inc.	2002	$25 M	9,816	$2.5 M (15 yrs.)
HNTB Architecture	2000	$40 M	11,092	$15 M (20 yrs.)
HOK Sports Facilities Group	1994	$22 M	15,500	$1.4M (10 yrs.)
GSGS&B	1989	$25 M	11,432	$1.1 M (3 yrs.)
HOK Sports Facilities Group	1997	$16 M	11,602	$2.8 M (20 yrs.)
E.L Mills & Associates	1960	$940,000	9,600	—
HNTB Architecture	2002	$39.2 M	10,000	$5 M (15 yrs.)
HOK Sports Facilities Group	1998	$37 M	11,000	$4 M (15 yrs.)

287

Architect	Opened	Cost (original)	Capacity (current)	Naming Rights (amt. & expiration)
Tetra Tech, Inc.	2002	$35 M	6,000	—
HKS Inc.	2007	$40.4 M	5,288	—
Jack L. Gordon Architects	2001	$35 M	8,000	—
Clarke, Caton and Hintz	2001	$20.5 M	6,425	$3 M (10 yrs.)
GSG Architecture	2001	$4 M	2,500	—
Heinlein Schrock Stearns	2002	$14 M	6,100	—
DLR Group with TWH Architects	2000	$10 M	6,157	$1 M (10 yrs.)

Minor League Ballparks

Other New Minor League Ballparks: 2000–07

Team	League/Affiliation	Stadium	Location
Clearwater Threshers	Class A Florida State League/ Philadelphia Phillies	Bright House Networks Field	Clearwater, FL
Corpus Christi Hooks	Class AA Texas League/ Houston Astros	Whataburger Field	Corpus Christi, TX
Dayton Dragons	Class A Midwest League/ Cincinnati Reds	Fifth Third Field	Dayton, OH
Frisco RoughRiders	Class AA Texas League/ Texas Rangers	Dr. Pepper/ Seven Up Ballpark	Frisco, TX
Gary SouthShore RailCats	Independent Northern League	The Steel Yard	Gary, IN
Great Lakes Loons	Class A Midwest League/ Los Angeles Dodgers	Dow Diamond	Midland, MI
Greensboro Grasshoppers	Class A South Atlantic League/ Florida Marlins	First Horizon Park	Greenboro, SC
Greenville Drive	Class A South Atlantic League/ Boston Red Sox	West End Field	Greenville, SC
Idaho Falls Chukars	Rookie Pioneer League/ Kansas City Royals	Melaleuca Field	Idaho Falls, ID
Jacksonville Suns	Class AA Southern League/ Los Angeles Dodgers	Baseball Grounds of Jacksonville	Jacksonville, FL
Joliet Jackhammers	Independent Northern League	Silver Cross Field	Joliet, IL
Kansas City T-Bones	Independent Northern League	CommunityAmerica Ballpark	Kansas City, KS
Lake County Captains	Class A South Atlantic/ Cleveland Indians	Classic Park	Eastlake, OH
Lakewood BlueClaws	Class A South Atlantic/ Philadelphia Phillies	FirstEnergy Park	Lakewood, NJ
Lancaster Barnstormers	Independent Atlantic League	Clipper Magazine Stadium	Lancaster, PA
Lexington Legends	Class A South Atlantic League/ Houston Astros	Applebee's Park	Lexington, KY
Lincoln Salt Dogs	Independent American Association	Haymarket Park	Lincoln, NE
Long Island Ducks	Independent Atlantic League	Citibank Park	Central Islip, NY
Midland RockHounds	Class AA Texas League/Oakland A's	Citibank Ballpark	Midland, TX
Mississippi Braves	Class AA Southern League/ Atlanta Braves	Trustmark Park	Pearl, MS

Architect	Opened	Cost (original)	Capacity (current)	Naming Rights (amt. & expiration)
HOK Sport + Venue + Event with EwingCole	2004	$32 M	7,000	$1.7 M (10 yrs.)
HKS Inc.	2005	$27.7 M	8,255	Undisclosed
HNTB Architecture	2000	$22.7 M	7,250	Undisclosed
David Schwarz/Architectural Services, Inc. with HKS Inc.	2003	$28 M	10,600	Undisclosed
HNTB Architecture	2003	$45 M	6,000	$875,000 (10 yrs.)
HOK Sport + Venue + Event	2007	$28 M	5,500	—
Moser Mayer Phoenix Associates	2005	$20 M	5,021	$3 M (10 yrs.)
DLR Group	2006	$14.5 M	5,700	—
Elliott Workgroup Architects	2007	$5.6 M	3,400	600,000
HOK Sport + Venue + Event	2003	$34 M	10,000	—
Sink Combs Dethlefs	2002	$27 M	6,915	$1.5 M (10 yrs.)
Heinlein Schrock Stearns	2003	$15 M	5,500	Undisclosed
DLR Group	2003	$19.5 M	7,273	$4.26 M (15 yrs.)
HNTB Architecture	2001	$20 M	6,588	$4.5 M (20 yrs.)
Tetra Tech, Inc.	2005	$23.4 M	6,500	$2.5 M (10 yrs.)
Brisbin Brook Beynon Architects (Canada)	2001	$13.5 M	6,994	$3 M (10 yrs.)
DLR Group	2001	$32 M	4,500	—
HNTB Architecture with Beatty Harvey Associates, Architects	2000	$14 M	6,200	Undisclosed
HOK Sport + Venue + Event	2002	$25 M	5,000	$2.1 M (25 yrs.)
HOK Sport + Venue + Event with Dale and Associates Architects	2005	$25 M	7,062	$25 M (10 yrs.)

Minor League Ballparks

Other New Minor League Ballparks: 2000–07

Team	League/Affiliation	Stadium	Location
Missoula Osprey	Rookie Pioneer League/ Arizona Diamondbacks	Ogren Park at Allegiance Field	Missoula, MT
Montgomery Biscuits	Class AA Southern League/ Tampa Bay Devil Rays	Montgomery Riverwalk Stadium	Montgomery, AL
New Hampshire Fisher Cats	Class AA Eastern League/ Toronto Blue Jays	Merchantsauto.com Stadium	Manchester, NH
Peoria Chiefs	Class A Midwest League/ Chicago Cubs	O'Brien Field	Peoria, IL
Rockford RiverHawks	Independent Frontier League	RiverHawks Stadium	Rockford, IL
Rome Braves	Class A South Atlantic/ Atlanta Braves	State Mutual Stadium	Rome, GA
Southern Illinois Miners	Independent Frontier League	Marion Stadium	Marion, IL
Springfield Cardinals	Class AA Texas League/ St. Louis Cardinals	Hammons Field	Springfield, MO
State College Spikes	Class A New York-Penn League/ Pittsburgh Pirates	Medlar Field at Lubrano Park	University Park, PA
Staten Island Yankees	Class A New York-Penn League/ New York Yankees	Richmond County Bank Ballpark at St. George	Staten Island, NY
Stockton Ports	Class A California League/ Oakland A's	Banner Island Ballpark	Stockton, CA
Tennessee Smokies	Class AA Southern League/ Chicago Cubs	Smokies Park	Kodak, TN
Traverse City Beach Bums	Independent Frontier League	Wuerfel Park	Traverse City, MI
Tri-City ValleyCats	Class A New York-Penn League/ Houston Astros	Joseph L. Bruno Stadium	Troy, NY
West Viginia Power	Class A South Atlantic League/ Milwaukee Brewers	Appalachian Power Park	Charleston, WV
York Revolution	Independent Atlantic League	Sovereign Bank Stadium	York, PA

Source: DesignIntelligence

Architect	Opened	Cost (original)	Capacity (current)	Naming Rights (amt. & expiration)
Heery International, Inc. with CTA Architects	2004	$10.2 M	3,500	$1 M
HOK Sport + Venue + Event	2004	$26 M	7,000	—
HNTB Architecture	2005	$20 M	7,000	Undisclosed
HNTB Architecture	2000	$24 M	7,500	—
CSHQA Architects/Engineers/Planners	2005	$7 M	4,000	—
Brisbin Brook Beynon Architects (Canada)	2003	$14.8 M	6,100	Undisclosed
360 Architecture	2007	$18 M	4,380	—
Pellham Phillips Hagerman	2004	$32 M	8,056	—
L. Robert Kimball & Associates; DLR Group	2006	$24 M	6,000	—
HOK Sport + Venue + Event	2001	$34 M	6,886	Undisclosed
HKS Inc.	2005	$14.5 M	5,000	—
HNTB Architecture	2000	$20 M	6,412	—
Fuller Nichols Architects	2006	$8 M	3,518	—
DLR Group	2002	$14 M	4,500	—
HNTB Architecture	2005	$23 M	4,500	$1.25 M (10 yrs.)
Tetra Tech, Inc.; Murphy and Dittenhafer, Inc.	2007	$32.5 M	5,200	$2.7 (10 yrs.)

Sports Stadiums

From classic ballparks to cutting-edge arenas and stadiums, the following charts provide statistical and architectural highlights for all major-league baseball, basketball, football, and hockey venues in the United States. All cost and architectural information refers to the stadiums as they were originally built and does not include additions, renovations, or expansions.

Baseball

Team	League	Stadium	Location	Opened
Arizona Diamondbacks	National	Chase Field	Phoenix, AZ	1998
Atlanta Braves	National	Turner Field	Atlanta, GA	1997
Baltimore Orioles	American	Oriole Park at Camden Yards	Baltimore, MD	1992
Boston Red Sox	American	Fenway Park	Boston, MA	1912
Chicago Cubs	National	Wrigley Field	Chicago, IL	1914
Chicago White Sox	American	US Cellular Field	Chicago, IL	1991
Cincinnati Reds	National	Great American Ball Park	Cincinnati, OH	2003
Cleveland Indians	American	Jacobs Field	Cleveland, OH	1994
Colorado Rockies	National	Coors Field	Denver, CO	1995
Detroit Tigers	American	Comerica Park	Detroit, MI	2000
Florida Marlins	National	Dolphins Stadium	Miami, FL	1987
Houston Astros	National	Minute Maid Park	Houston, TX	2000
Kansas City Royals	American	Kauffman Stadium	Kansas City, MO	1973
Los Angeles Angels of Anaheim	American	Angel Stadium of Anaheim	Anaheim, CA	1966
Los Angeles Dodgers	National	Dodger Stadium	Los Angeles, CA	1962
Milwaukee Brewers	National	Miller Park	Milwaukee, WI	2001
Minnesota Twins	American	Hubert H. Humphrey Metrodome	Minneapolis, MN	1982
New York Mets	National	Shea Stadium	Flushing, NY	1964
New York Yankees	American	Yankee Stadium	Bronx, NY	1923
Oakland A's	American	McAfee Coliseum	Oakland, CA	1966
Philadelphia Phillies	National	Citizens Bank Park	Philadelphia, PA	2004
Pittsburgh Pirates	National	PNC Park	Pittsburgh, PA	2001

Architect	Cost (original)	Capacity (current)	Roof Type	Naming Rights (amt. & expiration)
Ellerbe Becket with Bill Johnson	$355 M	49,033	Convertible	$33.1 M (30 yrs.)
Heery International, Inc.; Williams-Russell & Johnson, Inc.; Ellerbe Becket	$250 M	49,831	Open-Air	Undisclosed
HOK Sports Facilities Group with RTKL Associates Inc.	$210 M	48,876	Open-Air	—
Osborn Engineering Company	$365,000	33,871	Open-Air	—
Zachary Taylor Davis	$250,000	38,765	Open-Air	—
HOK Sports Facilities Group	$150 M	44,321	Open-Air	$68 M (20 yrs.)
HOK Sport + Venue + Event with GBBN Architects	$290 M	42,053	Open-Air	$75 M (30 yrs.)
HOK Sports Facilities Group	$173 M	43,345	Open-Air	$13.9 M (20 yrs.)
HOK Sports Facilities Group	$215 M	50,445	Open-Air	$15 M (indefinite)
HOK Sports Facilities Group; SHG Inc.	$300 M	40,637	Open-Air	$66 M (30 yrs.)
HOK Sports Facilities Group	$125 M	47,662	Open-Air	—
HOK Sports Facilities Group	$248.1 M	40,950	Retractable	$170 M (28 yrs.)
HNTB Architecture	$50.45 M	40,625	Open-Air	—
Robert A.M. Stern Architects	$25 M	45,050	Open-Air	—
Emil Praeger	$24.47 M	56,000	Open-Air	—
HKS Inc. with NBBJ and Eppstein Uhen Architects Inc.	$399.4 M	42,500	Retractable	$41 M (20 yrs.)
Skidmore, Owings & Merrill	$75 M	55,883	Dome	—
Praeger, Kavanaugh, Waterbury	$24 M	55,601	Open-Air	—
Osborn Engineering Company	$3.1 M	57,545	Open-Air	—
Skidmore, Owings & Merrill	$25.5 M	48,219	Open-Air	$6 M (5 yrs.)
EwingCole with HOK Sport + Venue + Event	$346 M	43,000	Open-Air	$57.5 M (25 yrs.)
HOK Sport + Venue + Event; L.D. Astorino Companies	$262 M	38,000	Open-Air	$30 M (20 yrs.)

Sports Stadiums

Baseball

Team	League	Stadium	Location	Opened
San Diego Padres	National	Petco Park	San Diego, CA	2004
San Francisco Giants	National	AT&T Park	San Francisco, CA	2000
Seattle Mariners	American	Safeco Field	Seattle, WA	1999
St. Louis Cardinals	National	Busch Stadium	St. Louis, MO	2006
Tampa Bay Devil Rays	American	Tropicana Field	St. Petersburg, FL	1990
Texas Rangers	American	Rangers Ballpark in Arlington	Arlington, TX	1994
Toronto Blue Jays	American	Rogers Centre	Toronto, ON, Canada	1989
Washington Nationals	National	RFK Stadium	Washington, DC	1961

Basketball

Team	Conference	Stadium	Location	Opened
Atlanta Hawks	Eastern	Philips Arena	Atlanta, GA	1999
Boston Celtics	Eastern	TD Banknorth Garden	Boston, MA	1995
Charlotte Bobcats	Eastern	Charlotte Bobcats Arena	Charlotte, NC	2005
Chicago Bulls	Eastern	United Center	Chicago, IL	1994
Cleveland Cavaliers	Eastern	Quicken Loans Arena	Cleveland, OH	1994
Dallas Mavericks	Western	American Airlines Center	Dallas, TX	2001
Denver Nuggets	Western	Pepsi Center	Denver, CO	1999
Detroit Pistons	Eastern	Palace of Auburn Hills	Auburn Hills, MI	1988
Golden State Warriors	Western	Oracle Arena	Oakland, CA	1966
Houston Rockets	Western	Toyota Center	Houston, TX	2003
Indiana Pacers	Eastern	Conseco Fieldhouse	Indianapolis, IN	1999
Los Angeles Clippers	Western	Staples Center	Los Angeles, CA	1999
Los Angeles Lakers	Western	Staples Center	Los Angeles, CA	1999
Memphis Grizzlies	Western	FedEx Forum	Memphis, TN	2004

Architect	Cost (original)	Capacity (current)	Roof Type	Naming Rights (amt. & expiration)
Antoine Predock Architect with HOK Sport + Venue + Event	$453 M	46,000	Open-Air	$60 M (22 yrs.)
HOK Sports Facilities Group	$345 M	40,800	Open-Air	$50 M (24 yrs.)
NBBJ	$517.6 M	46,621	Retractable	$40 M (20 yrs.)
HOK Sport + Venue + Event	$344 M	46,816	Open-Air	Undisclosed
HOK Sports Facilities Group; Lescher & Mahoney Sports; Criswell, Blizzard & Blouin Architects	$138 M	45,360	Dome	$30 M (30 yrs.)
David Schwarz/Architectural Services, Inc.; HKS Inc.	$190 M	49,115	Open-Air	—
Rod Robbie and Michael Allen	C$500 M	50,516	Retractable	C$20 M (10 yrs.)
Osborn Engineering Company	$24 M	56,692	Open-Air	—

Architect	Cost (original)	Capacity (current)	Naming Rights (amt. & expiration)
HOK Sports Facilities Group; Arquitectonica	$213.5 M	20,300	$180 M (20 yrs.)
Ellerbe Becket	$160 M	18,624	$138 M (20 yrs.)
Ellerbe Becket with Odell & Associates and The Freelon Group, Inc	$265 M	18,500	—
HOK Sports Facilities Group; Marmon Mok: W.E. Simpson Company	$175 M	21,711	$25 M (20 yrs.)
Ellerbe Becket	$152 M	20,562	Undisclosed
David Schwarz/Architectural Services, Inc. with HKS Inc.	$420 M	19,200	$40 M (20 yrs.)
HOK Sports Facilities Group	$160 M	19,309	$68 M (20 yrs.)
Rossetti Associates	$70 M	21,454	—
HNTB Architecture	n/a	19,200	$30 M (10 yrs.)
HOK Sports + Venue + Event	$175 M	18,300	Undisclosed
Ellerbe Becket	$183 M	18,345	$40 M (20 yrs.)
NBBJ	$330 M	20,000	$100 M (20 yrs.)
NBBJ	$330 M	20,000	$100 M (20 yrs.)
Ellerbe Becket with Looney Ricks Kiss	$250 M	18,165	$90 M (20 yrs.)

Sports Stadiums

Basketball

Team	Conference	Stadium	Location	Opened
Miami Heat	Eastern	American Airlines Arena	Miami, FL	1998
Milwaukee Bucks	Eastern	Bradley Center	Milwaukee, WI	1988
Minnesota Timberwolves	Western	Target Center	Minneapolis, MN	1990
New Jersey Nets	Eastern	Continental Airlines Arena	East Rutherford, NJ	1981
New Orleans Hornets	Western	New Orleans Arena	New Orleans, LA	1999
New York Knicks	Eastern	Madison Square Garden	New York, NY	1968
Orlando Magic	Eastern	Amway Arena	Orlando, FL	1989
Philadelphia 76ers	Eastern	Wachovia Center	Philadelphia, PA	1996
Phoenix Suns	Western	US Airways Center	Phoenix, AZ	1992
Portland Trail Blazers	Western	Rose Garden	Portland, OR	1995
Sacramento Kings	Western	Arco Arena	Sacramento, CA	1988
San Antonio Spurs	Western	AT&T Center	San Antonio, TX	2002
Seattle SuperSonics	Western	Key Arena at Seattle Center	Seattle, WA	1983
Toronto Raptors	Eastern	Air Canada Centre	Toronto, ON, Canada	1999
Utah Jazz	Western	EnergySolutions Arena	Salt Lake City, UT	1991
Washington Wizards	Eastern	Verizon Center	Washington, DC	1997

Football

Team	Conference	Stadium	Location	Opened
Arizona Cardinals	NFC	University of Phoenix Stadium	Glendale, AZ	2006
Atlanta Falcons	NFC	Georgia Dome	Atlanta, GA	1992
Baltimore Ravens	AFC	M&T Bank Stadium	Baltimore, MD	1998
Buffalo Bills	AFC	Ralph Wilson Stadium	Orchard Park, NY	1973
Carolina Panthers	NFC	Bank of America Stadium	Charlotte, NC	1996
Chicago Bears	NFC	Soldier Field	Chicago, IL	2003
Cincinnati Bengals	AFC	Paul Brown Stadium	Cincinnati, OH	2000
Cleveland Browns	AFC	Cleveland Browns Stadium	Cleveland, OH	1999
Dallas Cowboys	NFC	Texas Stadium	Irving, TX	1971

Architect	Cost (original)	Capacity (current)	Naming Rights (amt. & expiration)
Arquitectonica	$175 M	19,600	$42 M (20 yrs.)
HOK Sports Facilities Group	$90 M	18,717	—
KMR Architects	$104 M	19,006	$18.75 M (15 yrs.)
Grad Partnership; DiLullo, Clauss, Ostroski & Partners	$85 M	19,040	$29 M (12 yrs.)
Arthur Q. Davis, FAIA & Partners	$112 M	18,500	—
Charles Luckman	$116 M	19,763	—
Lloyd Jones Philpot; Cambridge Seven Associates	$98 M	17,248	$1.5 M (4 yrs.)
Ellerbe Becket	$206 M	20,444	$40 M (29 yrs.)
Ellerbe Becket	$90 M	19,023	$26 M (30 yrs.)
Ellerbe Becket	$262 M	21,538	—
Rann Haight Architect	$40 M	17,317	$7 M (10 yrs.)
Ellerbe Becket with Lake/Flato Architects and Kell Muñoz Architects	$186 M	18,500	$85 M (20 yrs.)
NBBJ	$67 M	17,072	$15.1 M (15 yrs.)
HOK Sports Facilities Group; Brisbin Brook Beynon Architects (Canada)	C$265 M	19,800	C$40 M (20 yrs.)
FFKR Architects	$94 M	19,911	$20 M (10 yrs.)
Ellerbe Becket	$260 M	20,674	$44 M (15 years)

297

Architect	Cost (original)	Capacity (current)	Roof Type	Naming Rights (amt. & expiration)
Peter Eisenman with HOK Sport + Venue + Event	$370.6 M	65,000	Retractable	$154.5 M (20 yrs.)
Heery International, Inc.	$214 M	71,149	Dome	—
HOK Sports Facilities Group	$220 M	69,084	Open-Air	$75 M (15 yrs.)
HNTB Architecture	$22 M	73,800	Open-Air	—
HOK Sports Facilities Group	$248 M	73,258	Open-Air	Undisclosed
Wood + Zapata, Inc. with Lohan Caprile Goettsch	$365 M	62,000	Open-Air	—
NBBJ	$400 M	65,535	Open-Air	—
HOK Sports Facilities Group	$283 M	73,200	Open-Air	—
Warren Morey	$35 M	65,846	Partial Roof	—

Sports Stadiums

Football

Team	Conference	Stadium	Location	Opened
Denver Broncos	AFC	Invesco Field at Mile High Stadium	Denver, CO	2001
Detroit Lions	NFC	Ford Field	Allen Park, MI	2002
Green Bay Packers	NFC	Lambeau Field	Green Bay, WI	1957
Houston Texans	AFC	Reliant Stadium	Houston, TX	2002
Indianapolis Colts	AFC	RCA Dome	Indianapolis, IN	1984
Jacksonville Jaguars	AFC	Jacksonville Municipal Stadium	Jacksonville, FL	1995
Kansas City Chiefs	AFC	Arrowhead Stadium	Kansas City, MO	1972
Miami Dolphins	AFC	Dolphins Stadium	Miami, FL	1987
Minnesota Vikings	NFC	Hubert H. Humphrey Metrodome	Minneapolis, MN	1982
New England Patriots	AFC	Gillette Stadium	Foxboro, MA	2002
New Orleans Saints	NFC	Louisiana Superdome	New Orleans, LA	1975
New York Giants	NFC	Giants Stadium	E. Rutherford, NJ	1976
New York Jets	AFC	Meadowlands	E. Rutherford, NJ	1976
Oakland Raiders	AFC	McAfee Coliseum	Oakland, CA	1966
Philadelphia Eagles	NFC	Lincoln Financial Field	Philadelphia, PA	2003
Pittsburgh Steelers	AFC	Heinz Field	Pittsburgh, PA	2001
San Diego Chargers	AFC	Qualcomm Stadium	San Diego, CA	1967
San Francisco 49ers	NFC	Monster Park	San Francisco, CA	1960
Seattle Seahawks	NFC	Qwest Field	Seattle, WA	2002
St. Louis Rams	NFC	Edward Jones Dome	St. Louis, MO	1995
Tampa Bay Buccaneers	NFC	Raymond James Stadium	Tampa, FL	1998
Tennessee Titans	AFC	LP Field	Nashville, TN	1999
Washington Redskins	NFC	FedEx Field	Landover, MD	1996

Architect	Cost (original)	Capacity (current)	Roof Type	Naming Rights (amt. & expiration)
HNTB Architecture with Fentress Bradburn Architects and Bertram A. Burton and Associates	$400.8 M	76,125	Open-Air	$120 M (20 yrs.)
SmithGroup	$500 M	64,355	Dome	$40 M (40 yrs.)
John Somerville	$960,000	60,890	Open-Air	—
HOK Sport + Venue + Event	$325 M	69,500	Retractable	$300 M (30 yrs.)
HNTB Architecture	$82 M	60,127	Dome	$10 M (10 yrs.)
HOK Sports Facilities Group	$138 M	73,000	Open-Air	—
Kivett and Meyers	$43 M	79,409	Open-Air	—
HOK Sports Facilities Group	$125 M	74,916	Open-Air	—
Skidmore, Owings & Merrill	$55 M	64,121	Dome	—
HOK Sport + Venue + Event	$325 M	68,000	Open-Air	Undisclosed
Curtis & Davis Architects	$134 M	69,065	Dome	—
HOK Sports Facilities Group	$75 M	79,670	Open-Air	—
HOK Sports Facilities Group	$75 M	79,670	Open-Air	—
Skidmore, Owings & Merrill	$25.5 M	62,026	Suspension (fixed)	$6 M (5 yrs.)
NBBJ	$320 M	66,000	Open-Air	$139.6 M (20 yrs.)
HOK Sport + Venue + Event with WTW Architects	$281 M	64,440	Open-Air	$58 M (20 yrs.)
Frank L. Hope and Associates	$27 M	71,294	Open-Air	$18 M (20 yrs.)
John & Bolles	$24.6 M	69,843	Open-Air	$6 M (4 yrs.)
Ellerbe Becket with LMN Architects	$360 M	67,000	Partial Roof	$75.27 M (15 yrs.)
HOK Sports Facilities Group	$280 M	66,000	Dome	$31.8 M (12 yrs.)
HOK Sports Facilities Group	$168.5 M	66,000	Open-Air	$32.5 M (13 yrs.)
HOK Sports Facilities Group	$290 M	67,000	Open-Air	$30 M (10 yrs.)
HOK Sports Facilities Group	$250.5 M	80,116	Open-Air	$205 M (27 yrs.)

299

Sports Stadiums

Hockey

Team	Conference	Stadium	Location	Opened
Anaheim Mighty Ducks	Western	Honda Center	Anaheim, CA	1993
Atlanta Thrashers	Eastern	Philips Arena	Atlanta, GA	1999
Boston Bruins	Eastern	TD Banknorth Garden	Boston, MA	1995
Buffalo Sabres	Eastern	HSBC Arena	Buffalo, NY	1996
Calgary Flames	Western	Pengrowth Saddledome	Calgary, AB, Canada	1983
Carolina Hurricanes	Eastern	RBC Center	Raleigh, NC	1999
Chicago Blackhawks	Western	United Center	Chicago, IL	1994
Colorado Avalanche	Western	Pepsi Center	Denver, CO	1999
Columbus Blue Jackets	Western	Nationwide Arena	Columbus, OH	2000
Dallas Stars	Western	American Airlines Center	Dallas, TX	2001
Detroit Red Wings	Western	Joe Louis Arena	Detroit, MI	1979
Edmonton Oilers	Western	Rexall Place	Edmonton, AB, Canada	1974
Florida Panthers	Eastern	BankAtlantic Center	Sunrise, FL	1998
Los Angeles Kings	Western	Staples Center	Los Angeles, CA	1999
Minnesota Wild	Western	Xcel Energy Center	Saint Paul, MN	2000
Montreal Canadiens	Eastern	Bell Centre	Montreal, QC, Canada	1996
Nashville Predators	Western	Nashville Arena	Nashville, TN	1997
New Jersey Devils	Eastern	Prudential Center	Newark, NJ	2007
New York Islanders	Eastern	Nassau Veterans Memorial Coliseum	Uniondale, NY	1972
New York Rangers	Eastern	Madison Square Garden	New York, NY	1968
Ottawa Senators	Eastern	Scotiabank Place	Kanata, ON, Canada	1996
Philadelphia Flyers	Eastern	Wachovia Center	Philadelphia, PA	1996
Phoenix Coyotes	Western	Jobing.com Arena	Glendale, AZ	2003
Pittsburgh Penguins	Eastern	Mellon Arena	Pittsburgh, PA	1961
San Jose Sharks	Western	HP Pavillion	San Jose, CA	1993
St. Louis Blues	Western	Scottrade Center	St. Louis, MO	1994
Tampa Bay Lightning	Eastern	St. Pete Times Forum	Tampa, FL	1996
Toronto Maple Leafs	Eastern	Air Canada Centre	Toronto, ON, Canada	1999
Vancouver Canucks	Western	General Motors Place	Vancouver, BC, Canada	1995
Washington Capitals	Eastern	Verizon Center	Washington, DC	1997

Source: DesignIntelligence

Architect	Cost (original)	Capacity (current)	Naming Rights (amt. & expiration)
HOK Sports Facilities Group	$120 M	17,174	$60 M (15 yrs.)
HOK Sports Facilities Group; Arquitectonica	$213.5 M	18,750	$180 M (20 yrs.)
Ellerbe Becket	$160 M	17,565	$138 M (20 yrs.)
Ellerbe Becket	$127.5 M	18,595	$24 M (30 yrs.)
Graham Edmunds; Graham McCourt	C$176 M	20,140	C$20 M (20 yrs.)
Odell & Associates	$158 M	18,176	$80 M (20 yrs.)
HOK Sports Facilities Group; Marmon Mok; W.E. Simpson Co.	$175 M	20,500	$25 M (20 yrs.)
HOK Sports Facilities Group	$160 M	18,129	$68 M (20 yrs.)
Heinlein Schrock Stearns; NBBJ	$150 M	18,500	$135 M (indefinite)
David Schwarz/Architectural Services, Inc. with HKS Inc.	$420 M	18,000	$40 M (20 yrs.)
Smith, Hinchmen and Grylls Associates	$57 M	18,785	—
Phillips, Barrett, Hillier, Jones & Partners with Wynn, Forbes, Lord, Feldberg & Schmidt	C$22.5 M	16,900	Undisclosed
Ellerbe Becket	$212 M	19,452	$27 M (10 yrs.)
NBBJ	$330 M	18,500	Undisclosed
HOK Sports Facilities Group	$130 M	18,064	$75 M (25 yrs.)
Consortium of Quebec Architects	C$280 M	21,273	$100 M (20 yrs.)
HOK Sports Facilities Group	$144 M	17,500	—
HOK Sport + Venue + Event with Morris Adjmi Architects	$375 M	17,615	$105.3 M (20 yrs.)
Welton Becket	$31 M	16,297	—
Charles Luckman	$116 M	18,200	—
Rossetti Associates	C$200 M	18,500	C$20 M (15 yrs.)
Ellerbe Becket	$206 M	18,168	$40 M (29 yrs.)
HOK Sport + Venue + Event	$220 M	17,653	$ 25 M (10 yrs.)
Mitchell and Ritchie	$22 M	17,323	$18 M (10 yrs.)
Sink Combs Dethlefs	$162.5 M	17,483	$55.8 M (18 yrs.)
Ellerbe Becket	$170 M	19,260	Undisclosed
Ellerbe Becket	$139 M	19,500	$25 M (12 yrs.)
HOK Sports Facilities Group; Brisbin Brook Beynon Architects (Canada)	C$265 M	18,800	C$40 M (20 yrs.)
Brisbin Brook Beynon Architects (Canada)	C$160 M	18,422	C$18.5 M (20 yrs.)
Ellerbe Becket	$260 M	19,700	$44 M (13 yrs.)

301

Tallest Buildings in the World

The following list ranks the world's 100 tallest buildings as determined by the Council on Tall Buildings and Urban Habitat. Buildings that have reached their full height but are still under construction are deemed eligible and are indicated with a UC in the year category along with the anticipated completion date, if known.

	Building	Yr.	Location	Height (ft./m.)	(# stories)	Architect
1	Taipei 101	2004	Taipei, Taiwan	1,670/509	101	C.Y. Lee & Partners (Taiwan)
2	Shanghai World Financial Center	2008	Shanghai, China	1,614/492	101	Kohn Pedersen Fox Associates; East China Architectural Design and Research Institute Co. Ltd. (China)
3	Petronas Tower 1	1998	Kuala Lumpur, Malaysia	1,483/452	88	Cesar Pelli & Associates
4	Petronas Tower 2	1998	Kuala Lumpur, Malaysia	1,483/452	88	Cesar Pelli & Associates
5	Sears Tower	1974	Chicago, IL	1,451/442	110	Skidmore, Owings & Merrill
6	Jin Mao Building	1999	Shanghai, China	1,381/421	88	Skidmore, Owings & Merrill
7	Two International Finance Centre	2003	Hong Kong, China	1,362/415	88	Cesar Pelli & Associates
8	CITIC Plaza	1996	Guangzhou, China	1,283/391	80	Dennis Lau & Ng Chun Man Architects & Engineers (China)
9	Shun Hing Square	1996	Shenzhen, China	1,260/384	69	K.Y. Cheung Design Associates (China)
10	Empire State Building	1931	New York, US	1,250/381	102	Shreve, Lamb & Harmon
11	Central Plaza	1992	Hong Kong, China	1,227/374	78	Ng Chun Man & Associates (China)
12	Bank of China	1989	Hong Kong, China	1,205/367	70	Pei Cobb Freed & Partners
13	Bank of America Tower	2008	New York, NY	1,000/366	54	Cook+Fox Architects; Adamson Associates Architects
14	Almas Tower	UC08	Dubai, UAE	1,181/360	68	WS Atkins & Partners (UK)
15	Emirates Tower One	1999	Dubai, UAE	1,165/355	54	Norr Group Consultants (Canada)
16	Tuntex Sky Tower	1997	Kaohsiung, Taiwan	1,140/348	85	C.Y. Lee & Partners (Taiwan); Hellmuth, Obata & Kassabaum
17	Aon Centre	1973	Chicago, IL	1,136/346	83	Edward Durrell Stone & Associates

Building	Yr.	Location	Height (ft./m.)	(# stories)	Architect
18 The Center	1998	Hong Kong, China	1,135/346	73	Dennis Lau & Ng Chun Man Architects & Engineers (China)
19 John Hancock Center	1969	Chicago, IL	1,127/344	100	Skidmore, Owings & Merrill
20 Rose Tower	UC07	Dubai, UAE	1,093/333	72	Khatib & Alami (Lebanon)
21 Shimao International Plaza	2006	Shanghai, China	1,093/333	60	Ingenhoven Architekten (Germany); East China Architectural Design and Research Institute Co. Ltd. (China)
22 Minsheng Bank Building	UC07	Wuhan, China	1,087/331	68	Wuhan Architectural Design Institute (China)
23 Ryugyong Hotel	*	Pyongyang, North Korea	1,083/330	105	Baikdoosan Architects & Engineers (North Korea)
24 China World Trade Center Tower III	2008	Beijing, China	1,083/328	69	Skidmore, Owings & Merrill
25 Q1 Tower	2005	Gold Coast, Australia	1,058/323	78	The Buchan Group (Australia)
26 Burj al Arab Hotel	1999	Dubai, UAE	1,053/321	60	WS Atkins & Partners (UK)
27 Nina Tower I	2006	Hong Kong, China	1,046/319	80	n/a
28 Chrysler Building	1930	New York, NY	1,046/319	77	William Van Alen
29 New York Times Tower	UC07	New York, NY	1,046/319	52	Renzo Piano Building Workshop (Italy); FXFOWLE Architects
30 Bank of America Plaza	1993	Atlanta, GA	1,039/317	55	Kevin Roche John Dinkeloo & Associates
31 US Bank Tower	1990	Los Angeles, CA	1,018/310	73	Pei Cobb Freed & Partners
32 Menara Telekom Headquarters	1999	Kuala Lumpur, Malaysia	1,017/310	55	Hijjas Kasturi Associates (Malaysia)
33 Emirates Tower Two	2000	Dubai, UAE	1,014/309	56	Norr Group Consultants (Canada)
34 One Island East	2008	Hong Kong, China	1,011/308	69	Wong & Ouyang (HK) Ltd. (China)
35 AT&T Corporate Center	1989	Chicago, IL	1,007/307	60	Skidmore, Owings & Merrill
36 Burj Dubai Lake Hotel	2008	Dubai, UAE	1,004/306	61	WS Atkins & Partners (UK)
37 JP Morgan Chase Tower	1982	Houston, TX	1,002/305	75	I.M. Pei & Partners
38 Baiyoke Tower II	1997	Bangkok, Thailand	997/304	85	Plan Architects Co. (Thailand)
39 Two Prudential Plaza	1990	Chicago, IL	995/303	64	Loebl Schlossman Dart & Hackl

303

* Topped out in 1995 but never completed

Tallest Buildngs in the World

	Building	Yr.	Location	Height (ft./m.)	(# stories)	Architect
40	Wells Fargo Plaza	1983	Houston, TX	992/302	71	Skidmore, Owings & Merrill
41	Kingdom Centre	2002	Riyadh, Saudi Arabia	992/302	41	Ellerbe Becket; Omrania & Associates (Saudi Arabia)
42	Aspire Tower	2006	Doha, Qatar	984/300	36	AREP Group (France) with Hadi Simaan Partners (Qatar)
43	First Canadian Place	1975	Toronto, ON, Canada	978/298	72	Bregman + Hamann Architects (Canada)
44	Eureka Tower	2006	Melbourne, Australia	975/297	91	Fender Katsalidis Architects (Australia)
45	Comcast Center	UC07	Philadelphia, PA	975/297	57	Robert A.M. Stern Architects with Kendall/ Heaton Associates Inc.
46	Landmark Tower	1993	Yokohama, Japan	971/296	70	The Stubbins Associates
47	Emirates Crown	2008	Dubai, UAE	971/296	63	n/a
48	311 South Wacker Drive	1990	Chicago, IL	961/293	65	Kohn Pedersen Fox Associates
49	SEG Plaza	2000	Shenzhen, China	957/292	71	Hua Yi Designing Consultants Ltd (China)
50	American International Building	1932	New York, NY	952/290	67	Clinton & Russell
51	Key Tower	1991	Cleveland, OH	947/289	57	Cesar Pelli & Associates
52	Plaza 66	2001	Shanghai, China	945/288	66	Kohn Pedersen Fox Associates with East China Architectural Design and Research Institute Co. Ltd. (China) and Frank C.Y. Feng Architects & Associates (China)
53	One Liberty Place	1987	Philadelphia, PA	945/288	61	Murphy/Jahn Architects
54	Millennium Tower	2006	Dubai, UAE	935/285	59	WS Atkins & Partners (UK)
55	Sunjoy Tomorrow Square	2003	Shanghai, China	934/285	55	John Portman & Associates
56	Columbia Center	1984	Seattle, WA	933/284	76	Chester Lindsey Architects
57	Cheung Kong Centre	1999	Hong Kong, China	929/283	63	Cesar Pelli & Associates; Leo A Daly
58	Chongqing World Trade Center	2005	Chongqing, China	929/283	60	Haines Lundberg Waehler
59	The Trump Building	1930	New York, NY	927/283	71	H. Craig Severance
60	Bank of America Plaza	1985	Dallas, TX	921/281	72	JPJ Architects
61	United Overseas Bank Plaza	1992	Singapore	919/280	66	Kenzo Tange Associates (Japan)

Building	Yr.	Location	Height (ft./m.)	(# stories)	Architect
62 Republic Plaza	1995	Singapore	919/280	66	Kisho Kurokawa Architect & Associates (Japan)
63 Overseas Union Bank Center	1986	Singapore	919/280	63	Kenzo Tange Associates (Japan)
64 Citigroup Center	1977	New York, NY	915/279	59	The Stubbins Associates
65 Hong Kong New World Tower	2002	Shanghai, China	913/278	61	Bregman + Hamann Architects (Canada)
66 Diwang International Commerce Center	2006	Nanning, China	906/276	54	n/a
67 Scotia Plaza	1989	Toronto, ON, Canada	902/275	68	The Webb Zerafa Menkes Housden Partnership (Canada)
68 Williams Tower	1983	Houston, TX	901/275	64	Johnson/Burgee Architects
69 Wuhan World Trade Tower	1998	Wuhan, China	896/273	60	Wuhan Architectural Design Institute (China)
70 The Cullinan North Tower	UC07	Hong Kong, China	886/270	68	n/a
71 The Cullinan South Tower	UC07	Hong Kong, China	886/270	68	n/a
72 Renaissance Tower	1975	Dallas, TX	886/270	56	Skidmore, Owings & Merrill
73 China International Center Tower B	UC07	Guangzhou, China	884/269	62	n/a
74 Dapeng International Plaza	2006	Guangzhou, China	883/269	56	Guangzhou Design Institute (China)
75 21st Century Tower	2003	Dubai, UAE	883/269	55	WS Atkins & Partners (UK)
76 Naberezhnaya Tower C	UC07	Moscow, Russia	881/268	61	RTKL Associates Inc.; ENKA Insaat ve Sanayi AS. (Russia)
77 Al Faisaliah Center	2000	Riyadh, Saudi Arabia	876/267	30	Foster and Partners (UK)
78 900 North Michigan Ave.	1989	Chicago, IL	871/265	66	Kohn Pedersen Fox Associates
79 Bank of America Corporate Center	1992	Charlotte, NC	871/265	60	Cesar Pelli & Associates
80 SunTrust Plaza	1992	Atlanta, GA	871/265	60	John Portman & Associates
81 BOCOM Financial Towers	1999	Shanghai, China	869/265	52	ABB Architekten (Germany)
82 Triumph Palace	2005	Moscow, Russia	866/264	61	TROMOS (Russia)
83 Bluescope Steel Centre	1991	Melbourne, Australia	866/264	52	Daryl Jackson Pty Ltd (Australia)
84 Shenzhen Special Zone Daily Tower	1998	Shenzhen, China	866/264	42	n/a

305

Tallest Buildngs in the World

	Building	Yr.	Location	Height (ft./m.)	(# stories)	Architect
85	Tower Palace Three, Tower G	2004	Seoul, South Korea	865/264	73	Skidmore, Owings & Merrill
86	Trump World Tower	2001	New York, NY	861/262	72	Costas Kondylis & Partners LLC Architects
87	Water Tower Place	1976	Chicago, IL	859/262	74	Loebl Schlossman Dart & Hackl
88	Grand Gateway Plaza I	2005	Shanghai, China	859/262	54	Callison Architecture; Frank C.Y. Feng Architects & Associates (China)
89	Grand Gateway Plaza II	2005	Shanghai, China	859/262	54	Callison Architecture; Frank C.Y. Feng Architects & Associates (China)
90	Aon Center	1974	Los Angeles, CA	858/262	62	Charles Luckman & Associates
91	Hotel Panorama	UC07	Hong Kong, China	856/262	64	DLN Architects & Engineers (China)
92	BCE Place-Canada Trust Tower	1990	Toronto, ON, Canada	856/261	53	Skidmore, Owings & Merrill; Bregman + Hamann Architects (Canada)
93	Dual Towers 1	2006	Manama, Bahrain	853/260	57	Ahmed Janahi Architects (Bahrain)
94	Dual Towers 2	2006	Manama, Bahrain	853/260	57	Ahmed Janahi Architects (Bahrain)
95	101 Collins Street	1991	Melbourne, Australia	853/260	50	Denton Corker Marshall (Australia)
96	Transamerica Pyramid	1972	San Francisco, CA	853/260	48	William Pereira
97	GE Building, Rockefeller Center	1933	New York, NY	850/259	70	Raymond Hood
98	Chase Tower	1969	Chicago, IL	850/259	60	C.F. Murphy Associates
99	Commerzbank Zentrale	1997	Frankfurt, Germany	850/259	56	Foster and Partners (UK)
100	Two Liberty Place	1990	Philadelphia, PA	848/258	58	Murphy/Jahn Architects

Note: Although at the time of printing the Burj Dubai building has surpassed the height of Taipei 101, official figures about its height have not been released.

Source: Council on Tall Buildings and Urban Habitat

SUSTAINABLE/ GREEN DESIGN

Recent winners of sustainable design awards (buildings, products, and leaders), organizations devoted to developing and promoting green design guiding principles, and a timeline of the history of this movement can be found in this chapter.

BSA Sustainable Design Awards

Every two years the Boston Society of Architects presents the Sustainable Design Awards to projects worldwide that positively impact the environment. The judging criteria includes environmental balance, energy-efficiency, appropriate land use, minimal ecological impact, reuse of existing buildings or facilities, the level of use of non-renewable resources, the use of recycled or renewable materials, and excellence in integrating sustainable concepts with traditional design requirements.

For more information, visit the Boston Society of Architects' website, *www.architects.org.*

2007 Winners

**Honor Award for Design
Excellence**
Sidwell Friends Middle School Addition
    and Renovation
Washington, DC
KieranTimberlake Associates

**Honor Award for
Renovation/Restoration**
Blackstone Station Adaptive Reuse,
    Harvard University
Cambridge, MA
Bruner/Cott & Associates, Inc.

Awards for Design
Provincetown Art Association and Museum
Provincetown, MA
Machado and Silvetti Associates

South Lake Union Discovery Center
Seattle, WA
Miller/Hull Partnership

Citation for Design
Sophia Gordon Hall, Tufts University
Medford, MA
William Rawn Associates Architects, Inc.

Santa Monica Library
Santa Monica, CA
Moore Ruble Yudell Architects & Planners

Atwater Commons, Middlebury College
Middlebury, VT
KieranTimberlake Associates

JURY
Dan Arons, Architerra
Ken Fisher, Gensler
Chris Garvin, Cook + Fox
Cynthia Greene, US Environmental Protection
    Agency
Rosemary Monahan, US Environmental
    Protection Agency

Source: Boston Society of Architects

309

BSA Sustainable Design Awards

310

Sophia Gordon Residence Hall at Tufts University, Medford, MA, by William Rawn Associates Architects, Inc. (Photos: *above*, Melody Ko for Tufts University and, *right*, Jodi Hilton for Tufts University)

Cradle to Cradle

As opposed to traditional cradle-to-grave production processes where materials eventually are landfilled or incinerated, Cradle to Cradle (C2C) is a model of sustainable production in which all waste materials are productively reincorporated into new production and use phases, or closed loops. This eco-effective production method seeks to solve rather than to merely manage the problems currently created by industry.

The C2C protocol assesses materials used in products and processes based on the Intelligent Products System, designed by the German chemist Michael Braungart and colleagues at the Environmental Protection Encouragement Agency. Materials are inventoried, evaluated, and placed in one of four categories—green, yellow, orange, or red—based on human health and environmental relevance criteria with the eventual goal of optimizing material use by selecting green-category replacements for red-category substances as they become available.

Green: Little or no risk. The chemical is acceptable.

Yellow: Low to moderate risk. The chemical is acceptable for use in the desired application until a green alternative is found.

Orange: No indication of a high-risk chemical. However, a complete assessment is not possible due to lack of information.

Red: High risk. Red chemicals should be phased out as soon as possible and include all known or suspected carcinogens, endocrine disruptors, mutagens, reproductive toxins, and teratogens.

In addition, McDonough Braungart Design Chemistry, the private sustainable product and process design consultancy founded by American architect William McDonough and Michael Braungart, offers C2C certification for products, which meet or exceed the C2C protocol.

More information about the C2C protocol and other C2C initiatives, including the Chemical Profiles Knowledge Base, can be obtained through GreenBlue at *www.greenblue.org.* For more about C2C certification, contact MBDC at *www.mbdc.com.*

311

Source: GreenBlue

Declaration of Interdependence for a Sustainable Future

Adopted by the International Union of Architects (UIA) at its 1993 World Congress of Architects, the Declaration of Interdependence for a Sustainable Future is a statement of commitment on behalf of design professionals worldwide to "place environmental and social sustainability at the core of our practice." To promote the realization of the declaration's ideas, a set of principles (included below) and practices was also composed.

The complete text can be found on the UIA's website, *www.uia-architectes.org.*

Principles

Principle 1: Individually and collectively the members of the Architecture Profession will advise their clients and assist with the education of the broader community on the environmental implications of development trends, strategies, and policies.

Principle 2: The Architecture Profession will engage with local communities in formulating appropriate strategies and design guidelines for sustainable human settlement that are economically and environmentally appropriate to their particular culture and place.

Principle 3: Architects will, through their work, seek to give full expression to a culture of interdependence with the environment.

Principle 4: Architects will advance ecologically sustainable development by contributing to and supporting appropriate designs, products, services, and technologies.

Principle 5: Architects should promote the development of an ecologically sustainable future for the planet and ensure that development strategies, design concepts, and innovations which are consistent with, or improve the prospect of, ecological sustainability are made available globally, including to disadvantaged groups and nations, with appropriate mechanism to protect intellectual property.

Principle 6: In developing ecologically sustainable building and settlement practices, all sources of relevant knowledge and methods, including those of indigenous people, should be considered.

Principle 7: Architects should promote healthy and environmentally responsible living and behavioral patterns and develop designs and technologies in support of such lifestyles.

Principle 8: Architects will promote development strategies and projects which anticipate the needs and recognize the rights of present and future generations.

Principle 9: Architects will, through their practices, implement the International Conventions and Agreements for protection of the rights and well being of the earth and its peoples; the integrity and diversity of the Cultural Heritage, Monuments, and Sites; and the biodiversity, integrity, and sustainability of the global ecosystem.

Principle 10: The initial education and Continuing Professional Development of Architects should recognize the need for a wide range of knowledge and insights from the arts, culture and humanities, the natural and social sciences, and the technologies as a basis for understanding the behavior and management of ecological systems, and for creating ecologically sustainable forms of production, development, and settlement.

Source: International Union of Architects

Pardon me, if when I want to tell the story of my life it's the land I talk about. This is the land. It grows in your blood. And you grow. If it dies in your blood you die out.

Pablo Neruda

Earth Day Product Awards

Presented by Green Building Pages, an online green resource guide, the Earth Day Product Awards recognize products and manufacturers that are advancing sustainable building practices. Entries are judged on their entire life cycle, with the exception of the Social Sustainability Award, which recognizes corporate social responsibility; the Global Climate Product Award, which recognizes solutions to global climate change; and the Innovative Achievement Award, which recognizes innovative solutions for creating a sustainable world.

Information about the winning products including a sustainability analysis, can be found online at *www.greenbuildingpages.com.*

2007 Winners

Production and Manufacturing
EcoTimber Hand-Scraped Flooring
EcoTimber

Installation, Use, and Maintenance
VitraStone
VitraStone

TrimTech
Trim Technologies

Dura-Loc Roofing
Allmet Roofing Products (Canada)

EcoTimber Exotics
EcoTimber

EcoTimber Hand-Scraped Flooring
EcoTimber

EcoTimber Classics
EcoTimber

Equaris BMRC Composting Toilet
Equaris Corporation

End of Product Life
Yarrow Sash & Door
Yarrow Sash & Door (Canada)

Social Sustainability
Timbon Premium Interior Moulding
Timbron International

Innovative Achievement
Interface

Planet, Inc. (Canada)

Global Climate Product
Interface FLOR

Sustainable Product
EcoTimber Hand-Scraped Floors
EcoTimber

Source: Green Building Pages

ED+C Excellence in Design Awards

Environmental Design + Construction's Excellence in Design Awards celebrate buildings that demonstrate a commitment to green building and sustainable design. Any architect, interior designer, contractor, building owner, or engineer is eligible to submit projects completed within the previous two years. A jury of professionals reviews entries for such green features as energy efficiency, indoor air quality, water conservation, sustainable or recycled materials, and site selection.

For additional information, visit ED+C on the Web at *www.edcmag.com*.

2007 Winners

Commercial
Banner Bank Building
Boise, ID
HDR, Inc.

Government
Gwinnett Environmental & Heritage
    Center
Buford, GA
Lord, Aeck, and Sargent, Inc.

Institutional
Kirsch Center for Environmental Studies,
    De Anza College
Cupertino, CA
Arup

Multi-Family Residential
The Vento
Calgary, AB, Canada
Busby Perkins+Will (Canada)

Single-Family Residential
BASF Near Zero Energy House
Patterson, NJ
BASF Corporation

315

JURY
S. Richard Fedrizzi, US Green Building Council
David Green, Lord, Aeck, and Sargent, Inc.
Peter Levasseur, EwingCole
Jim Nicolow, Lord, Aeck, and Sargent, Inc.
Carl Seville, National Association of Home
    Builders
Steven Winter, Steven Winter Associates, Inc.
Jerry Yudelson, Yudelson Associates

Source: Environmental Design + Construction

Environmental Stewardship Award

The Construction Specifications Institute's Environmental Stewardship Award (previously the Environmental Sensitivity Award) is presented to individuals, teams, chapters, regions, firms, and organizations for their initiatives to promote environmental awareness in the construction industry, practice sustainable design, or educate others about the advantages of designing for sustainability, or for work on a project that led to significant environmental preservation.

For additional information, visit CSI on the Web at *www.csinet.org*.

1996	BSW Green Team	2004	Cheryl C. Walker
1997	Ross G. Spiegel	2005	Mike Leonard
1998	Sandra Mendler	2006	Rebecca Foss
1999	Paolo Soleri		Mithun Architects + Designers + Planners
2000	City of Scottsdale's Green Building Program	2007	Dagmar B. Epsten
2001	LHB Engineers & Architects, Inc.		HGA Architects and Engineers
2002	Jonathan M. Miller		
2003	Lord, Aeck, and Sargent, Inc.		
	Sarah Nettleton Architects		

Source: Construction Specifications Institute

Trees are contagious; as soon as one neighborhood or street is planted, citizen pressure builds up for action from the next street.

William H. Whyte

Green Building Leadership Awards

The US Green Building Council's Green Building Leadership Awards recognize outstanding individuals and organizations that embody the principles of vision, leadership, and commitment to the evolution of green building design and construction. Awards are granted in such categories as advocacy, community, education, LEED, organizational excellence, and research. Recipients are honored in a ceremony at the USGBC's annual Greenbuild Conference & Expo.

For additional information, visit the USGBC's website at *www.usgbc.org.*

2006 Recipients

Advocacy Award, Organization
California Department of General Services

Advocacy Award, Individual
Maria Atkinson

Community Award, Individual
Robert Fox Jr.

Education Award, Organization
Alliance for a Sustainable Colorado

Education Award, Individual
Greg E. Franta

LEED Award, Organization
Liberty Property Trust

LEED Award, Individual
Gary Saulson

Organizational Excellence
Hellmuth, Obata and Kassabaum

Research Award
No award granted

317

Source: US Green Building Council

Architecture is about building for eternity, creating monuments, defying time, enclosing space, taming nature, defining roles, defining rules, controlling humanity, balancing reason and emotion: or rather it was once upon a time about all those things.

Andreas Papadakis

Green Roof Awards of Excellence

Green Roofs for Healthy Cities established the Green Roof Awards of Excellence to recognize green roof projects that exhibit leadership in integrated design and implementation and increase public awareness of the benefits of green roofs. Entries are evaluated for their aesthetic, economic, functional, and ecological components. In addition, the jury grants the Civic Award of Excellence and other special awards as warranted.

More information is available online at *www.greenroofs.org*.

2007 Winners

Extensive Residential
Feldman Residence, Santa Lucia Preserve
Carmel, CA
Rana Creek Living Architecture

Extensive Industrial/Commercial
Calamos Investments
Naperville, IL
Intrinsic Landscaping, Inc.

Extensive Institutional
Sanitation District No. 1
Ft. Wright, KY
Sanitation District No. 1

Intensive Residential
The Louisa
Portland, OR
Walker Macy Landscape Architects

Intensive Industrial/Commercial
ABN AMRO Plaza, 6th Floor Podium
Chicago, IL
Barrett Company

Intensive Institutional
Nashville Public Square
Nashville, TN
Hawkins Partners, Inc.

Civic Award of Excellence
Lisa Goodman

JURY
Paul Adelmann, Xcel Energy
Jeffrey L. Bruce, Jeffrey L. Bruce & Company
Paul Farmer, American Planning Association
Michael Gibbons, Architectural Systems Inc.
Monica Kuhn, architect
Ed Snodgrass, Green Roof Plants
Nancy Somerville, American Society of
   Landscape Architects

Source: Green Roofs for Healthy Cities

Did you know...

More than three million square feet of new green roofs were installed in North America in 2006, 25 percent more than the year before.

From the top: **The Louisa, Portland, OR, by Walker Macy Landscape Architects** (Photo courtesy of Green Roofs for Healthy Cities and Walker Macy Landscape Architects); **Nashville Public Square, Nashville, TN, by Hawkins Partners, Inc.** (Photo courtesy of Green Roofs for Healthy Cities and Hawkins Partners, Inc.)

Hannover Principles

Developed by sustainable design innovator William McDonough, the Hannover Principles were written to guide the environmentally sensitive construction of the Hannover, Germany, World's Fair 2000. The principles are universally recognized as a seminal expression on environmentally intelligent design and have inspired and influenced a wide array of works and documents, ranging from the UIA's Declaration of Interdependence to the US GSA's Guidelines for Sustainability.

To read the full text of the principles, go to *www.mcdonough.com/principles.pdf.*

Principles

1. **Insist on rights of humanity and nature to co-exist** in a healthy, supportive, diverse, and sustainable condition.

2. **Recognize interdependence.** The elements of human design interact with and depend upon the natural world, with broad and diverse implications at every scale. Expand design considerations to recognize even distant effects.

3. **Respect relationships between spirit and matter.** Consider all aspects of human settlement, including community, dwelling, industry, and trade, in terms of existing and evolving connections between spiritual and material consciousness.

4. **Accept responsibility for the consequences of design,** decisions upon human well-being, the viability of natural systems, and their right to co-exist.

5. **Create safe objects of long-term value.** Do not burden future generations with requirements for maintenance or vigilant administration of potential design due to the careless creation of products, processes, or standards.

6. **Eliminate the concept of waste.** Evaluate and optimize the full life-cycle of products and processes to approach the state of natural systems, in which there is no waste.

7. **Rely on natural energy flows.** Human designs should, like the living world, derive their creative forces from perpetual solar income. Incorporate this energy efficiently and safely for responsible use.

8. **Understand the limitations of design.** No human creation lasts forever, and design does not solve all problems. Those who create and plan should practice humility in the face of nature. Treat nature as a model or mentor, not as an inconvenience to be evaded or controlled.

9. **Seek constant improvement by the sharing of knowledge.** Encourage direct and open communication between colleagues, patrons, manufacturers, and users to link long-term sustainable considerations with ethical responsibility, and re-establish the integral relationship between natural processes and human activity.

Source: William McDonough + Partners

320

Holcim Award for Sustainable Construction

The Holcim Award for Sustainable Construction encourages future-oriented, tangible sustainable design initiatives in the building and construction industry. The competition was created by the Swiss-based Holcim Foundation for Sustainable Construction and is conducted in partnership with some of the world's leading technical universities. Prize money totaling $2 million per three-year competition cycle encourages and inspires achievements that go beyond convention to explore new ways and means.

For more information, visit the award online at *www.holcimfoundation.org*.

2006 Global Recipients

Gold
Main Station
Stuttgart, Germany
Ingenhoven Architekten (Germany)

Upgrading San Rafael-Unido, Urban
  Integration Project
Caracas, Venezuela
Proyectos Arqui 5 CA (Venezuela)

Silver
Waterpower – Renewal Strategy for the
  Mulini Valley
Amalfi and Scala, Italy
Centola & Associati and Mariagiovanna
  Riitano (Italy)

Bronze
Greening the Infrastructure at Benny Farm
Montreal, QC, Canada
L'OEUF (Canada)

JURY
Adèle Naudé Santos
Banasopit Mekvichai (Thailand)
Rachid Benmokthar Benabdellah (Morocco)
Olivia L. La O' Castillo (Philippines)
Claude Fussler (France)
Ashok B. Lall (India)
Hansjürg Leibundgut (Switzerland)
Urs Bieri (Switzerland)
Tim MacFarlane (UK)
Thom Mayne
Mohsen Mostafavi
Enrique Norten (Mexico)
Hans-Rudolf Schalcher (Switzerland)
Kaarin Taipale (Finland)

Source: Holcim Foundation for Sustainable Construction

321

IDSA Ecodesign Principles & Practices

Developed by the Ecodesign Section of the Industrial Designers Society of America to educate designers about an ecologically sensitive approach to developing environmentally conscious products, the Ecodesign Principles & Practices guidelines were officially adopted by the IDSA executive committee in 2001. The Ecodesign Section provides information and tools about ecologically sound practices, produces an introductory curriculum on ecological design, and promotes the topic of sustainability at IDSA conferences.

More information about the initiatives of the Ecodesign Section can be found on the IDSA's website at *www.idsa.org/whatsnew/sections/ecosection/*.

IDSA recognizes the following ecological principles:

Human society and the biosphere are interdependent.
Nature can survive without humanity, but society is dependent on the biosphere for crucial services. Society's systematic destruction of the biosphere threatens nature's health and its capacity to sustain human society.

Our biosphere requires protection on several levels.
Destructive substances from the Earth's interior must not accumulate in the biosphere (toxic metals, CO_2 from fossil fuels, etc.). Persistent synthetic substances must not be allowed to accumulate in the biosphere (PCBs, CFCs, radioactive isotopes, and so forth). The Earth's major habitats, productive natural cycles, and biological diversity must not be destroyed.

Meeting society's basic needs and reducing consumption is necessary.
Enabling people in less industrialized societies to meet their basic needs is required to slow population growth and to protect habitats. Fair and efficient use of resources can enable all people access to water, food, shelter, basic healthcare, and education. Environmentally friendly technologies can be developed to both meet basic needs in all societies and to reduce resource consumption in more industrialized societies.

IDSA recommends the following ecodesign practices:

Use ecodesign strategies appropriate to the product:
- Reduce overall material content and increase the percentage of recycled material in products.
- Reduce energy consumption of products that use energy.
- Specify sustainably grown materials when using wood or agricultural materials.
- Design disposable products or products that wear out to be more durable and precious.
- Eliminate unused or unnecessary product features.

- Design continuously transported products for minimal weight.
- Design for fast, economical disassembly of major components prior to recycling
- Design products so that toxic components (electronics, etc.) are easily removed prior to recycling.

Perform a comprehensive environmental assessment:

- Consider all of the ecological impacts from all of the components in the product over its entire life cycle, including extraction of materials from nature, conversion of materials into products, product use, disposal or recycling, and transport between these phases.
- Consider all ecological impacts, including global warming, acid rain, smog, habitat damage, human toxicity, water pollution, cancer causing potential, ozone layer depletion, and resource depletion.
- Strive to reduce the largest ecological impacts.
- Conduct a life-cycle impact assessment to comprehensively identify opportunities for improving ecological performance.

Encourage new business models and effective communication:

- Support product take-back systems that enable product upgrading and material recycling.
- Lease the product or sell the service of the product to improve long-term performance and end-of-life product collection.
- Communicate the sound business value of being ecologically responsible to clients and commissioners.
- Discuss market opportunities for meeting basic needs and reducing consumption.
- Present superior product quality claims (energy saving, contains less toxic waste, etc.) along with other performance features.

323

Source: Industrial Designers Society of America

Design is the patterning and planning of any act toward a desired, foreseeable end... any attempt to separate design, to make it a thing-by-itself works, counter to the fact that design is the primary underlying matrix of life.

Victor Papanek

LEED™ Green Building Rating System

The LEED (Leadership in Energy and Environmental Design) Green Building Rating System™ is a voluntary national standard for developing sustainable buildings that was developed by the US Green Building Council. The system establishes a common set of measurements for green building and provides a framework for assessing building performance and meeting sustainability goals. LEED emphasizes state-of-the-art strategies for sustainable site development, water conservation, energy efficiency, materials selection, and indoor environmental quality. Project certification, professional accreditation, training, and resources are all a part of the LEED program. LEED standards are currently available or under development for new construction and major renovation projects, existing building operations, commercial interiors, core and shell projects, homes, neighborhood development, retail, schools, healthcare facilities, and laboratories.

For more information, visit the USGBC's website at *www.usgbc.org.*

Did you know...

On July 5, 2007, the US Green Building Council's membership hit 10,000.

Lifecycle Building Challenge

The Lifecycle Building Challenge rewards projects that facilitate and advance the eventual recovery of building systems, components, and materials through adaptation, disassembly, or dismantling. Lifecycle thinking encompasses the idea of creating buildings that are stocks of resources for future buildings. The program is sponsored by the US Environmental Protection Agency. Winners are announced at the West Coast Green Conference.

Additional information is available online at *www.lifecyclebuilding.org*.

2007 Professional Winners

People's Choice Award
Sustainability by Design: Deconstruction
    and Adaptive Reuse at Haworth, Inc.
Holland, MI

Building, Built
Pavilion in the Park
Miller/Hull Partnership

Component, Built
Green-Zip-Tape™
Frank Little

Service, Built
ATHENA Assembly Evaluation Tool
ATHENA Institute

Building, Unbuilt
GreenMobile Factory-built Housing Units
    for the Southeast
Michael Berk
Mississippi State University

Component, Unbuilt
Deconstructable and Reusable Composite
    Slab
Mark D. Webster, Dirk M. Kestner, James
    C. Parker, and Matthew H. Johnson

2007 Student Winners

Building
groHome
Adam Fenner, Jason Bond, Thomas
    Gerhardt, Josh Canez, and Nick
    Schaider
Texas A&M University

Component
Guidelines for Building with Reusable
    Materials
Aaron Tvrdy
University of Nebraska–Lincoln

Tool and Service
Deconstruction Engineer
Keith Cullum and Paul Sargent
California Polytechnic State University, San
    Luis Obispo

JURY
Brad Guy, Pennsylvania State University
Lance Hosey, William McDonough + Partners
Vivian Loftness, Carnegie Mellon University
Martin J. Kooistra, Habitat for Humanity
Ann Kosmal, General Services Administration
Scott Shell, EHDD Architecture
Alex Wilson, BuildingGreen, Inc.

325

Source: US Environmental Protection Agency

Nantucket Principles and Santa Fe Priorities

In 2002, AEC leaders gathered in Nantucket, MA, to discuss the future of green building and sustainable design. The action agenda that resulted, the Nantucket Principles, has helped the profession integrate green principles into mainstream practice and raise awareness of sustainability. At the fifth-annual Leadership Summit on Sustainable Design in 2006, participants expanded the Nantucket Principles into a further call to action, the Santa Fe Priorities, for design professions and their clients, the media, and government officials.

Nantucket Principles

Current practices in the design and construction of the built environment are contributing to our accelerating environmental crises. The architecture, engineering, and interior design professions and their clients are a critical part of the solutions—solutions that point to a bright, alternative future. Recognizing the fragility of our environment, design firms and clients should redefine themselves:
- to engage,
- to listen,
- to learn,
- to educate, and
- to act toward a strong sustainable model.

It is time to operate under a new paradigm, a new set of values, a new set of ethics, and with new awareness of the impact of design.

Under these Nantucket Principles, design and construction organizations commit to the principles of sustainable development, including:
- environmental awareness,
- social/cultural equity,
- economic fitness,
- public policy, and
- technological ingenuity.

Design excellence shall incorporate, by definition, the meeting of sustainable principles. We believe that there is no conflict between sustainability and the art of architecture and design.

Our future and our solutions start here…today.
- It is time to redefine our conscience and look toward expansion.
- We must expand our view of the client to include tomorrow's child.
- We must expand our obligations to include the health of the public environment and the planet.
- We must expand our consideration of the community, site, and space to always include the larger systems and influences.

We will integrate these models of sustainability in our future work:
- Sustainable development is that which meets all the needs of the present without compromising the ability of future generations to meet their own needs.*
- Design for sustainability requires awareness of the full short- and long-term consequences of any transformation of the environment. Sustainable design is the conception and realization of environmentally sensitive and responsible expression as a part of the evolving matrix of nature.†

An action agenda...the next steps for architecture and design professionals and firms:

- Lead with vision and integrity.
- Hold a sustainable conference in your office to educate and empower your employees.
- Develop a plan of action for your firm's sustainable agenda.
- Mandate firm and staff accountability toward sustainable action.
- Empower internal champions to mentor staff and external champions to guide the firm to day-to-day sustainable action.
- Build a knowledge base on sustainability within your firm.
- Encourage your staff and fellow principals to actively participate in organizations that support green values.
- Identify measurements of success: life-cycle issues, user success, durability, connection to the larger community.

Broaden the profession:

- Become a more responsible professional and adopt the role of sustainable design educator within your firm, with your clients, and in your community.
- Engage with design schools and listen to student perspectives about sustainability.
- Communicate the benefits of sustainability to the client and community at large, including research, shared knowledge, and case studies.
- Connect with fellow design professionals, schools, and other contributors to the industry to plan future directions toward sustainability.

- Develop a process that points to a holistic approach to sustainability that involves all disciplines (i.e., community, public sector) and seemingly unrelated or unexpected disciplines that can add value.

Redefine success goals in terms of service:

- To the users.
- To the community.
- To your clients.

Collaborate with leaders in your region to align larger development strategies that are more in line with sustainable principles, including:

- Transit/development solutions.
- Preservation of larger natural eco-systems.
- Commitment to existing urban centers.
- Reducing dependence on fossil fuel.
- Promote the development and use of ecological sustainable building products and components.

Envision your future victory and celebrate each increment of success. Sustainability is now clearly an ethical issue for us as professionals. It shall be reflected in all of our future work.

*From the U.N. Brundtland Commission, 1987.

† Part of the Hannover Principles, 1992.

327

Nantucket Principles and Santa Fe Priorities

Santa Fe Priorities

1. As citizens, we will actively raise awareness in our respective communities about the impacts of pollution, global warming, and excessive energy consumption that threaten to upset the delicate balance of the environment that sustains us all.

2. As design and industry leaders, we will create new policies, protocols, and procedures that will enable us to inhabit the planet in sustainable, healthier, more responsible ways. Acting in concert, we will take steps to ensure that substantial progress will be made in mitigating and eventually repairing the environmental damage that has already been inflicted.

3. As parents and teachers, we will instill in successive generations an awareness of and high regard for the myriad interdependent natural systems that are required to sustain life on our planet.

4. We will work with leaders in business and technology to quantify and communicate the clear economic benefits of truly sustainable design. We will promote incentives to accelerate implementation of sustainable goals by key stakeholders.

5. We realize that the challenges facing us today transcend political, religious, economic, and cultural boundaries, whether real or imagined. Hence, our actions will be undertaken without regard to parochial interests, for the benefit of all.

Source: Design Futures Council

Did you know...

According to the US Green Building Council, the green building industry is worth more than $12 million.

National Award for Smart Growth Achievement

Through the National Award for Smart Growth Achievement, the US Environmental Protection Agency recognizes public entities that promote and achieve smart growth, thus creating better communities and initiating environmental benefits. The competition is open to local and state governments and other public-sector entities. Nonprofit or private organizations and individuals are not eligible for the award; however, when collaborating with a governmental or public-sector entity their participation is acknowledged.

For additional information, visit the EPA's website, *www.epa.gov.*

2006 Awards

Overall Excellence in Smart Growth
Massachusetts Office for Commonwealth
    Development

Built Projects
Old Town Wichita
Wichita, KS
City of Wichita

Policies and Regulations
Pennsylvania Fresh Food Financing
    Initiative
Pennsylvania Department of Community
    and Economic Development

Small Communities
Winooski Downtown Redevelopment
    Project
Winooski, VT
City of Winooski

Equitable Development
Bethel Center
Chicago, IL
Chicago Department of Planning and
    Development

Source: US Environmental Protection Agency

329

National Green Building Awards

The National Association of Home Builders presents the annual Green Building Awards to recognize leaders who have advanced green-home building. With this program, the NAHB hopes to encourage builders to incorporate green practices into their developments, designs, and construction methodologies and to speed the public's acceptance of sustainable, environmentally friendly building. A jury of industry professionals selects the winners, who are celebrated at the annual NAHB National Green Building Conference.

More information, can be found online at *www.nahb.org*.

2007 Winners

Single-Family Custom Home of the Year
W.H. Hull Company

Single-Family Luxury Home of the Year
Durano Construction

NAHB Model Green Home Building Guidelines Home of the Year
Stitt Energy Systems

Single-Family Concept Home of the Year
SunMountain Construction

Multifamily Project of the Year
High Point
Seattle, WA

Land Development Project of the Year
Pringle Creek Community

Green Product Marketing Project of the Year
Arch Wood Protection Inc.

Green Development Marketing Project of the Year
Wonderland Hill Development Company

Green Home Marketing Project of the Year
CMI Homes Inc.

Green Building Program of the Year
Built Green, Master Builders Association of King and Snohomish Counties (WA)

New Green Building Program of the Year
GreenBuilding Council of the Home Builders Association of St. Louis and Eastern Missouri

Builder Advocate of the Year
Don Ferrier

Remodeler Advocate of the Year
Carl Seville

Group Advocate of the Year
Cherokee Investment Partners

Source: National Association of Home Builders

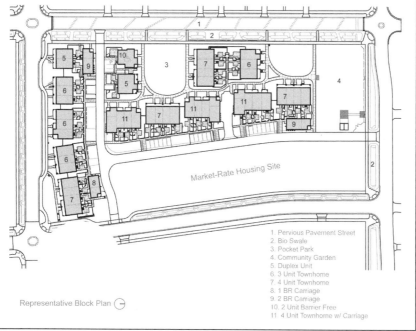

1. Pervious Pavement Street
2. Bio Swale
3. Pocket Park
4. Community Garden
5. Duplex Unit
6. 3 Unit Townhome
7. 4 Unit Townhome
8. 1 BR Carriage
9. 2 BR Carriage
10. 2 Unit Barrier Free
11. 4 Unit Townhome w/ Carriage

Market-Rate Housing Site

Representative Block Plan

High Point, Seattle, WA, by Mithun Architects + Designers + Planners (Photos courtesy of the National Association of Home Builders)

Phoenix Awards

The annual Phoenix Awards recognize excellence in brownfield redevelopment by honoring individuals, groups, companies, organizations, government bodies, and agencies that are working to solve the critical environmental challenge of transforming abandoned industrial sites into productive new uses. One winner is selected from each of the Environmental Protection Agency's 10 regions. Additional special winners may also be selected, such as projects that have had a significant impact on communities.

For more information, visit *www.phoenixawards.org*.

2006 Winners

Region 1
Kendall Square Redevelopment
Cambridge, MA

Region 2
Fulton Fish Market at Hunts Point
Bronx, New York

Region 3
Bethlehem Commerce Center
Bethlehem, PA

Region 4
Baldwin Park Redevelopment
Orlando, FL

Region 5
Toledo Loves Its Jeeps
Toledo, OH

Region 6
Heifer International Center
Little Rock, AR

Region 7
Alberici Corporate Headquarters
St. Louis, MO

Region 8
Murray Smelter Site
Murray, UT

Region 9
Lion Creek Crossings
Oakland, CA

Region 10
Trail of the Coeur d'Alenes
Panhandle Area, Idaho

Community Impact Winner
South Pier District
Sheboygan, WI

Green Building Winner
Alberici Corporate Headquarters
St. Louis, MO

Source: Phoenix Awards

SBIC Awards

The Sustainable Buildings Industry Council Awards have been granted annually since 2001 in two categories. The Exemplary Sustainable Building Awards recognize institutional, residential, and government buildings that demonstrate the successful application of the whole-building design approach. Each winning project makes an important contribution to the sustainable building movement. The Best Sustainable Practice Awards honor the exceptional contributions SBIC members are making to sustainability.

Additional information is available online at *www.sbicouncil.org*.

2006 Exemplary Building Awards

First Place
Cambridge City Hall Annex
Cambridge, MA
Consigli Construction Co., Inc.

Second Place
South Campus Headquarters, Toyota
    Motor Sales, U.S.A.
Torrance, CA
Turner Construction Company

Third Place
Genzyme Center
Cambridge, MA
Behnisch Architects; Behnisch Architekten
    (Germany)

Honorable Mention
Tom Ridge Environmental Center
Erie, PA
Wallace Roberts & Todd

Wal-Mart Experimental Store
Aurora, CO
Turner Construction Company

West Quad, University of South Carolina
Columbia, SC
Little with The Boudreaux Group

2006 Best Sustainable Practice Awards

**Sustainable Policy/Program
Initiatives**
Green GlobesTM
Green Building Initiative

Educational Initiatives
ASHRAE Promise: A Sustainable Future
ASHRAE

**Stimulating Demand through
Increased Consumer Awareness
Sustainable Practice Tools for
Creating a Market Transformation**
Green Building Pages

**Sustainable Research,
Development, Construction
Process, and Demonstration**
Honorable Mention
Insulation Strategies for Added Protection
    Against Severe Storms
ICYNENE

Source: Sustainable Buildings Industry Council

Show You're Green

The annual Show You're Green competition showcases outstanding housing projects that are both affordable and green. The jury reviews entries for their incorporation of the AIA Affordable Green Housing Guidelines: site and building design, water conservation, energy efficiency, sustainable material use, recycling during construction and post-occupancy, indoor environmental quality, and other innovative design strategies. The winning projects also demonstrate how regional, geographic, climatic, and cultural influences generate different responses to unique needs.

For photos and profiles of the winners, as well as green housing resources, visit *www.designadvisor.org*.

2007 Winners

150 Prospect Street
Somerville, MA
Boyes-Watson Architects

Denny Park Apartments
Seattle, WA
Runberg Architecture Group

Orchard Gardens
Missoula, MT
MacArthur, Means & Wells, Architects

Pine Ridge Townhomes
Ketchum, ID
Living Architecture

Eastern Village Cohousing
Bethesda, MD
EDG Architects

New Columbia
Seattle, WA
Mithun Architects + Designers + Planners

Little Ajax Affordable Housing
New York, NY
Peter L. Gluck and Partners, Architects

Trolley Square
Cambridge, MA
Mostue & Associates Architects

JURY
Dana Bourland, The Enterprise Foundation
Deane Evans, Center for Architecture and
    Building Science Research
Kira Gould, Gould Evans
Rick Schneider, Inscape Studio
Anne Tourney, City of Boroondara (Australia)
Andrea Traber, Architecture + Sustainability
Walker Wells, Global Green USA

Source: American Institute of Architects

Smart Environments Awards

The International Interior Design Association and *Metropolis* magazine launched the Smart Environments Awards program in 2006 to recognize the best design solutions from the past five years that fully integrate sustainable design strategies. The competition is open to interior designers and architects and aims to celebrate socially responsible, beautiful, functional designs that integrate design excellence, human well-being, and sustainability.

For more information, visit the *Metropolis* website, *www.metropolismag.com.*

2007 Winners

Navy Federal Credit Union Heritage Oaks
    Center
Pensacola, FL
ASD, Inc.

Stratus Vineyards
Niagara-on-the-Lake, ON, Canada
burdifilek (Canada)

Eco-Suite
Toronto, ON, Canada
Kantelberg Design (Canada)

IslandWood
Bainbridge Island, WA
Mithun Architects + Designers + Planners

United States Census Bureau Headquarters
Washington, DC
Skidmore, Owings & Merrill

JURY
Joe Pettipas, HOK Toronto
Shashi Caan, IIDA, The Collective
Hank Hildebrandt, the University of Cincinnati

Source: International Interior Design Association and Metropolis

335

Gardens are the result of a collaboration between art and nature.

Penelope Hobhouse

Sustainable/Green Design Timeline

As the effects of industrialized society are increasingly blamed for the erosion of the planet's health and the quality of life for its inhabitants, the green movement within the AEC industry continues to gain momentum. The following timeline traces the significant moments in the development of sustainable/green design.

1871 The Chicago Fire stimulates uniform municipal building codes and ordinances.

1890s William T. Love purchases land in New York for a proposed hydro-electric power project; a century later Love Canal becomes the poster child for hazardous waste cleanup.

1892 The Sierra Club is founded on May 28.

1893 The Colombian Exposition (Chicago World's Fair) celebrates the dawn of the Industrial Revolution.

1916 New York City passes the first ordinance for separation of land-use zones.

1936 Frank Lloyd Wright develops his concept of Broadacre City to accommodate the automobile.

The Urban Land Institute is founded.

1939 At the New York World's Fair, the Futurama exhibit, sponsored by Shell Oil and General Motors and designed by Norman Bel Geddes, takes visitors through a model of an idealized United States with cities of the future replete with seven-lane highways, dazzling skyscrapers, and elevated pedestrians walkways.

1945 Norman Bel Geddes unveils his "Toledo Tomorrow" master plan for Toledo, OH, that envisions a metropolis dissected by highways, relocation of heavy industry away from downtown, and manicured business parks—a harbinger of low-density, suburban sprawl.

1947 Levittown (NY) opens as the first large-scale speculative suburban housing development by a single builder/developer.

1956 The US Interstate Highway system is launched, justified on the basis of national defense (and with major support from the oil and automotive industries).

1960 OPEC (Organization of the Petroleum Exporting Countries) is formed by Iran, Iraq, Kuwait, Saudi Arabia, and Venezuela.

1962 Rachel Carson publishes *Silent Spring.*

1969 The Apollo Space Program provides distant images of Earth, heightening awareness of the planet as a living, interconnected system.

1970s Robert Davis inherits 80 acres of Gulf-front Florida Panhandle property from his grandfather that will eventually become Seaside.

1970 The First Earth Day is celebrated on April 22.

The Nixon administration forms the Environmental Protection Agency.

The Clean Air Act establishes emission standards.

1972 The first United Nations Conference on the Human Environment is held in Stockholm, Sweden.

The Pruitt Igoe public housing project in St. Louis is demolished after only 16 years. It is plagued by crime, disrepair, vandalism, and high vacancy rates, although it received a design award from the American Institute of Architects. The project's ruin symbolizes the loss of architects' credibility as problem solvers in the urban social domain.

1973 The Endangered Species Act protects plant and animal environments.

1977 President Jimmy Carter refers to the need for energy conservation as "the moral equivalent of war," calling the United States "the most wasteful nation on Earth."

The Clean Water Act is passed.

1978 The Love Canal contamination is discovered; after 11 years of cleanup, the land is declared habitable again.

1979 Portland, OR, establishes an urban growth boundary to prevent the "ravenous rampage of suburbia."

1980 The Superfund is established.

1982 The Energy and Environmental Building Association is formed.

1983 The World Commission on Environment and Development (commonly known as the Brundtland Commission, named for its chair Gro Harlem Brundtland) convenes at the behest of the United Nations to propose a global agenda for environmental problems. Their often-cited 1987 report defines sustainable development as "development that meets the needs of the present without compromising the ability of future generations to meet their own needs."

1985 A team of British scientists reports that there is a hole in the ozone layer over the Antarctic.

1988 The AIA Committee on the Environment is formed.

1990 The Washington State Growth Management Act requires fast-growing areas to create comprehensive, coordinated plans for future development.

1991 Austin, TX, starts the first organized green building program.

1992 Wendy E. Brawer creates the Green Apple Map for New York City, and a global effort follows (www.greenmap.org).

Environmental Building News publishes its first issue.

The US Department of Energy publishes a rating system (0–100) for home energy efficiency, with 100 being a home that is completely energy self-sufficient.

337

Sustainable/Green Design Timeline

The United Nations Conference on Environment and Development, or Earth Summit, in Rio de Janeiro, Brazil, brings together representatives from more than 170 nations who agree to work toward sustainable development of the planet.

1993 The US Green Building Council is formed.

The Rural Studio begins designing and building houses under the direction of Auburn University professors Samuel Mockbee and Dennis K. Ruth.

The Declaration of Interdependence for a Sustainable Future is signed by Olufemi Majekodunmi and Susan A. Maxman, presidents of the International Union of Architects and the American Institute of Architects.

1994 The EPA launches its Brownfields reclamation program.

Seattle announces a 20-year urban growth plan to limit sprawl.

1996 General Motors unveils its battery-powered EV-1 electric car.

The United Nations stages the second Habitat Conference in Istanbul and launches the global Best Practices Program for Sustainable Communities; it concurrently establishes the biennial Dubai Award.

William McDonough receives the Presidential Award for Sustainable Development.

The University of Virginia launches the Institute of Sustainable Design.

The Kyoto Protocol limits emissions of greenhouse gases from industrialized countries.

Architect John Hermannsson publishes the *Green Building Resource Guide* with cost comparison for choosing green vs. conventional products.

The American Planning Association publishes *Best Development Practices: Doing the Right Thing and Making Money at the Same Time.*

1998 The Energy Star Commercial Buildings program begins.

The AIA Committee on the Environment grants it first annual Top Green Projects awards.

The Sierra Club releases *The Dark Side of the American Dream*, listing the 20 cities most endangered by sprawl.

2000 New York becomes the first state to promote green building through tax credits.

The SmithGroup's Phillip Merrill Environmental Center for the Chesapeake Bay Foundation (Annapolis, MD) is the first project to achieve platinum status in the LEED Green Building Rating System™.

2002 The UN World Summit on Sustainable Development, a follow-up to the 1992 Earth Summit, is held in Johannesburg, South Africa.

R.S. Means publishes the first estimating handbook for green building.

2003 William McDonough launches the GreenBlue organization as a means to openly share his accumulated knowledge on sustainable design.

2005 McDonough Braungart Design Chemistry certifies the first six products in the Cradle to Cradle™ certification program, which evaluates and certifies the quality of products based on Cradle to Cradle™ Design principles by measuring their positive effects upon the environment, human health, and social equity.

2006 By early 2006, the US Green Building Council expands their LEED program to include separate rating systems for six different project types, including homes, neighborhoods, and interiors.

Source: DesignIntelligence

339

The action of time makes man's works into natural objects. In making them natural objects, time also gives to man's lifeless productions the brief quality of everything belonging to nature—life.

Vernon Lee

Sustainable Leadership Awards

The annual Sustainable Leadership Awards for Design and Development are presented jointly by the International Interior Design Association, the American Institute of Architects, and CoreNet Global. The programs honor outstanding sustainable practices by for-profit and not-for-profit organizations. The awards are given to designers and their clients for buildings that integrate sustainability with design excellence, and to organizations for policy, process, education, mentoring, or other sustainable development practices.

Additional information is available on the IIDA's website, *www.iida.org.*

2007 Recipients

Achievement in Sustainable Design Collaboration
Fuller Paint Company Warehouse
 conversion
Salt Lake City, UT
GSBS Architects and Big-D Construction

Achievement in Not-For-Profit Organizations
RAND Corporation Headquarters
Santa Monica, CA
DMJM Design and Rand Corporation

Achievement in Large Corporations
Hearst Tower
New York, NY
Hearst Corporation with Tishman Speyer
 Properties

Achievement in the Public Sector and Government
Federal Office Building
San Francisco, CA
US General Services Administration

Achievement in Small to Mid-Sized Enterprises
Platinum LEED™ Certification for the
 retrofit of the Adobe Headquarters
San Jose, CA
Adobe Systems Incorporated with
 Cushman & Wakefield

JURY
Nick Axford, C.B. Richard Ellis (UK, chair)
Sanford Smith, Toyota Motor Sales USA Inc.
Holly Henderson, H2EcoDesign
Penny Bonda, environmental writer and editor
Gail Lindsey, Design Harmony
Lynn Simon, Simon & Associates, Inc.
Kevin Sneed, OTJ Architects

Source: International Interior Design Association

Top Green Projects

The American Institute of Architects' Committee on the Environment annually selects the Top Green Projects to highlight viable architectural design solutions that protect and enhance the environment. Winning projects address significant environmental challenges, such as energy and water conservation, use of recycled materials, and improved indoor air quality. Responsible use of building materials, daylighting, efficient heating and cooling, and sensitivity to local environmental issues are some of the jury's considerations.

To view photos and descriptions of the winners, go to *www.aiatopten.org.*

2007 Winners

EpiCenter, Artists for Humanity
Boston, MA
Arrowstreet Inc.

Global Ecology Research Center
Stanford, CA
EHDD Architecture

Government Canyon Visitor Center
Helotes, TX
Lake/Flato Architects

Hawaii Gateway Energy Center
Kailua-Kona, HI
Ferraro Choi and Associates

Heifer International
Little Rock, AR
Polk Stanley Rowland Curzon Porter
    Architects

Sidwell Friends Middle School
Washington, DC
Kieran Timberlake Associates

Wayne L. Morse US Courthouse
Eugene, OR
Morphosis; DLR Group

Whitney Water Purification Facility
New Haven, CT
Steven Holl Architects

Willingboro Master Plan and Public
    Library
Willingboro, NJ
Croxton Collaborative Architects

Z6 House
Santa Monica, CA
LivingHomes, Raymond L. Kappe

Top Green Projects

2007 Honorable Mentions

William J. Clinton Presidential Center
Little Rock, AR
Polshek Partnership Architects

Gerding Theater at the Armory
Portland, OR
GBD Architects Inc.

Provincetown Art Association and Museum
Provincetown, MA
Machado and Silvetti Associates

Stillwell Avenue Terminal Train Shed
New York, NY
Kiss + Cathcart Architects

JURY
David Brems, Gillies Stransky Brems Smith
Alisdair McGregor, Arup
John Quale, University of Virginia School of
    Architecture
Traci Rose Rider, North Carolina State University
Anne Schopf, Mahlum Architects
Susan Szenasy, *Metropolis*

Source: American Institute of Architects

Creating an architectural structure means taking possession of the earth. It means transforming a condition of nature into a condition of culture through man's work and addressing the needs of the community.

Mario Botta

Z6 House, Santa Monica, CA, by LivingHomes
(Photos: CJ Berg/Sunshine Divis)

Top 10 Green Building Products

The Top 10 Green Building Products of the Year award recognizes the best products added to the *GreenSpec* directory during the past year as selected by editors of *Environmental Building News*. With more than 2,000 listings, the directory contains a wide range of materials, products, and equipment that can help reduce the environmental impact of a building. *GreenSpec* carefully evaluates all products; manufacturers do not pay to be listed, nor does the directory carry advertising.

Additional information is available from *GreenSpec*'s website at *www.buildinggreen.com.*

2006 Winners

Polished concrete system
RetroPlate

Underwater standing timber salvage
Triton Logging (Canada)

PaperStone Certified composite surface
    material
KlipTech Composites, Inc.

Varia and "100 Percent" recycled-content
    panel products
3form, Inc.

Recycled-content interior molding
Timbron International

SageGlass tintable glazing
Sage Electrochromics

Water-efficient showerhead with
    H2Okinetic technology
Delta

WeatherTRAK smart irrigation controls
HydroPoint Data Systems, Inc.

Coolerado Cooler advanced, indirect evap-
    orative air conditioner
Coolerado, LLC

Renewable Energy Credits
Community Energy, Inc.

Source: BuildingGreen

DESIGN &
HISTORIC
PRESERVATION

This chapter highlights many of the organizations
that assist individuals, communities, and professionals in their preservation efforts as well as advocacy
programs that alert the public to historic resources
in imminent danger of being lost. Preservation
award programs and their current winners are also
included.

Abbott Lowell Cummings Award

The Vernacular Architecture Forum's Abbott Lowell Cummings Award honors distinguished books about North American vernacular architecture and landscapes. Books are evaluated for their level of scholarship, use of fieldwork, and research methods. A founder of the VAF, Abbott Lowell Cummings was a prolific researcher and writer best known for his magnum opus *The Framed Houses of Massachusetts Bay, 1625–1725* (1979).

For more information, visit VAF online at *www.vernaculararchitectureforum.org*.

1983 "'In a Manner and Fashion Suitable to Their Degree': An Investigation of the Material Culture of Early Rural Pennsylvania," in *Working Papers from the Regional Economic History Research Center, Vol. 5 No. 1*
Jack Michel

1984 No award granted

1985 *Big House, Little House, Back House, Barn: The Connected Farm Buildings of New England*
Thomas Hubka
University Press of New England

1986 *Hollybush*
Charles Martin
University of Tennessee Press

1987 *Holy Things and Profane: Anglican Parish Churches in Colonial Virginia*
Dell Upton
Architectural History Foundation

1988 *Architecture and Rural Life in Central Delaware, 1700–1900*
Bernard L. Herman
University of Tennessee Press

1989 *Study Report for Slave Quarters Reconstruction at Carter's Grove*
Colonial Williamsburg Foundation

Study Report for the Bixby House Restoration
Old Sturbridge Village

1990 *Manhattan for Rent, 1785–1850*
Elizabeth Blackmar
Cornell University Press

Building the Octagon
Orlando Rideout
American Institute of Architects Press

1991 *Architects and Builders in North Carolina*
Catherine W. Bishir, Charlotte Vestal Brown, Carl R. Lounsbury, and Ernest H. Wood
University of North Carolina Press

1992 *Alone Together: A History of New York's Early Apartments*
Elizabeth Collins Cromley
Cornell University Press

A Place to Belong, Community, Order and Everyday Space in Calvert, Newfoundland
Gerald Pocius
University of Georgia Press

1993 *Homeplace: The Social Use and Meaning of the Folk Dwelling in Southwestern North Carolina*
Michael Ann Williams
University of Georgia Press

The Park and the People: A History of Central Park
Roy Rosenzweig and Elizabeth Blackmar
Cornell University Press

347

Abbott Lowell Cummings Award

1994   *The Stolen House*
       Bernard L. Herman
       University Press of Virginia

1995   *Living Downtown: The History of
       Residential Hotels in the United States*
       Paul Groth
       University of California Press

1996   *An Illustrated Glossary of Early
       Southern Architecture and Landscape*
       Carl R. Lounsbury
       Oxford University Press

1997   *Unplanned Suburbs: Toronto's
       American Tragedy, 1900–1950*
       Richard Harris
       Johns Hopkins University Press

1998   *City Center to Regional Mall:
       Architecture, the Automobile, and
       Retailing in Los Angeles, 1920–1950*
       Richard Longstreth
       MIT Press

1999   *The Myth of Santa Fe: Creating a
       Modern Regional Tradition*
       Chris Wilson
       University of New Mexico Press

       Architecture of the United States
       Dell Upton
       Oxford University Press

2000   *Delta Sugar: Louisiana's Vanishing
       Plantation Landscape*
       John B. Rehder
       Johns Hopkins University Press

       *Cheap, Quick & Easy: Imitative
       Architectural Materials, 1870–1930**
       Pamela H. Simpson
       University of Tennessee Press

       *Building Community, Keeping the Faith:
       German Catholic Vernacular Architecture
       in a Rural Minnesota Parish**
       Fred W. Peterson
       Minnesota Historical Society Press

2001   *Vernacular Architecture*
       Henry Glassie
       Indiana University Press

2002   *The Patina of Place: The Cultural
       Weathering of a New England
       Landscape*
       Kingston William Heath
       University of Tennessee Press

2003   *Theaters of Conversion: Religious
       Architecture and Indian Artisans in
       Colonial Mexico*
       Samuel Y. Edgerton
       University of New Mexico Press

2004   *A River and Its City: The Nature of
       Landscape in New Orleans*
       Ari Kelman
       University of California Press

2005   *Temple of Grace: The Material
       Transformation of Connecticut's
       Churches, 1790–1840*
       Gretchen Buggeln
       University Press of New England

2006   *Town House: Architecture and Material
       Life in the Early American City,
       1780-1830*
       Bernard L. Herman
       University of North Carolina Press

       *The Courthouses of Early Virginia:
       An Architectural History*
       Carl R. Lounsbury
       University of Virginia Press

2007   *Two Carpenters: Architecture and
       Building in Early New England,
       1799–1859*
       J. Ritchie Garrison
       University of Tennessee Press

* Honorable Mention

Source: Vernacular Architecture Forum

348

America's 11 Most Endangered Historic Places

The National Trust for Historic Preservation annually compiles a list of the most threatened historic sites in the United States. Since 1988, this program has highlighted more than 185 historic buildings, sites, and landscapes threatened by neglect, deterioration, insufficient funds, inappropriate development, or insensitive public policy. While being listed does not guarantee protection or financial support, the attention generated by the program has produced significant support for many of the threatened sites.

Photos and histories of each site are available at *www.nationaltrust.org/11most/*.

2007 America's 11 Most Endangered Historic Places

Industrial Waterfront
Brooklyn, NY

El Camino Real National Historic Trail
El Paso, TX, to San Juan Pueblo, NM

H.H. Richardson House
Brookline, MA

Hialeah Park
Hialeah, FL

Historic Places in Powerline Corridors
Delaware, Maryland, New Jersey, New York,
   Pennsylvania, Virginia, West Virginia

Historic Structures in Mark Twain National
   Forest
Missouri

Historic Route 66 Motels
Illinois to California

Minidoka Internment National Monument
Jerome County, ID

Philip Simmons Workshop and Home
Charleston, SC

Pinon Canyon
Colorado

Stewart's Point Rancheria
Sonoma County, CA

Source: National Trust for Historic Preservation

349

Did you know...

America's 11 Most Endangered Historic Places list has identified 189 sites since the program began 20 years ago. It has been so successful in galvanizing preservation efforts and rallying resources that in just two decades an astounding 52 percent of these one-of-a-kind landmarks have been saved and rehabilitated.

America's 11 Most Endangered Historic Places

From the top: **Pinon Canyon, Colorado** (Photo: Rebecca Goodwin)**; Markham Springs Wheel House at the Mark Twain National Forest, Missouri** (Photo: Jennifer Sandy, MWO Field Representative). (All photos courtesy of the NTHP)

Antoinette Forrester Downing Book Award

The Society of Architectural Historians grants the Antoinette Forrester Downing Book Award to outstanding publications in the field of historic preservation. Works published in the two years prior to the award are eligible. The award honors Antoinette Downing's tireless preservation advocacy efforts in Rhode Island, including her seminal book *The Architectural History of Newport.*

More information is available from the SAH website, *www.sah.org.*

1987	*Providence, A Citywide Survey of Historic Resources* William McKenzie Woodward and Edward F. Sanderson Rhode Island Historic Preservation Commission	1997	*A Guide to the National Road* and *The National Road* Karl B. Raitz Johns Hopkins University Press
1990	*East Cambridge: A Survey of Architectural History in Cambridge* Susan E. Maycock MIT Press	1998	*A Guide to the Historic Architecture of Eastern North Carolina* Catherine W. Bishir and Michael T. Southern University of North Carolina Press
1991	*Somerset: An Architectural History* Paul Baker Touart Maryland Historical Trust and Somerset County Historical Trust	1999	No award granted
		2000	*Boston's Changeful Times* Michael Holleran Johns Hopkins University Press
1994	*The Buried Past: An Archaeological History of Philadelphia* John L. Cotter University of Pennsylvania Press	2001	*Preserving Cultural Landscapes in America* Arnold R. Alanen and Robert Z. Melnick, editors John Hopkins University Press
1995	*Along the Seaboard Side: the Architectural History of Worcester County, Maryland* Paul Baker Touart Worcester County	2002	*A Building History of Northern New England* James Garvin University Press of New England
1996	*The Historic Architecture of Wake County, North Carolina* Kelly A. Lally Wake County Government	2003	No award granted

351

Antoinette Forrester Downing Book Award

2004   *Restoring Women's History Through Historic Preservation*
Gail Lee Dubrow and Jennifer B.
    Goodman, eds.
Johns Hopkins University Press
    and New Hampshire
    Preservation Alliance

2005   *A Richer Heritage: Historic Preservation in the Twenty-First Century*
Robert E. Stipe
North Carolina University Press

2006   No award granted

2007   *Earth Repair: A Transatlantic History of Environmental Restoration*
Marcus Hall
University of Virginia Press

Source: Society for Architectural Historians

Heritage places are not merely tangible evidence of the past as deemed important to a small, historically minded subset of society...they provide emotional anchors for the community as a whole.

Dirk H.R. Spennemann

Crowninshield Award

The National Trust for Historic Preservation's highest honor, the Louise DuPont Crowninshield Award, recognizes individuals and organizations that have demonstrated extraordinary lifetime achievement in the preservation of America's heritage. Winners are selected by the board of trustees' preservation committee.

Additional information is available online at *www.nationaltrust.org.*

1960	Mount Vernon Ladies Association
1961	Henry Francis DuPont
1962	Katherine Prentis Murphy
1963	Martha Gilmore Robinson
1964	Bertram and Nina Little
1965	Charles E. Peterson
1966	Ima Hogg
	Mary Gordon Latham Kellenberger
1967	*No award granted*
1968	St. Clair Wright
1969	Henry and Helen Flynt
1970	Frank L. Horton
1971	Frances R. Edmunds
1972	Alice Winchester
1973	Ricardo E. Alegria
1974	Jacob and Mary Morrison
1975	*No award granted*
1976	Katherine U. Warren
1977	San Antonio Conservation Society
1978	Helen Duprey Bullock
1979	Old Post Office Landmark Committee
1980	William J. Murtagh
	Ernest A. Connally
1981	Gordon C. Gray
1982	Helen Abell
1983	Historic American Buildings Survey of the National Park Service, US Department of the Interior, in cooperation with the American Institute of Architects and the Library of Congress, Washington, DC

1984	Leopold Adler
1985	James Marston Fitch
1986	Antoinette Forrester Downing
1987	Frank Blair Reeves
1988	Robert E. Stipe
1989	Frederick L. Rath Jr.
	Association of Junior Leagues
1990	Frederick Gutheim
1991	Robert R. Garvey Jr.
1992	Joan Bacchus Maynard
1993	Carl B. Westmoreland
	Arthur P. Ziegler Jr.
1994	Walter Beinecke Jr.
1995	Dana Crawford
1996	Richard H. Jenrette
1997	Marguerite Neel Williams
1998	Frederick Williamson
	Anice Barber Read
1999	Daniel Patrick Moynihan
2000	National Park Service
2001	George and Cynthia Mitchell
2002	John F. Seiberling
2003	Walter Nold Mathis
2004	Nancy Campbell
2005	J. Reid Williamson Jr.
2006	George B. Hartzog Jr.
	Stewart Udall
2007	Nellie Longsworth

Source: National Trust for Historic Preservation

353

European Union Prize for Cultural Heritage

The European Union Prize for Cultural Heritage/Europa Nostra Awards recognize outstanding heritage achievements in Europe. It aims to promote high standards and skills in conservation practices and to stimulate the cross-cultural exchange of information. Awards are granted for architectural heritage, cultural landscapes, works of art, and archaeological sites. A monetary prize of 10,000 euros is granted to the first-place winner; second place receives a medal, and third place, a diploma.

For more information, visit *www.europanostra.org* on the Internet.

2006 Architectural Heritage Recipients

Top Prize
Sarica Church
Cappadocia, Turkey

Medals
The Porthania, University of Helsinki
Helsinki, Finland

Church of the Virgin
Timotesubani, Georgia

Terminal 1, Ferihegy Airport
Budapest, Hungary

New York Palace & Café
Budapest, Hungary

Pont Trencat
Sant Celoni and Santa Maria de
   Palautordera, Spain

Roundhouse
London, UK

Diplomas
Stift Klosterneuburg
Klosterneuburg, Austria

Paradehuset, Gisselfeld Kloster
Haslev, Denmark

Texaco Service Station 1938
Skovshoved Harbour, Denmark

Belvedere on Pfingstberg Hill
Potsdam, Germany

Domus Academica, University of Oslo
Oslo, Norway

Pocarjeva Domacija
Mojstrana, Slovenia

San Juan de los Reyes
Granada, Spain

Eslöv Civic Hall
Eslöv, Sweden

St Paul's Church
Bristol, UK

Brunel's ss Great Britain
Bristol, UK

JURY
Federico Guasti (Italy, chair)
Philip Geoghegan, Architect (Ireland, vice-chair)
José-María Ballester (Spain)
Grigor Doytchinov (Austria/Bulgaria)
Tamás Fejérdy (Hungary)
Luc Fornoville, Architect (Belgium)
Eszter Gyarmathy (Switzerland)
Emil Hädler (Germany)
Alexander Kalligas (Greece)
Bente Lange (Denmark)
Sandra van Lochem (Netherland)
Tapani Mustonen (Finland)
Roberto Pasini (Italy)
Michael Thomas (UK)
Przemyslaw Urbanczyk (Poland)

Source: Europa Nostra

Pont Trencat in Sant Celoni and Santa Maria de Palautordera, Spain (Photos courtesy Europa Nostra Awards photo archives)

355

Great American Main Street Awards

Each year the National Trust for Historic Preservation's National Main Street Center celebrates five communities that have demonstrated considerable success with preservation-based revitalization. These towns have generated support from their residents and business leaders, drawn financial assistance from both public and private sources, and created innovative solutions for their unique situations. Winners receive $2,500 to fund further revitalization efforts, a bronze plaque, two road signs, and a certificate.

For more information, visit *www.mainstreet.org.*

1995	Clarksville, MO		2000	Coronado, CA
	Dubuque, IA			Keokuk, IA
	Franklin, TN			Newkirk, OK
	Sheboygan Falls, WI			Port Townsend, WA
	Old Pasadena, CA			St. Charles, IL
1996	Bonaparte, IA		2001	Danville, KY
	Chippewa Falls, WI			Elkader, IA
	East Carson Street Business District, Pittsburgh, PA			Enid, OK
				Mansfield, OH
	Saratoga Springs, NY			Walla Walla, WA
	Wooster, OH			
			2002	Cedar Falls, IA
1997	Burlington, VT			La Crosse, WI
	DeLand, FL			Milford, NH
	Georgetown, TX			Okmulgee, OK
	Holland, MI			Staunton, VA
	Libertyville, IL			
			2003	Greenville, SC
1998	Corning, IA			Littleton, NH
	Lanesboro, MN			Manassas, VA
	Morgantown, WV			Rome, GA
	Thomasville, GA			Wenatchee, WA
	York, PA			
			2004	Burlington, IA
1999	Bay City, MI			Encinitas, CA
	Cordell, OK			Paso Robles, CA
	Denton, TX			Rogers, AR
	Lafayette, IN			Westfield, NJ
	San Luis Obispo, CA			

356

2005   Barracks Row, Washington, DC
        Emporia, KS
        Frederick, MD
        New Iberia, LA
        Washington Gateway, Boston, MA

2006   El Reno, OK
        Lynchburg, VA
        Natchitoches, LA
        Parsons, KS

The National Main Street Center suspended the Great
American Main Street Awards for 2007 while the organization's award programs undergo an expansion.

Source: National Trust Main Street Center

357

Cities are shaped by their vernacular as much as their monuments.

Paul Goldberger

Guidelines for Architectural Historians Testifying on the Historical Significance of Properties

The following guidelines were adopted by the Society of Architectural Historians in 1986 to enhance professional standards in the preservation review process. In developing the guidelines, the SAH established a framework of acceptable conduct for those testifying as members of the discipline. The document was intended for wide circulation, to be used by the staffs and members of review bodies at the state and local levels and by all others concerned with the integrity of the review process.

Guidelines

Architectural historians engage in research into, and the dissemination of knowledge about, the evolution of the art and craft of architecture and its place in the history of civilization. The knowledge which they perpetuate, acquire, and spread is central to understanding human growth, for the buildings of any age reflect not only the visions of their designers and clients, but also the values of their era. Architectural historians have a special responsibility to the past, for their judgments as to the value of its artifacts often figure large in public and private decisions about what to preserve and what to destroy. That which is preserved nurtures the culture whose past it represents. That which is destroyed is lost forever.

Thus, the architectural historian has an awesome burden when called upon to speak to the value of a building, group of buildings, and other components of the man-made environment. It is essential to the integrity of the discipline that the architectural historian's testimony be based on sound scholarship, be an honest appraisal of all the pertinent circumstances, and be given with due regard for the gravity of its consequences.

Architectural historians testifying on the significance of historic properties before a duly constituted review board, commission, council, legislative committee, or court of law should:

- Make objective and truthful statements and eschew dissemination of untrue,

unfair, or exaggerated statements regarding the significance of any property or properties;

- Assess the significance of the property or properties in question according to applicable local, state, and/or federal criteria;

- Express their professional opinion only when it is founded upon adequate knowledge of the facts, upon expertise in pertinent areas of scholarship, and upon honest conviction;

- State specifically the circumstances under which they are presenting testimony, including whether they are taking, or at any time have taken, a fee for work related to the case in question; and

- Issue no statements on behalf of interested parties unless they indicate on whose behalf those statements are being made, the nature of any compensation related to the case, and any personal interest in the property or properties in question or in property which would be affected by the disposition of the property or properties in question.

Credentials

An individual who intends to testify as an expert on matters pertaining to architectural history before a duly constituted review board, commission, council, legislative committee, or court of law must have a demonstrated record of achievement in that discipline.

A full set of credentials applicable,

directly and indirectly, to the case should be presented in writing for the public record.

As credentials, it is appropriate to cite institutions attended, degrees earned, research conducted, scholarly work published, pertinent consulting projects completed or in progress, and past and present employment. Professional affiliations, offices, committees, and similar forms of service related to the discipline may be included, but it must be made explicit that all testimony presented reflects solely that individual's opinion unless he or she has been duly authorized by an organization, agency, or firm to speak on its behalf.

All parties involved in a given case should understand that architectural historians are not certified, registered, or licensed according to a uniform set of standards comparable to those employed in professions such as law, medicine, or architecture. Moreover, it should be understood that no one form of academic program is acknowledged to be the sole means by which an individual can become an architectural historian. Advanced degrees in art and architectural history form the primary bases for entering the discipline; nevertheless, comparable preparation in other fields such as American history, American studies, geography, archaeology, and folklife also may provide expertise in assessing aspects of the built environment in their historic context. Furthermore, architects, landscape architects, and others practicing in professional design and planning fields may have expertise in facets of architectural history. Finally, it is possible for a person to acquire such expertise with little or no formal education in the field.

From a legal standpoint, expert testimony must be based on specialized knowledge of a particular subject, surpassing that which might be acquired by the average, well-informed layperson. Therefore, in all the above cases, a demonstrated record of

achievement related to the historical subjects in question, rather than training or professional practice per se, should be considered the essential basis for one's qualifications to testify as an expert on matters pertaining to architectural history in a given case. Moreover, simply having an interest in old buildings or being involved with efforts to preserve them should not be considered an adequate basis for such testimony.

In presenting qualifications, architectural historians should be specific in enumerating their areas of expertise with respect to the case. Working in architectural history, or even in the sphere of North American architecture, does not always render an individual fully qualified to address all pertinent topical areas with authority. For example, a scholar of 18th-century North American architecture may not necessarily be well equipped to assess the significance of properties dating from later periods. Moreover, it is doubtful whether someone who knows little or nothing about the architecture of a given locale is in a good position to assess the local significance of a property or properties in that place.

Research

A foremost responsibility of an architectural historian intending to testify on the significance of a property or properties is to familiarize himself or herself with that work to the fullest extent possible. Under all circumstances, this effort should include onsite study. Interiors also should be examined whenever feasible and must be scrutinized when all or a portion of them are being considered in the case.

Furthermore, the architectural historian intending to testify should gain familiarity with as much additional information as possible concerning the property or properties. Of at least equal importance is knowledge of the context within which the property's significance may be evaluated.

359

Guidelines for Architectural Historians

Such contextual frameworks include, but are not necessarily limited to: other work of the period(s), type(s), and designer(s) involved; work employing similar materials, construction techniques, or systems; work commissioned by the same or comparable clients, occupied by the same or comparable clients, or occupied by the same or analogous groups; and the physical setting in both its historic and current dimensions. In cases involving one or more properties within a designated historic district, or a precinct that has the potential to become a historic district, the full nature of the contribution of the property or properties to that district should be carefully considered.

In some instances, the necessary research may already have been conducted for a case. The architectural historian intending to testify then has the responsibility to examine this material carefully, making sure that it is complete and accurate prior to preparing his or her scholarly evaluation. In other instances, additional research may be needed, and the architectural historian intending to testify either should undertake this work or wait until it is completed by another responsible party before preparing an assessment. Whenever possible, architectural historians intending to testify should also seek consultation from colleagues known for their research in specialized subject areas pertinent to the case.

It should be realized that many such subject areas have received little or no scholarly attention and that the absence of this research should not necessarily preclude responsible efforts to save significant properties. It further should be recognized that many cases cannot be researched in a definitive manner when such an undertaking would require far more time than can be allocated even under favorable circumstances. Nevertheless, in all cases, an architectural historian intending to testify should exercise his or her best professional judgment in determining whether adequate information is available and determining that no available information is being concealed from consideration.

Moreover, the architectural historian offering testimony should be explicit regarding the degree to which his or her statements are based on his or her own research or on the work of others. Under no circumstances should an architectural historian convey the impression that an assessment is his or her own when it has in fact been wholly or substantially prepared by another party.

Criteria for Evaluation

Architectural historians intending to testify should be thoroughly familiar with applicable local, state, and federal criteria for evaluation and gain a full understanding of the issues relating to significance that the testimony is intended to resolve. The criteria for the National Register of Historic Places and for most, if not all, local landmark and historic district ordinances specify that properties may be designated on the basis of local significance as well as by virtue of their significance to a state or the nation.

However, the concept of local significance is often ignored or distorted in testimony and thus deserves special consideration here. A given work may not rank among the finest designed by a distinguished architect, for example, but this does not necessarily undermine its significance for the locality in question. Similarly, comparative analysis of examples of a building type in different geographic regions does not necessarily provide insight on the local significance of examples in any one of those regions.

Furthermore, local significance should not be interpreted as meaning only the earliest, oldest surviving, best, or most unusual examples unless the applicable criteria for evaluation so state. The objective of national preservation legislation and most local ordinances is to foster a comprehensive plan for protecting historic properties. Indeed, significance often may be fully understood only after it is studied in relation to the local context. Failure to assess a property's or properties' significance in any of the above ways will undermine the credibility of the testimony and run counter to the intent of the national historic preservation program.

Fees

Taking a fee for testimony is legal under most circumstances and should not, in itself, be construed as diminishing the value of testimony. At the same time, an architectural historian who even unintentionally conveys the impression that his or her testimony is in any way affected by monetary compensation or personal reasons contrary to those of sound scholarship blemishes both preservation efforts and the discipline's integrity. Indeed, the entire basis for scholarship, along with its public reputation, rests on its independence.

Therefore, architectural historians should make every reasonable effort to demonstrate that their testimony is motivated solely by honest conviction, understanding of all relevant material, and scholarly expertise. In every instance, architectural historians testifying should state explicitly whether they are taking a fee for that testimony; whether they are taking, or at any time have taken, a fee for work related to the case; and the source or sources for same fees. They should further explicitly state all the circumstances under which they are presenting testimony in that case. In contractual agreements, which will, or may at some later date, include testimony, that agreement should stipulate that the underlying aim of the architectural historian's work is to arrive at an objective evaluation of the significance of the property or properties in question. The contracted fee should be structured according to the nature of the work undertaken for research, analysis, and preparation of findings in a report or other appropriate form and not according to the real or potential monetary value of the property or properties in question. Under some circumstances, it may be prudent to perform such work incrementally; that is, prepare preliminary findings, and, should the contracting parties so agree, then proceed with an in-depth study.

The contractual agreement should specifically preclude the contractor's later excerpting portions of the study in a manner that distorts the overall findings of that study. Furthermore, architectural historians should never agree "for monetary compensation or otherwise" to prepare a study that merely makes an argument pro or con without weighing all pertinent information and performing a full scholarly assessment.

No uniform set of standards should be established for such studies any more than for other forms of scholarly endeavor. Architectural historians should be guided by the same standards that are considered exemplary for other work in their discipline. A study too quickly prepared, lacking careful consideration of all aspects contributing to complete historical analysis, should be viewed as a serious breach of personal and professional integrity.

Summary

Architectural historians should regard testimony as a public service and as a constructive means of advocating the retention of significant components of the man-made environment in accordance with applicable local, state, and federal laws. All work done to prepare for testimony, as well as the testimony itself, also should reflect high scholarly standards and should not suggest personal gain of any sort acquired at the expense of these objectives.

The Society of Architectural Historians is the leading scholarly organization promoting the study and preservation of the built environment. For more information about the society, please visit its website at www.sah.org.

Source: © *Society of Architectural Historians. Reprinted with permission.*

Guidelines for the Treatment of Cultural Landscapes

The secretary of the interior developed the Guidelines for the Treatment of Cultural Landscapes to provide expert guidance for projects involving cultural landscapes. A cultural landscape is defined as "a geographic area, including both cultural and natural resources and the wildlife or domestic animals therein, associated with a historic event, activity, or person or exhibiting other cultural or aesthetic values."

Additional resources are available at *www.nps.gov/history/*.

1. Before undertaking project work, research of a cultural landscape is essential. Research findings help to identify a landscape's historic period(s) of ownership, occupancy, and development and bring greater understanding of the associations that make them significant. Research findings also provide a foundation to make educated decisions for project treatment and can guide management, maintenance, and interpretation. In addition, research findings may be useful in satisfying compliance reviews (e.g., Section 106 of the National Historic Preservation Act as amended).

2. Although there is no single way to inventory a landscape, the goal of documentation is to provide a record of the landscape as it exists at the present time, thus providing a baseline from which to operate. All component landscapes and features that contribute to the landscape's historic character should be recorded. The level of documentation needed depends on the nature and the significance of the resource. For example, plant material documentation may ideally include botanical name or species, common name, and size. To ensure full representation of existing herbaceous plants, care should be taken to document the landscape in different seasons. This level of research may most often be the ideal goal for smaller properties but may prove impractical for large, vernacular landscapes.

3. Assessing a landscape as a continuum through history is critical in assessing cultural and historic value. By analyzing the landscape changes over time—the chronological and physical "layers" of the landscape—can be understood. Based on analysis, individual features may be attributed to a discrete period of introduction, their presence or absence substantiated to a given date, and therefore the landscape's significance and integrity evaluated. In addition, analysis allows the property to be viewed within the context of other cultural landscapes.

4. In order for the landscape to be considered significant, character-defining features that convey its significance in history must not only be present, but they also must possess historic integrity. Location, setting, design, materials, workmanship, feeling, and association should be considered in determining whether a landscape and its character-defining features possess historic integrity.

5. Preservation planning for cultural landscapes involves a broad array of dynamic variables. Adopting comprehensive treatment and management plans, in concert with a preservation maintenance strategy, acknowledges a cultural landscape's ever-changing nature and the interrelationship of treatment, management, and maintenance.

Source: National Park Service

Historic Preservation Book Prize

Sponsored by the Center for Historic Preservation at the University of Mary Washington, the Historic Preservation Book Prize honors publications that have made significant contributions to the historic preservation field in the United States. A jury of preservation professionals reviews submissions for their efforts in breaking new ground and enhancing the intellectual vitality of the preservation movement. Winners receive a $500 prize and are invited to lecture at the school.

More information is available on the Center for Historic Preservation website, *www.umw.edu/cas_mwc/chp/*.

1989 *The Past is a Foreign Country*
David Lowenthal
Cambridge University Press

1990 *Saving America's Countryside: A Guide to Rural Conservation*
Samuel N. Stokes and A. Elizabeth Watson, et al.
Johns Hopkins University Press

Imagining the Past: East Hampton Histories
T. H. Breen
University of Georgia Press

1991 *Architects and Builders in North Carolina: A History of the Practice of Building*
Catherine W. Bishir, Charlotte Vestal Brown, Carl R. Lounsbury and Ernest H. Wood
University of North Carolina Press

1992 *Constructing Chicago*
Daniel Bluestone
Yale University Press

1993 *The Park and the People: A History of Central Park*
Roy Rosenzweig and Elizabeth Blackmar
Cornell University Press

1994 *The Politics of Public Memory: Tourism, History, and Ethnicity in Monterey, California*
Martha K. Norkunas
State University of New York Press

1995 *An Illustrated Glossary of Early Southern Architecture and Landscape*
Carl R. Lounsbury
Oxford University Press

1996 *Gender, Class, and Shelter: Perspectives in Vernacular Architecture*
Elizabeth Collins Cromley and Carter Hudgins
University of Tennessee Press

1997 *Mickey Mouse History and Other Essays on American Memory*
Mike Wallace
Temple University Press

1998 *Shadowed Ground: America's Landscapes of Violence and Tragedy*
Kenneth E. Foote
University of Texas Press

1999 *The Presence of the Past: Popular Uses of History in American Life*
Roy Rosenzweig
Columbia University Press

363

Historic Preservation Book Prize

2000   *The Drive-In, The Supermarket, and*
The Transformation of Commercial
Space in Los Angeles, 1914-1941
Richard Longstreth
MIT Press

2001   *Houses from Books: Treatises, Pattern*
Books, and Catalogs in American
Architecture, 1738–1950
Daniel Reiff
Pennsylvania State University Press

2002   *From Cottage to Bungalow: Houses*
and the Working Class in
Metropolitan Chicago 1869–1929
Joseph C. Bigott
University of Chicago Press

2003   *A Modern Arcadia: Frederick Law*
Olmsted Jr. and the Plan for Forest
Hills Gardens
Susan L. Klaus
University of Massachusetts Press

2004   *Gaining Ground: A History of*
Landmaking in Boston
Nancy S. Seasholes
MIT Press

2005   *Downtown America: A History of the*
Place and the People Who Made It
Alison Isenberg
University of Chicago Press

2006   *A Golden Haze of Memory:*
The Making of Historic Charleston
Stephanie E. Yuhl
University of North Carolina Press

Source: Center for Historic Preservation

One must always maintain one's connection to the past and yet ceaselessly pull away from it.

Gaston Bachelard

Historic Preservation Timeline

Evolving from isolated, private initiatives to a full-scale national movement, the history of preservation in the United States is comprised of grassroots efforts, landmark court cases, and numerous laws and economic incentives. This timeline marks some of those moments as the heroic efforts of pioneers have led to an organized and mature movement. Today, even the concept of endangered places has broadened to include not only historic buildings but entire neighborhoods, landscapes, and vernacular buildings.

1791   The Massachusetts Historical Society is established to collect and preserve resources for the study of American history.

1812   The first national historical organization, the American Antiquarian Society, is founded in Worcester, MA.

1816   Considered an early act of preservation, Philadelphia purchases the 1732 Independence Hall (Philadelphia State House) to rescue it from demolition.

1850   The New York legislature purchases the Hasbrouck House (1750), George Washington's headquarters in Newburgh, and opens it to the public as a historic house museum.

1853   Ann Pamela Cunningham founds the Mount Vernon Ladies' Association of the Union, the first private preservation organization in the United States, to save George Washington's Mount Vernon from destruction by neglect.

1857   Philadelphia's Carpenters' Hall (1744), site of the First Continental Congress, is restored and opened to the public.

1872   Congress sets aside Yellowstone as a national park.

1876   An early instance of preservation in an urban setting, Boston's Old South Meeting House (1729) is rescued from demolition and opened as a museum.

1889   The Association for the Preservation of Virginia Antiquities, the nation's first statewide preservation organization, is formed.

In the first instance of federal preservation spending, Congress provides $2,000 for protection of the prehistoric Casa Grande ruin in Arizona.

1890   Congress passes legislation to authorize the preservation of the Chickamauga and Chattanooga Battlefield in Georgia and Tennessee.

1896   In *US v. Gettysburg Electric Railway Company*, the first preservation case to go before the US Supreme Court, the condemnation of private property for a national memorial is upheld.

1906   The Antiquities Act is passed granting the president the power to designate national monuments and establishing penalties for destroying historic and cultural resources on federal land.

365

Historic Preservation Timeline

1910   The incorporation of the Society for the Preservation of New England Antiquities marks a broadening in preservation theory from preserving buildings with heroic associations to buildings that are "architecturally beautiful or unique."

1916   President Woodrow Wilson approves legislation establishing the National Park Service within the US Department of the Interior as the administrative agency responsible for sites designated as national park areas.

1925   The Vieux Carre Commission is established to protect New Orleans' historic French Quarter, laid out in 1721. However, it is not until a 1936 state constitutional amendment passes that the commission is granted true enforcement powers.

1926   Henry Ford begins assembling old buildings and artifacts, which trace 300 years of technological and cultural history, at his Dearborn, MI, Greenfield Village.

John D. Rockefeller Jr. begins funding the restoration and reconstruction of Williamsburg, VA.

1931   America's first municipal preservation ordinance to establish a historic district with regulatory control is passed in Charleston, SC, to protect the city's quickly vanishing heritage.

1933   Charles E. Peterson forms the Historic American Buildings Survey to document historic buildings through measured drawings, photographs, and written descriptions.

1935   Congress passes the National Historic Sites Act, which establishes historic preservation as a national policy and creates the National Historic Landmarks program.

1944   *This Is Charleston*, the country's first citywide inventory of public buildings, is published in Charleston, SC.

1946   Robert Moses proposes the Vieux Carre Expressway, an elevated riverfront highway passing through the architecturally significant historic French Quarter in New Orleans. The proposal is finally defeated in 1969.

1947   The first US preservation conference is held in Washington, DC.

1949   Congress charters the National Trust for Historic Preservation to lead private-sector preservation efforts.

1951   The National Trust for Historic Preservation acquires the 1805 Woodlawn Plantation in Alexandria, VA. Fifty-five years later, the organization operates 28 historic properties.

1952   *Historic Preservation* (now *Preservation*), the nation's first nationwide preservation magazine, is launched.

1959   *College Hill, A Demonstration Study of Historic Area Renewal for Providence, RI* is published and becomes a national model for using historic preservation as a means of community renewal.

1959 President Dwight Eisenhower approves a six-year, $650 million urban renewal appropriation that removes rather than rehabilitates old buildings and leaves a legacy of torn neighborhoods and discontinuity.

1960 The Mount Vernon Ladies' Association of the Union is named the inaugural recipient of the National Trust's Crowninshield Award, which honors a lifetime of achievement in the field of historic preservation.

1961 Jane Jacobs publishes *The Death and Life of Great American Cities*, a commentary on the increasing demise of America's urban environments that will remain relevant to issues of sprawl and the legacy of urban renewal into the 21st century.

1962 At their invitation, architect John Carl Warnecke meets with President John F. Kennedy and the First Lady to save Washington, DC's historic Lafayette Square from demolition, a collaboration that restores the square's 19th-century townhouses and the Renwick Gallery (1859). Warnecke also utilizes a pioneering context-sensitive approach in his design of the required federal buildings, which he inserts behind the restored townhouses.

1963 Despite widespread public outcry, the demolition of New York's Pennsylvania Station begins, a loss that galvanizes the preservation movement.

1964 Columbia University's School of Architecture offers the first graduate-level course in historic preservation.

William Matson Roth purchases the 1893 Ghirardelli Square, a former San Francisco chocolate factory, to save it from demolition. He restores the building and turns it into a retail center, a pioneering adaptive-use project.

1965 The International Council on Monuments and Sites is created to establish international standards for the preservation, restoration, and management of the cultural environment.

1966 *With Heritage So Rich* is published and becomes a seminal historic preservation book documenting American cultural resources and chronicling the preservation movement.

Congress passes the National Historic Preservation Act, a watershed for the preservation movement. It establishes the National Register of Historic Places and the Advisory Council on Historic Places, calls for broader federal funding of preservation activities and individual state historic preservation programs, encourages the creation of local historic districts and through Section 106 provides for the protection of preservation-worthy sites and properties threatened by federal activities.

The Department of Transportation Act prohibits the destruction or adverse use of historic sites (as well as parklands) by transportation projects unless there is no feasible and prudent alternative.

1967 The first state historic preservation officers and the first keeper of the National Register are appointed.

367

Historic Preservation Timeline

1968   The Association for Preservation Technology is founded as an inter-disciplinary clearinghouse for information and research about preservation techniques for historic structures.

New York City enacts an ordinance allowing the transfer of develop-ment rights, a tool that assists in the preservation of historic buildings.

1969   The National Environmental Policy Act requires federal agencies to prepare impact statements for proj-ects that may affect cultural, as well as natural, resources.

The Historic American Engineering Record is established as a sister program to HABS to document and record engineering and indus-trial sites.

1971   Executive Order 11593 requires federal agencies to inventory their lands for cultural and historic sites and to nominate places to the National Register.

The National Trust for Historic Preservation begins its annual Preservation Honor Awards pro-gram to recognize individuals, organizations, and projects that represent the best in preservation.

1972   Through the Surplus Real Property Act, Congress authorizes the trans-fer of surplus historic federal prop-erty to local public agencies for preservation.

The World Heritage List is founded by UNESCO to record cultural and natural properties with outstanding universal value.

1973   *Old House Journal* is launched as a newsletter for Brooklyn brownston-ers and quickly expands its editorial and readership nationwide. Thirty years later, it has more than 130,000 readers.

The first National Historic Preservation Week is celebrated, an annual event held in May.

The city of New York amends its Landmarks Preservation Law to authorize the Landmarks Commission to designate interior landmarks.

1974   Preservation Action is formed and to date is the only national preser-vation lobby in the United States.

1976   The Tax Reform Act of 1976 pro-vides the first major preservation tax incentives for the rehabilitation of certified historic income-produc-ing properties in the form of a 60-month amortization of rehabilita-tion costs.

The Public Buildings Cooperative Use Act encourages restoration and adaptive use of historic buildings for federal use by requiring the fed-eral government to obtain and rehabilitate, where possible, his-toric buildings for use as federal office space.

The Historic Preservation Fund, funded by Outer Continental Shelf mineral receipts, is established to provide preservation grants to the states.

1977   The National Trust's Main Street Project, forerunner of today's National Main Street Center, is launched in Galesburg, IL; Hot Springs, SD; and Madison, IN, to demonstrate the value of preservation as a tool for downtown revitalization. Twenty-five years later the program boasts the participation of more than 1,650 communities, a total reinvestment in these communities of $16 billion, the creation of 226,900 new jobs and 88,700 building rehabilitation projects.

1978   In *Penn Central Transportation Co. v. City of New York*, one of preservation's landmark rulings, the US Supreme Court upholds the right of the city to block construction over Grand Central Terminal, thus affirming the legitimacy of preservation ordinances and local governments' power to enforce such ordinances.

The Secretary of the Interior's Standards for Historic Preservation are released as the first professional standards to guide alterations and additions to historic buildings.

The Revenue Act of 1978 creates a 10 percent tax credit for the rehabilitation of qualified historic commercial properties.

Eero Saarinen's Dulles International Airport Terminal (Chantilly, VA) is deemed eligible for the National Register in 1978, only 16 years after its construction, breaking the typical 50-year rule.

1979   With the largest concentration of 1920s and 1930s resort architecture in the United States, Miami Beach becomes the first National Register Historic District comprised entirely of 20th-century buildings.

This Old House debuts on Boston Public Television and will eventually become one of the most popular PBS and home improvement shows in history, reaching more than 3.9 million viewers weekly.

1980   Amendments to the National Historic Preservation Act are passed that direct federal agencies to nominate and protect historic federal properties, broaden participation of local governments, and require owner consent for National Register listing.

The Vernacular Architecture Forum is founded to encourage the study and preservation of traditional structures and landscapes.

1981   The Economic Recovery Tax Act expands the rehabilitation tax credit program, offering a 25 percent credit for renovating certified historic properties, and prompts a surge in rehab work nationwide. It also abolishes the tax incentive for demolishing historic properties.

1982   The zero preservation funding proposed by the Reagan administration is fought, and funding is restored after an intensive nationwide campaign.

1983   After a zealous preservation protest, Congress approves a $48 million plan to restore the west front of the US Capitol rather than the planned $73 million addition that would have obscured the historic facade.

369

Historic Preservation Timeline

1985 McDonald's announces plans to restore the first roadside stand built by Ray Kroc in 1955 in Des Plaines, IL.

1986 After a nationwide campaign to save the rehabilitation tax credits, the Tax Reform Act of 1986 is passed, although the credits are reduced from the 1981 level.

1988 Manassas National Battlefield Park in Virginia is saved from a 1.2 million-square-foot shopping mall development. The park will face another battle in 1993 when Disney proposes a historic theme park, Disney's America, three miles from the Battlefield Park. After tremendous national outcry over concerns about the effect of the associated sprawl on the battlefield, Disney withdraws its proposal.

The National Trust issues its first 11 Most Endangered Historic Places List to bring attention to threatened historic sites and to generate local support. In the next 15 years, only one of the more than 160 listed sites will be destroyed.

DOCOMOMO (Documentation and Conservation of Buildings, Sites, Neighborhoods of the Modern Movement) is founded in the Netherlands in response to the increasing demolition of Modern architecture. The group documents and advocates for the preservation of Modern heritage.

1991 The passage of the Intermodal Surface Transportation Efficiency Act provides a significant source of federal funding for preservation projects.

1995 The World Monuments Fund establishes its biennial World Monuments Watch list of 100 worldwide cultural sites in urgent need of intervention.

1996 In response to looming development, the National Trust purchases the land directly across the Ashley River from its 1738 Drayton Hall plantation (Charleston, SC) in order to preserve the site's natural vistas and historic character.

1997 The state of Texas becomes a pioneer in the digitizing of preservation records with its launch of the Texas Historic Sites Atlas (http://atlas.thc.state.tx.us/), an online database of 238,000 historic and archeological site records documenting Texas history with integrated mapping software for locating the resources.

1998 Save America's Treasures, a public-private partnership, is founded to identify and rescue the enduring symbols of America and raise public awareness and support for their preservation.

The first 20th-century vernacular structure less than 50 years old, the 1959 Ralph Sr. and Sunny Wilson House in Temple, TX, built for the founder of Wilsonart International, is listed in the National Register of Historic Places.

The 1966 appropriation providing federal funding for the National Trust is terminated. The Trust has since relied on private-sector contributions.

1998   Arapahoe Acres in Englewood, CO, is the first post-World War II residential subdivision listed as a historic district in the National Register of Historic Places.

2001   By 2001, historic buildings provide approximately one-fourth of the General Services Administration's federally owned space.

2003   The National Trust is the first non-profit group to receive the National Humanities Medal.

New York City passes contextual zoning regulations in a number of neighborhoods to encourage sympathetically-scaled new buildings within historic districts.

2004   In a vigorous fund-raising campaign, preservationists purchase Mies van der Rohe's landmark 1951 Farnsworth House in Plano, IL, considered by many a masterpiece of modernism and one of the most important residential designs of the 20th century.

Source: DesignIntelligence

371

Did you know...

The Historic Columbia River Highway in Oregon was the first scenic highway constructed in the United States (1913–1922). The road, and its associated designed landscape, was a technical and civic achievement of its time, successfully mixing ambitious engineering with sensitivity to the magnificent landscape. In 2000, it became the first scenic highway to be designated a National Historic Landmark.

J. Timothy Anderson Awards

The J. Timothy Anderson Awards for Excellence in Historic Rehabilitation honor outstanding real estate projects that rehabilitate historic buildings using federal historic rehabilitation tax credits. Entries are judged for their overall design and quality, interpretation and respect of historic elements, impact on the community, and financial and market success. The National Housing & Rehabilitation Association named the competition in memory of Boston architect and preservation advocate J. Timothy Anderson.

More information is available online at *www.housingonline.com.*

2006 Winners

Affordable Housing, Large
New Holland Apartments
Danville, IL
Melotte – Morse – Leonatti, Ltd.;
   New Holland, L.P.

Affordable Housing, Small
Acushnet Commons
New Bedford, MA
Brown SouthCoast Architects; Women's
   Institute for Housing & Economic
   Development

Market-Rate Residential, Large
Peerless Lofts
Providence, RI
Durkee, Brown, Viveiros & Werenfels
   Architects; Cornish Associates

Mixed-Income Housing, Large
The Apartments at Boott Mills
Lowell, MA
The Architectural Team, Inc.; Winn
   Development

Mixed-Income Housing, Small
Liberty School Apartments
Glasgow, KY
Brandstetter Carroll; AU Associates

Most Innovative Adaptive Reuse and/or Commercial Rehabilitation
Masonic Temple (Tremont Grand)
Baltimore, MD
Murphy and Dittenhafer, Inc.; William C.
   Smith & Co.

Best Scattered-Site Development
Salem Historic Homes
Salem, NJ
Kitchen & Associates; Penrose Properties

Honorable Mentions
Mattapan Heights Phase II
Boston, MA
Bergmeyer Associates, Inc.; Trinity
   Financial

Cadillac Building
Seattle, WA
Stickney Murphy Romine Architects;
   Historic Seattle

JURY
Josh Anderson, Cathartes Private Investments
Lisa Burcham, Washington DC Office of
   Planning
John L. Kelly, Nixon Peabody
John Mackey, American Express Tax and
   Business Services
Paul McGinley, McGinley Kalsow & Associates
Karl Stumpf, RTKL Associates Inc.

Source: National Housing & Rehabilitation Association

Landslide Landscapes

The Cultural Landscape Foundation's annual thematic list of endangered cultural landscapes is intended to rally public support order to stimulate preservation of the sites. Nominations are accepted from local groups or individuals, professionals, government officials, and other interested parties. Past themes have included masterworks of landscape architecture, working landscapes, and garden landscapes.

For photos, site histories, status updates, and biographies, visit the CLF website, *www.tclf.org/landslide/*.

2007 Heroes of Horticulture

Desert Ironwood Tree, Arizona-Sonora
    Museum
Tucson, AZ

Cork Oak
Santa Cruz, CA

Bougainvillea
Glendora, CA

Paired Moreton Bay Fig Trees,
    Rancho Los Alamitos
Long Beach, CA

Banyan Tree Allée
Boca Grande, FL

Bamboo Jungle Garden
Avery Island, LA

Southern Live Oak
Baton Rouge, LA

American Sycamore, Antietam
Sharpsburg, MD

Bur Oak, Henry Ford Estate
Dearborn, MI

Tree Peonies, Linwood Gardens
Pavilion, NY

Chestnut Tree, Susan B. Anthony House
Rochester, NY

Pear Orchard, Ellwanger Garden
Rochester, NY

Azaleas, Airlie Gardens
Wilmington, NC

Baldcypress Grove, Spring Grove Cemetery
Cincinnati, OH

Big Leaf Maple Pow Wow Tree
Gladstone, OR

Rhododendron, Greendale Cemetery
Meadville, PA

Camellias, Magnolia Plantation
Charleston, SC

Southern Live Oak
Johns Island, SC

Live Oak Allée, Main Street
Houston, TX

Eucalyptus Tree, Washington Park
    Arboretum
Seattle, WA

Elms of the National Mall
Washington, DC

Source: Cultural Landscape Foundation

373

Most Popular Historic Houses 2008

Every year *DesignIntelligence*, in conjunction with the *Almanac of Architecture & Design*, polls America's historic house museums to determine which are the most popular destinations. For the purposes of this study, a house museum is defined as a historic house that is currently exhibited and interpreted as a dwelling place.

1. **Biltmore Estate**
   Asheville, NC
   Richard Morris Hunt, 1895

2. **Mount Vernon**
   Mount Vernon, VA
   George Washington, 1785–86

3. **Hearst Castle**
   San Simeon, CA
   Julia Morgan, 1927–1947

4. **Graceland**
   Memphis, TN
   Furbringer & Ehrman, 1939

5. **Arlington House, The Robert E. Lee Memorial**
   Arlington, VA
   George Hadfield, 1817

6. **Monticello, Home of Thomas Jefferson**
   Charlottesville, VA
   Thomas Jefferson, 1768–79, 1793–1809

7. **Vanderbilt Mansion**
   Hyde Park, NY
   McKim, Mead and White, 1898

8. **The Breakers**
   Newport, RI
   Richard Morris Hunt, 1895

9. **Betsy Ross House**
   Philadelphia, PA
   Architect unknown, 1740

10. **Paul Revere House**
    Boston, MA
    Architect unknown, c.1680

11. **The Edison and Ford Winter Estates**
    Fort Myers, FL
    Thomas Edison, 1886 (Edison home)
    Architect unknown, 1911 (Ford home)

12. **Lincoln Home**
    Springfield, IL
    Architect unknown, 1839

13. **The Hermitage, Home of President Andrew Jackson**
    Nashville, TN
    Architect unknown, 1819–1821; David Morrison, 1831–32; Joseph Reiff and William Hume, 1835–37

14. **Boldt Castle**
    Alexandria Bay, NY
    Hewitt, Stevens & Paist, 1900–04

15. **Fair Lane, The Henry Ford Estate**
    Dearborn, MI
    William H. Van Tine, 1915

16. **Marble House**
    Newport, RI
    Richard Morris Hunt, 1892

17. **Fallingwater**
    Mill Run, PA
    Frank Lloyd Wright, 1939

18. **Taliesen West**
    Scottsdale, AZ
    Frank Lloyd Wright, 1937

19. **The Elms**
Newport, RI
Horace Trumbauer, 1901

20. **House of the Seven Gables**
Salem, MA
Architect unknown, 1668

21. **Vizcaya**
Miami, FL
Burrall Hoffman, 1916

22. **Franklin D. Roosevelt Cottage**
Lubec, ME
William T. Sears, 1897

23. **Home of Franklin D. Roosevelt**
Hyde Park, NY
Architect unknown, 1826

24. **Rosecliff**
Newport, RI
Stanford White, 1902

25. **FDR's Little White House**
Warm Springs, GA
Henry Toombs, 1932

Source: DesignIntelligence

He who Loves an Old House Never Loves in Vain. How can an Old House Used to Sun and Rain, To Lilac and Larkspur, And an Elm above, Ever Fail to Answer The Heart that gives it Love.

Isabel Fiske Conant, 1903

National Main Street Leadership Awards

The National Trust for Historic Preservation's National Main Street Leadership Awards recognize exceptional accomplishments in the revitalization of America's downtowns and neighborhood commercial districts. The annual program honors key leaders, including elected officials, government staff persons, public agencies, and non-profit organizations with the Civil Leadership Award; small businesses and corporations with the Business Leadership Award; and individuals with the Main Street Heroes Award.

A list of past winners is available online at *www.mainstreet.org*.

2006 Recipients

Business Leadership Award
Connecticut Light and Power Company

Civic Leadership Award
Bill Grant

Main Street Heroes Award
Main Street communities affected by
  Hurricane Katrina and those that
  responded with support

The National Main Street Center suspended the
National Main Street Leadership Awards for 2007 while
the organization's award programs undergo an expansion.

Source: National Trust for Historic Preservation

Even though current design preferences should never influence the assessment of work from a historical perspective, taste persists as an influential, it not always acknowledged, undertow, especially when addressing work of the recent past.

Richard Longstreth

National Preservation Awards

The National Trust for Historic Preservation annually recognizes citizens, organizations, and public and private entities for their dedication to and support of historic preservation. A jury of preservation professionals selects the winners of the National Preservation Awards using such criterion as the projects' positive effect on the community, pioneering nature, quality, and degree of difficulty. Special interest is also placed on projects that use historic preservation as a method of revitalization.

For more information, visit the National Trust website, *www.nationaltrust.org*.

2007 Winners

The Arc Arkansas
Little Rock, AR

Bureau of Land Management, Eastern
    States, Bois Fort Band of Minnesota
    Chippewa, 1854 Treaty Authority
Minnesota

City of Iowa City and Friends of Historic
    Preservation
Iowa City, IA

Edith Wharton Restoration, Inc.
Lenox, MA

Griffith Observatory
Los Angeles, CA

Indiana Historic SPANs Task Force
Indianapolis, IN

Landmark Center
St. Paul, MN

Mercy Housing
Savannah, GA

Reggie Black
Golden, CO

Sabbathday Lake Village, Forest, and
    Farm Project
Sabbathday Lake, ME

Upstairs Downtown Program
Springfield, IL

Urban Outfitters Corporate Office Campus
Philadelphia, PA

WinShape Retreat at Berry College
    Mountain Campus
Rome, GA

Yale University Art Gallery
New Haven, CT

Source: National Trust for Historic Preservation

377

National Preservation Awards

From the top: **WinShape Retreat at Berry College Mountain Campus, Rome, GA** (Photo: Gabriel Benzur Photography)**; The Mount, Berkshires, MA** (Photo: Edith Wharton Restoration, Inc.). (All photos courtesy of the NTHP)

NTHP/HUD Secretary's Award for Excellence in Historic Preservation

The Secretary's Award for Excellence in Historic Preservation, conferred jointly by the National Trust for Historic Preservation and HUD, honors preservation projects that provide affordable housing or expanded economic opportunities for low- and moderate-income families and individuals. Nominations are reviewed for their impact on the community, quality and degree of difficulty, unusual or pioneering nature, affordable housing and economic development opportunities, and ability to fit within a community redevelopment plan.

More information is available at *www.huduser.org/research/secaward.html.*

1998	A.T. Lewis and Rio Grande Lofts Denver, CO	2003	Ziegler Estate/La Casita Verde Los Angeles, CA
1999	Belle Shore Apartments Chicago, IL	2004	Reviviendo Family Housing Lawrence, MA
2000	The city of Covington Kentucky	2005	Umpqua Community Development Corporation Roseburg, OR
2001	Notre Dame Academy Cleveland, OH	2006	Midtown Exchange Minneapolis, MN
2002	Hamilton Hotel Laredo, TX	2007	Hilliard Towers Apartments Chicago, IL

379

Source: National Trust for Historic Preservation

If we wish to have a future with greater meaning, we must concern ourselves...with the total heritage of the nation and all that is worth preserving from our past as a living part of the present.

With Heritage So Rich, 1966

Preserve America Presidential Awards

The Preserve America Presidential Awards honor organizations, business-es, government entities, and individuals for their exemplary accomplish-ments in the sustainable use and preservation of America's cultural or national heritage; the interpretation and integration of this heritage into contemporary community life; and innovative, creative, and responsible approaches to showcasing historic resources within the community.

For additional information, visit *www.preserveamerica.gov* online.

2007 Winners

Heritage Tourism
USS Midway Museum
San Diego, CA

Natchitoches-Cane River Region Heritage
    Tourism
Natchitoches, LA

Private Preservation
The History Channel, Save Our History
Nationwide and New York, NY

Downtown St. Louis Revitalization
St. Louis, MO

Source: Preserve America

People will not look forward to posterity, who never look backward to their ancestors.

Edmund Burke

From the top: **New York City Heritage Tourism Center, sponsored by the History Channel's Save Our History program** (Photo: Save Our History/History Channel)**; 1926 Paul Brown Building, St. Louis, MO** (Photo: Pyramid Companies). (All photos courtesy of Preserve America)

Secretary of the Interior's Standards for Rehabilitation

The Secretary of the Interior's Standards for Rehabilitation were developed to help protect the nation's irreplaceable cultural resources by promoting consistent preservation practices. They offer guidance on preserving the distinctive character of historic buildings and their sites while accommodating reasonable changes to meet new needs and uses. In order to be eligible for the 20 percent rehabilitation tax credit, projects must follow these guidelines.

For information about how to apply the standards, visit the National Park Service's website at *www.nps.gov/history/hps/tps/tax/rehabstandards.htm.*

1. A property shall be used for its historic purpose or be placed in a new use that requires minimal change to the defining characteristics of the building and its site and environment.

2. The historic character of a property shall be retained and preserved. The removal of historic materials or alteration of features and spaces that characterize a property shall be avoided.

3. Each property shall be recognized as a physical record of its time, place, and use. Changes that create a false sense of historical development, such as adding conjectural features or architectural elements from other buildings, shall not be undertaken.

4. Most properties change over time; those changes that have acquired historic significance in their own right shall be retained and preserved.

5. Distinctive features, finishes, and construction techniques or examples of craftsmanship that characterize a historic property shall be preserved.

6. Deteriorated historic features shall be repaired rather than replaced. Where the severity of deterioration requires replacement of a distinctive feature, the new feature shall match the old in design, color, texture, and other visual qualities and, where possible, materials. Replacement of missing features shall be substantiated by documentary, physical, or pictorial evidence.

7. Chemical or physical treatments, such as sandblasting, that cause damage to historic materials shall not be used. The surface cleaning of structures, if appropriate, shall be undertaken using the gentlest means possible.

8. Significant archeological resources affected by a project shall be protected and preserved. If such resources must be disturbed, mitigation measures shall be undertaken.

9. New additions, exterior alterations, or related new construction shall not destroy historic materials that characterize the property. The new work shall be differentiated from the old and shall be compatible with the massing, size, scale, and architectural features to protect the historic integrity of the property and its environment.

10. New additions and adjacent or related new construction shall be undertaken in such a manner that if removed in the future, the essential form and integrity of the historic property and its environment would be unimpaired.

Source: National Park Service

Threatened National Historic Landmarks

National Historic Landmarks are buildings, sites, districts, structures, and objects that are significant to American history and culture. Every two years the National Park Service compiles a list of the landmarks that are in eminent danger of destruction due to deterioration, incompatible new construction, demolition, erosion, vandalism, or looting in order to alert the federal government and Americans to this potential loss of their heritage.

For more information, visit the NPS's website at *www.nps.gov/history/nhl/*.

2006 Threatened Buildings and Historic Districts

Alaska
Amalik Bay Archeological District, King
    Salmon
Brooks River Archeological District,
    Naknek
Chilkoot Trail and Dyea Site, Skagway
Kennecott Mines, Kennecott

Arkansas
Bathhouse Row, Hot Springs
Centennial Baptist Church, Helena
Rohwer Relocation Center Cemetery,
    Rohwer

Colorado
Central City/Blackhawk Historic District,
    Central City
Cripple Creek Historic District, Cripple
    Creek

District of Columbia
Army Medical Museum and Library, Walter
    Reed Army Medical Center

Florida
Pensacola Naval Air Station Historic
    District, Pensacola

Georgia
Columbus Historic Riverfront Industrial
    District, Columbus
Sweet Auburn Historic District, Atlanta

Indiana
Joseph Bailly Homestead, Porter County

Iowa
Woodbury County Courthouse, Sioux City

Louisiana
Fort Jackson, Triumph

Massachusetts
Boston Naval Shipyard, Boston
Longfellow House, Cambridge
Lowell Locks and Canals Historic District,
    Lowell
Old State House, Boston
United First Parish Church (Unitarian) of
    Quincy, Quincy

Michigan
Calumet Historic District, Calumet
Highland Park Ford Plant, Highland Park
Quincy Mining Company Historic District,
    Hancock

Mississippi
Arlington, Natchez
Beauvoir, Biloxi
Lucius Q.C.Lamar House, Oxford
Old Mississippi State Capitol, Jackson
Siege and Battle of Corinth Sites, Corinth

383

Threatened National Historic Landmarks

Montana
Great Northern Railway Buildings, Glacier
    National Park

New Mexico
Pecos Pueblo, Pecos

Oklahoma
Boley Historic District, Boley
Fort Gibson

Ohio
Ohio and Erie Canal, Valley View Village

Pennsylvania
Albert Gallatin House, Point Marion
First Bank of the United States,
    Philadelphia

South Carolina
Church of the Holy Cross, Statesburg

Virginia
Exchange, Petersburg (Independent City)

Wyoming
Sheridan Inn, Sheridan

Source: National Park Service

It is only fair that future generations inherit a world that we have not shorn of
health and wealth.

David Lowenthal

UNESCO Asia-Pacific Heritage Awards

As a part of UNESCO's culture heritage program in Asia and the Pacific, the Awards for Culture Heritage Conservation celebrate the efforts of individuals and private-sector organizations to conserve and restore structures more than 50 years old. In addition, the Jury Commendation for Innovation recognizes newly built structures that demonstrate outstanding standards for contemporary architectural design that are well integrated into historic contexts.

Photos and descriptions of the winners, can be found online at *www.unescobkk.org/culture/heritageawards/*.

2007 Winners

Award of Excellence
Maitreya Temples
Ladakh, India

Award of Distinction
Convocation Hall, University of Mumbai
Mumbai, India

Altit Settlement
Gilgit, Pakistan

Galle Fort Hotel
Galle, Sri Lanka

Award of Merit
Bonython Hall, University of Adelaide
Adelaide, Australia

Lijiang Ancient Town
Lijiang, Yunnan Province, China

Little Hong Kong
Hong Kong SAR, China

Astana of Syed Mir Yahya
Skardu, Pakistan

Honorable Mention
Liu Family Civil Residence
Shanxi, China

Old St. Andrew's School
Singapore

Jury Commendation for Innovation
Whitfield Barracks
Hong Kong SAR, China

JURY
Susan Balderstone, Heritage Victoria (Australia)
William Chapman, University of Hawaii at Manoa
Richard A. Engelhardt UNESCO Bangkok
Pinraj Khanjanusthiti, Chulalongkorn University
   (Thailand)
Budi Lim, Budi Lim Architects (Indonesia)
Laurence Loh, Laurence Loh Architects
   (Malaysia)
David Lung, University of Hong Kong (China)
Chatvichai Promadhattavedi, Art and Culture
   Foundation of Bangkok and Pro-Space
   Company (Thailand)
Gurmeet Rai, Cultural Resource Conservation
   Initiative (India)
Johannes Widodo, National University of
   Singapore (Singapore)

Source: United Nations' Educational, Scientific and Cultural Organization

385

World Heritage List

The World Heritage List contains properties (such as forests, mountains, lakes, deserts, buildings, or cities) that possess outstanding universal value to the world's cultural and natural heritage. The World Heritage Committee selects sites for inclusion on the list. The committee also provides technical cooperation for the safe-guarding of World Heritage properties for entities whose resources are insufficient. Assistance with the nomination process, grants, and loans is also available.

For a full listing of all World Heritage properties, including photos, go to *http://whc.unesco.org.*

Historic Cities and Towns

Albania
Museum-City of Gjirokastra

Algeria
Kasbah of Algiers
M'Zab Valley

Austria
City of Graz – Historic Centre
Hallstatt-Dachstein Salzkammergut
    Cultural Landscape
Historic Centre of the City of Salzburg
Historic Centre of Vienna

Azerbaijan
Walled City of Baku with the Shirvanshah's
    Palace and Maiden Tower*

Belgium
Grand-Place, Brussels
Historic Centre of Brugge

Bolivia
City of Potosi
Historic City of Sucre

Bosnia and Herzegovina
Old Bridge Area of the Old City of Mostar

Brazil
Brasilia
Historic Centre of Salvador de Bahia
Historic Centre of São Luis
Historic Centre of the Town of Diamantina
Historic Centre of the Town of Goiás
Historic Centre of the Town of Olinda
Historic Town of Ouro Preto

Bulgaria
Ancient City of Nessebar

Canada
Lunenburg Old Town
Quebec (Historic Area)

Chile
Sewell Mining Town

China
Ancient City of Ping Yao
Historic Centre of Macao
Kaiping Diaolou and Villages
Old Town of Lijiang

Colombia
Historic Centre of Santa Cruz de Mompox
Port, Fortresses and Group of Monuments,
    Cartagena

DESIGN & HISTORIC PRESERVATION

Croatia
Historic City of Trogir
Historical Complex of Split with the Palace
    of Diocletian
Old City of Dubrovnik

Cuba
Old Havana and its Fortifications
Trinidad and the Valley de los Ingenios
Urban Historic Centre of Cienfuegos

Czech Republic
Historic Centre of Cesky Krumlov
Historic Centre of Prague
Historic Centre of Telc
Holasovice Historical Village Reservation
Kutná Hora: Historical Town Centre with
    the Church of St Barbara and the
    Cathedral of Our Lady at Sedlec

Dominican Republic
Colonial City of Santo Domingo

Ecuador
City of Quito
Historic Centre of Santa Ana de los Ríos de
    Cuenca

Egypt
Islamic Cairo

Estonia
Historic Centre (Old Town) of Tallinn

Ethiopia
Fortified Historic Town of Harar Jugol

Finland
Old Rauma

Former Yugoslav Republic of Macedonia
Ohrid Region with its Cultural and
    Historical Aspect and its Natural
    Environment

France
Historic Centre of Avignon
Historic Fortified City of Carcassonne
Historic Site of Lyons
Le Havre, the City Rebuilt by Auguste
    Perret
Paris, Banks of the Seine
Place Stanislas, Place de la Carrière and
    Place d'Alliance in Nancy
Port of the Moon, Bordeaux
Provins, Town of Medieval Fairs
Roman and Romanesque Monuments
    of Arles
Grande Ile, Strasbourg

Germany
Classical Weimar
Collegiate Church, Castle, and Old Town
    of Quedlinburg
Hanseatic City of Lübeck
Historic Centres of Stralsund and Wismar
Mines of Rammelsberg and Historic Town
    of Goslar
Old Town of Regensburg with Stadtamhof
Palaces and Parks of Potsdam and Berlin
Town of Bamberg

Greece
Historic Centre (Chorá) with the
    Monastery of Saint John "the
    Theologian" and the Cave of the
    Apocalypse on the Island of Pátmos
Medieval City of Rhodes
Old Town of Corfu

Guatemala
Antigua Guatemala

Holy See
Vatican City

Holy See/Italy
Historic Centre of Rome, the Properties
    of the Holy See in that City Enjoying
    Extraterritorial Rights and San Paolo
    Fuori le Mura

387

World Heritage List

Hungary
Budapest, the Banks of the Danube and
the Buda Castle Quarter

Iran
Meidan Emam, Esfahan

Israel
Old City of Acre

Italy
Assisi, the Basilica of San Francesco and
Other Franciscan Sites
Cathedral, Torre Civica and Piazza Grande,
Modena
City of Verona
City of Vicenza and the Palladian Villas of
the Veneto
Costiera Amalfitana
Crespi d'Adda
Ferrara, City of the Renaissance and its Po
Delta
Genoa: Le Strade Nuove and the system of
the Palazzi dei Rolli
Historic Centre of the City of Pienza
Historic Centre of Florence
Historic Centre of Naples
Historic Centre of San Gimignano
Historic Centre of Siena
Historic Centre of Urbino
I Sassi di Matera
Late Baroque Towns of the Val di Noto
(South-Eastern Sicily)
Portovenere, Cinque Terre, and the Islands
(Palmaria, Tino and Tinetto)
Syracuse and the Rocky Necropolis of
Pantalica
Venice and its Lagoon

Japan
Historic Monuments of Ancient Kyoto
(Kyoto, Uji and Otsu Cities)
Historic Monuments of Ancient Nara
Historic Villages of Shirakawa-go and
Gokayama

Jerusalem
Old City of Jerusalem and its Walls*

**Lao People's Democratic
Republic**
Town of Luang Prabang

Latvia
Historic Centre of Riga

Lebanon
Byblos

Libyan Arab Jamahiriya
Old Town of Ghadames

Lithuania
Vilnius Historic Centre

Luxembourg
City of Luxembourg: its Old Quarters and
Fortifications

Mali
Old Towns of Djenné
Timbuktu

Malta
City of Valletta

Mauritania
Ancient Ksour of Ouadane, Chinguetti,
Tichitt and Oualata

Mexico
Historic Centre of Mexico City and
Xochimilco
Historic Centre of Morelia
Historic Centre of Oaxaca and
Archaeological Site of Monte Alban
Historic Centre of Puebla
Historic Centre of Zacatecas
Historic Fortified Town of Campeche
Historic Monuments Zone of Querétaro
Historic Monuments Zone of Tlacotalpan
Historic Town of Guanajuato and Adjacent
Mines

Morocco
Historic City of Meknes
Ksar of Ait-Ben-Haddou
Medina of Essaouira (formerly Mogador)
Medina of Fez
Medina of Marrakesh
Medina of Tétouan (formerly known as
    Titawin)
Portuguese City of Mazagan (El Jadida)

Mozambique
Island of Mozambique

Nepal
Kathmandu Valley*

Netherlands
Historic Area of Willemstad, Inner City
    and Harbour, Netherlands Antilles
Droogmakerij de Beemster (Beemster
    Polder)

Norway
Bryggen
Røros

Panama
Historic District of Panamá, with the Salón
    Bolivar

Peru
City of Cuzco
Historic Centre of Lima
Historical Centre of the City of Arequipa

Philippines
Historic Town of Vigan

Poland
Cracow's Historic Centre
Historic Centre of Warsaw
Medieval Town of Torun
Old City of Zamosc

Portugal
Central Zone of the Town of Angra do
    Heroismo in the Azores
Cultural Landscape of Sintra
Historic Centre of Evora
Historic Centre of Guimarães
Historic Centre of Oporto

Republic of Korea
Kyongju Historic Areas

Romania
Historic Centre of Sighisoara
Villages with Fortified Churches in
    Transylvania

Russian Federation
Historic and Architectural Complex of
    the Kazan Kremlin
Historic Centre of Saint Petersburg and
    Related Groups of Monuments
Historical Centre of the City of Yaroslavl
Historic Monuments of Novgorod and
    Surroundings
Kremlin and Red Square, Moscow

Senegal
Island of Saint-Louis

Slovakia
Banska Stiavnica
Bardejov Town Conservation Reserve

Spain
Alhambra, Generalife and Albayzin,
    Granada
Archaeological Ensemble of Mérida
Historic Centre of Cordoba
Historic City of Toledo
Historic Walled Town of Cuenca
Ibiza, biodiversity and culture
Monuments of Oviedo and the Kingdom
    of the Asturias
Old City of Salamanca
Old Town of Avila with its Extra-Muros
    Churches
Old Town of Caceres
Old Town of Segovia and its Aqueduct

389

World Heritage List

San Cristóbal de La Laguna
Santiago de Compostela (Old town)
University and Historic Precinct of Alcalá de
    Henares

Sri Lanka
Old Town of Galle and its Fortifications
Sacred City of Kandy

Suriname
Historic Inner City of Paramaribo

Sweden
Church Village of Gammelstad, Luleå
Hanseatic Town of Visby
Naval Port of Karlskrona

Switzerland
Old City of Berne

Syrian Arab Republic
Ancient City of Aleppo
Ancient City of Bosra
Ancient City of Damascus

Tunisia
Kairouan
Medina of Sousse
Medina of Tunis

Turkey
City of Safranbolu
Historic Areas of Istanbul

Turkmenistan
Kunya-Urgench

Ukraine
L'viv – the Ensemble of the Historic Centre

**United Kingdom of Great Britain
and Northern Ireland**
City of Bath
Historic Town of St George and Related
    Fortifications, Bermuda
Liverpool – Maritime Mercantile City
New Lanark
Old and New Towns of Edinburgh
Saltaire

United Republic of Tanzania
Stone Town of Zanzibar

United States of America
La Fortaleza and San Juan Historic Site in
    Puerto Rico

Uruguay
Historic Quarter of the City of Colonia del
    Sacramento

Uzbekistan
Itchan Kala
Historic Centre of Bukhara
Historic Centre of Shakhrisyabz
Samarkand – Crossroads of Culture

Venezuela
Coro and its Port

Vietnam
Complex of Hué Monuments
Hoi An Ancient Town

Yemen
Historic Town of Zabid*
Old City of Sana'a
Old Walled City of Shibam

Yugoslavia
Natural and Culturo-Historical Region
    of Kotor

* Indicates the site is also on the World Heritage in
  Danger list as determined by the World Heritage
  Committee.

Source: UNESCO, World Heritage Committee

World's 100 Most Endangered Sites

The World Monuments Fund's biennial list of the 100 Most Endangered Sites contains architectural sites and monuments most in danger of destruction. For many sites, inclusion on this list is their only hope for survival. Limited financial support is also available and is awarded on a competitive basis. The World Monuments Fund is a private, nonprofit organization that fosters awareness and preservation of the world's cultural, artistic, and historic resources.

For photos and descriptions of each site, visit the World Monuments Fund's website, *www.wmf.org*.

2008 Endangered Sites

Afghanistan
Buddhist Remains of Bamiyan, Bamiyan
Murad Khane, Kabul
Tepe Narenj, Kabul

Algeria
Medracen and el-Khroub Numidian Royal
    Mausolea, Constantine

Antarctica
Scott's Hut and the Explorers' Heritage of
    Antarctica, Ross Island

Argentina
Brener Synagogue, Moises Ville

Armenia
Kumayri District, Alexandrapol

Australia
Dampier Rock Art Complex, Burrup
    Peninsula

Azerbaijan
Khinalyg Village

Bangladesh
Sonargaon-Panam City

Bosnia/Herzegovina
Sarajevo City Hall, Sarajevo

Brazil
Porangatu Historic District, Porangatu

Bulgaria
Novae Archaeological Site, Svishtov

Burkina Faso
Loropeni Ruins, Loropeni

Canada
Herschel Island, Yukon Territory

Chile
Montemar Institute of Marine Biology,
    Vina del Mar

China
Modern Shanghai
Xumishan Grottoes, Guyuan County

Cyprus
Famagusta Walled City

Egypt
Aqsunqur Mosque (Blue Mosque), Cairo
Shunet el-Zebib, Abydos
West Bank of the Nile, Luxor

Eritrea
Derbush Tomb, Massawa

391

World's 100 Most Endangered Sites

Ethiopia
Mohammadali House, Addis Ababa

France
Epailly Chapel of the Order of the Temple,
    Courban

Georgia
Gelati Monastery and Academy, Kutaisi

Ghana
Wa Naa's Palace, Wa

Greece
Lesvos Historic Churches, Lesvos
Pella Macedonian Tombs, Pella

Guatemala
Capitanes Generales Palace, Antiqua
    Guatemala
Ceibal Archaeological Site, Sayaxche

India
Amber Town, Rajasthan
Chettinad, Chennai
Jantar Mantar, Jaipur
Leh Old Town, Ladakh
Srinigar Heritage Zone, Srinigar

Indonesia
Kotagede Heritage District, Kotagede

Iraq
Cultural Heritage Sites of Iraq

Ireland
Tara Hill, Meath
Vernon Mount, Cork

Italy
Transhumance Cultural Landscape, Molise
    Region
Farnese Nymphaeum, Rome
Fenestrelle Fortress, Turin
Viscontian Bridge-Dam, Valleggio sul
    Mincio

Jamaica
Falmouth Historic Town, Falmouth

Jordan
Khirbet et-Tannur, Tafilah
Qusayr 'Amra, al-'Azraq

Jordan/Israel
Jordan River Cultural Landscape

Libya
Wadi Mathendous Rock Art, Fezzan

Macedonia
Mother of God Peribleptos Church, Ohrid

Madagascar
Fianarantsoa Old City, Fianarantsoa

Malta
Fort St. Elmo, Valletta

Mauritania
Chinguetti Mosque, Chinguetti

Mexico
Huaca Historic Neighborhood, Veracruz
Chihuahua Missions, Chihuahua
Monte Alban Archaeological Site, Oaxaca
Teuchtitlan-Guachimontones
    Archaeological Zone, Teuchtitlan

Morocco
Al-Azhar Mosque, Fez

Nigeria
Ikom Monoliths of Cross River State, Ikom

Pakistan
Shikarpoor Historic City Center,
    Shikarpoor

Palestinian Territories
Church of the Holy Nativity, Bethlehem

New York State Pavilion, Queens, NY (Photos courtesy of the World Monument Fund)

World's 100 Most Endangered Sites

Peru
Laraos Terraces, Laraos
Lima Historic City Center, Lima
Machu Picchu Historic Sanctuary,
    Urubamba Valley
Macusani-Corani Rock Art, Macusani
    and Corani
San Pedro Apostol de Andahuaylillas
    Church, Andahuaylillas
Santa Catalina Monastery, Arequipa

Russia
Icon of the Mother of God of the Sign
    Church, Teplovo
Mendeleev Tower, St. Petersburg
St. Petersburg Historic Skyline

Senegal
Saint-Louis Island

Sierra Leone
Freetown Historic Monuments, Freetown

Slovakia
Banská Stiavnica Calvary Complex, Banská
    Stiavnica

Somaliland
Las Geel Rock Art, Las Geel District

Spain
Joan Miró Foundation, Barcelona

Sri Lanka
Kandy Sacred City, Kandy

Sweden
Ljungberg Hall, Borlange City

Syria
Cyrrhus (Nebi Houri), Azaz
Old Damascus

Tanzania
Kilwa Historic Sites, Kilwa

Turkey
Çukur Han, Ankara
Hasankeyf
Istanbul Historic Walls, Istanbul
Meryem Ana (Mother of God) Church,
    Göreme, Cappadocia
Red Church, Güzelyurt, Sivrihisar,
    Cappadocia

Ukraine
Pidhirtsi Castle, Pidhirtsi

United Kingdom
Mavisbank House, Midlothian, Scotland
Richhill House, Armagh City, Northern
    Ireland
St. Peter's College, Cardross, Scotland
Wilton's Music Hall, London

United States
Florida Southern Historic Campus,
    Lakeland, FL
Historic Neighborhoods of New Orleans,
    LA
Historic Route 66
Main Street Modern, various locations
New York State Pavilion, Queens, NY
Salk Institute, San Diego, CA
Tutuveni Petroglyph Site, Hopi Tribal
    Land, AZ

Uzbekistan
Ayaz Kala, Ellikala
Madrasa Rashid, Bukhara

Zimbabwe
Bumbusi National Monument,
    Matabeleland

Source: World Monuments Fund

DESIGN
EDUCATION

Current and prospective design students will find many valuable resources in this chapter, including design and recognition award programs for students and educators in architecture, industrial design, interior design, landscape architecture, and planning.

ACSA Distinguished Professor Award

The Association of Collegiate Schools of Architecture presents the Distinguished Professor Award to honor sustained creative achievement in architectural education, whether through teaching, design, scholarship, research, or service. Eligible candidates must be a living faculty member at an ACSA member school for a minimum of 10 years or be otherwise allied with architectural education at an ACSA member school.

Additional information can be found on ACSA's website, *www.acsa-arch.org*.

1984–85 Alfred Caldwell, Illinois Institute of Technology
Robert S. Harris, Univ. of Southern California
E. Fay Jones, University of Arkansas
Charles Moore, University of Texas at Austin
Ralph Rapson, University of Minnesota

1985–86 James Marston Fitch, Columbia University
Leslie J. Laskey, Washington University
Harlan E. McClure, Clemson University
Edward Romieniec, Texas A&M University
Richard A. Williams, University of Illinois, Urbana–Champaign

1986–87 Christopher Alexander, University of California, Berkeley
Harwell Hamilton Harris, North Carolina State University
Stanislawa Nowicki, University of Pennsylvania
Douglas Shadbolt, University of British Columbia
Jerzy Soltan, Harvard University

1987–88 Harold Cooledge Jr., Clemson University
Bernd Foerster, Kansas State University
Romaldo Giurgola, Columbia University
Joseph Passonneau, Washington University
John G. Willams, University of Arkansas

1988–89 Peter R. Lee Jr., Clemson University
E. Keith McPheeters, Auburn University
Stanley Salzman, Pratt Institute
Calvin C. Straub, Arizona State University
Blanche Lemco van Ginkel, University of Toronto

1989–90 Gunnar Birkerts, University of Michigan
Olivio C. Ferrari, Virginia Polytechnic Institute and State University
George C. Means Jr., Clemson University
Malcolm Quantrill, Texas A&M University

397

ACSA Distinguished Professor Award

1990–91 Denise Scott Brown, University of Pennsylvania
Panos G. Koulermos, University of Southern California
William G. McMinn, Cornell University
Forrest Wilson, Catholic University of America
David G. Woodcock, Texas A&M University

1991–92 M. David Egan, Clemson University
Robert D. Dripps, University of Virginia
Richard C. Peters, University of California, Berkeley
David L. Niland, University of Cincinnati

1992–93 Stanley W. Crawley, University of Utah
Don P. Schlegel, University of New Mexico
Thomas L. Schumacher, University of Maryland

1993–94 George Anselevicius, University of New Mexico
John Harold Box, University of Texas at Austin
Peter McCleary, University of Pennsylvania
Douglas Rhyn, Univ. of Wisconsin–Milwaukee
Alan Stacell, Texas A&M University

1994–95 Blake Alexander, University of Texas at Austin
Robert Paschal Burns, North Carolina State University
Robert Heck, Louisiana State University
Ralph Knowles, University of Southern California

1995–96 James Barker, Clemson University
Mui Ho, University of California, Berkley
Patricia O'Leary, University of Colorado
Sharon E. Sutton, University of Michigan
Peter D. Waldman, University of Virginia

1996–97 Colin H. Davidson, University of Montreal
Michael Fazio, Mississippi State University
Ben J. Refuerzo, Univ. of California, Los Angeles
Max Underwood, Arizona State University
J. Stroud Watson, University of Tennessee

1997–98 Roger H. Clark, North Carolina State University
Bob E. Heatly, Oklahoma State University
John S. Reynolds, University of Oregon
Marvin E. Rosenman, Ball State University
Anne Taylor, University of New Mexico

1998–99 Ralph Bennett, University of Maryland
Diane Ghirardo, University of Southern California
Robert Greenstreet, University of Wisconsin–Milwaukee
Thomas Kass, University of Utah
Norbert Schoenauer, McGill University
Jan Wampler, Massachusetts Institute of Technology

1999–2000 Maelee Thomson Foster,
University of Florida
Louis Inserra, Pennsylvania
State University
Henry Sanoff, North Carolina
State University

2000–01 Ikhlas Sabouni, Prairie View
A&M University
Raymond J. Cole, University of
British Columbia

2001–02 Steven Paul Badanes, University
of Washington
Raymond Lifchez, University of
California, Berkeley
Marvin J. Malecha, North
Carolina State Universty
Enrique Vivoni Farage,
Universidad de Puerto Rico
James P. Warfield, University of
Illinois, Urbana–Champaign

2002–03 Sherry Ahrentzen, University of
Wisconsin–Milwaukee
Lance Jay Brown, City College
of New York, CUNY
David A. Crane, University of
South Florida
Lars Lerup, Rice University
Edward Steinfeld, University at
Buffalo, SUNY

2003–04 Michael Benedikt, University
of Texas at Austin
Georgia Bizios, North Carolina
State University
William C. Miller, University
of Utah

2004–05 Stephen Verderber, Tulane
University

2005–06 *No award granted*

2006–07 George Dodds, University of
Tennessee, Knoxville
Paul J. Donnelly, Washington
University in St. Louis
Geraldine Forbes Isais, University
of New Mexico
Ferdinand S. Johns, Montana
State University
Harry Van Oudenallen,
University of Wisconsin–
Milwaukee

Source: Association of Collegiate Schools of Architecture

399

Space is nothing—a mere negation of the solid. And thus we come to
overlook it.

Geoffrey Scott

ACSP Distinguished Educator Award

The ACSP Distinguished Educator Award is presented by the Association of Collegiate Schools of Planning to recognize exemplary service in planning education and practice. Nominations are welcomed from chairs and faculty at ACSP member schools. Recipients are chosen for their scholarly contributions, teaching excellence, service to the profession, and significant contributions to planning education or practice.

Further information is available from the ACSP's website, *www.acsp.org*.

1983	Harvey S. Perloff, University of California, Los Angeles	1996	Martin Meyerson, University of Pennsylvania
1984	John Reps, Cornell University	1997	Lloyd Rodwin, Massachusetts Institute of Technology
1985	*No award granted*	1998	Michael Teitz, University of California, Berkeley
1986	F. Stuart Chapin Jr., University of North Carolina at Chapel Hill	1999	Lisa Redfield Peattie, Massachusetts Institute of Technology
1987	John Friedmann, University of California, Los Angeles	2000	Melvin M. Webber, University of Calfornia, Berkeley
1988	*No award granted*	2001	*No award granted*
1989	John Dyckman, Johns Hopkins University	2002	David R. Godschalk, University of North Carolina at Chapel Hill
1990	Barclay Gibbs Jones, Cornell University	2003	Paul Niebanck, University of Washington
1991	C. Britton Harris, University of Pennsylvania	2004	Susan Fainstein, Rutgers, The State University of New Jersey
1992	Melville C. Branch, University of Southern California	2005	Lawrence E. Susskind, Massachusetts Institute of Technology
1993	Ann Strong, University of Pennsylvania	2006	Martin Wachs, University of California, Berkeley
1994	John A. Parker, University of North Carolina at Chapel Hill	2007	Lewis D. Hopkins, University of Illinois at Urbana–Champaign
1995	Alan Feldt, University of Michigan		

Source: Association of Collegiate Schools of Planning

AIA Education Honor Awards

The annual Education Honor Awards, presented by the American Institute of Architects, recognize outstanding teachers and celebrate educational excellence in the classroom, laboratory, or studio or through community work. The jury selects the winners based on the entries' development of exceptional, innovative, and intellectually challenging courses, initiatives, or programs that address broad issues and advance architectural education and practice.

For more information, visit the AIA's website, *www.aia.org.*

2007 Winners

ecoMOD
University of Virginia
John Quale and Paxton Marshall

SCI-TECH I-IV
Iowa State University
Jason Alread and Thomas Leslie

Visioning Rail Transit in Northwest
    Arkansas: Lifestyles and Ecologies
University of Arkansas and Washington
    University in St Louis
Stephen Luoni, Aaron Gabriel, Jeffrey
    Huber, Eric Kahn, William Conway,
    Tahar Messadi, Greg Herman

JURY
Ann Chaintreuil, Chaintreuil, Jensen & Stark
    Architects (chair)
Anthony Costello, AIA Ohio Valley
Catherine McNeel, American Institute of
    Architecture Students/Mississippi State
    University
Michaele Pride, University of Cincinnati
Michael Rotondi, Roto Architects and Southern
    California Institute of Architecture

Source: American Institute of Architects

401

You can never learn less, you can only learn more.

R. Buckminster Fuller

AIA Education Honor Awards

Visioning Rail Transit in Northwest Arkansas: Lifestyles and Ecologies by the University of Arkansas and Washington University in St Louis (Images courtesy of the University of Arkansas)

AIAS Educator Honor Award

The Educator Honor Award is the most prestigious award conferred by the American Institute of Architecture Students on an educator. It recognizes educators who have made outstanding contributions to the formal education of architecture students, provided exemplary education to the public on the virtues of excellence in architecture and the environment, and made exceptional contributions to the academic and career counseling of architecture students.

For more information, visit the AIAS on the Internet at *www.aias.org.*

1991   Leighton Lin
University of Hawaii at Manoa

1992   Frank Bosworth
Bowling Green State University

1993   David M. Scott
Washington State University

1994   Spencer A. Leineweber
University of Hawaii at Manoa

1995   Tom Hoffman
Andrews University

1996   James G. Fausett
Southern Polytechnic State
University

1997   Joyce M. Noe
University of Hawaii at Manoa

1998   Shannon Criss
Mississippi State University

1999   Laura H. Lee
Carnegie Mellon University

2000   William J. Carpenter
Southern Polytechnic State
University

2001   Vivian Loftness
Carnegie Mellon University

2002   Rumiko Handa
University of Nebraska–Lincoln

2003   Rusty Smith
Auburn University

Mike Andrejasich
University of Illinois at
Urbana–Champaign

2004   Mohammed Bilbeisi
Oklahoma State University

2005   Neil Frankel
University of Wisconsin–
Milwaukee

2006   *No award granted*

2007   David W. Hinson
Auburn University

403

Source: American Institute of Architects Students

AICP Outstanding Student Awards

With its Outstanding Student Awards, the American Institute of Certified Planners recognizes outstanding students graduating from accredited university planning programs, both at the undergraduate and graduate levels. Recipients have been selected for this honor by their school's department head and colleagues following criteria that include an emphasis on the quality of students' coursework and the likelihood of success as a professional planner.

Additional information can be found online at *www.planning.org.*

2007 Recipients

Bachelor's Degree

Thomas Coleman, Alabama A&M University

Susan Marie DeBlieck, Iowa State University

Christopher Eaton, Ball State University

Sara Elinor Foster, University of Virginia

John Hemmerle, University of Cincinnati

Cari Lynn Meyer, California Polytechnic State University, San Luis Obispo

Sarah Elizabeth Murray, East Carolina University

Martin Palaniuk, Eastern Washington University

Emilie Pannell, University of Illinois at Urbana–Champaign

Hector Solis, California State Polytechnic University, Pomona

Milena Stoeva, Michigan State University

Master's Degree

Kate Bender, New York University

Matthew Henson Brinkley, Michigan State University

Ava Bromberg, University of California at Los Angeles

Jajean Rose Burney, University at Buffalo, SUNY

Jonah Katz Chiarenza, University of Virginia

Craig Cipriano, Rutgers, The State University of New Jersey

Katherine Cote, University of Washington

Anuttama Dasgupta, University of Illinois at Urbana–Champaign

Neil Creagh Dixon, University of Wisconsin–Madison

Sarah Lynn Downing, Kansas State University

Jeremy A. Emerson, University of Nebraska–Lincoln

Fred Evander, Eastern Washington University

Alan Fogg, Virginia Polytechnic Institute & State University

Samuel H. Fox, University of Oregon

Amy Gilder-Busatti, Morgan State University

Derek Hanson, University of Kansas

Elizabeth Hayden, Tufts University

Ryan Herchenroether, Hunter College, CUNY

Kara Homan, University of Iowa

Stephanie Jennings, University of Pennsylvania

Lynda Jordan, Alabama A&M University

Michael Kennedy, California State Polytechnic University, Pomona

David L. Lewis, Virginia Commonwealth University

Brandie Miklus, Florida State University
Benjamin G. Miller, Clemson University
Israel Jose Monsanto Diaz, University of
Massachusetts Amherst
Timothy L. Moreland, University of
Memphis
James Scott Muscatello, Cleveland State
University
Richard Norton, University of Southern
California
Alicia Parker, San Jose State University
Iris Patten, University of Florida

Emily Rosendall, Ball State University
Mary Troyan, University of Oklahoma
Esther Valle, California Polytechnic State
University, San Luis Obispo
Katherine Hay Wallace, Massachusetts
Institute of Technology
Lucy M. Wilkinson, Iowa State University
Nicole Davis Woerner, Auburn University
Sarah Donahue Wolff, University of North
Carolina at Chapel Hill
Katy E. Wyerman, University of Cincinnati

Source: American Institute of Certified Planners

405

Whenever and wherever societies have flourished and prospered rather than stagnated and decayed, creative and workable cities have been at the core of the phenomenon....Decaying cities, declining economies, and mounting social troubles travel together. The combination is not coincidental.

Jane Jacobs

AICP Outstanding Student Project Awards

The American Institute of Certified Planners recognizes distinctive student achievement that advance the planning field with its annual Outstanding Student Project Awards. Students or student teams in accredited planning programs may enter a paper or class project in one of three categories: contemporary issues, the application of the planning process, and applied research. No more than three awards are granted each year.

Additional information is available online at *www.planning.org.*

2007 Winners

Application of the Planning Process
Two Squares, One Place
Abigail Emison, Jonathan Leit, Dina
  Mackin, Masatomo Miyazawa, Alison
  Novak, Gena Peditto, Ommeed Sathe,
  Antonina Simeti, Charu Singh, Shanny
  Spraus, James Stevens, Moshahida
  Sultana, and Ritesh Warade
Massachusetts Institute of Technology

Applied Research
Changing of the Guard: A New Vision for
  Fort Monmouth
Peilin Chen, Yiun Lin Chong, Nicole M.
  Clare, Thomas Hastings, Geoffrey W.
  Long, Elizabeth Ann McQueen, Michael
  Smart, Julia A. Taylor, Jocelyn Torio,
  and Melinda G. Watts
University of Pennsylvania

Contemporary Issue
Going Public! Strategies for Meeting
  Public Restroom Need in Portland's
  Central City
Josh Ahmann, Kevin Bond, Warren
  Greaser, Sarah Selden, Amber
  Springberg, Kartik Srinivas, and
  Jon Swae
Portland State University

JURY
Robert E. Blanchard, Bob Blanchard Consulting
Lucia E. Garsys, Hillsborough County
David Ortiz, Philadelphia City Planning
  Commission
Veronica Rosales, City of El Paso

Source: American Institute of Certified Planners

The chief function of the city is to convert power into form, energy into culture, dead matter into the living symbols of art, biological reproduction into social creativity.

Lewis Mumford

Alpha Rho Chi Bronze Medal

The Alpha Rho Chi Bronze Medal was established in 1931 to encourage professional leadership, promote the ideals of professional service, and stimulate professional merit by commending qualities not necessarily pertaining to scholarship. Each year more than 100 schools of architecture, whose faculty select a graduating senior who best exemplifies these qualities, participate. Alpha Rho Chi is a national co-ed professional fraternity for architecture and the allied arts.

Additional information may be found on the fraternity's website, *www.alpharhochi.org.*

2007 Recipients

Andrews University
Christine Arnold

Arizona State University
Alexis Briana Flores

Auburn University
Steven Keith Wall

Ball State University
Joseph Michael Littrell

Boston Architectural College
William Leo Patterson

California College of the Arts
Mary Desing

California Polytechnic State University, San Luis Obispo
Naomi Szto

California State Polytechnic University, Pomona
Courtney A. Hukel

Carnegie Mellon University
Read J. Langworthy

Catholic University of America
Ana M. McKernan

City College of New York, CUNY
Carlos Feliz

Clemson University
Jessica Erin Latour; Curt Hjalmar Berg

Columbia University
Sabri Farouki

Cooper Union
David C. Petersen

Cornell University
Jonathan Douglas Moody; Namita Vijay Dharia

Dalhousie University
Kingman Brewster

Drexel University
Anthony William Harper

Drury University
Jason August Hudspeth; Lalima Hangma Chemjong

Florida A&M University
Denise Francis

Harvard University
Sarah Jacoby; Ying Zhou

407

Alpha Rho Chi Bronze Medal

Illinois Institute of Technology
Janel Fung

Iowa State University
Bradley Edward Baer

Kansas State University
Shalece L. Charles

Louisiana State University
Nicole Brannon

Louisiana Tech University
Brandy M. Blanchard

Massachusetts Institute of Technology
Jeffrey Anderson

McGill University
Andrea Heather Tsang

Miami University
Michelle Bennett

Mississippi State University
David Christopher Donovan

Montana State University
Russell Schutte

New York Institute of Technology
Rachelle O. Ybarbo

NewSchool of Architecture and Design
Nathaniel B. Hudson; Michael G. Watts

North Dakota State University
Brock T. Martinson

Norwich University
Moriah Arrato Gavrish

Ohio State University
Ronnie G. Parsons

Oklahoma State University
Jennifer B. Bohan

Parsons The New School of Design
Parker B. Lee

Pennsylvania State University
Jennifer L. Whary

Pratt Institute
Artem Motvitskiy

Princeton University
Marc Francis Louis McQuade

Rensselaer Polytechnic Institute
Anthony Malacarne

Rhode Island School of Design
Benjamin Garcia Saxe

Rice University
Scott Stark

Roger Williams University
Amanda M. Roy

Savannah College of Art and Design
Paul Kenneth Schwartzkopf

Southern University and A&M College
Christopher Williams

Syracuse University
Douglas Jack

Temple University
Emmanuel Pierre Jordon Gee

Texas A&M University
Jennifer Wong

Texas Tech University
Oliver Earl Cox III

Tulane University
Kimberly Michele Patrie

University of California, Los Angeles
Liesl Schaper Margolin

University at Buffalo, SUNY
Nathaniel Russell Cornman

University of Arizona
Melissa Kegan Tom

University of Arkansas
Jared Charles Hueter

University of British Columbia
Julie Bogdanowicz

University of Colorado at Denver
Rori Dee Knudtson

University of Detroit Mercy
Amy M. Szewczyk

University of Florida
Sheila M. Moenart

University of Hawaii at Manoa
Heidi Newton

University of Idaho
Shannon Nichole Brown

University of Illinois at Chicago
Darya Minosyants; Linda Just

University of Illinois at Urbana-Champaign
Hector M. Hernandez

University of Kansas
Lincoln Landon Lewis

University of Manitoba
Liane Veness

University of Maryland
Jessica Lynn Leonard

University of Memphis
Anthea Jane Selkirk; Kamesha Letrece Hervey

University of Miami
Jason Gadson; Megan McLaughlin

University of Michigan
Joshua David Bard

University of Minnesota
Daniel Handeen

University of Nebraska-Lincoln
William Jason DeRoin

University of North Carolina at Charlotte
Bradford Ryan Butler

University of Pennsylvania
Jackie C. Wong

University of South Florida
Daryl Raymond Croi

University of Southern California
Bruce Jia-Chi Chan

University of Tennessee, Knoxville
Margaux Elizabeth Verdera

University of Texas at Arlington
Josephine Elizabeth Fitzgibbons

University of Texas at Austin
Anh Hang Nguyen

University of Toronto
Andrew Donald Sinclair

University of Utah
Rachel McKenzie

Alpha Rho Chi Bronze Medal

University of Virginia
Allison Whitney Dryer

University of Washington
Ryan Carl Wong

University of Waterloo
Jonathan Tyrrell

Virginia Polytechnic Institute and State University
Kelley Denise White

Washington University in St. Louis
Nicole Triden Ostrander

Wentworth Institute of Technology
Tom Kuczynski

Woodbury University
Serjick Issagholian

Yale University
James Michael Tate

Source: Alpha Rho Chi

I'm interested in the moment when two objects collide and generate a third. The third object is where the interesting work is.

Bruce Mau

ASLA National Student Design Competition

The American Society of Landscape Architects annually conducts a competition to identify and recognize outstanding works of design and research by students. Any landscape architecture student or student team in the United States or Canada is eligible to enter. Awards are granted at the jury's discretion. Winning students and their advisers are honored at ASLA's annual conference.

For additional information, visit ASLA's website at *www.asla.org*.

2007 Award of Excellence Winners

General Design
Plugging In: Bringing the Stream Back to Watts
Toshihiko T. Karato, Elissa Rosenberg (adviser), and Elizabeth Meyer (adviser)
University of Virginia

Residential Design
Prairie Roots: Site Design for Solar Decathlon Project Solar Home
Mark Ruzicka, Celine Andersen, Stephanie Rolley (adviser), and Tim Keane (adviser)
Kansas State University

Analysis and Planning
The Sea of Galilee Coast: From Line to Space
Ilana Smolyar, Tal Alon-Mozes (adviser), Nava Regev (adviser), Anat Sade (adviser), and Amir Mueller (adviser)
Israel Institute of Technology (Israel)

Community Service
Planting for the Future: Improving Math Skills through Landscape Architecture
Reyna Baeza, Alfredo Cornejo, Alvaro Figueroa, Terry Lu, J. Marshall Mason, Donna Yeung, Jennifer Yi, and Gerald Taylor Jr. (adviser)
California State Polytechnic University, Pomona

411

2007 Honor Award Winners

General Design
"Living Corridor"—from Ditch to Greenway: Chinghe Riverfront Landscape Renovation
Zhenqing Que, Rui Yang (adviser), Laurie D. Olin (adviser), Ron Henderson (adviser), and Colin Franklin (adviser)
Tsinghua University (China)

island is land
Yu Kwon, Joon-ho Shin, Jeong-sam Kwon, Hyo-jin Kim, and Jihyun Lee, Kyu-mok Lee (adviser), Ah-yeon Kim (adviser), and Jung-min Choi (adviser)
University of Seoul (South Korea)

(In)Security: Access and Anxiety in the Wall Street Financial District
Bret C. Wieseler, Dean Abbott (adviser), Rebecca Krinke (adviser), Lance Nekar (adviser), and Richard Hansen (adviser)
University of Minnesota

ASLA National Student Design Competition

Pte Oyate Academy
Megumi Aihara, Eric Gordon, Takuma
   Ono, Julia Watson, and Scheri Fultineer
   (adviser)
Harvard University

SWALESCAPES
Noah Z. Levy, David Gouverneur (adviser),
   and Lucinda R. Sanders (adviser)
University of Pennsylvania

Residential Design
Dream Balloons
Tang Xiaolu, Han Xiaoxi, Cao Yiyun, and
   Dong Nannan (adviser)
Tongji University (China)

Analysis and Planning
Remodeling Renewal
Leslie Webster, Randolph T. Hester
   (adviser), Linda Jewell (adviser), Marcia
   McNally (adviser), Louise Mozingo
   (adviser), and Michael Southworth
University of California, Berkeley

Repairing the Local Food System: Long-
   Range Planning for People's Grocery
Alethea Marie Harper, Charles Sullivan
   (adviser), Michael Southworth (advis-
   er), and Robert L. Thayer
University of California, Berkeley

Perkins Road Underpass: Reconnecting
   Across Barriers
Douglas Thompson, Wes Michaels
   (adviser), and Brad Cantrell (adviser)
Louisiana State University

The Landscape of the Informal City: A
   Landscape Approach to Upgrading an
   Informal Settlement in Kingston,
   Jamaica
Karyn Williams and Alissa North (adviser)
University of Toronto (Canada)

Event Landscape: Halifax Harbour Festival
Van Thi Diep and John Danahy (adviser)
University of Toronto (Canada)

Research
Cross-Cultural Perceptions of the Cultural
   Landscape in American Suburban-Strip
   Chinatowns
Yun Cao, Richard C. Rome (adviser),
   Alfredo B. Lorenzo (adviser), Matthew
   Powers (adviser), and Andrew Chin
   (adviser)
Florida A&M University

Visual Preference for Stormwater Pond
   Edge Treatments
Kimberly S. Heiss, Les Linscott (adviser),
   and Gary Purdum (adviser)
University of Florida

Living Lightly: Minimizing Impact and
   Maximizing Function of Suburban Yards
Mike Teed, Ronald Kellett (adviser), and
   Patrick Condon (adviser)
University of British Columbia (Canada)

Communications
The Digital Art on Campus Project
Grant Thompson, Allison Sheridan
   (adviser), Michael Martin (adviser), and
   Ann Marie VanDerZanden (adviser)
Iowa State University

lunch: dialect
Shanti Levy, David Malda, Ryan Moody,
   Elizabeth K. Meyer (adviser), and
   Phoebe Crisman (adviser)
University of Virginia

RESPOND: A Residential Oil Spill in St.
   Bernard Parish, LA
Katherine Foo, Heather Gott, Meredith
   Haamen, Suzanne Perry, Bunyan Bryant
   (adviser), and Gregory Button (adviser)
University of Michigan

Community Service

Safe Passage Entry Garden
Amanda Bell, Paul Chasan, Terri Chiao,
    Arielle Farina Clark, Hilary Clark,
    Jocelyn L. Freilinger, Ryan Ihm, Jeff
    Kurtz, Vanessa Lee, David Marshall,
    Noriko Marshall, Justin Martin, Michael
    Michalek, Nicole Mikesh, Elizabeth
    Umbanhowar, and Daniel Winterbottom
    (adviser)
University of Washington

Collaboration

Wild Urbanism
Anna Hook, Heather Rusch, Brook Muller
    (adviser), and Ron Lovinger (adviser)
University of Oregon

Navigating Nature
Ryan Bitzegaio, Megan Caylor, Elizabeth
    Clay, Alex Corn, Charles Estell,
    Francesca Hernandez, Ashley Keith,
    Christopher Patten, Nicole Randolph,
    Nadia Roumie, Adam Voirin, Kelly
    Woodward, and Martha Hunt (adviser)
Ball State University

Toolboxes for Learning
Cortney Kirk, Student Affiliate, Roger Wei,
    Mike Hahn, and Nadine Gerdts
    (adviser)
Rhode Island School of Design

JURY

Todd D. Johnson, Design Workshop (chair)
Joan Honeyman, Jordan Honeyman Landscape
    Architecture
Dean Hill, Terratecture
Leonard J. Hopper, New York City Public
    Housing Authority
Shannon R. Nichol, Gustafson Guthrie Nichol,
    Ltd
Mark Rios, Rios Clementi Hale Studios
Lolly Tai, Temple University

Source: American Society of Landscape Architects

413

Almost any garden, if you see it at just the right moment, can be confused with paradise.

Henry Mitchell

Berkeley Prize Competition

The Berkeley Prize Competition consists of two awards: In the Berkeley Prize Essay Competition, architecture students from around the world are invited to submit an essay that responds to that year's theme around architecture as a social art. All semi-finalists in the essay competition may then submit a proposal for the Berkeley Prize Travel Fellowship explaining how participation in that year's travel program would enhance their education and career.

Information about the competition and the winners is available online at *www.berkeleyprize.org.*

2007 Essay Competition Winners

This year's competition question asked, What do you believe is the most needed project in your town that, when built, would better the social situation for a population in need?

First Prize
Sara Navrady and Erica Moore
University of Waterloo (Canada)

Second Prize
Matthew Clarke
University of Kentucky

Third Prize
Talha Khwaja
Oklahoma State University

Fourth Prize
Budoor Bukhari
American University of Sharjah (UAE)

JURY
Rodney Harber, Harber & Associates, University of Natal (South Africa)
Nguyen Chi Tam, Renzo Piano Building Workshop (France)
Elizabeth Ogbu, Public Architecture
Ron Van Oers, Delft University of Technology (Netherlands)

2007 Travel Fellowship Winner

The winner will attend the People Building Better Cities and the Global Studio conferences in Johannesburg, South Africa.

Winner
Budoor Bukhari
American University of Sharjah (UAE)
.

Honorable Mention
Gabriela Sorda
University of Buenos Aires (Argentina)

JURY
Raymond Lifchez, University of California, Berkeley
John Peterson, Public Architecture and Peterson Architects
Adriano Pupilli, architect (Australia)
Leslie Van Duzer, University of Minnesota

Source: Berkeley Prize Endowment

414

Charles E. Peterson Prize

The Charles E. Peterson Prize, named for the founder of the Historic American Buildings Survey program, recognizes the best set of measured drawings prepared by students following HABS standards. Drawings must be of a building that has not yet been recorded by HABS or an addendum to existing HABS drawings that furthers the understanding of the building's significant features. Awards totaling $7,000 are granted each year.

Additional information is available at *www.nps.gov/history/*.

2007 Winners

First Place
W. Arms Museum
Youngstown, OH
Ross Andrysco, Jeremy Artzner, Brian
    Boggs, Nicholas Bradac, Scott Clifford,
    Danelle Durig, Bryan Eaton, Patrick
    Fox, Lauren Frey, Jessie Hawkins, Daniel
    Judy, Mindy Kalac, Michael Kessel,
    Christopher Loeser, Alexander Matsov,
    Eric Phillips, Michael Sanbury,
    Nathaniel Winfield, and Elizabeth
    Corbin Murphy (instructor)
Kent State University

Second Place
Othniel Beale House
Charleston, SC
Katie Lawrence, Hilary King, Jamie
    Zwolack, Will Hamilton, Julius
    Richardson, Meg Richardson, Kim
    Jones, Natalie Ford, Jason Grismore,
    and Ashley Robbins (instructor)
Clemson University and College of
    Charleston

Third Place
Magazine Building, Fort Sam Houston
San Antonio, TX
Juan Rueda, Nimisha Thakur, Pamela
    Moczygemba, and Sue Ann Pemberton
    (instructor)
University of Texas at San Antonio

Fourth Place
J A Ranch
Palo Duro, TX
Tammy Cooper, Tahir Demiecioglu, Omar
    Garcia, Matt Jasper, Shana Kelso,
    Eugenia Magann, Jorge Pareja-Diaz,
    Valerie Sewell, Angela Steffensmeier,
    Elizabeth Vasquez, Troy Ainsworth, Gary
    Lindsey, Guy Giersch, and John P. White
    (instructor)
Texas Tech University

Honorable Mention
First Congregational Church of Western
    Springs
Western Springs, IL
Scott Berger, Elizabeth Blasius, Carla
    Bruni, Weston Davey, Young Jin Kim,
    Kelly Little, Jessamyn Miller, Mira Patel,
    Gregory Rainka, Jennifer Reep,
    Benjamin Roberts, Nicole Seguin,
    Robert Shymanski, Nicola Spasoff,
    Andrea Trickey, Rebecca Young, and
    Charles Pipal (instructor)
School of the Art Institute of Chicago

G.B. Cooley House
Monroe, LA
Brandy M. Blanchard, David M. Bruce,
    Martin Dale Bryant, Christie Jones,
    Jenny LaBatt, Melody McNabb, Kerry
    Soniat, Shelly Strange, Alan Thomas,
    Brian Wyatt, and Guy W. Carwile
    (instructor)
Louisiana Tech University

415

Source: Historic American Buildings Survey

Educator of Distinction

The American Society of Interior Designers' Educator of Distinction Award recognizes an individual, institution, or research project that has made a lasting and significant contribution to the interior design profession. It is granted on an annual basis as merited. Recipients are selected by a jury of professionals and are presented with an engraved crystal award.

For additional information, visit the ASID on the Web at *www.asid.org*.

2003	Buie Harwood Virginia Commonwealth University
2004	Dianne Jackman University of Manitoba
2005	Rural Studio Auburn University
2006	Janine M. Benyus

Source: American Society of Interior Designers

Design is a plan for arranging elements in such a way as best to accomplish a particular purpose.

Charles Eames

Eye for Why Student Design Competition

The Eye for Why Student Design Competition, sponsored by Dyson, Inc. and the Industrial Designers Society of America, challenges students to reinvent everyday household objects to reflect the Dyson philosophy: a commitment to intelligent, function-first design. Students in industrial design programs accredited by the National Association of Schools of Art & Design and individual student members of IDSA are eligible to enter.

For more information, visit the IDSA on the Internet at *www.idsa.org.*

2007 Winners

First Place
Excubo
Matthew Gale
California College of the Arts

Second Place
CheckIt
Joe Urich
California College of the Arts

Sluice
Brett Belock
University of Notre Dame

Third Place
No award granted

Honorable Mentions
Arium
Janna Prilutsky
Cleveland Institute of Art

RainDrop
Bob Lewin
Philadelphia University

JURY
Katherine Bennett, Katherine Bennett Industrial
    Design
Carol Catalano, Catalano Design
Emma Jane Heatley, Dyson
Pascal Malassigné, Milwaukee Institute of Art &
    Design
Craig Scherer, Insight Product Development
Maria Weber, Webb Scarlett de Vlam

417

Source: Industrial Designers Society of America

It is always important to me that a product does not just exist in the here and now, but that it shows a way into the future.

Florian Hufnagl

Eye for Why Student Design Competition

Excubo by Matthew Gale (Photos courtesy of the Industrial Designers Society of America)

Gabriel Prize

Awarded by the Western European Architecture Foundation, the Gabriel Prize encourages the study of classical architecture and landscapes in France. George Parker Jr., the founder of the prize and the foundation, believed in the humanizing power of classical architecture. Winners receive a $17,500 grant to finance a three-month individualized study of French architecture.

Additional information is available from the competition's website, *www.gabrielprize.org.*

1991	Ralph T. Jackson	1999	Melissa Weese Goodill
1992	Amy E. Gardner	2000	Mirelle Roddier
1993	David T. Mayernik	2001	Richard Chenoweth
1993	Kimberly R. Kohlhaas	2002	Alexander Fernandez
1994	Stephen A. Bross	2003	David E. Gamble
1995	Errol Barron	2004	Victor Agran
1996	Stephen W. Harby	2005	Michael Reardon
1997	Ron Witte	2006	Mario C. Cortes
1998	Alexander Ortenberg	2007	Joyce Rosner
1999	Erik Thorkildsen		

Source: Western European Architecture Foundation

419

Architecture is only concerned with the erection of public buildings and monuments, with the construction of public squares, sites and memorials. Architecture and building are not objects of consumption but objects of use. They can only be reconstructed in a perspective of material permanence. Without such permanence, without architecture transcending the life span of its builders, no public space, no collective expression such as art is ever possible.

Léon Krier

Gerald D. Hines Student Urban Design Competition

The Gerald D. Hines Competition, named in honor of the urban development pioneer, is open to graduate students who are pursuing real estate-related studies at North American schools. In the first stage, teams devise a solution to that year's problem during an 11-day charrette. Four finalist teams refine their solutions in the second stage. The winning team receives a $50,000 prize; the three runners-up share a $30,000 prize.

Further information is available from the Urban Land Institute's website, *www.udcompetition.uli.org.*

2007 Winners

This year's competition charged participants with forming a quasi-public agency to redevelop Los Angeles' East First Street corridor from Alameda to Mariachi Plaza.

First Prize
Techtonics
Christopher Lollini, Andrea Gaffney, Robert McCracken, Aditi Rao, Brooke Ray Smith, John Landis (adviser), and Clark Wilson (adviser)
University of California, Berkeley

Runners-up
Confluencia
Todd Bjerkaas, Anuttama Dasgupta, DongJun Lim, Leah Ostenberg, Samantha Singer, Brian Deal (adviser), and Mark Dixson (adviser)
University of Illinois at Urbana–Champaign

Spanning the Divide
Christina Mullins, Zhenqing Que, Samuel Rong Kuo, Ling Zeng, Shiyi Zhang, Rick Peiser (adviser), and James Kostaras (adviser)
Harvard University

East First Street Los Angeles
Raymond Kwok, Michelle Lauterwasser, Cheng-Yang Lee, Esther Mei-Shan Liu, Dong Woo Yim, Richard Peiser (adviser)
Harvard University

JURY
William Chilton, Pickard Chilton
James J. Curtis III, Bristol Group
Edward A. Feiner, Skidmore, Owings & Merrill
William A. Gilchrist, Department of Planning, Birmingham, AL (chair)
Mark W. Johnson, Civitas
Anne Vernez Moudon, University of Washington, Seattle
Evan Rose, SMWM
Yaromir Steiner, Steiner + Associates

Source: Urban Land Institute

Gerckens Prize

The Society for American City and Regional Planning History awards its biennial Gerckens Prize to educators who have demonstrated sustained excellence in teaching planning history. The prize is named after its first recipient, Professor Emeritus Laurence C. Gerckens, who helped define city planning history as a discipline and was a founder of SACRPH.

More information is available online at *www.dcp.ufl.edu/sacrph/*.

2001	Laurence C. Gerckens
	Ohio State University
2003	David Schuyler
	Franklin & Marshall College
2005	Mary Corbin Sies
	University of Maryland
2007	Christopher Silver
	University of Florida

Source: Society for American City and Regional Planning History

421

What thrill can be as great as a design carried through, a building created in three dimensions, partaking of painting in color and detail, partaking of sculpture in shape and mass. A building for people, people other than one-self, who can rejoice together over the creation.

Philip Johnson

Henry Adams Medal

Each year the Henry Adams Medal honors the top-ranking graduates of accredited BArch and MArch programs. Formerly The School Medal, the program began in 1914 and eventually evolved into the Henry Adams Medal, named for the noted historian and journalist. The top-ranking student(s) is listed below first, followed by the second-ranked student(s). Not all schools participate each year; nor do they always honor a second-ranked student.

More information is available from the American Architectural Foundation, *www.archfoundation.org.*

2007 BArch Recipients

Andrews University
Daniel Acevedo
Jonathan Harrison

Auburn University
Cayce Bean
Lindsey Butler

Boston Architectural College
Alec Rudolph Tesa
Elizabeth Bazzazi

California College of the Arts
Joseph Barajas
Michael Packer

California State Polytechnic University, Pomona
Michael E. Idoine
Bijan Shoeleh

Carnegie Mellon University
Andrew Caruso
Emily Rice

City College of New York, CUNY
Fatmir Hodzic
Natalia Galvis

Cooper Union
Julian H. Louie
Daria A. Khapalova

Cornell University
Patricia Maria Brizzio
Jason Teck Chye Lim

Drexel University
George Poulin
Kristopher Harris

Drury University
Jennie McGinnis Hill
Chandra Ann McAllister

Florida A&M University
Ava Joseph
Trevor Walker

Illinois Institute of Technology
Michael Krauss
Joseph Dietz

Kansas State University
Andrea Nickisch
Matthew Teismann

Louisiana State University
Henry David Louth
Sarah Louise Calandro

Louisiana Tech University
Kerry Soniat
Sascha Tobias Poeschl, Chuck D. Lejune

New Jersey Institute of Technology
Patrick Candalla
Daniel Sernotti

New York Institute of Technology
Shmuel Flaum
Andrew K. Williams

NewSchool of Architecture and Design
Nathaniel B. Hudson
John Thomas Sadari

North Dakota State University
Ron Randell
Kevin Thueringer

Norwich University
Blake C. Civiello
Erika S. Satteson

Oklahoma State University
Christina Glasgow
Rob Brown

Pennsylvania State University
Paul A. Boccadoro
Gillean M. Denny

Pratt Institute
Jennifer Dempsey
Alexander Gryger

Rensselaer Polytechnic Institute
Alison Duncan
Mary Kate Cahill

Roger Williams University
Chelsey Emery Killam
Gregory R. Ralph

Syracuse University
Nicholas C. Hunt
Margaret R. Mink

Temple University
Dustin Tyler Tobias
Khalid Gabriel Carmichael

Texas A&M University
Jennifer Wong
Mariano Ortiz Ratkovic

Tulane University
John Jason Heinze
Blake Douglas Fisher

University at Buffalo, SUNY
Volker Braun-Kolbe
William Carrie Helm II

University of Arizona
Savannah G. Gammon
Alexis Hawanczak Carver

University of Arkansas
Kara Elizabeth Pegg
Cari L. Paulus

University of Detroit Mercy
Carl M. Bolofer
Rachel E. Clark

University of Hawaii at Manoa
Grata Koo

University of Houston
Gilford Michael Allen
Rashida Mustafa Mogri

University of Idaho
Somdebda Flavien Sawadogo
Steven Lamar Clark

University of Kansas
Emily C. Finch, Andrew J. Harrington
Megan P. Hunziker

University of Miami
Ryan Losch
Michael R. McGrattan

University of North Carolina at Charlotte
Natalie Jones Morgan
Dawn Elizabeth Pryor

423

Henry Adams Medal

University of Southern California
Ashley Merchant
Albert Lam

University of Tennessee, Knoxville
Geoffrey Goodmiller
Bradford Raines

University of Texas at Austin
Jonas Niels Philipsen
Kimberly Nicole Rice

Woodbury University
Masami Honda
Thomas Dylan Saunders, Sam Farhangazad

2007 MArch Recipients

Arizona State University
Neeta Pandey
Alexis Briana Flores, Steven M. Jakub

Boston Architectural College
Tobin Shulman
Aimee Savard

California State Polytechnic University, Pomona
Adrianne Price
Junjian Compeau

Carleton University
Allan Paul Banina
Ana Lukas

Catholic University of America
Dana M. Pallante, Marisa J. Schaffer
  (one-year program)
Elisa M. Garcia (two-year program)
Craig Martin, William V. Putnam
  (three-year program)

Clemson University
Jason M. Gibson
David Ruthven

Columbia University
Robert Lee Brackett III
Alexandra Scott Young

Dalhousie University
Jane Abbott
Marcin Sztaba

Florida A&M University
Somer Spencer
Denise Francis

Georgia Institute of Technology
Jihan Stanford
Nathan Stone

Harvard University
Andrew Witt
Grace Leung

Illinois Institute of Technology
Barbara De Gregorio, Melissa Kaiser

Louisiana State University
Sean Early David
Annese Kathleen Gronowski

Massachusetts Institute of Technology
Rebecca M. Edson
Sandra A. Baron

McGill University
Shih-Huei Sherry Huang
Maria Javornik

Miami University
Janine Mejia-Diaz
Kelly Ann Alter, Jeffrey David Martin

Montana State University
Veronica Schreibeis
Lindsey Olson, Allison Orr, Joshua Vernon

New Jersey Institute of Technology
Peter Mason
Adam Secola

NewSchool of Architecture and Design
Tyler J. Van Stright, Kevan Michael Potter
Marie Jean Clark

Ohio State University
Nicholas E. Lewis
Scott Thomas Dobbe

Parsons The New School for Design
Kailin M. Gregga
Kip Issac

Polytechnic University of Puerto Rico
Celina Bocanegra González
Eileen Díaz Lamboy

Princeton University
Steve Shoei-Sheng Chen
Eric Michael Rothfeder, Rosalyne F. Shieh

Rensselaer Polytechnic Institute
Derek Keil
Joseph Banks

Rhode Island School of Design
Janine Kathryn Soper
Jonathan Michael Powell, Sebastian Tobias Snyder, Milton Ethan Barlow

Rice University
Linh Dan Do
Joseph Lim

Savannah College of Art and Design
Meghan McDermott
Karisfi Indra Hartano

Syracuse University
Dena M. Wangberg
Danielle S. Pactovis

Tulane University
Michael William Ball
Emmanuelle Chammah

University of British Columbia
Anna Lisa Meyboom

University of California, Berkeley
Grant Adams
Laura Allen

University of California, Los Angeles
Michael Leaveck
Neil Cook

University of Colorado at Denver
Jay Paul Fourniea
Jordan Nicole Lucy

University of Florida
Jennifer C. Daniels
Stella Hofer

University of Hawaii at Manoa
Hong Wei Xue
Jennifer Toba

University of Houston
Kevin Matthew Walton
Catherine Marian Callaway

University of Illinois at Chicago
Heidi Dahle
John Wolters

University of Kansas
Ryan P. Walters
Nathan A. Mast

University of Manitoba
Andrea Flynn
Anna Katerina Hlynsky

University of Maryland
Kristina Rebecca Crenshaw
Michael Paul Binder

425

Henry Adams Medal

University of Miami
Kimberly Clemente
Thomas Bagby IV

University of Michigan
Nicholas Haddick Robertson
Rachel C. Rush

University of Montreal
Nancy Briere
Hubert Pelletier

University of Nebraska–Lincoln
William Jason DeRoin
Lisa Marie Satter

University of Nevada, Las Vegas
Abhilasha Wadhwa
Daniel Overbey

University of North Carolina at Charlotte
Andrew Wendell Bryant
Bradford Ryan Butler

University of Pennsylvania
Peter W. Rae
Nicholas Hollot

University of South Florida
Daryl Raymond Croi

University of Southern California
Alberto Galindo, Russell Morse
Corey Mollet

University of Tennessee, Knoxville
David Baker
Heather Stone

University of Texas at Arlington
Andrew James Adkison
Yesenia M. Blandon

University of Texas at San Antonio
Russell H. Kenyon
Niki D. Manning

University of Toronto
Graeme Stewart
Joshua Samuel Cohen

University of Utah
Michael Dolan
John Oderda

University of Virginia
James John Richardson
Benjamin James Thompson

University of Washington
Katherine J. Idziorek
Todd R. Beyreuther, Ray Glen Villanueva

University of Waterloo
Fan-ju Susan Tang
Kyle Sanvictores

University of Wisconsin–Milwaukee
Cory Kamholz
Franz Heitzer

Washington University in St. Louis
Michael Douglas Browning
Rachel Aileen Doniger

Yale University
Weston Woodward Walker
Mathew Dryden Razook

Source: American Architectural Foundation

426

IDP Outstanding Firm Award

The American Institute of Architects grants the IDP (Intern Development Program) Firm Award to firms that exhibit an exemplary commitment to interns through in-house training opportunities, mentoring, continuing education programs, and adherence to the Intern Development Program. Entrants are reviewed in one of three categories based on size—small firm (nine or fewer employees), medium firm (10 to 49), and large firm (50 or more)—with an overall winner chosen from the finalists.

For additional information, visit the AIA online at *www.aia.org*.

1991   Askew Nixon Ferguson,
            Memphis, TN
        Clark Nexsen Owen Barberi
            Gibson, Norfolk, VA
        Gilley–Hinkel Architects,
            Bristol, CT
        Kekst Architecture, Cleveland, OH
        RTKL, Baltimore, MD

1992   HKS, Inc., Dallas, TX
        Luey Architects, Tigard, OR

1993   Jeffrey S. Conrad, Architect,
            Oxnard, CA
        CUH2A, Princeton, NJ
        Earl Swensson Associates,
            Nashville, TN
        Western Michigan University,
            Kalamazoo, MI

1994   Albert Kahn Associates, Inc.,
            Detroit, MI
        Cynthia Easton, Sacramento, CA
        Johnson, Laffen, Meland, Grand
            Forks, ND
        Klipp Colussy Jenks DuBois,
            Denver, CO

1995   BSW International, Tulsa, OK
        Einhorn Yaffee Prescott,
            Washington, DC
        Naval Facilities Engineering
            Command, Alexandria, VA

1996   Collins Rimer & Gordon,
            Cleveland, OH
        Schmidt Associates, Inc.,
            Indianapolis, IN
        Watkins Hamilton Ross
            Architects, Inc., Bellaire, TX

1997   Giattina Fisher Aycock Architects,
            Birmingham, AL

1998   Everton Oglesby Askew,
            Nashville, TN
        Loebl Schlossman & Hackl/
            Hague Richards, Chicago, IL

        Honorable Mention
        BWBR Architects, St. Paul, MN
        Caldwell Architects, Marina del
            Rey, CA
        RTKL Associates, Baltimore, MD

1999   NBBJ, Columbus, OH

        Honorable Mention
        The Hillier Group, Princeton, NJ

2000   *No awards granted*

2001   Gorman Richardson Architects,
            Inc., Hopkinton, MA

        Honorable Mention
        Kling-Lindquist, Philadelphia, PA

427

IDP Outstanding Firm Award

2002	Payette Associates, Boston, MA	2005	Stahl Architects, Fargo, ND

2002 Payette Associates, Boston, MA

Honorable Mention
Flad & Associates, Madison, WI

2003 James, Harwick + Partners, Dallas, TX

Finalists
TTV Architects, Jacksonville, FL
FreemanWhite, Inc., Charlotte, NC

2004 InVision Architecture, Sioux City, IA
FEH Associates, Sioux City, IA

Finalist
KKE Architects, Inc., Minneapolis, MN

2005 Stahl Architects, Fargo, ND

Finalists
Caldwell Architects, Marina del Ray, CA
Torti Gallas and Partners, Silver Springs, MD

2006 Gould Evans Associates, Kansas City, MO
Cannon Design, Inc., Grand Island, NY

2007 Baskervill, Richmond, VA
Scott and Globe Architects Inc., Tulsa, OK

Source: American Institute of Architects

You know you've achieved perfection in design, not when you have nothing more to add, but when you have nothing more to take away.

Antoine de Saint Exupery

IDSA Education Award

The Industrial Designers Society of America grants the Education Award to recognize excellence in industrial design education. Educators are presented this award in honor of significant and distinguished contributions.

For additional information, visit the IDSA on the Internet at *www.idsa.org*.

1988	Arthur J. Pulos Syracuse University
1989	Robert Lepper Carnegie Mellon University
1990	Edward J. Zagorski University of Illinois at Urbana– Champaign
1991	James M. Alexander Art Center College of Design
1992	Strother MacMinn Art Center College of Design Robert E. Redmann University of Bridgeport
1993	Vincent M. Foote North Carolina State University Herbert H. Tyrnauer California State University, Long Beach
1994	Hin Bredendieck Georgia Institute of Technology Joseph Koncelik Ohio State University
1996	Toby Thompson Rochester Institute of Technology
1997	Marc Harrison Rhode Island School of Design

1998	Bruce Hannah Pratt Institute
1999	Michael Nielsen Arizona State University
2000	Katherine J. McCoy Illinois Institute of Technology Michael McCoy Illinois Institute of Technology
2001	James J. Pirkl Syracuse University
2002	Steven Skov Holt California College of the Arts
2003	*No award granted*
2004	Joe Ballay Carnegie Mellon University
2005	Carl Garant Columbus College of Art & Design
2006	Noel Mayo Ohio State University
2007	Thomas David Milwaukee Institute of Art & Design A. Charles Wallschlaeger Ohio State University

Source: Industrial Designers Society of America

429

Jot D. Carpenter Medal

The American Society of Landscape Architects bestows the Jot D. Carpenter Medal to university educators who have made sustained and significant teaching contributions to a landscape architecture program at a school with an official ASLA student chapter. The award began in 2000 to honor the memory of Ohio State University professor Jot D. Carpenter and his contributions to landscape architecture education and the profession.

For additional information, visit *www.asla.org* on the Web.

2000	Roy H. DeBoer Rutgers, The State University of New Jersey
2002	Alton A. Barnes Jr. Kansas State University
2003	Craig W. Johnson Utah State University
2004	Marvin I. Adleman Cornell University
2005	Robert S. (Doc) Reich Louisiana State University
2006	Donald L. Collins Clemson University
2007	Terence G. Harkness University of Illinois at Urbana– Champaign

Source: American Society of Landscape Architects

To see the universe within a place is to see a garden; to see it so is to have a garden; not to prevent its happening is to build a garden.

James Rose

NCARB Prize

The NCARB Prize for Creative Integration of Practice and Education in the Academy celebrates architecture programs that emphasize the continuum between practice and education. Jurors evaluate submissions for their creative, innovative approach to integrating the academy and the profession within a studio curriculum. The grand prize comes with a $25,000 award, and the prize winners each receive $7,500.

More information is available from NCARB's website, *www.ncarb.org*.

2007 Winners

Grand Prize
ecoMOD
University of Virginia

Prize Winners
Habitat Trails: From Infill Housing to
    Green Neighborhood Design
University of Arkansas

Re-expanding Architectural Practice
University of Southern California

Learning Barge
University of Virginia

Reweaving the Neighborhood Fabric: How
    Modular Housing Can Build Affordable
    and Dignified Communities
University of Wisconsin–Milwaukee

Research: Practice-based Study in the
    Academy
Washington University in St. Louis

JURY
Arnold J. Aho, Norwich University
Joseph Bilello, Ball State University
Michiel M. Bourdrez, NCARB
Frances Bronet, University of Oregon
Joseph L. Bynum, The Ritchie Organization
T. Rexford Cecil, Kentucky State Board of
    Examiners and Registration of Architects
H. Carleton Godsey, Godsey Associates Architects
Frank M. Guillot, Guillot Vivian Viehmann
    Architects
Clark Llewellyn, Montana State University
Demetrius Norman, NCARB
Garth Rockcastle, University of Maryland
Barbara A. Sestak, Portland State University
    (chair)
Jeff Shannon, University of Arkansas
George Thrush, Northeastern University

Source: National Council of Architectural Registration Boards

431

Presidents of the American Institute of Architecture Students

The American Institute of Architecture Students is a nonprofit, student-run organization that seeks to promote excellence in architecture education, training, and practice, as well as to organize architecture students and promote the study of architecture. More than 150 chapters at US and Canadian colleges and universities support members with professional development seminars, community projects, curriculum advisory committees, guest speakers, and many other programs.

To locate a chapter, visit the AIAS website, *www.aias.org.*

1956–57	James R. Barry Rice University	1972–73	Fay D'Avignon Boston Architectural Center
1957–58	Robert S. Harris Princeton University	1973–74	Fay D'Avignon Boston Architectural Center
1958–59	Paul J. Ricciutti Case Western Reserve University	1974–75	Patric Davis Boston Architectural Center
1959–60	Charles Jones University of Arizona	1975–76	Ella Hall North Carolina State University
1960–61	Ray Gaio University of Notre Dame	1976–77	Jerry Compton Southern California Inst. of Architecture
1961–62	Donald L. Williams University of Illinois at Urbana–Champaign	1977–78	Charles Guerin University of Houston
1962–63	Carl Schubert California State Polytechnic University	1978–79	John M. Maudlin-Jeronimo University of Miami
1964–65	Joseph Morse Howard University	1979–80	Richard Martini Boston Architectural Center
1965–66	Kenneth Alexander Pratt Institute	1980–81	Alejandro Barbarena University of Houston
1966–67	Jack Worth III Georgia Institute of Technology	1981–82	Bill Plimpton University of California, Berkeley
1967–68	Morten Awes University of Idaho	1982–83	Robert Klancher University of Cincinnati
1968–69	Edward Mathes University of Southwestern Louisiana	1983–84	Robert Fox Temple University
1969–70	Taylor Culver Howard University	1984–85	Thomas Fowler IV New York Inst. of Tech.–Old Westbury
1970–71	Michael Interbartolo Boston Architectural Center	1985–86	Scott Norberg University of Nebraska–Lincoln
1971–72	Joseph Siff Rice University	1986–87	Scott Norberg University of Nebraska–Lincoln

1987–88	Kent Davidson	1998–99	Jay M. Palu
	University of Nebraska–Lincoln		University of Nebraska–Lincoln
1988–89	Matthew W. Gilbertson	1999–00	Melissa Mileff
	University of Minnesota		University of Oklahoma
1989–90	Douglas A. Bailey	2000–01	Scott Baldermann
	Montana State University		University of Nebraska–Lincoln
1990–91	Alan D.S. Paradis	2001–02	Matt Herb
	Roger Williams College		University of Maryland
1991–92	Lynn N. Simon	2002–03	Lawrence Fabbroni
	University of Washington		Carnegie Mellon University
1992–93	Courtney E. Miller	2003–04	Wayne Mortenson
	University of Maryland		University of Nebraska–Lincoln
1993–94	Garen D. Miller	2004–05	Jacob Day
	Drury College		University of Maryland
1994–95	Dee Christy Briggs	2005–06	Eric W. Zaddock
	City College of New York, CUNY		Andrews University
1995–96	Robert J. Rowan	2006-07	Jonathan Bahe
	Washington State University		University of Minnesota
1996–97	Raymond H. Dehn	2007–08	Andrew Caruso
	University of Minnesota		Carnegie Mellon University
1997–98	Robert L. Morgan		
	Clemson University		

Source: American Institute of Architects Students

433

Architecture arouses sentiments in man. The architect's task therefore, is to make those sentiments more precise.

Adolf Loos

Rotch Travelling Scholarship

Established in 1883 by the sons and daughters of Benjamin Smith Rotch, an active arts patron, the Rotch Travelling Scholarship affirms the value of foreign travel to the development and training of architects. The winners receive $35,000 to support a minimum of eight months of travel and study abroad and $3,500 upon completion of their travel journal, which is archived at the Massachusetts Institute of Technology.

For more information, visit the program's website, *www.rotchscholarship.org*.

1884	Clarence Howard Blackall	1921	Frank Somerville Carson
1885	Samuel Walker Mead	1922	Wallace K. Harrison
1886	George Frederick Newton	1923	Isidor Richmond
1887	Edgar A. Josselyn	1924	Eugene Francis Kennedy
1888	Austin Willard Lord	1925	Walter F. Bogner
1889	Henry Bacon	1926	Louis Skidmore
1890	William Thomas Partridge	1927	Edward Durrell Stone
1891	Robert Closon Spenser	1928	Ralph E. Winslow
1892	John Watrous Case	1929	Charles St. George Pope
1893	Walter Harrington Kilham	1930	Barnett Sumner Gruzen
1894	Harold Van Bruen Manonigle	1931	Carney Goldberg
1895	Will Stein Aldrich	1932	Carroll Coletti
1896	Louis Holmes Boynton	1933	George Stephen Lewis
1897	Henry Bodge Pennell	1934	Newbhard N. Culin
1898	Louis Chapel Newhall	1935	Gordon Bunshaft
1899	Louis Warren Pulsifer	1936	Leon Hyzen
1900	William Leslie Welton	1937	John A. Valtz
1901	William Luther Mowll	1938	Malcolm C. Robb
1902	James Ford Clapp	1939	William E. Hartmann
1903	Edward T. Foulkes	1940	George R. McClellan
1904	Frederick Charles Hirons	1941	J. Martin Rosse
1905	William DeForrest Crowell	1942	*No award granted*
1906	Leroy Pearls Burnham	1943	*No award granted*
1907	Otto Faelten	1944	*No award granted*
1908	Isreal P. Lord	1945	*No award granted*
1909	Horace G. Simpson	1946	Melvern Coates Ensign
1910	Joseph McGinniss	1947	Dale C. Byrd
1911	Niels Hjalmar Larsen	1948	Victor A. Lundy
1912	Charles Cameron Clark	1949	Eduard H. Bullerjahn
1913	William Leo Smith	1950	Robert L. Bliss
1914	Ralph Johnson Batchelder	1951	Bruce A. Abrahamson
1915	Frederick Roy Witton	1952	Norman M. Klein
1916	Ralph Thomas Walker	1953	Richard C. Brigham Jr.
1917	James Newhall Holden	1954	Paul J. Corrol
1918	*No award granted*	1955	Robert T. Coles
1919	*No award granted*	1956	James Stageberg
1920	Robert Murray Blackall	1957	John I. Schlossman

1958	W. Byron Ireland	1983	John K. McLaughlin Jr.
1959	Gardner Ertman	1984	Eric Liebmann
1960	Jack Chun	1985	Thomas M. Walsh
1961	John O. Cotton	1986	J. Scott Kilbourne
1962	Thomas N. Larson	1987	Mark A. Engberg
1963	James T. Flynn	1988	Thomas Carlson-Reddig
1964	Harry F. Eagan	1989	Joseph Mamavek
1965	John W. Cuningham	1990	Mark Moeller
1966	Dennis Walsh	1991	Joslin Stewart
1967	William E. Roesner	1992	Debi L. McDonald
1968	James Sandell	1993	David T. Nagahiro
1969	Michael P. Buckley	1994	Craig Mutter
1970	Gary Lowe	1995	Jose Sama
1971	John P. Sheehy	1996	Nicholas Isaak
1972	Valdis Smits	1997	Andrew James Davis
1972	Richard J. Green	1998	Julia Holmes McMorrough
1973	Craig D. Roney	1999	Robert Linn
1974	Nelson Scott Smith	2000	Patricia Anahory
1975	Philip Dangerfield	2001	Lorenzo Mattii
1976	Duane E. Kell	2002	Kari Silloway
1977	Patrick M. Sullivan	2003	Bradley Shanks
1978	Ernest F. Cirangle	2004	Aaron Follett
1979	Glenn Matsumoto	2005	Zachary Hinchliffe
1980	Marvin J. Malecha	2006	Elizabeth Leidy
1981	William A. McGee	2007	Mason Pritchett
1982	John M. Reimnitz		

Source: Rotch Travelling Scholarship

435

A building must have a strong idea that is architectural rather than sculptural or painterly—one that is related to the activity in the building.

Edward Larrabee Barnes

Solar Decathlon

In the Solar Decathlon competition, multidisciplinary student teams from colleges and universities from around the world design, build, and operate houses that are powered entirely by the sun. The houses must be attractive, effective, and energy efficient and produce enough energy to power an electric car. Finalists transport their houses to the National Mall in Washington, DC, where final judging takes place under the direction of the US Department of Energy, the competition's sponsor.

Photos of all the winners are available online at *www.solardecathlon.org*.

2005 Winners

First Place
University of Colorado, Denver and Boulder
Drew Bailey, Frank Burkholder, Mark Cruz, Kristin Field, Jeff Lyng, John Previtali, Jacob Uhl, Kerrie Badertscher (faculty), Mike Brandemuehl (faculty), Julee Herdt (faculty), Rick Sommerfeld (faculty)

Second Place
Cornell University
Joshua Bonaventura, Timothy Fu, Ted Haffner, Stephanie Horowitz, Larissa Kaplan, Marc Miller, Benjamin Uyeda, Matthew Ulinski (faculty), Zellman Warhaft (faculty)

Third Place
California Polytechnic State University
Nicholas Holmes, Robert Johnson, Austin Quig-Hartman, Jesse Maddren (faculty), Rob Peña (faculty), Sandy Stannard (faculty)

Architecture and Dwelling
Virginia Polytechnic Institute and State University
Brian Atwood, Mike Christopher, Alec Clardy, Chip Clark, Nathan Gabriele, Dan Gussman, Phil Hassell, Nancy Hodges, Chuck Hoover, Nick King, Brandon Ligenfelser, Kyle Longbrake, Ben Mohr, Nick Monday, Brett Moss, David Rairden, Tom Shockey, Alan Todd, Adam Tomey, Matt Wagner, Seanene White, Robert Dunay (faculty), Mike Ellis (faculty), Michael Ermann (faculty), Ben Gauslin (faculty), Ben Johnson (faculty), Robert Schubert (faculty), Greg Tew (faculty), Joe Wheeler (faculty)

Documentation, Communications, and Getting Around
University of Colorado, Denver and Boulder
Drew Bailey, Frank Burkholder, Mark Cruz, Kristin Field, Jeff Lyng, John Previtali, Jacob Uhl, Kerrie Badertscher (faculty), Mike Brandemuehl (faculty), Julee Herdt (faculty), Rick Sommerfeld (faculty)

Comfort Zone and Hot Water
Cornell University
Joshua Bonaventura, Timothy Fu, Ted
Haffner, Stephanie Horowitz
Larissa Kaplan, Marc Miller, Benjamin
Uyeda, Matthew Ulinski (faculty),
Zellman Warhaft (faculty)

Appliances and Lighting
California Polytechnic State University
Nicholas Holmes, Robert Johnson, Austin
Quig-Hartman, Jesse Maddren (faculty),
Rob Peña (faculty), Sandy Stannard
(faculty)

Energy Balance
Crowder College
Vickie Boyt, Gale Perry, Art Boyt (faculty),
Kevin Newby (faculty)

Florida International University
Marcelino Alonso, Charles Bowden,
Eugenia De Marco, Raul A. Chinga,
Jimmy Feng, Josh Freese, Leslie A.
Goldberg, Javier Guerrero, Carlos
Hernandez, Michael L. Lopez, Diane
Marshall, Ryan Moreno, Robert Perez,
David Samayoa, Marcela Tejedor, Keqian
Xing, Jikang Zha, Ronald A. Baier (fac-
ulty), Nathaniel Quincy Belcher (facul-
ty), Jason Chandler (faculty), Stephanie
Strange (administrator), Yong X. Tao
(faculty)

University of Missouri–Rolla
Allison Arnn, Nick Bristow, Brandon Cotter,
Swarnali Ghosh, Alex James, Chris
Krueger, Joel Lamson, Natalie McDonald,
Dustin Nottage, Joe Schaefer, Adam
Tiehes, Patrick Williams, Chris Wright,
Stuart Baur (faculty), Chuck Berendzen
(faculty), Jeff Birt (faculty), Paul Hirtz
(faculty), Bob Phelan (faculty), Eric
Showalter (faculty)

JURY
Dennis Askins, Karim Rashid Design
Steve Badanees, Jersey Devil
Doug Balcomb, New Mexico Solar Energy
Association
Philip Bernstein, Autodesk
Howard Brandston, The Brandston Partnership
Inc.
Mike Deru, National Renewable Energy
Laboratory
Steve Emmerich, National Institute of Standards
and Technology
Ben Finzel, Fleishman-Hillard International
Communications
Ethan Goldman, BuildingGreen
Sam Grawe, *Dwell*
Pete Jacobs, Architectural Energy Corporation
Kim Master, What's Working Inc.
Edward Mazria, Mazria Odems Dzurec, Inc.
John W. Mitchell, University of
Wisconsin–Madison
Kathryn Tyler Prigmore, HDR Architecture Inc.
Katherine Salant, columnist
Craig Savage, Building Media Inc.
Grant Simpson, RTKL Associates Inc.
Gary Steffy, Gary Steffy Lighting Design Inc.
Sandra Stashik, Grenald Waldron Associates
Sarah Susanka, Mulfinger, Susanka, Mahady &
Partners Inc.
Russ Taylor, Steven Winter Associates
Terry Townsend, Townsend Engineering
Jaime Van Mourik, National Building Museum
Norm Weaver, InterWeaver Consulting
Alan Wickstrom, BuildingOnline Inc.
Ken Wilson, Envision Design

Source: Solar Decathlon

437

SOM Foundation Traveling Fellowships

The SOM Foundation Traveling Fellowships offer recent graduates the opportunity to conduct in-depth research, collaborate with other designers, and pursue independent study. The SOM Prize, for architecture, design, and urban design graduates, carries a $50,000 research and travel stipend; the runner-up receives a $20,000 travel fellowship. The winner of the Structural Engineering Travel Fellowship receives $10,000. The programs of the SOM Foundation are funded by an endowment established by the partners of Skidmore, Owings & Merrill.

More information can be found online at *www.somfoundation.som.com.*

2007 Recipients

SOM Prize
Amanda Hallberg
Illinois Institute of Technology

SOM Prize Runner-up
Hugh Hayden
Cornell University

SOM PRIZE JURY
John Maeda, MIT Media Lab
Monica Ponce de Leon, Office dA
Hashim Sarkis, Hashim Sarkis Architecture
Jorge Silvetti, Machado and Silvetti Associates
Ross Wimer, Skidmore, Owings & Merrill

Structural Engineering Travel Fellowship
Kiley M. Rode
Stevens Institute of Technology

STRUCTURAL ENGINEERING JURY
Tom Powers, Chicago Bureau of Bridges and Transit
Susan Conger-Austin, Illinois Institute of Technology
William Baker, Skidmore, Owings & Merrill

Source: SOM Foundation

438

For me, making architecture is the same as thinking.

Tadao Ando

Left: **SOM Prize recipient Amanda Hallberg.** *Top:* **Proposal for a new home for Facets Multimedia Cinematheque Videotheque in Wicker Park, Chicago, by Amanda Hallberg.**

Student Sustainable Design Competition

The annual Student Sustainable Design Competition, sponsored by the International Interior Design Association, recognizes outstanding sustainable design by students enrolled in post-secondary interior design programs. Designs are judged for their innovative character, responsible use of materials, practical application, visual comfort, and sustainable material application. Awards include a $3,500 grand prize, a $1,500 first prize, and a gift certificate for the honorable mention.

Additional information is available from the IIDA's website, *www.iida.org*.

2007 Winners

Best of Competition
Whitford Oncology and Hematology
   Center
Jennifer Rheaume
Endicott College

Award of Excellence
Urban Incubator
Nicole Goulet
Washington State University

Honorable Mention
Green Leaf Fitness Center
Meera P. Bahukutumbi
International Academy of Design &
   Technology–Chicago

Taliesin West
Yong-Chan Kim
Academy of Art University

Campsite Summer Vacation Home
Tami Clark
Canada College (Canada)

Source: International Interior Design Association

440

Good design is making something intelligible and memorable. Great design is making something memorable and meaningful.

Dieter Rams

Topaz Medallion

The American Institute of Architects and the American Collegiate Schools of Architecture jointly award the Topaz Medallion to honor an instructor for outstanding co ntributions in architectural education. Candidates may be nominated by colleagues, students, and former students. Recipients have made a significant imprint on architecture, expanded into fields beyond their specialty, and made a lasting impact on their students.

For additional information, visit the AIA's website at *www.aia.org.*

1976	Jean Labatut Princeton University	1993	Mario G. Salvadori Columbia University
1977	Henry Kamphoefner North Carolina State University	1994	Harlan E. McClure Clemson University
1978	Lawrence Anderson Massachusetts Institute of Technology	1995	Henry N. Cobb Harvard University
1979	G. Holmes Perkins University of Pennsylvania	1996	Denise Scott Brown University of Pennsylvania
1980	Serge Chermayeff Yale University	1997	Donlyn Lyndon University of California, Berkeley
1981	Marcel Breuer Harvard University	1998	Werner Seligmann Syracuse University
1982	Joseph Esherick University of California, Berkeley	1999	W. Cecil Steward University of Nebraska–Lincoln
1983	Charles E. Burchard Virginia Polytechnic Institue and State University	2000	Alan H. Balfour Rensselaer Polytechnic Institute
1984	Robert Geddes Princeton University	2001	Lee G. Copeland Washington College/University of Pennsylvania
1985	Colin Rowe Cornell University	2002	Jerzy Soltan Harvard University
1986	Vincent J. Scully Yale University	2003	Marvin J. Malecha North Carolina State University
1987	Ralph Rapson University of Minnesota	2004	Stanford Anderson Massachusetts Institute of Technology
1988	John Hejduk Cooper Union	2005	Edward Allen University of Oregon
1989	Charles Moore University of California, Berkeley	2006	William G. McMinn Cornell University/Florida International University
1990	Raymond L. Kappe Southern California Institute of Architecture	2007	Lance Jay Brown City College of New York, CUNY
1991	Kenneth Frampton Columbia University		* Honored posthumously
1992	Spiro Kostof* University of California, Berkeley		*Source: American Institute of Architects*

441

Topaz Medallion

Lance Jay Brown (Photo: Bill Summers)

ORGANIZATIONS

The history, purpose, and membership benefits of major national and international design associations can be found in this chapter, along with a summary listing of numerous design and building-related organizations and government agencies.

AIGA, the professional association for design

One of the oldest and largest membership associations for professionals engaged in visual communication and graphic design, AIGA, the professional association for design was founded in 1914 as the American Institute of Graphic Arts. Its more than 20,000 members include professional designers, educators, and students in traditional communication design fields, such as type and book design, as well as such newer disciplines as interaction design, experience design, and motion graphics. In addition, AIGA supports the interests of those involved in designing from other disciplines, professions, and business who are committed to advancing the understanding of the value of design. AIGA serves as a hub of information and activity within the design community through conferences, competitions, exhibitions, publications, educational activities, and its website.

the professional association for design

Address ———————————————————
164 Fifth Avenue
New York, NY 10010
(212) 807-1990
www.aiga.org

Mission ———————————————————
AIGA's mission is to advance designing as a professional craft, strategic tool, and vital cultural force.

American Architectural Foundation

The American Architectural Foundation is a national nonprofit 501(c)(3) organization that educates individuals and communities about the power of architecture to transform lives and improve the places where we live, learn, work, and play. The AAF's programs include the Mayors' Institute on City Design and *Great Schools by Design*—highly regarded initiatives that help improve the built environment through the collaboration of thought leaders, designers, and local communities. Through its outreach programs, grants, exhibitions, and educational resources, the AAF helps people become thoughtful and engaged stewards of the world around them. The AAF is headquartered in The Octagon, an 1801 Federal-style home designed by William Thornton.

American
Architectural
Foundation

Address

1799 New York Avenue NW
Washington, DC 20006
(202) 626-7318
www.archfoundation.org

Mission

The American Architectural Foundation's mission is to educate the public on the power of architecture to improve lives and transform communities. The AAF is a national resource that helps provide information and best practices to communities and leaders, promotes collaboration, and encourages design excellence.

American Institute of Architects

Representing the professional interests of America's architects since 1857, the American Institute of Architects provides education, government advocacy, community redevelopment, and public outreach activities with and for its 80,000 members. With more than 300 local and state AIA organizations, the institute closely monitors legislative and regulatory actions at all levels of government. It provides professional development opportunities, industry standard contract documents, information services, and a comprehensive awards program.

Address

1735 New York Avenue NW
Washington, DC 20006
(202) 626-7300
www.aia.org

Mission

The American Institute of Architects is the voice of the architecture profession dedicated to serving its members, advancing their value, and improving the quality of the built environment.

American Planning Association

The American Planning Association promotes good planning practices to build better communities, while protecting the environment so residents have choices in housing, transportation, and employment. The 39,000 members include engaged citizens, planning professionals, and elected and appointed officials. The APA strives to engage all citizens in the planning process so it is open, transparent, and reflects the needs and desires of all community members. The association has offices in Washington, DC, and Chicago. It operates local chapters across the country and interest-specific divisions, and provides extensive research, publications, and training opportunities. The APA's professional institute, the American Institute of Certified Planners, certifies planners and promotes high ethical standards of professional practice.

Address ────────────────────────────

122 South Michigan Avenue, Suite 1600
Chicago, IL 60603
(312) 431-9100
www. planning.org

1776 Massachusetts Avenue NW, Suite 400
Washington, DC 20036
(202) 872-0611
www.planning.org

Mission ────────────────────────────

The American Planning Association is a nonprofit public interest and research organization committed to urban, suburban, regional, and rural planning. The APA and its professional institute, the American Institute of Certified Planners, advance the art and science of planning to meet the needs of people and society.

American Society of Interior Designers

The American Society of Interior Designers was formed in 1975 by the consolidation of the American Institute of Designers and the National Society of Interior Designers. It serves more than 38,000 members with continuing education and government affairs departments, conferences, publications, online services, and more. Members include residential and commercial designers; 2,500 manufacturers of design-related products and services, also known as industry partners; and 12,000 interior design students. ASID operates 48 local chapters throughout the United States.

Address

608 Massachusetts Avenue NE
Washington, DC 20002
(202) 546-3480
www.asid.org

Mission

The mission of the American Society of Interior Designers is to advance the interior design profession through knowledge generation and sharing, advocacy of interior designers' right to practice, professional and public education, and expansion of interior design markets.

American Society of Landscape Architects

Representing the landscape architecture profession in the United States since 1899, the American Society of Landscape Architects currently serves more than 16,000 members through 48 chapters across the country. The ASLA's goal is to advance knowledge, education, and skill in the art and science of landscape architecture. The benefits of membership include a national annual meeting, *Landscape Architecture* magazine, continuing education credits, seminars and workshops, professional interest groups, government advocacy, and award programs. In addition, the US Department of Education has authorized the Landscape Architectural Accreditation Board of the ASLA as the accrediting agency for landscape architecture programs at US colleges and universities.

 AMERICAN
SOCIETY OF
LANDSCAPE
ARCHITECTS

Address ————————————————————
636 Eye Street NW
Washington, DC 20001
(202) 898-2444
www.asla.org

Mission ————————————————————
The mission of the American Society of Landscape Architects is to lead, to educate, and to participate in the careful stewardship, wise planning, and artful design of our cultural and natural environments.

Design Futures Council

The Design Futures Council is a think tank of design and building industry leaders who collaborate through a series of regular meetings, summits, and *DesignIntelligence*, a monthly journal. The group shares information among its members on best practices and new trends in the design community in order to help member organizations anticipate change and increase competitive fitness. Recent summit topics have included sustainable/green design and creativity (with the Salk Institute). Members include leading architecture and design firms; dynamic manufacturers; service providers; and small, forward-thinking AEC companies taking an active interest in their future.

Address
25 Technology Parkway South, Suite 101
Atlanta, GA 30092
(800) 726-8603
www.di.net

Mission
The Design Futures Council is a think tank with the mission to explore trends, changes, and new opportunities in design, architecture, engineering, and building technology for the purpose of fostering innovation and improving the performance of member organizations.

Industrial Designers Society of America

Founded in 1965, the Industrial Designers Society of America is a professional association of industrial designers, educators, and students dedicated to the promotion of the profession. By fostering innovation and high standards of design, the IDSA communicates the value of design to the public and mentors young designers in their professional career development. The organization serves its constituency through the professional journal *Innovation*, award programs, an annual conference, research sponsorship and collection, networking opportunities, and promotion of the practice at all levels of government.

Address

45195 Business Court, Suite 250
Dulles, VA 20166
(703) 707-6000
www.idsa.org

Mission

The mission of the Industrial Designers Society of America is to lead the profession by expanding our horizons, connectivity and influence, and our service to members; inspire design quality and responsibility through professional development and education; and elevate the business of design and improve our industry's value.

International Interior Design Association

The International Interior Design Association provides a variety of services and benefits to its more than 10,000 members through eight specialty forums, nine regions, and more than 30 chapters around the world. This professional networking and educational association promotes the interior design practice to the public and serves its members as a clearinghouse for industry information. The IIDA was founded in 1994 as the result of a merger of the Institute of Business Designers, the International Society of Interior Designers, and the Council of Federal Interior Designers. The goal of the merger was to create an international association with a united mission that would represent interior designers worldwide.

INTERNATIONAL INTERIOR DESIGN ASSOCIATION

Address
222 Merchandise Mart Plaza
Suite 567
Chicago, IL 60654
(312) 467-1950
www.iida.org

Mission
The International Interior Design Association is committed to enhancing the quality of life through excellence in interior design and advancing interior design through knowledge. The IIDA advocates for interior design excellence, provides superior industry information, nurtures a global interior design community, maintains educational standards, and responds to trends in business and design.

National Trust for Historic Preservation

The National Trust for Historic Preservation is a private, nonprofit membership organization dedicated to saving historic places and revitalizing America's communities. Since its founding in 1949, it has worked to preserve historic buildings and neighborhoods through leadership, educational programs, publications, financial assistance, and government advocacy. Staff at the Washington, DC, headquarters, six regional offices, and 28 historic sites work with the its 270,000 members and thousands of preservation groups nationwide to protect the irreplaceable places that tell America's story. The NTP also publishes the award-winning *Preservation* magazine, hosts the nation's largest preservation conference, sponsors a number of award programs to celebrate outstanding preservation achievements, operates a number of community revitalization programs (such at the National Main Street Center), and provides technical training (such as the heritage tourism and rural heritage programs).

NATIONAL TRUST
for HISTORIC PRESERVATION*

Address

1785 Massachusetts Avenue, NW
Washington, DC 20036
(202) 588-6000
www.nationaltrust.org

Mission

The National Trust for Historic Preservation is a privately funded, nonprofit organization that provides leadership, education, advocacy, and resources to save America's diverse historic places and revitalize our communities.

Society for Environmental Graphic Design

The Society for Environmental Graphic Design is a nonprofit organization formed in 1973 to promote public awareness of and professional development in environmental graphic design. This interdisciplinary field encompasses the talents of many design professionals, including graphic designers, architects, landscape architects, product designers, planners, interior designers, and exhibition designers, in the planning and design of graphic elements that shape our built and natural environments. Practitioners design graphic elements to help identify, direct, inform, interpret, and visually enhance our surroundings. From wayfinding systems and mapping to exhibit design and themed environments, environmental graphic design impacts our experiences everywhere. The SEGD offers its members an interdisciplinary network to support and enhance their efforts in this growing discipline, a quarterly color magazine, a bi-monthly newsletter, an annual conference, a design award program, technical bulletins, job bank listings, and many other formal and informal resources.

Address

1000 Vermont Avenue, Suite 400
Washington, DC 20005
(202) 638-5555
www. segd.org

Mission

The Society for Environmental Graphic Design is an international nonprofit educational organization providing resources for design specialists in the field of environmental graphic design; architecture; and landscape, interior, and industrial design.

Society for Marketing Professional Services

Established in 1973, the Society for Marketing Professional Services is a network of 5,700 marketing and business development professionals representing architectural, engineering, planning, interior design, construction, and specialty consulting firms throughout the United States and Canada. The society's benefits include a certification program (Certified Professional Services Marketer), an annual marketing and management conference (www.buildbusiness.org), an annual marketing communications competition, educational programs, resources, and publications highlighting the latest trends and best practices in professional services marketing in the AEC industry. SMPS is supported by 50 chapters in the United States.

Address

99 Canal Center Plaza, Suite 330
Alexandria, VA 22314
(800) 292-7677
www.smps.org

Mission

The mission of the Society for Marketing Professional Services is to advocate for, educate, and connect leaders in the building industry.

Society of Architectural Historians

Since its founding in 1940, the Society of Architectural Historians has sought to promote the history of architecture. The membership of the SAH ranges from professional, such as architects, planners, preservationists, and academics, to those simply interested in architecture. The society produces a quarterly journal and monthly newsletter and organizes study tours and an annual conference. There are also a number of associated, although independent, local chapters. The SAH's national headquarters is located in Chicago's architecturally significant Charnley-Persky House, which was designed in 1891 by the firm of Dankmar Adler and Louis Sullivan. Guided tours of the house are offered.

Address

1365 North Astor Street
Chicago, IL 60610
(312) 573-1365
www.sah.org

Mission

The mission of the Society of Architectural Historians is to advance knowledge and understanding of the history of architecture, design, landscape, and urbanism worldwide.

Urban Land Institute

Formed in 1936 as a research arm of the National Association of Real Estate Boards (now the National Association of Realtors), the Urban Land Institute is an independent organization for those engaged in the entrepreneurial and collaborative process of real estate development and land-use policymaking. ULI has more than 30,000 members worldwide and a $27-million operating budget. The ULI members are the people that plan, develop, and redevelop neighborhoods, business districts, and communities across the United States and around the world, working in private enterprise and public service. The institute's activities include research, forums and task forces, awards, education, and publishing.

Address

1025 Thomas Jefferson Street NW
Suite 500 West
Washington, DC 20007
(202) 624-7000
www.uli.org

Mission

The mission of the Urban Land Institute is to provide responsible leadership in the use of land to enhance the total environment.

US Green Building Council

The US Green Building Council was formed in 1993 to integrate, educate, and provide leadership for building industry leaders, environmental groups, designers, retailers, and building owners as they strive to develop and market products and services that are environmentally progressive and responsible. The council includes nearly 8,500 worldwide organizations and 75 regional chapters with a common interest in green building practices, technologies, policies, and standards. Its most visible program, the LEED™ Green Building Rating System, is a voluntary, consensus-based rating system that provides a national standard on what constitutes a green building. It also offers professional accreditation to certify individuals who have demonstrated their ability to serve on a LEED project team and provide detailed knowledge of LEED project certification requirements and processes.

Address ——————————————————
1015 18th Street NW, Suite 805
Washington, DC 20036
(202) 828-7422
www.usgbc.org

Mission ——————————————————
The US Green Building Council's core purpose is to transform the way buildings and communities are designed, built, and operated, enabling an environmentally and socially responsible, healthy, and prosperous environment that improves the quality of life.

Design & Building-Related Organizations

The following associations, organizations, and government agencies offer a variety of information and support for the design and construction industry.

Associations & Organizations

Acoustical Society of America
2 Huntington Quadrangle, Suite 1NO1
Melville, NY 11747
(516) 576-2360
http://asa.aip.org

Air-Conditioning & Refrigeration Institute
4100 North Fairfax Drive, Suite 200
Arlington, VA 22203
(703) 524-8800
www.ari.org

Air Conditioning Contractors of America
2800 Shirlington Road, Suite 300
Arlington, VA 22206
(703) 575-4477
www.acca.org

Alliance to Save Energy
1850 M Street NW, Suite 600
Washington, DC 20036
(202) 857-0666
www.ase.org

American Arbitration Association
1633 Broadway, 10th Floor
New York, NY 10019
(212) 716-5800
www.adr.org

American Architectural Manufacturers Association
1827 Walden Office Square, Suite 550
Schaumburg, IL 60173
(847) 303-5664
www.aamanet.org

American Concrete Institute
38800 Country Club Drive
Farmington Hills, MI 48331
(248) 848-3700
www.aci-int.org

American Council of Engineering Companies
1015 15th Street NW, 8th Floor
Washington, DC 20005
(202) 347-7474
www.acec.org

American Forest Foundation
1111 Nineteenth Street NW, Suite 780
Washington, DC 20036
(202) 463-2462
www.affoundation.org

American Gas Association
400 North Capitol Street NW, Suite 400
Washington, DC 20001
(202) 824-7000
www.aga.org

American Hardware Manufacturers Association
801 North Plaza Drive
Schaumburg, IL 60173
(847) 605-1025
www.ahma.org

American Horticultural Society
7931 East Boulevard Drive
Alexandria, VA 22308
(703) 768-5700
www.ahs.org

American Institute of Building Design
7059 Blair Road NW, Suite 201
Washington, DC 20012
(800) 366-2423
www.aibd.org

American Institute of Steel Construction
One East Wacker Drive, Suite 700
Chicago, IL 60601
(312) 670-2400
www.aisc.org

American Lighting Association
2050 Stemmons Freeway, Suite 10046
Dallas, TX 75342
(800) 605-4448
www.americanlightingassoc.com

American National Standards Institute
1819 L Street NW, Sixth Floor
Washington, DC 20036
(202) 293-8020
www.ansi.org

American Nursery & Landscape Association
1000 Vermont Avenue NW, Suite 300
Washington, DC 20005
(202) 789-2900
www.anla.org

American Resort Development Association
1201 15th Street NW, Suite 400
Washington, DC 20005
(202) 371-6700
www.arda.org

American Society for Horticulture Science
113 South West Street, Suite 200
Alexandria, VA 22314
(703) 836-4606
www.ashs.org

American Society for Testing & Materials
100 Barr Harbor Drive
West Conshohocken, PA 19428
(610) 832-9585
www.astm.org

American Society of Civil Engineers
1801 Alexander Bell Drive
Reston, VA 20191
(800) 548-2723
www.asce.org

American Society of Consulting Arborists
15245 Shady Grove Road, Suite 130
Rockville, MD 20850
(301) 947-0483
www.asca-consultants.org

American Society of Golf Course Architects
125 North Executive Drive, Suite 106
Brookfield, WI 53005
(262) 786-5960
www.asgca.org

American Society of Heating, Refrigerating & Air-Conditioning Engineers
1791 Tullie Circle NE
Atlanta, GA 30329
(404) 636-8400
www.ashrae.org

American Society of Mechanical Engineers
Three Park Avenue
New York, NY 10016
(800) 843-2763
www.asme.org

American Society of Plumbing Engineers
8614 Catalpa Avenue, Suite 1007
Chicago, IL 60656
(773) 693-2773
www.aspe.org

American Society of Professional Estimators
2525 Perimeter Place Drive, Suite 103
Nashville, TN 37214
(615) 316-9200
www.aspenational.com

American Subcontractors Association, Inc.
1004 Duke Street
Alexandria, VA 22314
(703) 684-3450
www.asaonline.com

461

American Textile Manufacturers Institute
1130 Connecticut Avenue NW
Washington, DC 20036
(202) 862-0500
www.textileweb.com

APA – The Engineered Wood Association
7011 South 19th Street
Tacoma, WA 98466
(253) 565-6600
www.apawood.org

Design & Building-Related Organizations

Architectural Research Centers Consortium
c/o Brooke Harrington Architecture
Program
Temple University
1947 North 12th Street
Philadelphia, PA 19122
(215) 204-4300
www.arccweb.org

Architectural Woodwork Institute
46179 Westlake Drive, Suite 120
Potomac Falls, VA 20165
(571) 323-3636
www.awinet.org

ASFE
8811 Colesville Road, Suite G106
Silver Spring, MD 20910
(301) 565-2733
www.asfe.org

Asphalt Roofing Manufacturers Association
1156 15th Street NW, Suite 900
Washington, DC 20005
(202) 207-0917
www.asphaltroofing.org

Associated Builders & Contractors
4250 North Fairfax Drive, 9th Floor
Arlington, VA 22203
(703) 812-2000
www.abc.org

Associated General Contractors of America
2300 Wilson Boulevard, Suite 400
Arlington, VA 22201
(703) 548-3118
www.agc.org

Associated Owners & Developers
PO Box 4163
McLean, VA 22103
(703) 734-2397
www.constructionchannel.net/aod

Association for Contract Textiles
PO Box 101981
Fort Worth, TX 76185
(817) 924-8048
www.contracttextiles.org

Association for Facilities Engineering
8160 Corporate Park Drive, Suite 125
Cincinnati, OH 45242
(513) 489-2473
www.afe.org

Association for the Advancement of Cost Engineering
209 Prairie Avenue, Suite 100
Morgantown, WV 26501
(304) 296-8444
www.aacei.org

Association of Architecture School Librarians
William R. Jenkins Architecture
and Art Library
University of Houston
Houston, TX 77204
www.architecturelibrarians.org

Association of Energy Engineers
4025 Pleasantdale Road, Suite 420
Atlanta, GA 30340
(770) 447-5083
www.aeecenter.org

Association of Higher Education Facilities Officers
1643 Prince Street
Alexandria, VA 22314
(703) 684-1446
www.appa.org

Association of Pool and Spa Professionals
2111 Eisenhower Avenue
Alexandria, VA 22314
(703) 838-0083
www.theapsp.org

Association of the Wall & Ceiling Industry
513 West Broad Street, Suite 210
Falls Church, VA 22046
(703) 534-8300
www.awci.org

Brick Industry Association
1850 Centennial Park Drive, Suite 301
Reston, VA 20191
(703) 620-0010
www.bia.org

Building Codes Assistance Project
1850 M Street NW, Suite 600
Washington, DC 20036
(202) 857-0666
www.bcap-energy.org

Building Futures Council
2300 Wilson Boulevard, Suite 400
Arlington, VA 22201
(703) 837-5365
www.thebfc.com

Building Owners & Managers Association International
1201 New York Avenue, Suite 300
Washington, DC 20005
(202) 408-2662
www.boma.org

Building Stone Institute
551 Tollgate Road, Suite C
Elgin, IL 60123
(847) 695-0170
www.buildingstoneinstitute.org

California Redwood Association
405 Enfrente Drive, Suite 200
Novato, CA 94949
(415) 382-0662
www.calredwood.org

Carpet and Rug Institute
730 College Drive
Dalton, GA 30720
(706) 278-3176
www.carpet-rug.com

Cedar Shake and Shingle Bureau
PO Box 1178
Sumas, WA 98295
(604) 820-7700
www.cedarbureau.org

Center for Health Design
1850 Gateway Boulevard, Suite 1083
Concord, CA 94520
(925) 521-9404
www.healthdesign.org

Color Association of the United States
315 West 39th Street, Studio 507
New York, NY 10018
(212) 947-7774
www.colorassociation.com

Composite Panel Association/Composite Wood Council
18922 Premiere Court
Gaithersburg, MD 20879
(301) 670-0604
www.pbmdf.com

Construction Management Association of America
7926 Jones Branch Drive, Suite 800
McLean, VA 22102
(703) 356-2622
www.cmaanet.org

Construction Specifications Institute
99 Canal Center Plaza, Suite 300
Alexandria, VA 22314
(703) 684-0300
www.csinet.org

Copper Development Association
260 Madison Avenue, 16th Floor
New York, NY 10016
(212) 251-7200
www.copper.org

Council of Professional Surveyors
1015 15th Street NW, 8th Floor
Washington, DC 20005
(202) 347-7474
www.acec.org/coalitions/COPS/

Council on Tall Buildings and Urban Habitat
Illinois Institute of Technology
S.R. Crown Hall
3360 South State Street
Chicago, IL 60616
(312) 567-3307
www.ctbuh.org

463

Design & Building-Related Organizations

Deep Foundations Institute
326 Lafayette Avenue
Hawthorne, NJ 07506
(973) 423-4030
www.dfi.org

Design-Build Institute of America
1100 H Street NW, Suite 500
Washington, DC 20005
(202) 682-0110
www.dbia.org

Design Management Institute
29 Temple Place, 2nd Floor
Boston, MA 02111
(617) 338-6380
www.dmi.org

Door & Hardware Institute
14150 Newbrook Drive, Suite 200
Chantilly, VA 20151
(703) 222-2010
www.dhi.org

Edison Electric Institute
701 Pennsylvania Avenue NW
Washington, DC 20004
(202) 508-5000
www.eei.org

EIFS Industry Members Association
3000 Corporate Center Drive, Suite 270
Morrow, GA 30260
(800) 294-3462
www.eima.com

Electrical Power Research Institute
3420 Hillview Avenue
Palo Alto, CA 94304
(800) 313-3774
www.epri.com

Gas Technology Institute
1700 South Mount Prospect Road
Des Plaines, IL 60018
(847) 768-0500
www.gastechnology.org

Glass Association of North America
2945 SW Wanamaker Drive, Suite A
Topeka, KS 66614
(785) 271-0208
www.glasswebsite.com

GreenBlue
600 East Water Street, Suite C
Charlottesville, VA 22901
(434) 817-1424
www.greenblue.org

Hardwood Plywood & Veneer Association
1825 Michael Faraday Drive
Reston, VA 20195
(703) 435-2900
www.hpva.org

Hearth, Patio & Barbecue Association
1901 North Moore Street, Suite 600
Arlington, VA 22209
(703) 522-0086
www.hpba.org

Human Factors and Ergonomics Society
1124 Montana Avenue, Suite B
Santa Monica, CA 90403
(310) 394-1811
www.hfes.org

Illuminating Engineering Society of North America
120 Wall Street, 17th Floor
New York, NY 10005
(212) 248-5000
www.iesna.org

Institute of Electrical & Electronics Engineers, Inc.
3 Park Avenue, 17th Floor
New York, NY 10016
(212) 419-7900
www.ieee.org

Institute of Store Planners
25 North Broadway
Tarrytown, NY 10590
(914) 332-0040
www.ispo.org

**International Association of
Lighting Designers**
Merchandise Mart
200 World Trade Center, Suite 9-104
Chicago, IL 60654
(312) 527-3677
www.iald.org

International Code Council
500 New Jersey Avenue NW, 6th Floor
Washington, DC 20001
(888) 422-7233
www.iccsafe.org

**International Facility Management
Association**
1 East Greenway Plaza, Suite 1100
Houston, TX 77046
(713) 623-4362
www.ifma.org

**International Furnishings and Design
Association**
150 South Warner Road, Suite 156
King of Prussia, PA 19406
(610) 535-6422
www.ifda.com

International Society of Arboriculture
1400 West Anthony Drive
Champaign, IL 61821
(217) 355-9411
www.isa-arbor.com

International Wood Products Association
4214 King Street, West
Alexandria, VA 22302
(703) 820-6696
www.iwpawood.org

Irrigation Association
6540 Arlington Boulevard
Falls Church, VA 22042
(703) 536-7080
www.irrigation.org

**ISA–The Instrumentation, Systems,
and Automation Society**
67 Alexander Drive
Research Triangle Park, NC 27709
(919) 549-8411
www.isa.org

**Joslyn Castle Institute for Sustainable
Communities**
3902 Davenport Street
Omaha, NE 68131
(402) 595-1902
www.ecospheres.org

Light Gauge Steel Engineers Association
1201 15th Street NW, Suite 320
Washington, DC 20005
(202) 263-4488
www.lgsea.com

Maple Flooring Manufacturers Association
60 Revere Drive, Suite 500
Northbrook, IL 60062
(847) 480-9138
www.maplefloor.org

Marble Institute of America
28901 Clemens Road, Suite 100
Cleveland, OH 44145
(440) 250-9222
www.marble-institute.com

Metal Building Manufacturers Association
1300 Sumner Avenue
Cleveland, OH 44115
(216) 241-7333
www.mbma.com

**National Association of Environmental
Professionals**
389 Main Street, Suite 202
Malden, MA 02148
(781) 397-8870
www.naep.org

National Association of Home Builders
1201 15th Street NW
Washington, DC 20005
(202) 266-8200
www.nahb.org

465

Design & Building-Related Organizations

National Center for Preservation Technology & Training
645 University Parkway
Natchitoches, LA 71457
(318) 356-7444
www. ncptt.nps.gov

National Clearinghouse for Educational Facilities
1090 Vermont Avenue NW, Suite 700
Washington, DC 20005
(202) 289-7800
www.edfacilities.org

National Concrete Masonry Association
13750 Sunrise Valley Drive
Herndon, VA 20171
(703) 713-1900
www.ncma.org

National Conference of States on Building Codes & Standards
505 Huntmar Park Drive, Suite 210
Herndon, VA 20170
(703) 437-0100
www.ncsbcs.org

National Council of Acoustical Consultants
7150 Winton Drive, Suite 300
Indianapolis, IN 46268
(317) 328-0642
www.ncac.com

National Electrical Contractors Association
3 Bethesda Metro Center, Suite 1100
Bethesda, MD 20814
(301) 657-3110
www.necanet.org

National Electrical Manufacturers Association
1300 North 17th Street, Suite 1752
Rosslyn, VA 22209
(703) 841-3200
www.nema.org

National Fire Protection Association
1 Batterymarch Park
Quincy, MA 02169
(617) 770-3000
www.nfpa.org

National Fire Sprinkler Association
40 Jon Barrett Road
Patterson, NY 12563
(845) 878-4200
www.nfsa.org

National Glass Association
8200 Greensboro Drive, Suite 302
McLean, VA 22102
(866) 342-5642
www.glass.org

National Institute of Building Sciences
1090 Vermont Avenue NW, Suite 700
Washington, DC 20005
(202) 289-7800
www.nibs.org

National Lighting Bureau
8811 Colesville Road, Suite G106
Silver Spring, MD 20910
(301) 587-9572
www.nlb.org

National Kitchen & Bath Association
687 Willow Grove Street
Hackettstown, NJ 07840
(800) 843-6522
www.nkba.org

National Organization of Minority Architects
c/o School of Architecture and Design
College of Engineering, Architecture and Computer Sciences
Howard University
2366 6th Street NW, Room 100
Washington, DC 20059
(202) 686-2780
www.noma.net

National Paint & Coatings Association
1500 Rhode Island Avenue NW
Washington, DC 20005
(202) 462-6272
www.paint.org

National Preservation Institute
PO Box 1702
Alexandria, VA 22313
(703) 765-0100
www.npi.org

National Society of Professional Engineers
1420 King Street
Alexandria, VA 22314
(703) 684-2800
www.nspe.org

National Sunroom Association
1300 Sumner Avenue
Cleveland, OH 44115
(216) 241-7333
www.nationalsunroom.org

National Wood Flooring Association
111 Chesterfield Industrial Boulevard
Chesterfield, MO 63005
(800) 422-4556
www.woodfloors.org

New Buildings Institute, Inc.
PO Box 2349
142 East Jewett Boulevard
White Salmon, WA 98672
(509) 493-4468
www.newbuildings.org

NOFMA: The Wood Flooring Manufacturers Association
22 North Front Street, Suite 660
Memphis, TN 38103
(901) 526-5016
www.nofma.org

North American Insulation Manufacturers Association
44 Canal Center Plaza, Suite 310
Alexandria, VA 22314
(703) 684-0084
www.naima.org

North American Steel Framing Alliance
1201 15th Street NW, Suite 320
Washington, DC 20005
(202) 785-2022
www.steelframingalliance.com

NSSN: A National Resource for Global Standards/American National Standards Institute
25 West 43rd Street
New York, NY 10036
(212) 642-4980
www.nssn.org

Plumbing Manufacturers Institute
1340 Remington Road, Suite A
Schaumburg, IL 60173
(847) 884-9764
www.pmihome.org

Portland Cement Association
5420 Old Orchard Road
Skokie, IL 60077
(847) 966-6200
www.cement.org

Precast/Prestressed Concrete Institute
209 West Jackson Boulevard #500
Chicago, IL 60606
(312) 786-0300
www.pci.org

Preservation Trades Network, Inc.
PO Box 249
Amherst, NH 03031
(866) 653-9335
www.ptn.org

Professional Construction Estimators Association of America
PO Box 680336
Charlotte, NC 28216
(877) 521-7232
www.pcea.org

Professional Landcare Network (PLANET)
950 Herndon Parkway, Suite 450
Herndon, VA 20170
(703) 736-9666
www.landcarenetwork.org

Rocky Mountain Institute
1739 Snowmass Creek Road
Snowmass, CO 81654
(970) 927-3851
www.rmi.org

Design & Building-Related Organizations

Society of American Registered Architects
14 East 38th Street, 11th Floor
New York, NY 10016
(888) 385-7272
www.sara-national.org

Society of Fire Protection Engineers
7315 Wisconsin Avenue, Suite 620E
Bethesda, MD 20814
(301) 718-2910
www.sfpe.org

Society for Marketing Professional Services
99 Canal Center Plaza, Suite 330
Alexandria, VA 22314
(800) 292-7677
www.smps.org

Sustainable Buildings Industry Council
1112 16th Street NW, Suite 240
Washington, DC 20036
(202) 628-7400
www.sbicouncil.org

Tile Council of America, Inc.
100 Clemson Research Boulevard
Anderson, SC 29625
(864) 646-8453
www.tileusa.com

Tree Care Industry Association
3 Perimeter Road, Unit 1
Manchester, NH 03103
(603) 314-5380
www.treecareindustry.org

Vernacular Architecture Forum
PO Box 1511
Harrisonburg, VA 22803-1511
www.vernaculararchitectureforum.org

Underwriters Laboratories Inc.
333 Pfingsten Road
Northbrook, IL 60062
(847) 272-8800
www.ul.com

Vinyl Institute
1300 Wilson Boulevard, Suite 800
Arlington, VA 22209
(703) 741-5670
www.vinylinfo.org

Waterfront Center
1622 Wisconsin Avenue NW
Washington, DC 20007
(202) 337-0356
www.waterfrontcenter.org

Window & Door Manufacturers Association
1400 East Touhy Avenue, Suite 470
Des Plaines, IL 60018
(847) 299-5200
www.wdma.com

468

Government Agencies

Army Corps of Engineers
441 G Street NW
Washington, DC 20314
(202) 761-0011
www.usace.army.mil

Bureau of Land Management
Office of Public Affairs
1849 C Street, Room 406-LS
Washington, DC 20240
(202) 452-5125
www.blm.gov

U.S. Census Bureau Manufacturing and Construction Division
Washington, DC 20233
(301) 763-5160
www.census.gov/const/www

Department of Agriculture
1400 Independence Avenue SW
Washington, DC 20250
 202) 720-2791
www.usda.gov

Department of Energy
Forrestal Building
1000 Independence Avenue SW
Washington, DC 20585
(800) 342-5363
www.energy.gov

Department of Labor
Frances Perkins Building
200 Constitution Avenue NW
Washington, DC 20210
(866) 487-2365
www.dol.gov

Department of the Interior
1849 C Street NW
Washington, DC 20240
(202) 208-3100
www.doi.gov

Department of Transportation
400 7th Street SW
Washington, DC 20590
(202) 366-4000
www.dot.gov

Environmental Protection Agency
Ariel Rios Building
1200 Pennsylvania Avenue NW
Washington, DC 20460
(202) 272-0167
www.epa.gov

Federal Emergency Management Agency
500 C Street SW
Washington, DC 20472
(202) 566-1600
www.fema.gov

General Services Administration
1800 F Street NW
Washington, DC 20405
(800) 333-4636
www.gsa.gov

**National Institute of Standards
& Technology**
100 Bureau Drive, Stop 1070
Gaithersburg, MD 20899
(301) 975-6478
www.nist.gov

United States Access Board
1331 F Street NW, Suite 1000
Washington, DC 20004
(202) 272-0080
www.access-board.gov

International Organizations

Architects' Council of Europe
Rue Paul Emile Janson, 29
B-1050 Brussels, Belgium
+32 2 543 11 40
dwww.ace-cae.org

Architecture Institute of Japan
26-20, Shiba 5-chome, Minato-ku
Tokyo 108-8414, Japan
+81-3-3456-2051
www.aij.or.jp

DOCOMOMO International
Institute Français d'Architecture
Palais de la Porte Dorée
273, avenue Daumesnil
F-75012 Paris, France
+33 1 58 51 52 65
www.docomomo.com

**International Centre for the Study of the
Preservation and Restoration of Cultural
Property**
Via di San Michele 13
I-00153 Rome, Italy
+39 06 585531
www.iccrom.org

469

Design & Building-Related Organizations

International Council of Societies of Industrial Design
455 St-Antoine West, Suite SS10
Montreal, QC, H2Z 1J1
Canada
(514) 448-4949
www.icsid.org

International Council on Monuments and Sites
49-51 rue de la Fédération
75015 Paris, France
+33 (0) 1 45 67 67 70
www.icomos.org

International Federation of Interior Architects/Designers
140 Hill Street 5th Storey
MICA Building
Singapore 179369
+65 63386974
www.ifiworld.org

International Federation of Landscape Architects
Kaceni 6
CZ-772 00 Olomouc
Czech Republic
+420 585 207 778
www.iflaonline.org

International Union of Architects
51, rue Raynouard
F-75016 Paris, France
+33 (1) 45 24 36 88
www.uia-architectes.org

Japan Institute of Architects
Kenchikuka Kaikan
2-3-18, Jingumae
Shibuya-ku, Tokyo 150-0001
Japan
+81-3-3408-7125
www.jia.or.jp

Royal Architectural Institute of Canada
330-55 rue Murray Street
Ottawa, ON, K1N 5M3
Canada
(613) 241-3600
www.raic.org

Royal Australian Institute of Architects
Level 2, 7 National Circuit
Barton ACT 2600
Australia
(02) 6121 2000
www.architecture.com.au

Royal Institute of British Architects
66 Portland Place
London W1B 1AD
UK
+44 (0)20 7580 5533
www.riba.org

United Nations Human Settlements Programme (HABITAT)
PO Box 30030, GPO
Nairobi, 00100, Kenya
(254-20) 7623120
www.unchs.org

Source: DesignIntelligence

DESIGN
RESOURCES

This chapter contains a variety of concise, informative entries, from a fully updated Salary and Compensation Guide, registration and licensure laws, architectural outreach opportunities, to lists of design-oriented bookstores, journals and magazines, and museums.

Architectural Outreach

Countless volunteer opportunities abound for architects, designers, and others interested in the built environment, ranging from disaster relief and recovery to community empowerment, restoration, and historic preservation. The following is a partial list of organizations, coalitions, and resources aimed at the coordination and operation of national and international volunteer programs that are focused on architecture, planning, design, and community development initiatives.

Aang Serian

Room 110, 3rd Floor, Mollel House
Stadium Road
Arusha, Tanzania
+255 754318548
www.aangserian.org.uk

Aang Serian (House of Peace) is a registered Tanzanian cultural association to promote, preserve, and document the traditional cultures of East Africa; to build self-esteem among youth; and to uphold the rights of indigenous peoples. This project is offered under a "Teach and Learn" program aimed at building two-way dialogues between Africa and the West.

AIA Disaster Assistance Program

1735 New York Avenue, NW
Washington, DC 20006
(202) 626-7300
www.aia.org/liv_volunteerform

Initiated as a part of the American Institute of Architects' response to Hurricane Katrina and the Asian Tsunami, the AIA Disaster Assistance program is seeking volunteers to participate in recovery and rebuilding efforts on an as-needed basis. With a database of professionals, the goal of the program is to be prepared to respond to future disasters by employing the expertise of qualified members.

Architects Without Borders

295 Neva Street
Sebastopol, CA 95472
(707) 823-2724
www.awb.iohome.net

Architects Without Borders is an international coalition of non-governmental, non-profit, volunteer humanitarian relief organizations. They support communities in developing visionary planning, leadership, and self determination models upon which communities can define and achieve their own aspirations.

Architecture for Humanity

900 Bridgeway, Suite 2
Sausalito, CA 94965
(415) 332-6273
www.architectureforhumanity.org

Architecture for Humanity promotes architectural and design solutions to global, social, and humanitarian crises. Through competitions, workshops, educational forums, partnerships with aid organizations, and other activities, Architecture for Humanity creates opportunities for architects and designers from around the world to help communities in need.

473

Architectural Outreach

Builders Without Borders

119 Main Street
Kingston, NM 88042
(505) 895-5400
www.builderswithoutborders.org

With volunteers, including architects, engineers, contractors, and others in the AEC
field, Builders Without Borders specializes
in affordable housing, both domestically
and abroad, emphasizing sustainable structures built with locally available materials.
Generally, BWB provides technical assistance to improve designs.

Building with Books

PO Box 16741
Stamford, CT 06905
(203) 585-5390
www.buildingwithbooks.org

Building with Books enhances education
and empowers youth in the United States
to make a positive difference in their communities while helping people of developing countries increase their self-reliance
through education and the development of
educational resources.

Caribbean Volunteer Expeditions

PO Box 388
Corning, NY 14830
(607) 962-7846
www.cvexp.org

Caribbean Volunteer Expeditions is a non-
profit agency dedicated to the preservation
and documentation of the historical heritage of the Caribbean. Members and volunteers measure and document historical
plantations, windmills, and other structures
to help local Caribbean agencies keep a
record of their architectural heritage.
Professional assistance is appreciated.

Habitat for Humanity International

121 Habitat Street
Americus, GA 31709
(229) 924-6935
www.habitat.org

Habitat for Humanity International seeks
to eliminate poverty housing and homeless-
ness from the world and to make decent
shelter a matter of conscience and action.
Through volunteer labor and donations of
money and materials, Habitat builds and
rehabilitates simple, decent houses with the
help of the homeowner (partner) families.

Heritage Conservation Network

1557 North Street
Boulder, CO 80304
(303) 444-0128
www.heritageconservation.net

Heritage Conservation Networks' hands-on
building conservation workshops bring
people to historic sites around the world to
provide much-needed labor and technical
assistance to preservation projects.
Participants work with and learn from
experts in the field of heritage conservation; all levels of experience are welcome.

La Sabranenque

rue de la Tour de l'Oume
30290 Saint Victor la Coste
France
www.sabranenque.com

La Sabranenque works toward the preservation of the traditional Mediterranean habitat
and architecture. Working with volunteers, it
preserves, restores, and rebuilds sites that
can range from a simple village path to a
complex of buildings using traditional construction techniques while introducing volunteers to the values of vernacular architecture and traditional construction.

National Park Service Volunteers-In-Parks Program
1849 C Street NW
Washington, DC 20240
(202) 208-6843
www.nps.gov

The Volunteers-In-Parks Program provides a vehicle through which the National Park Service can accept and utilize voluntary help and services from the public.

Open Architecture Network
Architecture for Humanity
900 Bridgeway, Suite 2
Sausalito, CA 94965
(415) 332-6273
www.openarchitecturenetwork.org

The Open Architecture Network is an online, open-source community dedicated to improving living conditions through innovative and sustainable design. Here designers of all persuasions can share their ideas, designs and plans; view and review designs posted by others; collaborate to address specific design challenges; manage design projects from concept to implementation; protect their intellectual property rights using the Creative Commons licensing system; and build a more sustainable future.

Peace Corps
1111 20th Street NW, 8th Floor
Washington, DC 20526
(202) 692-2170
www.peacecorps.gov

Peace Corps Volunteers serve in countries across the globe: Africa, Asia, the Caribbean, Central and South America, Europe, and the Middle East. Collaborating with local community members, volunteers work in such areas as education, youth outreach and community development, the environment, and information technology.

Public Architecture 1% Solution
1211 Folsom Street, 4th Floor
San Francisco, CA 94706
(415) 861-8200
www.theonepercent.org
www.publicarchitecture.org

The 1% Solution program grew out of a realization that there are no formal mechanisms supporting or recognizing pro bono architectural work within the profession. The goal of the 1% Solution is to direct one percent of all architects' working hours to matters of public interest, pro bono.

Rebuilding Together
1536 16th Street NW
Washington, DC 20036
(202) 483-9083
www.rebuildingtogether.org

Rebuilding Together preserves and revitalizes houses and communities, assuring that low-income homeowners, from the elderly and disabled to families with children, live in warmth, safety, and independence. Its goal is to make a sustainable impact in partnership with the community.

Red Feather Development Group
PO Box 907
Bozeman, MT 59771
(406) 585-7188
www.redfeather.org

Red Feather educates and empowers American Indian nations to create sustainable solutions to the severe housing crisis within reservation communities. Red Feather teaches affordable, replicable, and sustainable approaches to home construction, working with volunteers alongside tribal members to build desperately needed homes.

475

Architectural Outreach

Shelter For Life International
7767 Elm Creek Boulevard, Suite 310
Maple Grove, MN 55369
(888) 426-7979
www.shelter.org

Shelter for Life International is a faith-based humanitarian organization that enables people affected by conflict and disaster to rebuild their communities and restore their lives through appropriate shelter and community development programs. Shelter for Life has occasional volunteer opportunities in project management, construction, community development, engineering, architecture, and cross-cultural relations.

slowLab
c/o New York Foundation for the Arts
155 Avenue of the Americas, 14th Floor
New York, NY 10013
(212) 366-6900
www.slowlab.org

The goal of slowLab is to promote slowness as a positive catalyst of individual, socio-cultural, and environmental well-being. Current and future programs include public lectures, discussions and exhibitions, a dynamic online project observatory and communication portal, academic programs, and publishing projects.

Southface Energy Institute
241 Pine Street NE
Atlanta, GA 30308
(404) 872-3549
www.southface.org

Southface promotes sustainable homes, workplaces, and communities through education, research, advocacy, and technical assistance.

United Nations Volunteers
One United Nations Plaza (UN#7)
New York, NY 10017
(212) 906-3639
www.unvolunteers.org

The United Nations Volunteers supports sustainable human development globally through the promotion of volunteerism, including the mobilization of volunteers. It serves the causes of peace and development through enhancing opportunities for participation by all people.

World Hands Project
(505) 989-7000
www.worldhandsproject.org

The World Hands Project is a group of concerned citizen-activists from diverse backgrounds that works worldwide creating solutions that address the basic needs for clean water, food production, sanitation, and shelter. Through workshops and studios, participants work with communities to establish a better quality of life by combining technical knowledge and skills with the traditional wisdom of indigenous peoples.

World Shelters for Humanitarian Needs
550 South G Street
Arcata, CA 95521
(707) 822-6600
www.worldshelters.org

World Shelters designs, produces, and delivers temporary and permanent structures for both emergency response and long-term humanitarian needs.

Source: DesignIntelligence

Architecture Critics

Below is a listing of the major US newspapers, as well as a few magazines and online publications, that regularly feature architectural writing and criticism. Some publications have a staff architecture critic while others an art critic or critic-at-large who routinely covers architecture stories.

Arizona Republic
Richard Nilsen
Fine Arts Critic
200 East Van Buren Street
Phoenix, AZ 85004
(602) 444-8000
www.azcentral.com

Atlanta Journal-Constitution
Catherine Fox
Architecture Critic
72 Marietta Street NW
Atlanta, GA 30303
(404) 526-5151
www.ajc.com

Austin American-Statesman
Jeanne Claire van Ryzin
Arts Writer
305 South Congress Avenue
Austin, TX 78704
(512) 445-3500
www.statesman.com

Baltimore Sun
Edward Gunts
Architecture Critic
501 North Calvert Street
Baltimore, MD 21278
(410) 332-6000
www.baltimoresun.com

Bergen Record
John Zeaman
Art Critic
150 River Street
Hackensack, NJ 07601
(201) 646-4000
www.bergen.com

Boston Globe
Robert Campbell
Architecture Critic
135 Morrissey Boulevard
Boston, MA 02125
(617) 929-2000
www.boston.com

Boston Herald
David Eisen
Architecture Critic
One Herald Square
Boston, MA 02118
(617) 426-3000
www.bostonherald.com

Charleston Post and Courier
Robert Behre
Architecture & Preservation Critic
134 Columbus Street
Charleston, SC 29403
(843) 577-7111
www.charleston.net

Charlotte Observer
Allen Norwood
Home Editor
600 South Tryon Street
Charlotte, NC 28202
(704) 358-5000
www.charlotte.com

Chicago Sun-Times
Kevin Nance
Architecture Critic
350 North Orleans Street
Chicago, IL 60654
(312) 321-3000
www.suntimes.com

Architecture Critics

Chicago Tribune
Blair Kamin
Architecture Critic
777 West Chicago Avenue, FC300
Chicago, IL 60610
(312) 222-3232
www.chicagotribune.com

Cleveland Plain Dealer
Steven Litt
Art & Architecture Critic
Plain Dealer Plaza
1801 Superior Avenue
Cleveland, OH 44114
(216) 999-4500
www.plaindealer.com

Dallas Morning News
David Dillon
Architecture Critic
508 Young Street
Dallas, TX 75202
(214) 977-8861
www.dallasnews.com

Dayton Daily News
Terry A. Morris
Arts Critic
45 South Ludlow Street
Dayton, OH 45402
(937) 222-5700
www.daytondailynews.com

Denver Post
Kyle MacMillan
Critic-at-Large
1560 Broadway
Denver, CO 80202
(303) 820-1201
www.denverpost.com

Detroit Free Press
John Gallagher
Architecture Critic
615 West Lafayette Boulevard
Detroit, MI 48226
(313) 222-5000
www.freep.com

Los Angeles Times
Christopher Hawthorne
Architecture Critic
202 West First Street
Los Angeles, CA 90012
(213) 237-5000
www.latimes.com

Louisville Courier-Journal
Diane Heilenman
Visual Arts Critic
525 West Broadway
Louisville, KY 40201
(502) 582-4011
www.courier-journal.com

Milwaukee Journal Sentinel
Whitney Gould
Architecture Reporter
333 West State Street
Milwaukee, WI 53203
(414) 224-2000
www.jsonline.com

New York Times
Nicolai Ouroussoff
Architecture Critic
229 West 43rd Street
New York, NY 10036
(212) 556-1234
www.nytimes.com

Newark Star-Ledger
Dan Bischoff
Art Critic
1 Star-Ledger Plaza
Newark, NJ 07102
(973) 392-4141
www.starledger.com

Newport News Daily Press
Mark St. John Erickson
Arts/Museum/History Reporter
7505 Warwick Boulevard
Newport News, VA 23607
(757) 247-4600
www.dailypress.com

Philadelphia Inquirer
Inga Saffron
Architecture Critic
400 North Broad Street
Philadelphia, PA 19130
(215) 854-2000
www.philly.com

Pittsburgh Post-Gazette
Patricia Lowry
Architecture Critic
34 Boulevard of the Allies
Pittsburgh, PA 15222
(412) 263-1100
www.post-gazette.com

Portland Oregonian
Pending
Architecture Critic
1320 SW Broadway
Portland, OR 97201
(503) 221-8100
www.oregonian.com

Providence Journal
Bill Van Siclen
Art Critic
75 Fountain Street
Providence, RI 02902
(401) 277-7000
www.projo.com

Raleigh News & Observer
Pending
Features Editor
215 South McDowell Street
Raleigh, NC 27602
(919) 829-4500
www.newsobserver.com

Rocky Mountain News
Mary Chandler
Art & Architecture Critic
101 West Colfax Avenue
Suite 500
Denver, CO 80202
(303) 892-5000
www.rockymountainnews.com

San Antonio Express-News
Mike Greenberg
Architecture and Classical Music Critic
301 Avenue E
San Antonio, TX 78205
(210) 250-3000
www.mysanantonio.com

San Diego Union-Tribune
Ann Jarmusch
Architecture Critic
350 Camino de la Reina
San Diego, CA 92108
(619) 299-3131
www.signonsandiego.com

San Francisco Chronicle
John King
Urban Design Writer
901 Mission Street
San Francisco, CA 94103
(415) 777-1111
www.sfgate.com

San Jose Mercury News
Alan Hess
Architecture Writer
750 Ridder Park Drive
San Jose, CA 95190
(408) 920-5000
www.mercurynews.com

Seattle Post-Intelligencer
Regina Hackett
Art Critic
101 Elliot Avenue West
Seattle, WA 98119
(206) 448-8000
http://seattlepi.nwsource.com

Seattle Times
Sheila Farr
Art Critic
1120 John Street
Seattle, WA 98109
(206) 464-2111
http://seattletimes.nwsource.com

Architecture Critics

South Florida Sun-Sentinel
Emma Trelles
Arts Writer
200 East Las Olas Blvd
Fort Lauderdale, FL 33301
(954) 356-4000
www.sun-sentinel.com

St. Paul Pioneer Press
Larry Millett
Architecture Critic
345 Cedar Street
St. Paul, MN 55101
(651) 222-1111
www.twincities.com

Wall Street Journal
Ada Louise Huxtable
Architecture Critic
200 Liberty Street
New York, NY 10281
(212) 416-2000
www.wsj.com

Washington Post
Philip Kennicott
Culture Critic
1150 15th Street NW
Washington, DC 20071
(202) 334-6000
www.washingtonpost.com

Source: DesignIntelligence

Bookstores

The following is a list of US architecture and design bookstores, including rare and out-of-print dealers that specialize in design titles.

ARIZONA

Builder's Book Depot
1001 East Jefferson, Suite 5
Phoenix, AZ 85034
(800) 284-3434
www.buildersbookdepot.com

CALIFORNIA

Arcana: Books on the Arts
1229 Third Street Promenade
Santa Monica, CA 90401
(310) 458-1499
www.arcanabooks.com

Builder's Book
8001 Canoga Avenue
Canoga Park, CA 91304
(800) 273-7375
www.buildersbook.com

Builders Booksource
1817 Fourth Street
Berkeley, CA 94710
(800) 843-2028
www.buildersbooksource.com

Hennessey + Ingalls
214 Wilshire Boulevard
Santa Monica, CA 90401
(310) 458-9074
www.hennesseyingalls.com

J.B. Muns Fine Arts Books
1162 Shattuck Avenue
Berkeley, CA 94707
(510) 525-2420

MAK Center for Art and Architecture Bookstore
835 North Kings Road
West Hollywood, CA 90069
(323) 651-1510 x13
www.makcenter.com

Moe's Books
2476 Telegraph Avenue
Berkeley, CA 94702
(510) 849-2087
www.moesbooks.com

Potterton Books
Pacific Design Center, G154
8687 Melrose Avenue
West Hollywood, CA 90069
(310) 289-1247
www.pottertonbooks.co.uk

Sullivan Goss
7 East Anapamu Street
Santa Barbara, CA 93101
(805) 730-1460
www.sullivangoss.com

William Stout Architectural Books
804 Montgomery Street
San Francisco, CA 94133
(415) 391-6757
www.stoutbooks.com

COLORADO

Tattered Cover Bookstore
2955 East Colfax Avenue
Denver, CO 80206
(303) 322-7727
www.tatteredcover.com

CONNECTICUT

Reid & Wright
287 New Milford Turnpike
New Preston, CT 06777
(860) 868-7706
www.reidbook.com

DISTRICT OF COLUMBIA

AIA Bookstore
1735 New York Avenue NW
Washington, DC 20006
(202) 626-7475
www.aia.org/store

481

Bookstores

Franz Bader Bookstore
1911 I Street NW
Washington, DC 20006
(202) 337-5440

National Building Museum Shop
401 F Street NW
Washington, DC 20001
(202) 272-7706
www.nbm.org

ILLINOIS
Chicago Architecture Foundation Bookstore
224 South Michigan Avenue
Chicago, IL 60604
(312) 922-3432
www.architecture.org/shop

Prairie Avenue Bookshop
418 South Wabash Avenue
Chicago, IL 60605
(800) 474-2724
www.pabook.com

INDIANA
Architectural Center Bookstore
50 South Meridian
Suite 100
Indianapolis, IN 46204
(317) 634-3871
www.aiaindiana.org

MARYLAND
Baltimore AIA Bookstore
11 1/2 West Chase Street
Baltimore, MD 21201
(410) 625-2585
www.aiabalt.com

MASSACHUSETTS
Ars Libri
500 Harrison Avenue
Boston, MA 02118
(617) 357-5212
www.arslibri.com

Charles B. Wood III Antiquarian Booksellers
PO Box 2369
Cambridge, MA 02238
(617) 868-1711
www.cbwoodbooks.com

F.A. Bernett
144 Lincoln Street
Boston, MA 02111
(617) 350-7778
www.fabernett.com

MISSOURI
St. Louis AIA Bookstore
911 Washington Avenue
Suite 100
St. Louis, MO 63101
(314) 621-3484
www.aia-stlouis.org

NEW YORK
Argosy Bookstore
116 East 59th Street
New York, NY 10022
(212) 753-4455
www.argosybooks.com

Cooper-Hewitt Museum Bookstore
2 East 91st Street
New York, NY 10128
(212) 849-8355
www.ndm.si.edu/shop/

Hacker Art Books
248 Flushing Avenue
Brooklyn, NY 11205
(718) 802-0443

Neue Galeria Bookstore
1048 Fifth Avenue
New York, NY 10028
(212) 628-6200
www.neuegalerie.org

New York School of Interior Design Bookstore
170 East 70th Street
New York, NY 10021
(212) 472-1500
www.nysid.edu

Potterton Books
D & D Building
Lobby Level
979 Third Avenue
New York, NY 10022
(212) 644-2292
www.pottertonbooks.co.uk

Rizzoli Bookstore
31 West 57th Street
New York, NY 10019
(212) 759-2424
www.rizzoliusa.com

Royoung Bookseller
564 Ashford Avenue
Ardsley, NY 10502
(914) 693-6116
www.royoung.com

Strand Book Store
828 Broadway
New York, NY 10003
(212) 473-1452
www.strandbooks.com

Urban Center Books
457 Madison Avenue
New York, NY 10022
(212) 935-3595
www.urbancenterbooks.com

Ursus Books
981 Madison Avenue
New York, NY 10021
(212) 772-8787
www.ursusbooks.com

OREGON
Powell's City of Books
1005 West Burnside
Portland, OR 97209
(503) 228-4651
www.powells.com

PENNSYLVANIA
AIA Bookstore & Design Center
117 South 17th Street
Philadelphia, PA 19103
(215) 569-3188
www.aiaphila.org

Joseph Fox Bookshop
1724 Sansom Street
Philadelphia, PA 19103
(215) 563-4184

TEXAS
Brazos Bookstore
2421 Bissonnet Street
Houston, TX 77005
(713) 523-0701
www.brazosbookstore.com

WASHINGTON
AIA Spokane Bookstore
335 West Sprague Avenue
Spokane, WA 99201
(509) 747-5498
www.aiaspokane.org

Hink & Wall
760 Hemlock Street
Edmonds, WA 98020
(800) 561-1203
www.gardenhistory.com

Peter Miller Architecture and Design Books
1930 First Avenue
Seattle, WA 98101
(206) 441-4114
www.petermiller.com

483

Source: DesignIntelligence

Journals & Magazines

The following is a list of major architecture and design journals and magazines from around the world, ranging from the mainstream to the cutting edge. Whether looking for periodicals that take a less-traditional approach or for exposure to the most recent projects and design news, this list is intended to provide an opportunity to explore new ideas and perspectives about design and expand your knowledge about the profession.

US Publications

Architect's Newspaper
21 Murray Street, Fifth Floor
New York, NY 10013
(212) 966-0630
www.archpaper.com
Published monthly.

Architectural Digest
6300 Wilshire Boulevard
Los Angeles, CA 90048
(800) 365-8032
www.archdigest.com
Published monthly by Condé Nast
Publications, Inc.

Architectural Record
Two Penn Plaza, Ninth Floor
New York, NY 10121
(212) 904-2594
www.architecturalrecord.com
The official magazine of the AIA, published monthly by the McGraw-Hill
Companies.

Architect
One Thomas Circle NW, Suite 600
Washington, DC 20005
(202) 452-0800
www.architectmagazine.com
Published monthly by Hanley Wood, LLC.

ASID ICON
608 Massachusetts Avenue NE
Washington, DC 20002
(202) 546-3480
www.asid.org
The magazine of the American Society of
Interior Designers, published quarterly.

Contract
770 Broadway, 4th Floor
New York, NY 10003
(847) 763-9050
www.contractmagazine.com
Published monthly by VNU Business
Publications, USA, Inc.

Common Ground
1849 C Street, NW
Washington, DC 20240
(202) 354-2277
http://commonground.cr.nps.gov/
Published quarterly by the National Park
Service for the heritage community.

Communication Arts
110 Constitution Drive
Menlo Park, CA 94025
(650) 326-6040
www.commarts.com/ca
Published eight times per year.

**CRM: The Journal of Heritage
Stewardship**
National Park Service
1849 C Street NW (2286)
Washington, DC 20240
(202) 354-2277
http://crmjournal.cr.nps.gov
Published twice a year by the National Park
Service.

Dwell
40 Gold
San Francisco, CA 94133
(415) 373-5100
www.dwellmag.com
Published 10 times per year.

eco-structure
1415 Highway 54 W., Suite 105
Durham, NC 27707
(919) 402-9300
www.eco-structure.com
Published eight times a year.

Engineering News Record
Two Penn Plaza, 9th Floor
New York, NY 10121
(212) 512-2000
www.enr.com
Published weekly by McGraw-Hill
Companies.

Faith & Form
Michael J. Crosbie
c/o SWA
50 Washington Street
Norwalk, CT 06854
(203) 857-0200, ext. 210
www.faithandform.com
The leading interfaith journal on religious
art and architecture, published quarterly.

Fine Homebuilding
Taunton Press
63 South Main Street
Newtown, CT 06470
(203) 426-8171
www.taunton.com/fh/
Published eight times a year by Taunton
Press.

Harvard Design Magazine
48 Quincy Street
Cambridge, MA 02138
(617) 495-7814
www.gsd.harvard.edu/research/
publications/hdm/
Published twice a year by the Harvard
University Graduate School of Design.

I.D.
38 East 29th Street, Floor 3
New York, NY 10016
(212) 447-1400
www.idonline.com
Published eight times per year.

Innovation
45195 Business Court, Suite 250
Dulles, VA 20166
(703) 707-6000
www.innovationjournal.org
Quarterly journal of the Industrial
Designers Society of America.

Interior Design
360 Park Avenue South, Floor 17
New York, NY 10010
(646) 746-6400
www.interiordesign.net
Published 15 times a year by Reed Business
Information.

Interiors & Sources
615 Fifth Street SE
Cedar Rapids, IA 52401
(319) 364-6167
www.isdesignet.com
Published nine times a year by Stamats
Business Media, Inc.

Journal of Architectural Education
Association of Collegiate Schools
of Architecture
1735 New York Avenue, NW
Washington, DC 20006
(202) 785-2324
www.jaeonline.ws
Published quarterly by Blackwell Publishing
for the ACSA.

Journal of Interior Design
Interior Design Educators Council, Inc.
7150 Winton Drive, Suite 300
Indianapolis, IN 46268
(317) 328-4437
www.idec.org/publication/jid/html
Published biannually by the Interior Design
Educators Council.

485

Journals & Magazines

Journal of the American Planning Association
City and Regional Planning
Georgia Institute of Technology
245 Fourth Street NW, Suite 204
Atlanta, GA 30332
(404) 894-1628
www.planning.org/japa/
Published quarterly by the American Planning Association.

Journal of the Society of Architectural Historians
1365 North Astor Street
Chicago, IL 60610
(312) 573-1365
www.sah.org
Published quarterly by the Society of Architectural Historians.

Landscape Architecture
636 Eye Street NW
Washington, DC 20001
(202) 898-2444
www.asla.org
Published monthly by the American Society of Landscape Architects.

Metropolis
61 West 23rd Street, 4th Floor
New York, NY 10010
(212) 627-9977
www.metropolismag.com
Published 11 times a year.

Old House Journal
1000 Potomac Street NW, Suite 102
Washington, DC 20007
(202) 399-0744
www.oldhousejournal.com
Published bimonthly by Restore Media, LLC.

Perspective
222 Merchandise Mart Plaza, Suite 1540
Chicago, IL 60654
(888) 799-4432
www.iida.org
Published quarterly by the International Interior Design Association.

Places
Center for Environmental Design Research
University of California, Berkeley
College of Environmental Design
390 Wurster Hall, #1839
Berkeley, CA 94720
(510) 642-2896
www.cedr.berkeley.edu
Published three times a year by the Design History Foundation.

Preservation
1785 Massachusetts Avenue NW
Washington, DC 20036
(800) 944-6847
www.nationaltrust.org
Published bimonthly by the National Trust for Historic Preservation.

International Publications

Abitare
Via Portuense 1555
00148 Ponte Galeria (RM), Italy
+39 06 65000808
www.abitare.it
Monthly magazine in Italian and English.

AD (Architectural Design)
1 Oldlands Way
Bognor Regis
West Sussex, PO22 9SA, UK
+44 01243 843 335
Published bi-monthly by John Wiley and Sons, Ltd.

AJ (Architects' Journal)
151 Rosebery Avenue
London, EC1R 4GB, UK
+44 020 7505 6700
www.ajplus.co.uk
Published by EMAP Construct.

l'Arca
Via Valcava, 20155
Milano, 6, Italy
+39 02 325246
www.arcadata.com
Published 11 times a year.

**Architectural History: The Journal
of the Society of Architectural Historians
of Great Britain**
Simon Green
RCA HMS, 16 Barnard Terrace
Edinburgh, EH8 9NX
Scotland, UK
www.sahgb.org.uk
Published annually.

Architectural Review
151 Rosebery Avenue
London, EC1R 4GB, UK
+44 020 7505 6622
www.arplus.com
Published by EMAP Construct.

Architecture Australia
Level 3, 4 Princes Street
Port Melbourne, Victoria
Australia 3207
+61 (03) 9646 4760
www.archmedia.com.au/aa/
Official magazine of the RAIA published
six times a year.

l'Architecture d'Aujourd'hui
3, rue Lhomond
75005 Paris, France
+33 1 44320590
www.jeanmichelplace.com/fr/
Published six times a year in French
and English.

Arkitektur
Box 4296
SE102 66 Stockholm, Sweden
+46 8 702 7850
www.arkitektur.se
Published eight times yearly; with English
summaries.

a+u magazine
2-31-2 Yushima, Bunkyo-ku
Tokyo, 113-0034, Japan
+81 33816-2935
www.japan-architect.co.jp
Published monthly in Japanese and English
by A+U Publishing Co., Ltd.

Blueprint
Design4design
14 Underwood Street
London, N1 7JQ, UK
www.blueprintmagazine.co.uk
+44 01245 4917 17
Published monthly by Wilmington Media
Ltd.

Canadian Architect
12 Concorde Place, Suite 800
Toronto, ON, M3C 4J2, Canada
(416) 510-6845
www.canadianarchitect.com
Published monthly by Business Information
Group, a division of Hollinger Canadian
Newspapers, LP.

Casabella
D. Trentacoste 7
Milan, 20134, Italy
+39 02 66 21 56 31
Published monthly in Italian with an
English summary.

El Croquis
Avda de los Reyes Catolicos 9
E-28280 El Escorial
Madrid, Spain
+34 91 8969410
www.elcroquis.es
Published bimonthly in Spanish and
English.

Domus
Via Achille Grandi 5/7
Rozzano
Milan, 20089, Italy
+39 0282472276
www.domusweb.it
Published monthly in Italian and English.

Hinge
24/F, Empire Land Commerical Centre
81 Lockhart Road
Wanchai
Hong Kong, China
+852 2520 2468
www.hingenet.com
Published monthly.

487

Journals & Magazines

Japan Architect
2-31-2 Yushima, Bunkyo-ku
Tokyo, 113-8501, Japan
+81 3 3816-2532
www.japan-architect.co.jp
Published quarterly in Japanese and
English.

Journal of Architecture
Building Four
Milton Park
Abingdon
Oxfordshire OX14 4RN, UK
+44 20 7017 6000
www.tandf.co.uk/journals/routledge/
Published five times a year by RIBA and
Routledge, an imprint of Taylor & Francis.

Journal of Sustainable Product Design
Centre for Sustainable Design
University College for the Creative Arts
Farnham Campus
Faculty of Design
Falkner Road
Farnham
Surrey GU9 7DS, UK
+44 (0)1252 89 2772
www.cfsd.org.uk/journal/index.html
A quarterly journal published by Kluwer
Academic Publishers in partnership with
the Centre for Sustainable Design.

Journal of Urban Design
Building Four
Milton Park
Abingdon
Oxfordshire OX14 4RN, UK
+44 20 7017 6000
Published three times a year by Routledge,
Taylor & Francis Group.

Ottagono
Via Stalingrado, 97/2
40128 Bologna, Italy
+39 051 3540 111
www.ottagono.com
Published monthly in bilingual text
(Italian and English).

Volume
Archis Foundation
Hamerstraat 20 A
1021 JV Amsterdam, Netherlands
31 20 3203926
www.archis.org
Bilingual magazine published six times
each year by Stichting Archis in association
with the Netherlands Architecture
Institute.

Wallpaper
Blue Fin Building
110 Southwark Street
London, SE1 0SU, UK
+44 20 3148 5000
www.wallpaper.com
Published 10 times a year.

Source: DesignIntelligence

Museums

There are many museums around the world devoted solely to architecture and design. In addition, many major museums maintain strong design collections and regularly host architecture and design-related exhibits. The following contains the contact information for these organizations.

US Museums

A+D Architecture and Design Museum
5900 Wilshire Boulevard
Los Angeles, CA 90010
(213) 381-5210
www.aplusd.org

Art Institute of Chicago
111 South Michigan Avenue
Chicago, IL 60603
(312) 443-3600
www.artic.edu/aic/

Athenaeum of Philadelphia
219 South Sixth Street
Philadelphia, PA 19106
(215) 925-2688
www.philaathenaeum.org

Center for Architecture
536 LaGuardia Place
New York, NY 10012
(212) 683-0023
www.aiany.org/centerforarchitecture/

Chicago Architecture Foundation
224 South Michigan Avenue
Chicago, IL 60604
(312) 922-3432
www.architecture.org

Cooper-Hewitt, National Design Museum, Smithsonian Institution
2 East 91st Street
New York, NY 10128
(212) 849-8400
www.ndm.si.edu

Heinz Architectural Center
Carnegie Museum of Art
4400 Forbes Avenue
Pittsburgh, PA 15213
(412) 622-3131
www.cmoa.org

MAK Center for Art & Architecture L.A.
The Schindler House
835 North Kings Road
West Hollywood, CA 90069
(323) 651-1510
www.makcenter.org

Museum of Arts & Design
40 West 53rd Street
New York, NY 10019
(212) 956-3535
www.madmuseum.org

Museum of Contemporary Art, Los Angeles
MOCA at California Plaza
250 South Grand Avenue
Los Angeles, CA 90012
(213) 626-6222
www.moca-la.org

Museum of Design
Marquis II Office Tower
285 Peachtree Center Avenue
Atlanta, GA 30303
(404) 979-6455
www.museumofdesign.org

Museum of Modern Art
11 West 53rd Street
New York, NY 10019
(212) 708-9400
www.moma.org

Museums

National Building Museum
401 F Street NW
Washington, DC 20001
(202) 272-2448
www.nbm.org

Octagon Museum
1799 New York Avenue NW
Washington, DC 20006
(202) 638-3221
www.theoctagon.org

Price Tower Arts Center
510 Dewey Avenue
Bartlesville, OK 74003
(918) 336-4949
www.pricetower.org

San Francisco Museum of Craft + Design
550 Sutter Street
San Francisco, CA 94102
(415) 773-0303
www.sfmcd.org

San Francisco Museum of Modern Art
151 Third Street
San Francisco, CA 94103
(415) 357-4000
www.sfmoma.org

Skyscraper Museum
39 Battery Place
New York, NY 10280
(212) 968-1961
www.skyscraper.org

Storefront for Art and Architecture
97 Kenmare Street
New York, NY 10012
(212) 431-5795
www.storefrontnews.org

Van Alen Institute
30 West 22 Street
New York, NY 10010
(212) 924-7000
www.vanalen.org

Virginia Center for Architecture
2501 Monument Avenue
Richmond, VA 23220
(804) 644-3041
www.virginiaarchitecture.org

International Museums

Alvar Aalto Museum
(Alvar Aalto Museo)
Alver Aallon katu 7
Jyväskylä, Finland
+358 14 624 809
www.alvaraalto.fi

Architectural Museum, Basel
(Architekturmuseum Basel)
Steinenberg 7
Postfach 911
CH-4001 Basel, Switzerland
+41 61 261 1413
www.architekturmuseum.ch

Architecture Center of Vienna
(Architekturzentrum Wien)
Museumsplatz 1, im MQ
A-1070 Vienna, Austria
+43 522 3115
www.azw.at

Architecture Museum of Lithuania
(Architekturos muziejus)
9 Sv. Mykolo St
LT-01124, Vilnius, Lithuania
+370 (5) 2610456
www.muziejai.lt/Vilnius/architekturos_
muziejus.en.htm

Bauhaus Archive/Museum of Design
(Bauhaus-Archiv/Museum für Gestaltung)
Klingelhöferstraße 14
10785 Berlin, Germany
+49 30 254 00 20
www.bauhaus.de

Canadian Centre for Architecture
1920, rue Baile
Montreal, QC, Canada H3H 2S6
(514) 939-7026
www.cca.qc.ca

International Center for Urbanism
(Centre International pour la Ville,
l'Architecture et le Paysage)
Rue de l'Ermitage 55 Kluisstraat
Brussels 1050, Belgium
+32 (0)2 642 24 50
www.civa.be

Danish Architecture Center
(Dansk Arkitektur Center)
Strandgade 27B
1401 Copenhagen K, Denmark
+45 32 57 19 30
www.dac.dk

Danish Design Center
(Dansk Design Center)
27 H C Andersens Boulevard
1553 Copenhagen V, Denmark
+45 33 69 33 69
www.ddc.dk

Design Museum, Finland
(Designmuseo)
Korkeavuorenkatu 23
00130 Helsinki, Finland
+35 89 622 0540
www.designmuseum.fi

Design Museum, London
28 Shad Thames
London SE1 2YD, UK
+44 87 0833 9955
www.designmuseum.org

Design Museum at the
Cultural Center of Belém
(Museu do Design, Centro Cultural
de Belém)
Praça do Império
1499-003 Lisbon, Portugal
+351 213 612 400
www.ccb.pt

German Centre for Architecture
(Deutsches Architektur Zentrum)
Direktorin Kristien Ring
Köpenicker Straße 48/49 Aufgang A
10179 Berlin, Germany
+49 30 278799-28
www.daz.de

German Architecture Museum
(Deutsches Architektur Museum)
Schaumainkai 43
60596 Frankfurt am Main
Germany
+49 69-212 38844
www.dam-online.de

The Lighthouse: Scotland's Centre
for Architecture, Design & the City
11 Mitchell Lane
Glasgow, G1 3NU, Scotland
United Kingdom
+44 141 221 6362
www.thelighthouse.co.uk

Museum of Architecture in Wroclaw
(Muzeum Architektury we Wroclawiu)
ul. Bernardynska 5
PL 50-156 Wroclaw, Poland
+48 (71) 343 36 75
www.ma.wroc.pl

Museum of Estonian Architecture
(Eesti Arhitektuurimuuseum)
Arts centre
Rotermann's Salt Storage
Ahtri 2, Tallinn 10151
tel. +372 625 7000
www.arhitektuurimuuseum.ee

491

Museums

Museum of Finnish Architecture
(Suomen Rakennustaiteen Museo)
Kasarmikatu 24, 00130
Helsinki, Finland
+358 9 8567 5100
www.mfa.fi

Netherlands Architecture Institute
(Nederlands Architectuurinstituut)
Museumpark 25
3015 CB Rotterdam, Netherlands
+3110-4401200
www.nai.nl

**National Museum of Art,
Architecture and Design**
(Nasjonalmuseet for Kunst,
Arkitektur og Design)
Kristian Augusts gate 23
Oslo, Norway
+47 21 98 20 00
www.nationalmuseum.no

Palladio Centre and Museum
(Centro Internazionale di Studi di
Architettura Andrea Palladio)
Contra' Porti 11
I-36100 Vicenza, Italy
+39 (04) 44 32 30 14
www.cisapalladio.org

RIBA Architecture Gallery
66 Portland Place
London W1B 1AD, UK
+44 20 7580 5533
www.architecture.com

**Röhsska Museum of Design
and Applied Art**
(Röhsska Museet för Konsthantverk
och Design)
Vasagatan 37-39
SE-400 15 Göteborg, Sweden
+46 31-61 38 50
www.designmuseum.se

Schusev State Museum of Architecture
Vozdvizhenka str., 5
119019 Moscow, Russia
+7-095-291-21-09
www.muar.ru

Swedish Museum of Architecture
(Arkitekturmuseet)
Skeppsholmen
SE-111 49 Stockholm, Sweden
+46 8 587 270 00
www.arkitekturmuseet.se

Victoria and Albert Museum
Cromwell Road
London SW7 2RL, UK
+44 20 7942 2000
www.vam.ac.uk

Vitra Design Museum
Charles-Eames-Str. 1
D-79576 Weil am Rhein
Germany
+49 7621 702 32 00
www.design-museum.de

Zurich Museum of Design
(Museum für Gestaltung Zürich)
Ausstellungsstrasse 60
8005 Zürich, Switzerland
+41 43 446 67 67
www.museum-gestaltung.ch

Source: DesignIntelligence

Registration Laws: Architecture

Following is a brief overview of state licensure requirements for architects. Due to the complexity of the laws, contact the individual state boards for the most accurate information. The National Council of Architectural Registration Boards also provides information its website, *www.ncarb.org*.

State Boards		Type of Law		Initial Requirements			Ongoing Req.
		Title Act	Practice Act	College Degree Required	Internship Required	ARE Exam Required	Continuing Education Required
Alabama	(334) 242-4179	■	■	■	■	■	■
Alaska	(907) 465-1676	■			■	■	
Arizona	(602) 364-4937	■	■			■	
Arkansas	(501) 682-3171	■	■	■	■	■	■
California	(916) 574-7220	■	■		■	■	
Colorado	(303) 894-7775	■	■			■	
Connecticut	(860) 713-6145	■	■	■	■	■	
Delaware	(302) 744-4505	■	■	■	■	■	■
Dist. of Columbia	(202) 442-4320		■	■	■	■	
Florida	(850) 487-1395	■	■	■	■	■	■
Georgia	(478) 207-2440	■	■		■	■	■
Hawaii	(808) 586-2702	■	■		■	■	■
Idaho	(208) 334-3233	■	■		■	■	■
Illinois	(217) 524-3211	■	■	■	■	■	■
Indiana	(317) 234-3022	■	■	■	■	■	■
Iowa	(515) 281-7362	■	■	■	■	■	■
Kansas	(785) 296-3053	■	■	■	■	■	■
Kentucky	(859) 246-2069	■	■	■	■	■	■
Louisiana	(225) 925-4802	■	■	■	■	■	■
Maine	(207) 624-8522	■	■			■	
Maryland	(410) 230-6261	■	■		■	■	■
Massachusetts	(617) 727-3072	■	■	■	■	■	■
Michigan	(517) 241-9253	■	■	■	■	■	
Minnesota	(651) 296-2388	■	■	■	■	■	■
Mississippi	(601) 856-4652	■	■	■	■	■	■
Missouri	(573) 751-0047	■	■	■	■	■	

493

Registration Laws: Architecture

State Boards		Type of Law		Initial Requirements			Ongoing Req.
		Title Act	Practice Act	College Degree Required	Internship Required	ARE Exam Required	Continuing Education Required
Montana	(406) 841-2367	■	■	■	■	■	
Nebraska	(402) 471-2021	■	■		■	■	■
Nevada	(702) 486-7300	■	■	■	■	■	
New Hampshire	(603) 271-2219	■	■		■	■	
New Jersey	(973) 504-6385	■	■	■	■	■	■
New Mexico	(505) 982-2869	■	■	■	■	■	■
New York	(518) 474-3817	■	■		■	■	■
North Carolina	(919) 733-9544	■	■	■	■	■	■
North Dakota	(701) 223-3540	■	■	■	■	■	
Ohio	(614) 466-2316	■	■	■	■	■	■
Oklahoma	(405) 949-2383	■	■	■	■	■	■
Oregon	(503) 763-0662	■	■	■	■	■	■
Pennsylvania	(717) 783-3397	■	■	CB	■	■	
Rhode Island	(401) 222-2565	■	■	■	■	■	■
South Carolina	(803) 896-4412	■	■	■	■	■	■
South Dakota	(605) 394-2510	■	■	■	■	■	■
Tennessee	(615) 741-3221	■	■	CB	■	■	■
Texas	(512) 305-8535	■	■	CB	■	■	■
Utah	(801) 530-6720	■	■	■	■	■	
Vermont	(802) 828-2373	■	■		■	■	■
Virginia	(804) 367-8514	■	■	■	■	■	
Washington	(360) 664-1388	■	■		■	■	
West Virginia	(304) 528-5825	■	■	■	■	■	■
Wisconsin	(608) 261-4486	■	■		■	■	
Wyoming	(307) 777-7788	■	■	■	■	■	■

CB: Contact Board
Source: National Council of Architectural Registration Boards

Registration Laws: Interior Design

Following is a brief overview of state registration requirements for interior designers. Note that not all states regulate the interior design profession. Due to the complexity of the laws, contact the individual state boards for the most accurate information. The American Society of Interior Designers also provides information on its website, *www.asid.org.*

State Boards		Type of Law		Initial Requirements			Ongoing Req.
		Title Act	Practice Act	College Degree Required	Internship Required	NCIDQ Exam Required	Continuing Education Required
Alabama	(205) 879-4232	■	■	■	■	■	■
Arkansas	(870) 226-6875	■		■	■	■	■
California	(760) 761-4734	*			■	■	■
Colorado	(303) 894-7784	†		‡	■	■	
Connecticut	(860) 713-6145	■		■	■	■	
Dist. of Columbia	(202) 727-1372	■	■	‡	■	■	■
Florida	(850) 487-1395	■	■	‡	■	■	■
Georgia	(478) 207-2440	■		■		■	■
Illinois	(217) 785-0800	■		‡	■	■	
Iowa	(515) 281-7362	■		‡	■	■	■
Kentucky	(859) 246-2069	■		■	■	■	■
Louisiana	(504) 828-6800	■	■	‡	■	■	■
Maine	(207) 624-8603	■		■	■	■	
Maryland	(410) 230-6322	■		■	■	■	■
Minnesota	(651) 296-2388	■		CB	■	■	■
Missouri	(573) 522-4683	■		‡	■	■	■
Nevada	(702) 486-7300	■	■	■	■	■	
New Jersey	(973) 504-6385	■		‡	■	■	■
New Mexico	(505) 476-4865	■		‡	■	■	■
New York	(518) 474-3817	■		‡	■	■	
Oklahoma	(405) 949-2383	■			■	■	
Tennessee	(615) 741-3221	■		‡	■	■	■
Texas	(512) 305-9000	■		‡	■	■	■
Virginia	(804) 367-8512	■		■	■	■	
Wisconsin	(608) 266-5511	■		‡	■	■	■

* Self-certification act   † Permitting statute   ‡ Two years post-high school education required   CB: Contact Board
Source: American Society of Interior Designers

495

Registration Laws: Landscape Architecture

Following is a brief overview of state licensure requirements for landscape architects. Note that not all states regulate the landscape architecture profession. Due to the complexity of the laws, contact the individual state boards for the most accurate information. The Council of Landscape Architectural Registration Boards and the American Society of Landscape Architects also provide information on their websites, *www.clarb.org* and *www.asla.org*.

State Boards		Type of Law		Initial Requirements				Ongoing Req.
		Title Act	Practice Act	Non-LAAB Accred. Degree Accepted	Non-LA Degree with Exp. Accepted	Exp. Only Accepted	LARE Exam Required	Cont. Educ. Required
Alabama	(334) 262-1351		■	■	■	■	■	■
Alaska	(907) 465-2540		■	■	CB	■	■	
Arizona	(602) 364-4930		■	■	■	■	■	
Arkansas	(501) 682-3112		■	■	■	■	■	■
California	(916) 575-7230		■	■			■	
Colorado	(303) 894-7800			■		■	■	
Connecticut	(860) 713-6145		■			■	■	■
Delaware	(302) 744-4537		■				■	■
Florida	(850) 487-1395		■			■	■	■
Georgia	(478) 207-2440		■				■	■
Hawaii	(808) 586-2702		■	■	■	■	■	
Idaho	(208) 334-3233		■			■	■	
Illinois	(217) 782-8556	■					■	
Indiana	(317) 234-3022		■				■	■
Iowa	(515) 281-4126		■	■	■	■	■	■
Kansas	(785) 296-3053		■				■	■
Kentucky	(859) 246-2753		■				■	■
Louisiana	(225) 952-3770		■	■	■	■	■	■
Maine	(207) 624-8522	■		CB	CB	CB	■	
Maryland	(410) 230-6322		■			■	■	
Massachusetts	(617) 727-3072	■				■	■	
Michigan	(517) 241-9288	■				■	■	

State Boards		Type of Law		Initial Requirements				Ongoing Req.
		Title Act	Practice Act	Non-LAAB Accred. Degree Accepted	Non-LA Degree with Exp. Accepted	Exp. Only Accepted	LARE Exam Required	Cont. Educ. Required
Minnesota	(651) 296-2388		■	■	■	■	■	■
Mississippi	(601) 856-4652		■	■	■	■	■	■
Missouri	(573) 751-0047		■				■	
Montana	(406) 841-2351		■				■	
Nebraska	(402) 471-2407		■			■	■	■
Nevada	(775) 688-1316		■	■	■	■	■	
New Hampshire	(603) 271-2219		■	■	■		■	■
New Jersey	(973) 504-6385	■			CB		■	■
New Mexico	(505) 476-4607		■	■	■		■	■
New York	(518) 474-3817		■	■	■		■	■
North Carolina	(919) 850-9088		■	■	■		■	■
North Dakota	(701) 223-3540		■	■	■	■	■	
Ohio	(614) 466-2316		■				■	■
Oklahoma	(405) 949-2383		■				■	■
Oregon	(503) 589-0093		■	■	■	■	■	■
Pennsylvania	(717) 772-8528		■			■	■	■
Rhode Island	(401) 222-1892		■	CB	CB	■	■	
South Carolina	(803) 734-9131		■			■	■	
South Dakota	(605) 394-2510		■				■	■
Tennessee	(615) 741-3221		■				■	■
Texas	(512) 305-9000		■				■	■
Utah	(801) 530-6628		■			■	■	
Virginia	(804) 367-8506	■		■	■	■	■	
Washington	(360) 664-1497	■		■	■	■	■	
West Virginia	(304) 727-5501		■			■	■	■
Wisconsin	(608) 266-2112	■		CB			■	
Wyoming	(307) 777-5403		■			■	■	■

497

CB: Contact board   LAAB: Landscape Architecture Accrediting Board

Source: Council of Landscape Architectural Registration Boards and American Society of Landscape Architects

Salary and Compensation Guide

Every year *DesignIntelligence* tracks the hiring of design professionals. Its annual *Compensation and Benefits Survey* includes benchmark compensation statistics from national and international design firms, coverage of employment issues, and discussions of human resources trends. Please use caution with the below information, an extract from the 2007 study. Regional variations, micro-economic fluctuations within certain professions and building types, and many other factors will cause deviations from these figures.

Additional salary statistics and compensation-related information can be found in the 2007 *Compensation and Benefits Survey* available at *www.di.net.*

Executive Staff

CEO
High Mean: $212,348.06
Low Mean: $173,270.65

Principal, non-owner
High Mean: $136,078.62
Low Mean: $104,258.00

COO
High Mean: $185,100.00
Low Mean: $152,088.10

Associate Principal
High Mean: $117,271.62
Low Mean: $92,240.28

Partner, owner
High Mean: $173,982.63
Low Mean: $128,798.74

Note: The above are pre-bonus figures. In the current economy, most principals receive a significant bonus with target bonuses often ranging from 25 to 100 percent or higher. The most common target bonus for partners/owners in the 2007 survey was 20 percent; the second-most-common was in excess of 100 percent.

Technical Staff

Project Manager, 15+ years exp.
High Mean: $108,496.21
Low Mean: $80,328.15

Architect, 5+ years exp.
High Mean: $64,518.96
Low Mean: $51,709.11

Project Manager, 10+ years exp.
High Mean: $86,116.06
Low Mean: $74,793.43

Interior Designer, 15+ years exp.
High Mean: $89,078.48
Low Mean: $70,867.17

Architect, 15+ years exp.
High Mean: $96.928.18
Low Mean: $72,678.28

Interior Designer, 10+ years exp.
High Mean: $69,575.31
Low Mean: $57,966.09

Architect, 10+ years exp.
High Mean: $79,918.73
Low Mean: $62,608.29

Interior Designer, 5+ years exp.
High Mean: $56,865.90
Low Mean: $45,983.98

Landscape Architect, 15+ years exp.
High Mean: $87,643.20
Low Mean: $74,000.77

Landscape Architect, 10+ years exp.
High Mean: $67,496.30
Low Mean: $60,085.19

Landscape Architect, 5+ years exp.
High Mean: $58,672.92
Low Mean: $48,077.60

Product Designer, 15+ years exp.
High Mean: $86,000.00
Low Mean: $66,500.00

Product Designer, 10+ years exp.
High Mean: $69,400.00
Low Mean: $57,600.00

Product Designer, 5+ years exp.
High Mean: $51,375.00
Low Mean: $44,333.33

IT Manager
High Mean: $81,195.81
Low Mean: $69,476.57

Note: The above are pre-bonus figures. In the current economy, most technical staff receive a bonus often ranging from 4 to 30 percent or higher.

Non-Technical Staff

Marketing Director
High Mean: $87,647.87
Low Mean: $73,894.43

Marketing Associate
High Mean: $63,969.90
Low Mean: $51,192.78

Marketing Assistant
High Mean: $46,988.69
Low Mean: $38,202.45

Office Manager
High Mean: $66,604.08
Low Mean: $52,878.95

Administrative Assistant
High Mean: $46,696.19
Low Mean: $33,821.30

Architecture Interns, Year 1

East
High Mean: $39,688
Low Mean: $35,468

West
High Mean: $41,687
Low Mean: $35,767

Midwest
High Mean: $37,751
Low Mean: $32,419

South
High Mean: $38,983
Low Mean: $34,282

499

Source: DesignIntelligence

10

OBITUARIES

This chapter is a celebration of the lives and contributions of the design and preservation leaders, patrons, and advocates who died between Aug. 1, 2006, and July 31, 2007.

Laurie Baker, 90

Laurie Baker, a British-born architect who spent his career in India building homes for the poor, died April 1, 2007. A meeting with Gandhi while passing through India during World War II inspired Baker, raised a Quaker, to later return to the country and apply his skills to help those less fortunate. A citizen of India since 1988, Baker's environmentally friendly structures utilized traditional Indian building methods. He rarely used steel or concrete, preferring locally availably materials, such as mud, brick, stone, terracotta tile, and coconut thatch. In addition to more than 2,000 houses, Baker designed educational, healthcare, industrial, and religious structures. In 1985 he co-founded the Centre of Science and Technology for Rural Development, a non-profit group that has built homes for more than 10,000 poor families.

Peter Blake, 86

Peter Blake, a German émigré who went on to become an architect, editor and author, museum curator, and a friend to many of the great minds in Modern art and architecture, died December 5, 2006. Born Peter Jost Blach, he fled with his family to England during Hitler's rise to power. He eventually moved to the United States, served as an Army intelligence officer, changed his name to Blake, and studied architecture at the University of Pennsylvania. During this period he formed friendships with some of the prominent names in art and architecture, including Jackson Pollack, Charles Eames, and Louis Kahn, who he briefly worked for. Blake was curator of architecture and design at the Museum of Modern Art from 1948 to 1950, then edited *Architectural Forum* until the magazine's demise in 1972. He founded his own journal, *Architecture Plus*, which was published until 1975. Blake then moved into academia, chairing the architecture departments at the Boston Architectural Center, 1975–79, and Catholic University. All the while he also practiced. His best-known projects are modernist homes on Long Island, some designed with Julian Neski, as well as a never-built museum for Jackson Pollack called the Ideal Museum. Blake authored numerous books, including a monograph on Marcel Breuer, *The Master Builders: Le Corbusier, Mies van der Rohe, Frank Lloyd Wright*; *Form Follows Fiasco: Why Modern Architecture Hasn't Worked*; and his 1993 memoir, *No Place Like Utopia: Modern Architecture and the Company We Kept.*

503

First row, from top left: **Sheldon Fox**, **Gregory Clement**, **Richard Blinder** (Photo: Chia Messina)
Second row, from top left: **Alan Fletcher** (Photo: Martin Dunkerton, courtesy of the Fletcher family)
Third row, from top left: **Julie Thoma Wright**, **Thomas Galloway**, **Margaret Helfand**
Fourth row, from top left: **Gerrard Haworth**, **Hans Wegner**, **Bill Stumpf** (Photo courtesy of Herman Miller)

Richard L. Blinder, 71

Richard Blinder, a founding partner of the New York firm Beyer Blinder Belle, died September 7, 2006. Best known for historic preservation work, such as the Ellis Island Immigration Museum and the renovation of Grand Central Station, the firm was also responsible for many new design projects. With a passion for museum and theater projects, Blinder took the lead on such projects as the Rubin Museum of Art in Chelsea, Manhattan, and the Ford Center for the Performing Arts (now Hilton Theater) in Times Square. A 1960 graduate of the Harvard Graduate School of Design, Blinder started the firm with John Belle and John H. Beyer in 1968, and all had been working at the time in the New York office of Victor Gruen. Inspired by Jane Jacobs' preservation work and a new interest in New York's historic architecture, the firm developed a niche in preservation work. Some of Blinder's other projects with the firm included the renovation of a building for the Japan Society, the Center for Jewish History, and the Henry Luce III Center for the Study of American Culture at the New York Historical Society, all in Manhattan. A 1979 inductee into the American Institute of Architects College of Fellows, he founded the James Martston Finch Charitable Trust to support historic preservation projects. Beyer Blinder Belle won the national AIA Firm Award in 1995.

Colin Boyne, 85

British architecture critic Colin Boyne died September 28, 2006. Famous for his rigorous interest in social architecture, the utopian ideas of modernism, wise planning, and, later, environmental design, Boyne's writing initiated discourse and influenced designers in England and the British Isles for many years. He joined the staff of the *Architects' Journal* in 1947 and served as the magazine's editor from 1953 to 1970. After leaving the publication, Boyne became chairman of the Architectural Press' editorial board, which controlled *Architects' Journal* and its sister publication *Architectural Review*, until 1982. Boyne was named a fellow of the Royal Institute of British Architects in 1977.

Giulio Castelli, 86

Giulio Castelli, a chemical engineer who founded the Italian design firm Kartell with his wife Anna Castelli Ferrieri in 1949, died October 6, 2006. Famous for its expansive line of mostly high-end plastic furniture and housewares from marquee designers such as Phillipe Starck, Ron Arad, Ettore Sottsass, and Joe Columbo, Kartell was originally a manufacturer of car accessories. Studying under Nobel Prize-winning chemist Giulio Natta, Castelli expanded polymer research into industrial products and was a leading force in reducing the cost of plastics. Castelli was also a founder of the Italian Association for Industrial Design and helped organize the Compasso d'Oro award, which promotes Italian design worldwide. Castelli opened the Kartell Museum in Milan in 2000, and, at the time of his death, was working on a book about Italian design entrepreneurs.

Giorgio Cavaglieri, 95

Giorgio Cavaglieri, a New York City architect and preservation pioneer, died May 15, 2007. An Italian Jew, born in Venice, who designed airfields for Mussolini before fleeing to the United States, Cavaglieri helped define New York City's preservation movement. He founded his own firm in New York in the early 1950s. An advocate of adaptive reuse as opposed to slavish re-creations, Cavaglieri's projects generated both extreme praise and criticism. His most notable project was the transformation of the Jefferson Market Library in Greenwich Village in the mid-1960s, a project often credited as the first successful preservation initiative in New York City following the failed efforts to save Penn Station. Cavaglieri was also a leader in the battle to save Grand Central Station. To celebrate his achievements, the New York Landmarks Conservancy presented Cavaglieri with the Lucy G. Moses Preservation Leadership Award in 2002.

Gregory Clement III, 56

Kohn Pedersen Fox Associates managing partner Gregory Clement died April 11, 2007. Clement joined the firm in 1984, after working at I.M. Pei & Partners, and became managing partner in 1993. He oversaw several of the firm's most important projects during his tenure there, including the Rodin Museum and the New Songdo City Master Plan, both in South Korea, and the renovation of the Museum of Modern Art in New York, with Yoshio Taniguchi. Clement was named a fellow of the American Institute of Architects in 2005.

Eli W. Cohen, 80

Chicago structural engineer Eli Cohen died May 2, 2007. His lengthy career included work for some of the premier architects of the day, Philip Johnson, Helmut Jahn, Tadao Ando, Cesar Pelli, Ricardo Bofill, and design innovations that allowed for more creative and efficient construction methods for tall buildings. Cohen integrated construction techniques used for power plant cooling towers, which he learned early in his career, into high-rise buildings, centralizing functionality within a concrete core. This allowed large, column-free spans on the exterior and room for greater architectural expression. After fighting for the independence of Israel in the late 1940s, Cohen came to the United States and graduated from the University of Illinois at Urbana–Champaign. He joined the Chicago firm Paul Rogers Associates, becoming partner in 1965, and then became a partner at Cohen-Barreto-Marchertas, which merged with the Thornton-Tomasetti Group in 1993. Between 1969 and 1973, CBM provided the structural engineering on more than 350 projects, including 70 high-rise buildings.

George Edson Danforth, 90

George Danforth, a former student of Mies van der Rohe's and his successor as head of the School of Architecture at the Illinois Institute of Technology, died June 5, 2007. Danforth began his studies under Mies at the then Armour Institute in 1936, when he was 17. He earned his bachelor's degree in 1940 and a graduate degree in 1943. From 1939 to 1944, Danforth was a draftsman in Mies' office, and from 1941 to 1953 he taught at IIT. He subsequently taught at Western Reserve University (now part of Case Western Reserve University) in Cleveland, OH. When he left IIT in 1959, Mies van der Rohe suggested Danforth as his replacement, and his former student served as the architecture school's director until 1975. Danforth also practiced architecture from 1949 to 1980. He was elected to the American Institute of Architects' College of Fellows in 1967.

Marian Despres, 97

Marian Despres, a founder of the Chicago Architecture Foundation and a leading preservationist in that city, died January 4, 2007. The wife of former Chicago Alderman Leon Despres and daughter of architect Alfred S. Alschuler, Despres had a working knowledge of both politics and architecture. She earned a PhD in psychology from the University of Chicago and taught until her children were young. As they got older, she began pursuing her interest in architecture, helping to save Henry Hobson Richardson's Glessner House and to found the Chicago Architecture Foundation, which bought and restored the historic structure. Her many other efforts included protests to stop the expansion of Lakeshore Drive through Jackson Park and prevent the demolition of Louis Sullivan's Garrick Theater and old Chicago Stock Exchange. Despres developed the first docent training course for the

CAF's tour guides; today there are more than 450 active docents leading 50 different city tours. Despres also served on the Chicago Landmarks Commission from 1985 to 2000.

Norman Kemmerer Dorf, 68

Norman Dorf, an architect and educator who dedicated his career to helping students pass the Architectural Registration Exam, died June 28, 2007. Dorf spent 16 years on the ARE committee of the National Council of Architectural Registration Boards, creating and grading exams and authoring study guides. He wrote the study guide *Solutions,* prepared a home study course for students, and traveled around the country lecturing and teaching exam candidates. As chair of the NCARB Research and Development Committee, Dorf led the design of the new computerized test. He also served two years on the NCARB Board of Directors. Following graduation from the Massachusetts Institute of Technology in 1963, Dorf joined Marcel Breuer's practice, working on the Whitney Museum in New York and the Abbey Church for St. John's University in Collegeville, MN. He then joined Davis, Brody & Associates where he was the project manager for the 1982 restoration of the New York Public Library and the Hoyt Biochemical Sciences Lab at Princeton University.

James W. Elmore, 89

James Elmore, the founding dean of the College of Architecture at Arizona State University, died April 19, 2007. Following service in the Army Corps of Engineers during World War II, he received a master's degree in architecture from Columbia University. In 1948 Elmore moved to Phoenix, opening a practice and teaching at Arizona State College in Tempe. There he helped organize the university's architecture and landscape architecture program. He was also instrumental in the realization of the Rio Salado project, a restoration of over 30 miles of river corridor in Phoenix. Elmore was involved in transportation issues for the area, as well as championing light rail, solar energy, and sustainability initiatives. He was a founding member of the environmental group Valley Forward. Elmore was elected to the American Institute of Architects' College of Fellows in 1966.

Avery C. Faulkner, 78

Avery Faulkner, a Washington, DC-based architect responsible for buildings at George Washington University, the Smithsonian Institution, American

University, and the National Zoo, died February 21, 2007. The son and nephew of renowned architects Waldron and Winthrop Faulkner, respectively, the younger Faulkner received bachelor's and master's degrees in architecture from Yale University. He was a winner of the Rome Prize but declined it to accept the Yale Traveling Fellowship. He worked for the firm Faulkner, Kingsbury and Stenhouse before becoming senior partner of Faulkner, Fryer and Vanderpool architects in 1968. Faulkner was elected to the American Institute of Architects' College of Fellows in 1980 and was appointed by President Ronald Reagan to the Advisory Council on Historic Preservation in 1987. In addition to numerous AIA awards, he received a GSA Biennial Design Award for his 1971 lion and tiger exhibit at the National Zoo.

Alan Fletcher, 75

Renowned British graphic designer and a founder of Pentagram, Alan Fletcher died September 21, 2006. Described by the *New York Times* as a "powerhouse of contemporary British business and cultural graphic design," his client list included Reuters, Olivetti, Pirelli, Cunard, the Victoria and Albert Museum, and Lloyds of London. In 1972 he co-founded Pentagram, a pioneering multidisciplinary design firm, with Colin Forbes, Theo Crosby, Kenneth Grange, and Mervyn Kurlansky. (Previously, Fletcher and Forbes had partnered with Bob Gill in the firm Fletcher/Forbes/Gill.) Pentagram became famous for branding and book and logo design; though by 1991 Fletcher chose to leave the company to focus on small, engaging projects. He became creative director of Phaidon in 1994, designing numerous books, including his own 2001 book *The Art of Looking Sideways*. In November 2006 the publisher posthumously issued *Alan Fletcher: Picturing & Poeting*. That same month, London's Design Museum, the institution to which Fletcher donated his archive, presented the first retrospective of his work.

Norman C. Fletcher, 89

Norman Fletcher, a co-founder with Walter Gropius and six other architects, of The Architects Collaborative, died May 31, 2007. A graduate of Yale University, Fletcher worked briefly for Skidmore, Owings & Merrill and then Saarinen, Swanson & Associates before establishing TAC in Boston in 1945. For 60 years, the firm operated an egalitarian practice, with each partner receiving the same compensation. Fletcher directed many projects for the firm, including buildings for Harvard and Clark universities; many schools in New England; offices for IBM; a planned community for 60,000 in Redwood

City, CA; and the Sterling and Francine Clark Art Institute in Williamstown, MA, with Pietro Belluschi. However, Fletcher's favorite project was the 1972 headquarters for the American Institute of Architects in Washington, DC. In 1964 TAC was the second firm to receive the American Institute of Architects' Firm Award, the highest honor bestowed on a firm. Fletcher was also a fellow of the AIA.

Sheldon Fox, 76

Kohn Pedersen Fox Associates co-founder Sheldon Fox died December 16, 2006. The New York-based firm was founded in 1976 and has since won more than 200 awards for its urban projects worldwide. After many years with Kahn & Jacobs, Architects, Fox joined the firm of John Carl Warnecke & Associates in 1972 as a senior vice president. There he met A. Eugene Kohn and William Pedersen. Later the three launched their own firm, Kohn Pedersen Fox, with Kohn acting as marketing principal, Pederson as design principal, and Fox as managing principal. The firm's many outstanding projects include the World Bank headquarters in Washington, DC; 333 West Wacker Drive in Chicago; Proctor & Gamble's Cincinnati headquarters, and a group of six buildings on New York's west side for ABC television. Fox was a fellow of the American Institute of Architects and the Architectural League of New York.

Thomas D. Galloway, 67

Thomas Galloway, dean of the College of Architecture at the Georgia Institute of Technology, died March 11, 2007. He is credited with enhancing the program through outreach to alumni, the Atlanta community, and international institutions, as well as developing new research initiatives and programs of study. Galloway joined Georgia Tech in 1992 from Iowa State University, where he was the dean of the College of Design. During his tenure at Georgia Tech, he forged study-abroad partnerships with universities in France and China and worked to develop a College of Engineering and Design with the University of Abu Dhabi in the United Arab Emirates. Two endowed chairs were created under him: the Harry West Chair for Quality Growth and Regional Development and the Thomas W. Ventulett III Distinguished Chair in Architectural Design. Galloway earned his master's and PhD in urban planning from the University of Washington. He was also a senior fellow of the Design Futures Council.

Richard Giegengack, 65

Washington, DC, architect Richard Giegengack died January 11, 2007. He joined Skidmore, Owings & Merrill's DC office in 1973 and later worked in the firm's New York and London offices before openning his own DC firm in 1993. During his career with SOM, Giegengack worked on the 1976 bicentennial master plan for the Mall and Constitution Gardens and the Northeast Corridor Improvement Project, which included the restoration of eight National Historic Landmark railroad stations between Boston and Washington. He designed a new railroad station for Providence, RI, and was instrumental in planning the renovation of Washington's Union Station. Since 1994 he had become engaged in working on the restoration and preservation of Camp Topridge in New York's Adirondacks, a 105-acre compound with 40 buildings once owned by Marjorie Merriweather Post. Giegengack earned his architecture degree from Yale University.

Ludwig Glaeser, 76

Ludwig Glaeser, a Mies van der Rohe expert and the first curator of his archive at the Museum of Modern Art, died September 27, 2006. Raised and educated in Germany, Glaeser moved to New York in 1963 to join MoMA's Department of Architecture and Design as an associate curator. In 1968, Mies van der Rohe gave the museum all the surviving documents, nearly 20,000 items, from his Berlin office, and Glaeser was appointed the archive's first curator. He held this position until 1980 when he departed to become the first director of the new Canadian Centre for Architecture in Montreal. In addition to numerous articles and papers, Glaeser wrote several books about Mies, including *Mies van der Rohe: Drawings in the Collection of the Museum of Modern Art* and *Ludwig Mies van der Rohe: Furniture and Furniture Designs from the Design Collection and the Mies van der Rohe Archive.*

Gerrard Wendell Haworth, 95

The founder and chairman of Michigan-based Haworth, Inc., a leading American manufacturer of office environments, Gerrard Haworth died October 25, 2007. He began the company in 1948 working from his garage; Haworth would grow to become a $1.4 billion corporation and one of the 400 largest private US companies, according to *Forbes* magazine. The company is credited with revolutionizing the office furniture industry with the invention of the pre-wired office furniture panel. The University of Michigan honored Haworth as the 1993 Entrepreneur of the Year. He also received

511

Western Michigan University's Distinguished Alumni Award in 1986 and was awarded a honorary doctorate from the Kendall College of Art and Design in 1987. In 1989 the Haworth family gave $5 million to Western Michigan University, and in appreciation, the school named its business school the Haworth College of Business.

Ray Hebert, 86

Former *Los Angeles Times* reporter Ray Hebert died April 26, 2007. Herbert was one of the first journalists in the country to cover city and regional planning. He wrote about water issues, sprawl, and traffic problems from 1960 until his retirement in 1988. His 1965 series on traffic congestion "Are We Losing Our Mobility?" seems especially prescient today. Hebert joined the staff of the *LA Times* in 1951, following work for United Press International.

Margaret Helfand, 59

Margaret Helfand, a Manhattan-based architect and planner, died June 20, 2007. Helfand had operated her own firm, Helfand Architects, since 1981 and was known for her use of natural materials and modernist forms and the integration of her buildings into the landscape. Among Helfand's noteworthy projects were the United Science Center at Swarthmore College (with Einhorn Yaffee Prescott) in Pennsylvania; the Automated Trading Desk office complex in Mount Pleasant, SC (with McKellar & Associates); the New York and Chicago headquarters for *Time Out* magazine; the NYU Stern School of Business; and the Friends Seminary School in Manhattan. Helfand become a fellow of the American Institute of Architects in 1998 and served as president of the AIA's New York chapter in 2001. Following the destruction of the World Trade Center, she chaired New York New Visions, an advisory group to governmental agencies on design and planning guidelines for the redevelopment of Lower Manhattan.

Jules Horton, 87

Architectural lighting design pioneer Jules Horton died February 23, 2007. In 1968 Horton founded Jules G. Horton Lighting Design, now Horton Lees Brogden Lighting Design. Renowned for innovations in lighting design for signage, streets, and architectural applications, Horton took equipment used in other applications and applied it to lighting design. His projects included the Dallas/Fort Worth International Airport, Jeddah International Airport, the University of Petroleum and Minerals in Saudi Arabia, and Tour de Credit

Lyonais in Lyon, France. Horton was honored posthumously at the IALD (International Association of Lighting Designers) Awards Dinner in May 2007.

Richard H. Howland, 96

Leading US architectural historian and preservationist Richard Howland died October 24, 2006. Following service with the Office of Strategic Service identifying areas of high cultural value in Europe during World War II, Howland earned his doctorate in classical archeology from Johns Hopkins University. He remained on the faculty at the university and became chair of its new Department of Art History, which he helped organize in 1947. While in Baltimore, he researched the city's 19th-century architecture and co-authored, with Eleanor Patterson Spencer, the 1953 *The Architecture of Baltimore*. He left Baltimore to head the National Trust, from 1956 to 1960, and then joined the Smithsonian Institution's Department of Civil History, first as head curator, then chairman. Smithsonian secretary Dillon Ripley tapped Howland to serve as his special assistant in 1968, a position he held until his retirement in 1985. Howland was also a co-founder, and later vice president, of the Society of Architectural Historians and a founding member of the International Council on Monuments and Sites. During his career, he served as a trustee of the Athenaeum in Philadelphia, National Building Museum, and Victorian Society in America, of which he was later its president. He was also a member of the US Park Service's consulting committee for National Historic Landmarks and served on the Mount Vernon advisory committee. His work to support the British National Trust resulted in the award of the Order of the British Empire by Queen Elizabeth in 1991.

Sam Huddleston, 92

Nationally noted landscape architect and regional planner Sam Huddleston died January 5, 2007. His firm, Sam L. Huddleston and Associates, was in business for 35 years. He believed in using native plants and that people should adapt their lifestyles to be in harmony with the environment. In 1975, he co-authored the book, with Michael Hussey, *Grow Native: Landscaping with Native and Apt Plants of the Rocky Mountains*, which pre-dated widespread interest in xeriscaping and the water conservation movement. He was also a co-founder of the Colorado chapter of the American Society of Landscape Architects and was named a national fellow of the group in 1962. He was also a member of the American Institute of Certified Planners.

John Hutton, 59

Former Donghia design director John Hutton died August 17, 2006. Hutton joined the high-end textile and furniture company in 1978 and left in 1998 to establish his own firm. While at Donghia, Hutton produced more than 200 designs, including the Anziano chair, originally designed for the American Academy in Rome. His work combined contemporary design with a classical foundation, with a particular affinity for the 18th-century Italian architect Palladio. With offices in West Islip, NY, and Nancy, France, Hutton's own firm designed collections for Sutherland Teak, Hickory Business Furniture, Flexform, and Holly Hunt, among others. During the 1980s, Hutton, with Donghia and interior designer Brian Stoner, helped furnish homes for Diana Ross, Liza Minelli, Steve Martin, Ralph Loren, Mary Tyler Moore, and Barbara Walters. He also worked for commercial clients, including Sony, the American Center in Paris, and several cruise ship lines. Many of his designs have been collected by such institutions as the Brooklyn Museum and the Houston Museum of Fine Arts.

Huson Jackson, 93

Longtime Harvard Graduate School of Design professor Huson Jackson died October 1, 2006. He had also been a partner in the Cambridge, MA, firm of Sert Jackson & Associates with José Lluis Sert, who had worked in Le Corbusier's atelier in the 1940s and was a dean of the Harvard GSD. Following work with Charles Eames during the 1930s, Jackson studied under Walter Gropius and Marcel Breuer at the Harvard Graduate School of Design, earning a master's degree in architecture in 1939. He joined the Harvard faculty in 1953, where he taught until 1970. In 1958 he and Sert formed Sert Jackson & Associates, which earned the AIA Firm Award in 1977. Their commissions included projects for Harvard, Boston University, MIT, and Princeton, as well as multifamily housing projects worldwide. In Barcelona, their building for the Joan Miro Foundation, completed in 1975, received an AIA Honor Award in 1979 and the AIA Twenty-five Year Award in 2002. Their Peabody Terrace student-housing complex at Harvard won an AIA Honor Award in 1965; in 1979 the Undergraduate Science Center at Harvard was recognized with an Honor Award, as was a housing project on New York's Roosevelt Island in 1981. Le Corbusier chose the firm as collaborating architects for his only US building, the Carpenter Center for the Visual Arts at Harvard. Jackson was elected to the American Institute of Architects' College of Fellows in 1975.

Lady Bird Johnson, 94

Lady Bird Johnson, former First Lady and wife of President Lyndon Baines Johnson, died July 11, 2007. Known as the "Environmental First Lady," she was a tireless advocate for national beautification. She is credited as the driving force behind President Johnson's many environmental initiatives, including the Beautification Act of 1965, which called for control of outdoor advertising and removal of roadside trash and encouraged scenic enhancement of roadways. Under the Johnson administration nearly 200 laws affecting the environment were passed adding momentum to a growing national conservation movement. Though she felt the term "beautification" trivialized the issue of environmental stewardship, Lady Bird formed the Committee for a More Beautiful Capital in 1964 to make Washington, DC, a model for the nation. The result was a privately funded bevy of flower and tree planting projects that still enhance the city. Lady Bird visited historic sites across the country with the media, calling attention to areas such as the Hudson River Valley in New York, historic sites in Virginia, and the California Redwood forests. Upon returning to Texas, Lady Bird focused her efforts there, culminating in the establishment of the National Wildflower Research Center, later renamed the Lady Bird Johnson Wildflower Center, a leading center for research and education projects related to wildflower located in Austin. She was also an honorary member of the American Society of Landscape Architects.

Warren D. Jones, 92

Warren D. Jones, a professor emeritus in the College of Architecture and Landscape Architecture at the University of Arizona, died April 7, 2007. He joined the university in 1966 shortly after the landscape architecture department was established, retiring in 1984. During his tenure, he planted nearly 400 tree species, a total of almost 5,000 trees, on the campus, testing their suitability for landscaping uses in the climate. Many were exotic heritage trees since designated Great Trees of Arizona. Following his retirement, Jones served as an adviser to the Arizona-Sonora Desert Museum and as a board member of the Boyce Thompson Arboretum. The author of several books on developing plants for dry climates, Jones was named a Master of the Southwest by *Phoenix Home & Garden* magazine in 1992.

515

Warren W. Jones, 78

Author, educator, and city planner Warren W. Jones died May 10, 2007. He was the founder of Solano Press, a California publisher specializing in titles related to land use, planning law, urban affairs, and environmental issues. In the late 1950s he worked as an assistant city planner for Berkeley and Santa Cruz while finishing his master's work at the University of California, Berkeley. He established his own firm, Warren W. Jones & Associates in 1961, and five years later joined Douglas Duncan in practice, changing the firm's name to Duncan and Jones. While practicing, Jones taught city planning classes in the UC Extension Division, and he wrote the university's first correspondence course in city planning. He stopped practicing in 1974 and devoted himself full-time to the extension programs. Jones founded Solano Press in 1985.

George Kovacs, 80

George Kovacs, a design innovator who introduced modern lighting fixtures to the US market, died June 22, 2007. His half-century of work as a designer, manufacturer, importer, and sales outlet for cutting-edge lighting made him a household name in the lighting industry and to aficionados of modernism. A native of Austria who spent the war years in the United States, Kovacs began importing Austrian Kalmar lamps in the mid-1950s. He eventually opened three retail stores on the East side of Manhattan and began manufacturing fixtures in a facility in Queens. In addition to his own designs, Kovacs marketed the work of such designers as Ingo Maurer, Isamu Noguchi, and Karim Rashid. Kovacs is credited with introducing the now-ubiquitous halogen torchiere to the US. He retired in 2000.

Denis G. Kuhn, 65

Denis Kuhn, a principal in Ehrenkrantz Eckstut & Kuhn Architects and a specialist in preservation and adaptive reuse architecture, died May 10, 2007. Kuhn was responsible for the restoration of Cass Gilbert's 1900 Beaux-Arts Custom House in Lower Manhattan, now the Smithsonian Institution's National Museum. He also helped transform the former New York Police Department headquarters in Little Italy into luxury apartments, a project critic Paul Goldberger wrote in 1990 was "probably the grandest Manhattan apartment residence south of the Dakota." Also in New York he was instrumental in renovations of the Federal Reserve Bank of New York, the Equitable Building, and the Astor Library. He also designed the Hollywood and Highland, a Los Angeles entertainment complex that includes the Kodak Theater, home of the Academy Awards. A Pratt Institute graduate, Kuhn joined Ehrenkrantz Eckstut & Whitelaw in 1979; the firm became Ehrenkrantz Eckstut & Kuhn in 1997. The winner of many local and national design and preservation awards, Kuhn was elected to the American Institute of Architects' College of Fellows in 1993.

Walter Charles Leedy Jr., 64

Cleveland State University professor and medieval architecture expert Walter Leedy died November 7, 2006. His 1980 book *Fan Vaulting: A Study of Form, Technology, and Meaning* has become the definitive tome on this medieval construction technique. Following study in Poland as a graduate student, Leedy received his doctorate from the Courtauld Art Institute in London in 1972. That year he joined the faculty of Cleveland State, quickly rising to chair of a combined art and art history department. He began to study and write about the built environment in Cleveland while developing a large collection of postcards and other brochures from the city's past. He later donated his collection to the Cleveland State University library and endowed a fund for the continued acquisition of documents of this kind. A longtime member of the Society of Architectural Historians, Leeds served on the SAH board from 1982 to 1984. He was also on the board of the Medieval Society of America.

William J. LeMessurier, 81

Structural engineer William LeMessurier died June 14, 2007. He is best known as the designer of the structural systems for Manhattan's 1977 Citicorp building, designed by Hugh Stubbins & Associates. LeMessurier designed a unique framing system for the tower and utilized the first tuned mass damper (a block of concrete floating on a film of oil and linked to the top of the frame by springs) to reduce wind vibration. Shortly after the building was completed, he discovered that the bracing on the outside of the building was inadequate, leaving it prone to hurricane-force winds. He quietly worked with the architect and the building's owner to repair the problem. The 900-foot-tall building is now fortified to withstand not only a hurricane of the force that might occur every 16 years, but a 700-year storm. The problem with the tower and its subsequent structural work was not known by the public, thanks in part to a 1978 newspaper strike, until a 1995 *New Yorker* article by Joe Morgenstern revealed the story. LeMessurier is generally regarded as a hero by other structural engineers for discovering, fixing, and

517

acknowledging the design flaw. He was trained as an architect at the Harvard Graduate School of Design before receiving his master's degree in engineering from the Massachusetts Institute of Technology in 1953. He started his own firm in 1961 and worked on a variety of marquee projects during his career. LeMessurier also taught at Harvard and MIT for many years.

Ivan Luini, 46

Ivan Luini, the president of Kartell U.S. Inc., died September 15, 2006. Luini had been largely responsible for the rapid and successful US expansion of Kartell, the Italian design firm known for its high-concept plastic furniture and housewares in collaboration with some of the world's A-list designers. Luini joined Kartell in 1998 and opened the first American Kartell showroom in New York, soon after rolling out stores in Miami, San Francisco, Atlanta, Boston, and Los Angeles. These outlets allowed buyers to take home high-end pieces of contemporary design with no lead time, much as Kartell founder Giulio Castelli did in the 1950s when he helped formulate plastics polymers that lowered the material's cost and increased its use in industrial design. Before joining Kartell, Luini worked for B&B Italia; helped introduce European design companies Cappellini, Flexorm, Ingo Maruer, and Fontana Arte to the United States through his company I.L. Euro, Inc.; and co-founded the lighting company Luceplan USA.

Tucker Madawick, 89

Industrial designer Tucker Madawick died September 13, 2006. His lengthy design career included automotive and airplane design as well as consumer and electronic products. He was a member of the first class of industrial designers at Pratt Institute, graduating in 1938. He joined Ford, working on its automotive team then on the B-24 bomber project. Following work for Corvair on the B-36 bomber, he joined Lippincott & Margulies, where he was a member of the design team for the ill-fated Tucker automobile. In 1947 Madawick went to work for Raymond Loewy Associates, where he established the firm's London office. Loewy sent him to join the Studebaker Starliner design team in South Bend, IN, in 1950. Unveiled in 1953, the automobile established Studebaker as a leader in automotive style innovation. Madawick then began a long career with RCA in 1959, hired as the manager of radio, phonograph, tape, and television design. His multidisciplinary approach produced some of the company's most enduring and innovative concepts. He retired in 1980 as vice president of consumer electronic products. A 1964 fel-

low of the Industrial Designers Institute, he was later president of its successor organization, the Industrial Designers Society of America. He was also
awarded a lifetime achievement award from the Cooper-Hewitt, National
Design Museum.

Vico Magistretti, 86

Industrial designer Vico Magistretti died September 19, 2006. An architect
and teacher as well as a designer of furniture and lighting, Magistretti was
born in Milan and worked for many years there, initially on post-war architecture projects and later on industrial design projects, many of them plastic,
which was then a cutting-edge material. His numerous projects, including
the Carimate chair, the Atollo table lamp, the Selene chair, and the
Maralunga sofa, were produced by Kartell, Cassina, Artemide, and other premier European manufacturers. He is credited for several design innovations
related to the use of plastics, and 12 of his designs are in the permanent collection of the Museum of Modern Art in New York. Eighty percent of his
work remains in production today. As an architect, Magistretti is renown for
his simple, modern, humanistic designs for office and municipal buildings
around Milan, as well as the Milano-San Felice planned community. He also
taught at the Royal College of Arts in London for 20 years.

Martin Meyerson, 84

Planner, author, and former president of the University of Pennsylvania,
Martin Meyerson died June 2, 2007. While dean of the College of
Environmental Design at the University of California, Berkeley, Meyerson was
chosen as the school's interim chancellor during 1964–65. He then served
four years as president of the Buffalo campus of the State University of New
York before joining Penn in 1970. Meyerson retired from Penn in 1981, leaving a legacy of international expansion and community outreach and a commitment to the role of the liberal arts at a research university. Educated at
Columbia and Harvard, Meyerson worked briefly for the Philadelphia
Planning Commission before joining the faculty of the University of Chicago
in 1948. He then taught at Penn, Harvard, and Berkeley. He was the first
director of the MIT-Harvard Joint Center for Urban Studies. Meyerson also
wrote several books, including *Politics, Planning, and Public Interest* with
Edward C. Banfield. Meyerson was a fellow of the American Academy of Arts
and Sciences, the American Association for the Advancement of Science, the
Royal Society of Arts in Great Britain, and the American Institute of Certified

Planners. The University of Pennsylvania's Graduate School of Fine Arts is named Meyerson Hall in his honor.

Valerius Leo Michelson, 90

University of Minnesota professor and acclaimed Modern architect Valerius (Val) Michelson died August 3, 2006. Born Valerius Mikhelson in Russia, he was captured by the Germans during World War II and later immigrated to the United States where he studied architecture. From 1952 to 1960 he worked for Marcel Breuer in New York. When Breuer's office designed Abbey Church for St. John's University in Collegeville, MN, Michelson was the supervising architect. Afterward, he stayed in Minnesota and joined the faculty of the University of Minnesota, where he taught design and architectural structure for 22 years. During that time he also led an active practice, designing St. Paul's Monastery in Maplewood, MN; buildings for the Itasca Community College in Grand Rapids, MI; and the Bierman Field Stadium at the University of Minnesota, among others. He was elected to the American Institute of Architects' College of Fellows in 1979. Michelson also served as adviser to Minnesota's Capitol Area Architectural and Planning Board from 1983 to 1997.

Joseph Miller, 88

Joseph Miller, an architect and longtime Catholic University professor, died September 26, 2007. Miller was a graduate of Catholic University, and as a member of its faculty he served as professor, director of the urban design program, and associate dean of graduate studies. He also helped found an autonomous School of Architecture and Planning at the university. A proponent of socially responsible architecture, Miller impressed upon his students the need to use their skills to benefit communities. Operating his own practice for more than 35 years, Miller's projects, more than 110 of them, included work for charitable and community organizations, school systems, low-rent housing initiatives, synagogues, preservation projects, and commercial facilities. He served 17 years in the D.C. Redevelopment Land Agency and was an arbitrator for the American Arbitration Association on architecture and construction-related matters.

Dan Saxon Palmer, 86

Architect Dan Palmer, best known as a prolific designer, with William Krisel, of 1950s modernist tract homes in Southern California, died December 22, 2006. From 1950 to 1964, Palmer and Krisel capitalized on the need for affordable housing in booming Los Angeles and its surrounding, working mostly for developers George and Bob Alexander. By designing for maximum cost efficiency, the architects proved to the developer that modern homes could be developed in tract situations at a high profit margin. And buyers snapped them up. With flat or butterfly roofs, open spaces, and modern amenities, more than 20,000 of the architects' homes were built, not only in California but also in Arizona, Nevada, Texas, and Florida. Palmer and Krisel had worked together in the L.A. office of Victor Gruen before partnering. The body of Palmer's work includes custom homes, apartments, commercial office buildings, and hospitals.

Timo Sarpaneva, 79

Finnish glassmaker and designer Timo Sarpaneva died October 2, 2006. His modern designs, with those of contemporaries such as Tapio Wirkkala and Alvar Aalto, helped define the crafted, organic look of mid-century Scandinavian glass. Trained as a graphic designer, he joined the Iittala Glassworks in 1950. He even designed the company's distinctive logo, with its lowercase "i" in front of a red circle. His work there included innovating techniques for coloring glass and using molds for textured effects. In 1962 he opened his own office in Helsinki, designing everything from dishware to pans to textiles. Sarpaneva won several Milan Triennale prizes for his designs and received honorary degrees from the Royal Society of Arts in London, the University of Mexico City, and the University of Art and Design in Helsinki. He was also the subject of an exhibit that traveled to New York, Chicago, Los Angeles, and Washington, DC, in 1994 and 1995.

Ruth P. Shellhorn, 97

Modernist landscape architect Ruth Shellhorn died November 3, 2006. She spent her 57-year career working in Southern California for clients such as Bullock's department stores and the Walt Disney Company. Her husband left his job in banking to run her practice, which blossomed after a consulting job for Bullock's led to commissions for most of the chain's stores as well as work for Walt Disney. Shortly before the opening of Disneyland in Anaheim, she designed the landscaping for Main Street, the Town Square, and the Plaza Hub, as well as designed the pedestrian traffic plan. In 1956 she was selected as landscape architect for a new University of California campus in Riverside. Shellhorn was named a fellow of the American Society of Landscape Architects in 1971.

Sylvan R. Shemitz, 82

Lighting design innovator Sylvan Shemitz died July 5, 2007. A leader in both the design and manufacturing of architectural lighting, Shemitz held more than 30 patents for products he developed. In 1963 he founded Sylvan R. Shemitz Designs in New Haven, CT. As a designer, Shemitz helped light the Jefferson Memorial in Washington, DC, and the façade of Grand Central Station in New York. In the 1980s, he worked with architect Helmut Jahn on the lighting of his United Airlines Terminal at Chicago's O'Hare airport. *The New York Times* reported that the two created a "glowing glass shed intended as a modern take on a grand European rail station." He also lit the Schneider Children's Medical Center of Israel, the Yale Law Library, and CN Tower in Toronto, Canada. Shemitz designed asymmetric lighting, marketed under the Elliptipar brand. He also invented Tambient ambient office lighting. He was a fellow of the Illuminating Engineering Society of North America.

Louis G. Silano, 80

Louis Silano, a longtime engineer for Parsons Brinckerhoff, died July 24, 2007. He retired in January 2007 as a senior vice president and technical director for structures at the firm, which he joined in 1951. During his lengthy career, Silano led the design and construction of a number of bridges and tunnels, including the Newport-Pell Bridge in Rhode Island; the Fremont Bridge in Portland, OR; and the 63rd St. Queens Connector and the renovation of the Atlantic Avenue Subway station, both in New York City. He had been Parsons Brinckerhoff's engineering manager for the Central Artery/Tunnel project in Boston, where he helped with initial designs for the Ted Williams Tunnel and the Fort Point Channel tunnel under Boston Harbor. Silano was honored by the American Society of Civil Engineers with the Roebling Award for lifetime achievement in bridge engineering in 1994 and the Lifetime Achievement Award in Design in 2005.

Pieter Singelenberg, 88

Architectural theorist, art historian, and author Pieter Singelenberg died in early 2007. The Dutch scholar became an expert on Hendrik Petrus Berlage, the father of Danish modernism, spending decades researching and writing about him, including *H.P. Berlage, Idea and Style: The Quest for Modern Architecture.* Singelenberg was the major contributor to a catalog for the exhibit Berlage: 1856–1934. The exhibition was held in The Hague, Netherlands, at the Gemeentemuseum, which Berlage designed and Singelenberg wrote about in *H.P. Berlage's Haags Gemeentemuseum.* A visitor to the United States as a teacher and lecturer, Singelenberg taught at the University of Louisville for a year in 1986. He also attended and lectured at meetings of the Society of Architectural Historians and visited the buildings of Frank Lloyd Wright, whom he came to admire greatly. In Holland, he was director of the University of Utrecht's Art Historical Institute and chair of its architectural history program from 1965 to 1978. He also established the Art Historical Institute at the University of Nijmegen and taught there for many years.

Bill Stumpf, 70

Bill Stumpf, most famous as the designer, with Don Chadwick, of Herman Miller's innovative Aeron ergonomic task chair, died August 30, 2006. Selected for the permanent design collection of the Museum of Modern Art a month before its official introduction in 1994, the Aeron was the first mass-produced chair with no hard shell for support. It relied on an aluminum frame covered with breathable, shape-hugging polyester mesh. Stumpf's affiliation with Herman Miller began in 1970 when he joined the staff. Two years later he opened his own firm, Stumpf, Weber & Associates, in Minneapolis, though many of his designs were produced for and by the Zeeland, MI, company. Stumpf designed the first modern ergonomic work chair, the Ergon, for Herman Miller in 1976, and in 1984, again with Chadwick, the Equa chair. His firm also designed Pur Water Filtration products and items for Lexmark International, among others. He authored the 1998 book *The Ice Palace that Melted Away* about the loss of civility in American discourse. Stumpf received a Personal Recognition Award from the Industrial Designers Society of America and was posthumously awarded the 2006 National Design Award for product design by the Smithsonian Institution's Cooper-Hewitt, National Design Museum.

Melvin M. Webber, 86

Melvin Webber, a city planning and transportation expert and longtime University of California, Berkeley professor, died November 25, 2006. Webber joined the university's department of city and regional planning in 1959. During his career, he headed UC Berkeley's Institute of Urban and Regional Development and the University of California Transportation Center, and was one of the planners of Bay Area Rapid Transit in the 1950s. He also helped establish a PhD program in planning at the university. Webber had been an editor of the *Journal of the American Institute of Planners* and founded the journal *Access* to distill complex analyses of policy issues. Among the honors he received was the Berkeley Citation in 1990 and the Distinguished Planning Educator Award from the Association of Collegiate Schools of Planning in 2000.

Hans J. Wegner, 92

Danish designer Hans Wegner died January 26, 2007. Famous for his chair designs, Wegner was a master craftsman whose designs, mostly in oak, ash, and teak, became icons of mid-century Danish modern design. Though none of his pieces were named by him (referred to only by catalog number), his signature designs have acquired names, such as the Ox chair, with its tubular roll across the top of the back that simulates horns; the Peacock chair, a refined take on the Windsor chair with a tall proud back and a fan of wooden insets; the Wishbone chair, a low-back wood chair with a Y-shaped inset for back support; and The Chair, a bentwood modern design with caned seat used for the 1960 Nixon-Kennedy debate. Believing that comfort and craftsmanship must come before aesthetic beauty, Wegner's chairs are renown for their success in both structure and design. Of the estimated 500 chairs he designed, 80 remain in production. The son of a cobbler in Denmark, Wegner was a design student in Copenhagen when he was hired by Arne Jacobsen and Erik Moller to design furniture for their town hall project in Aarhus. He stared his own firm shortly after that, and by the mid-1940s he had already produced several of his most enduring designs.

Sir Colin St. John Wilson, 85

British architect Sir Colin St. John (Sandy) Wilson died May 14, 2007. Best known as the architect of the beleaguered British Library, completed in 1997, Wilson was the former director of the Cambridge School of Architecture and a leading collector of 20th-century modern art. For 35 years he worked to get the British Library constructed, through public debates on style and location, administration changes, budget cuts, bureaucratic obstacles, and technical problems. Finally located next to St. Pancras Station in London, the controversial brick building has been both heralded as an inspiring piece of civil architecture and derided as a cold monolithic behemoth. He joined the Cambridge faculty in the 1960s, departing briefly to teach at Yale University and then the Massachusetts Institute of Technology. He began designs for the British Library project in 1962. One of his final projects was the Pallant House Gallery in Winchester, which houses his art collection. Wilson was knighted in 1998.

Julie Thoma Wright, 49

Interior designer and co-founder, with her husband Richard, of the Chicago auction house Wright, Julie Thoma Wright died June 11, 2007. An interior designer with a flourishing practice, Wright and her husband founded the boutique auction house in 2000, specializing in 20th-century art and design. The company, a private dealer in mid-century design for many years, has grown into a $25 million enterprise operating from a 60,000 square-foot building. A native of Iowa, Wright graduated from Iowa State University and moved to Chicago, where she joined Arlene Semel & Associates. She started her own firm, Julie Thoma Inc. in 1985 and won an AIA award for her creative design for a launderette. In 1989 Wright joined Interior Space Design, later Interior Space International, where she rose to vice president, leading the firm's commercial projects in Mexico City. She reestablished her own firm, Thoma Wright Ltd. in 1995. She has been credited as the creative force behind Wright, the auction house, developing exceptional catalogs, promoting the company, and managing its growth.

George Yu, 43

Architect, educator, and technology innovator George Yu died July 7, 2007. With Jason King, Yu operated the firm Design Office, maintaining offices in Los Angeles and Vancouver. Previously he ran his own practice, George Yu Architects, and between the two firms, he was responsible for the completion of more than 65 projects, most noteworthy for their use of cutting-edge digital and materials technologies. These included workspaces for IBM e-business in Chicago, New York, and Atlanta and the Honda Advanced Design Studio in Pasadena, CA. Yu was also a faculty member at the Southern California Institute of Architecture from 1988 until his death. In addition to having his work featured in a number of exhibitions, Yu and King were honored in *Architectural Record's* Design Vandguard issue in 2000. Yu received the Prix de Rome, the Canada Council's highest award for architecture, in 2000.

Name Index

Name Index

Name Index

Name Index

Name Index

Close, Robert A., 175
CMH Architects Inc., 139
CMI Homes Inc., 330
CO Architects, 94
Cobb, David, 118
Cobb, Henry N., 22, 170, 441
Cochran, Andrea C., 175
Cochran, Stephenson & Donkervoet, 279
Cochrane, Richard, 35
Cockerell, Charles Robert, 132, 192
Coffin, David, 10
Cogen Architects, 195
Cohagen, Chandler C., 189
Cohen, E. Gresley, 191
Cohen, Eli W., 506–507
Cohen, Joshua Samuel, 426
Cohen, Preston Scott, 14
Cohen-Barreto-Marchertas, 507
Coia, Jack Antonio, 133
Cole, Raymond J., 399
Cole, Robert I., 23
Coleman, Joseph R., 171
Coleman, Thomas, 404
Coles, Robert T., 162, 169, 434
Coletti, Carroll, 434
Colgan Perry Lawler Architects, 216
Collaborative Designworks, 69, 131
Collard, Max Ernest, 191
Collcutt, Thomas Edward, 132, 192
College of Charleston, 415
Collier, John, 128
Collins, Donald L., 430
Collins, Ellen, 219
Collins Rimer & Gordon, 427
Colon, Sheila, 19
Colonial Williamsburg Foundation, 347
Color Association of the United States, 463
Colter, Mary Jane, 248
Columbia University
    degrees/programs, 367
    staff, 183, 397, 441
    students/alumni, 249, 251, 407, 424, 508, 519
Columbus College of Art & Design, 429
COMEX, 87
Common Ground, 484
Communication Arts, 484
Communication Arts, Inc., 177
Compasso d'Oro, 506
Compeau, Junjian, 424
Composite Panel Association/Composite Wood Council, 463
Compton, Jerry, 432
Comune di Giussano, 57
Conant, Kenneth J., 10
Concordia, 263
Condon, Patrick, 412
Congress for the New Urbanism, 39
Connally, Ernest A., 353
Connecticut Light & Power Company, 376
Connolly Architects Inc., 195
Connor, Rose, 250
Consigli Construction Co., Inc., 333
Consortium of Quebec Architects, 301
Construction Management Association of America, 463
Construction Specifications Institute, 105, 316, 463
Constructive Communications, Inc., 103
Continuum, 35, 45, 81
Contract, 15, 33, 52, 66, 92, 484
Convention Center Associates, Architects, 281
Convention Center Design Group, 283
Conway, Patricia, 52
Conway, William, 401

Cook, Neil, 425
Cook, Peter, 87
Cook, Walter, 180
Cook + Fox Architects, 302
Cooledge, Harold, Jr., 397
Coolerado, LLC, 344
Coolidge, Shepley, Bulfinch and Abbott, 268
Coon, Burwell R., 190
Coop Himmelb(l)au, 267, Plates 36–38
Cooper, Douglas, 76
Cooper, Sir Edwin, 133
Cooper, Robertson & Partners, 273
Cooper, Tammy, 415
Cooper Carry, Inc., 103, 139
Cooper Union, 407, 422, 441
Cooper-Hewitt, National Design Museum, 109, 116, 138, 489
Cooper-Hewitt Museum Bookstore, 482
Copeland, Lee G., 441
Copper Development Association, 463
Corberó, Xavier, 106
Corbett, Harrison & MacMurray, 154, 236, 240
CoreNet Global, 340
Corgan Associates, Inc., 258
Corker, Bill, 123
Corn, Alex, 413
Cornejo, Alfredo, 411
Cornell University
    staff, 183, 184, 253, 398, 400, 430, 441
    students/alumni, 247, 248, 407, 422, 436–437, 438
Corner, James, 14
Cornish Associates, 372
Cornman, Nathaniel Russell, 409
Corona Martin, Ramon, 188
Corpus Christi Design Associates, 265
Correa, Charles, 119, 133, 146, 156, 170
Corrigan, Peter, 123
Corrol, Paul J., 434
Cortes, Mario C., 419
Costa, Lucio, 145
Costas Kondylis & Partners LLC Architects, 306
Costello, Elaine, 173
Cote, Katherine, 404
Cotera Kolar Negrete & Reed Architects, 279
Cottam Hargrave Architecture and Construction, 153
Cottee Parker Architects, 54
Cotter, Brandon, 437
Cotter, John L., 351
Cottier, Keith, 123
Cotton, John O., 435
Council of Architectural Component Executives, 185
Council of Education Facility Planners International, 60
Council of Landscape Architectural Registration Boards, 496
Council of Professional Surveyors, 463
Council on Tall Buildings and Urban Habitat, 100, 302, 463
Courtauld Institute, 517
Courtenay, Roger G., 175
Cowgill, Clinton H., 189
Cox, Oliver Earl, III, 408
Cox, Philip S., 123
Cox, Virginia Louise, 191
Cox & Associates, 64
Coxe, Weld, 102
Cradle to Cradle, 311, 339
Cram, Ralph Adams, 274
Cram, Stephen, 162
Cramer, James P., 176, 185
Cranbrook Academy of Art, 50
Crane, David A., 399
Crankshaw, Ned, 27

Name Index

Name Index

Name Index

Name Index

Name Index

Name Index

Name Index

Name Index

Name Index

Name Index

Name Index

Name Index

Prince of Wales, 161
Princeton University, 408, 425, 432, 441
Pringle, Jack, 192
Pringle Creek Community, 330
Pritchett, Mason, 435
Pritzker, Cindy, 108, 120
Pritzker, Jay, 108, 120
Pritzker Architecture Prize, 120, *121*
Pritzker Family, 90
Professional Construction Estimators Association of
    America, 467
Professional Landcare Network, 467
Progressive Architecture, 114
Propeller, 126
Prosse, Richard McClure, 162
Protoscar SA, 80
Prouvé, Jean, 30
Providence Journal, 479
Provine, Loring, 183
Proyectos Arqui 5 CA, 321
PRR, 58
Pryor, Dawn Elizabeth, 423
Pryse, Joe, *21*
P&T Architects and Engineers Ltd., 47, *49*, 94
Public Architecture, 77, 176
Public Architecture 1% Solution, 475
Public Buildings Cooperative Use Act, 368
Public Initiatives Development Corporation, 73
Public Lands Commission, 220
Pugh, David A., 169
Pugh + Scarpa Architects, 5, 8
Pulitzer, Joseph, 122
Pulitzer Prize for Architectural Criticism, 122
Pullman, George, 219
Pulos, Arthur J., 186, 429
Pulsifer, Louis Warren, 434
Purdum, Gary, 412
Purnell, Marshall E., 180
Purtill Family Business, 72
Puryear, Martin, 76
Pushelberg, Glenn, 52
Putman, Andrée, 149
Putnam, William V., 424
PWL Partnership Landscape Architects Inc., 58
PWP Landscape Architecture, 26

Q

QPK Design, 195
QUADERNS, 87
Quale, John, 401
Quantrill, Malcolm, 397
Quarry, Neville, 87, 123
Que, Zhenqing, 411, 420
Quebe, Lisbeth, 102
Quig-Hartman, Austin, 436, 437
Quilici, Andrea, 19
Quinn, Patrick, 184
Quinn, Richard W., 189

R

Rademan, Myles, 173
Al-Radi, Selma, 3
Radziner, Ronald B., 171
Rae, Peter W., 426
Rafael Viñoly Architects, 196, 272, 279
Rafferty Rafferty Tollefson Lindeke Architects, 128
RAIA Gold Medal, 123
RAIC Gold Medal, 124

Raines, Bradford, 424
Rainka, Gregory, 415
Rairden, David, 436
Raitz, Karl B., 351
Rajkovich, Thomas N., 23
Rakkolainen, Ismo, 35
Raleigh News & Observer, 479
Ralph, Gregory R., 423
Ralph Appelbaum Associates, 143, Plate 35
Ramirez Vazquez, Pedro, 87
Rams, Dieter, 440
Rana Creek Living Architecture, 318
Ranalli, Giancarlo, 18
Rand, Patrick, 171
Rand, Peter A., 185
RAND Corporation, 157
Randall Stout Architects, 271
Randell, Ron, 423
Randolph, Nicole, 413
Randy Brown Architects, 6
Rann Haight Architect, 297
Ransome, Ernest J., 270
Rao, Aditi, 420
Rapson, Ralph, 397, 441
Rashid, Karim, 149, 516
Rast, Joel, 93
Rath, Frederick L., Jr., 353
Ratkovik, Mariano Ortiz, 423
Ratner, Albert B., 86
Ray, Ronald Todd, 165
Rayle, Martha Garriott, 181
Raymond, Eleanor, 249
Raymond Loewy Associates, 518
Razook, Mathew Dryden, 426
RCA, 518
Read, Anice Barber, 353
Reardon, Michael, 71, 419
Rebuild Downtown Our Town (R.Dot), 253
Rebuilding Together, 475
Reconnecting America, 39
Record, James, 71
red dot design awards, 125–126, *127*
Red Feather Development Group, 475
Redmann, Robert E., 429
Reep, Jennifer, 415
Rees, Peter, 100
Reese, Frances S., 138
Reeves, Frank Blair, 353
Refuerzo, Ben J., 398
Regan, J. Thomas, 183
Regev, Nava, 411
Rehder, John B., 348
Reich, Robert S. (Doc), 25, 430
Reiff, Daniel, 364
Reilly, Sir Charles Herbert, 133
Reimnitz, John M., 435
Reiner, Thomas, 229
Reinhard & Hofmeister, 154, 236, 240
Reiser, Jesse, 14
Related, 108
Religious Art & Architecture Design Awards, 128–129
Remedios Siembieda, 61
Rendigs, Panzer and Martin, 269
Rensselaer Polytechnic Institute, 184, 408, 423, 425, 441
Renwick, James, Jr., 274
Renzo Piano Building Workshop, 207, 259, 270, 271, 272,
    303
Reps, John, 211, 230, 233, 400
Repucci, Demian, 84
residential architect, 130
residential architect Design Awards, 130–131, *131*

Name Index

Name Index

Name Index

Name Index

Timbron International, 314, 344
Timur Designs, 42
Tishman Speyer Properties, 340
Tishman, 64
Tite, Sir William, 132, 192
Tittle, James D., 169
Toba, Jennifer, 425
Tobata Women's Association, 59
Tobias, Dustin Tyler, 423
Tod Williams Billie Tsien & Associates, 252, 266, 275
Todd, Alan, 436
Toker, Franklin, 11
Tolar LeBartard Denmark Architects, 40
Toledano, Roulhac, 11
Tolene, Bryce, 19
Toll Brothers, 31
Tom, Melissa Kegan, 409
Tomey, Adam, 436
Tompkins, David D., 186
Tompkins, Doug, 175
Tongji University, 412
Tools Design, 125
Top 10 Green Building Products, 338, 344
Top Green Projects, 341–342, *343*
Top Ranked Buildings, 240–244
Topaz Medallion, 441, *442*
Topelson de Grinberg, Sara, 188
TOPOS-The International Review of Landscape
    Architecture and Urban Design, 28
Torio, Jocelyn, 406
Torti Gallas and Partners, 9, 39, *41*, 70, 428
Toscani, Chiara, 57
Touart, Paul Baker, 351
Toukonen, Kayne, 143
Town, A. Hays, 23
Town, Ithiel, 274
TRA Architects, 257, 283
Trachtenberg, Marvin, 11, 12
Traugott, Alan, 177
Trautwein Associates, Architects and Planners, 285
Traxon Technologies Ltd., 47
Treberspurg, Martin, 146
Tree Care Industry Association, 468
Tregre, Louis, 51
Treib, Marc, 117
Trelles, Emma, 480
Trickey, Andrea, 415
Trim Technologies, 314
Trinity Financial, 372
Triton Logging, 344
Trivers Associates, 89
TROMOS, 305
Troyan, Mary, 405
Truex, Van Day, 50
Trumbauer, Horace, 272
TSA, Inc., 176
Tsang, Andrea Heather, 408
Tschumi, Jean, 188
Tsien, Billie, 22, 152, 170, 252
Tsinghua University, 411
Tsoi/Kobus & Associates, Inc., 66, 196
Tsurumaki, Marc, *85*
TTV Architects, 428
Tuck Hinton Architects, 95, 268
Tucker, Beverly R., Jr., 153
Tucker, Randolph W., 102
Tucker, Robert, 177
Tucker Design Awards, 153
Tucker Sadler Architects, 283
Tufts University, 404
Tugwell, Rexford Guy, 211, 225
Tulane University, 183, 399, 409, 423, 425

Tuohy Furniture Corp., 33
Turner, John F. C., 146
Turner, Paul Venable, 12
Turner, William, 183
Turner Construction Company, 68, 333
Turnscape, 26
Turrell, James, 152
TVA Architects, 63
Tvrdy, Aaron, 325
TVS-D&P-Mariani PLLC, 283
Twenty-Five Year Award, 154–155
20-20 Technologies, 34
TWH Architects, 287
Tylevich Studio, Inc., 128, 129
Tyrnauer, Herbert H., 429
Tyrrell, Jonathan, 410
Tzannes, Alec, 191

U

Udagawa, Masamichi, 88
Udall, Stewart, 353
Uhl, Jacob, 436
UIA Gold Medal, 156
ULI Awards for Excellence, 157–158
Ulinski, Matthew, 436, 437
Ulrich, Roger, 175
Umbanhowar, Elizabeth, 413
Umemoto, Nanako, 14
Umpansiriratana, Suriya, 18
Underwood, Max, 398
Underwriters Laboratories Inc., 468
UNESCO, 368, 385
UNESCO Asia-Pacific Heritage Awards for Culture
    Heritage Conservation, 385
United Nations Centre for Human Settlements (HABI-
    TAT), 338, 470
United Nations Volunteers, 476
United States Institute for Theatre Technology, 159
Universidad de Puerto Rico, 399
University at Buffalo, SUNY, 399, 404, 409, 423
University of Arizona, 409, 423, 432, 515
University of Arkansas, 397, 401, *402*, 409, 423, 431
University of Arkansas Community Design Center, 40, 114
University of Bridgeport, 429
University of British Columbia, 397, 399, 409, 412, 425
University of Buenos Aires, 414
University of California, Berkeley
    awards/honors, 91
    degrees/programs, 73
    staff, 176, 183, 397, 398, 399, 400, 441, 519, 523
    students/alumni, 247, 250, 412, 420, 425, 432, 516
University of California, Los Angeles, 398, 400, 404, 409,
    425
University of California Extension, 516
University of Chicago, 507, 519
University of Cincinnati, 82, 398, 404, 432
University of Colorado at Boulder, 183, 436–437
University of Colorado at Denver, 409, 425, 436
University of Detroit Mercy, 409, 423
University of Florida, 184, 399, 409, 412, 421, 425
University of Hawaii at Manoa, 403, 409, 423, 425
University of Houston, 184, 423, 425, 432
University of Idaho, 409, 423, 432
University of Illinois at Chicago, 183, 409, 425
University of Illinois at Urbana-Champaign
    degrees/programs, 221
    staff, 183, 397, 399, 400, 403, 429, 430
    students/alumni, 247, 249, 404, 409, 420, 432, 507
University of Iowa, 404
University of Kansas, 183, 404, 409, 423, 425

Name Index

Name Index

X

Y

Z

Site Index

Site Index

Site Index

Site Index

Site Index

Site Index

Site Index

Site Index

Site Index

Site Index

V

VENEZUELA
VIETNAM

Y

YEMEN
YUGOSLAVIA

Z

ZIMBABWE

About the Editors

James P. Cramer is the founder and chairman of The Greenway Group, Inc.; co-chair of the Washington DC-based think-tank, the Design Futures Council; editor of *DesignIntelligence*, a journal on trends, strategies, and changes in the A/E/C industry published by the Design Futures Council and Greenway Communications. He researches, consults, and gives seminars for leading professional firms around the world and is the author of more than 135 articles and several books, including *Design + Enterprise, Seeking a New Reality in Architecture*. He is co-author of *How Firms Succeed, A Field Guide to Management Solutions* and *The Next Architect: A New Twist on the Future of Design*. Cramer is the former chief executive of the American Institute of Architects, past president of the American Architectural Foundation, and a former publisher of *Architecture* magazine. He is also a fellow of the Western Behavioral Sciences Institute in La Jolla, CA, a senior fellow of the Design Futures Council, and a Richard Upjohn Fellow of the American Institute of Architects.

Jennifer Evans Yankopolus is the co-editor of the *Almanac of Architecture & Design* and an architectural historian. She is also the editor of the Archidek series of collectable, educational architecture trading cards and an editor for the Östberg press where she helps projects to achieve the imprint's goal of promoting design excellence. She has a master's degree in architecture history from the Georgia Institute of Technology. She also studied at Drake University, where she received her BS in business administration and earned a master's degree in heritage preservation from Georgia State University. As a researcher, architectural historian, and project director, she brings a historical perspective to Greenway's initiatives.

Marvin J. Malecha is the dean of the College of Design at North Carolina State University. Prior to this appointment in 1994, he served as the dean of the College of Environmental Design at California State Polytechnic University, Pomona (1982–1994). At NC State he has fostered the development of a branch campus in Prague and championed new academic programs and partnerships. Presently, he is a member of the national board of the American Institute of Architects and the board for AIA North Carolina, and will serve as the AIA national president in 2009. He is a fellow of the AIA and an honorary member of the European Association for Architectural Education. In 1999 he received the Alumni Distinguished Achievement Award from the University of Minnesota and in 2002 was named a Distinguished Professor by the Association of Collegiate Schools of Architecture. He is also the recipient of the 2003 AIA/ACSA Topaz Medallion for excellence in architectural education.

östberg™

Library of Design Management

Every relationship of value requires constant care and commitment. At Östberg, we are relentless in our desire to create and bring forward only the best ideas in design, architecture, interiors, and design management. Using diverse mediums of communications, including books and the Internet, we are constantly searching for thoughtful ideas that are erudite, witty, and of lasting importance to the quality of life. Inspired by the architecture of Ragnar Östberg and the best of Scandinavian design and civility, the Östberg Library of Design Management seeks to restore the passion for creativity that makes better products, spaces, and communities. The essence of Östberg can be summed up in our quality charter to you: "Communicating concepts of leadership and design excellence."